C0-CEE-322

George Brown
College

HOSPITALITY FINANCIAL MANAGEMENT

CANADIAN EDITION

Robert E. Chatfield
College of Business
University of Nevada, Las Vegas

Michael C. Dalbor
William F. Harrah College of Hotel Administration
University of Nevada, Las Vegas

Paul A. Willie
School of Hospitality & Tourism Management
Niagara College

PEARSON

Prentice
Hall

Toronto

Library and Archives Canada Cataloguing in Publication

Chatfield, Robert E., 1953–
Hospitality financial management / Robert E. Chatfield, Michael C. Dalbor
  and Paul A. Willie. — 1st Canadian ed.

Includes index.
ISBN 978-0-13-613933-1

 1. Hospitality industry—Canada—Finance.   I. Dalbor, Michael C., 1961–
II. Willie, Paul A., 1960–   III. Title.

TX911.3.F5C53 2009   647.94068'1   C2008-903351-5

Copyright © 2009 by Pearson Education Canada, a division of Pearson Canada Inc., Toronto, Ontario.

Pearson Prentice Hall. All rights reserved. This publication is protected by copyright and permission should be obtained from the publisher prior to any prohibited reproduction, storage in a retrieval system, or transmission in any form or by any means, electronic, mechanical, photocopying, recording, or likewise. For information regarding permission, write to the Permissions Department.

Original edition published by Pearson Education, Inc., Upper Saddle River, New Jersy, USA. Copyright 2005 by Pearson Education, Inc. This edition is authorized for sale only in Canada.

ISBN-13: 978-0-13-613933-1
ISBN-10: 0-13-613933-7

Vice-President, Editorial Director: Gary Bennett
Editor-in-Chief: Ky Pruesse
Acquisitions Editor: Chris Helsby
Marketing Manager: Loula March
Senior Developmental Editor: Joel Gladstone
Production Editor: Claire Horsnell
Copy Editor: Kelli Howey
Proofreaders: Martin Townsend, Judy Phillips
Production Coordinator: Avinash Chandra
Composition: Integra
Art Director: Julia Hall
Cover and Interior Design: Anthony Leung
Cover Image: Getty Images/Justin Pumfrey

1 2 3 4 5   12 11 10 09 08

Printed and bound in the United States.

In memory of my father, William O. Chatfield, and to my mother, Ellie M. Chatfield, who have both taught me many valuable life-long lessons.

Robert E. Chatfield

This book is dedicated to my father and mother, John B. Dalbor and Dorothy G. Dalbor.
La manzana cae cerca del arbol

Michael C. Dalbor

This book is dedicated in memory of my father, Sylvester Alvin Willie, and to my mother, Amy Roberta Willie, who both consistently and affectionately instilled within me the importance as well as the value of education.

Paul A. Willie

Brief Contents

Contents

Brief Biographies

Robert E. Chatfield is professor of finance and director of MBA programs at the College of Business, University of Nevada, Las Vegas. Previously, he was an associate professor of finance at Texas Tech University and an assistant professor of finance at the University of New Mexico.

Professor Chatfield has been teaching financial management for over 25 years and has taught financial management to hospitality students at UNLV for the past 15 years. He has worked as a financial consultant to the gaming industry in Las Vegas. He has also received teaching excellence awards both at Texas Tech University and Purdue University.

Professor Chatfield has been a productive researcher, publishing in a number of leading finance journals, including *Financial Management, Journal of Financial and Quantitative Analysis*, the *Financial Review, International Journal of Forecasting, Journal of Money, Credit and Banking, Quarterly Journal of Business and Economics*, and *Journal of Economics and Business*.

Professor Chatfield enjoys athletics and especially likes to participate in tennis and white-water rafting, and is a novice ballroom dancer.

Michael C. Dalbor is an assistant professor in the William F. Harrah College of Hotel Administration at the University of Nevada, Las Vegas. He holds a B.S. in Food Service and Housing Administration from the Pennsylvania State University and an M.B.A. in finance from Loyola College in Maryland. He also holds a Ph.D. in Hotel, Restaurant, and Institutional Finance from the Pennsylvania State University.

He has published articles in the *Journal of Hospitality Tourism Research*, the *Cornell Hotel and Restaurant Administration Quarterly*, the *Appraisal Journal*, the *International Journal of Hospitality Management*, and the *Journal of Hospitality Financial Management*. He is active in the Association of Hospitality Financial Management Education and the Council on Hotel, Restaurant, and Institutional Education. He has worked in various management positions in the hospitality industry, including food and beverage management, and as a purchasing agent. He has also conducted numerous market analyses and feasibility studies as a hotel consultant and has been a commercial real estate appraiser specializing in hotel valuation.

Paul A. Willie is an accounting and finance professor at the School of Hospitality and Tourism Management, Niagara College, Canada.

Professor Willie has been teaching finance for more than 20 years. He has worked as a general manager in hotels and restaurants and has held a wide variety of managerial positions in accounting and finance. When not in the classroom, he is actively engaged as a management consultant. He has provided his expertise and services across Canada, the Caribbean, and South America.

He is a graduate of the University of Guelph, School of Hospitality and Tourism Management (Bachelor of Commerce in Hotel and Food Administration), and Nova Southeastern University, The Wayne Huizenga School of Business and Entrepreneurship, where he obtained his M.B.A. and is now a doctoral candidate. He is a Certified Financial Manager (CFM), Certified Management Accountant (CMA), Certified Hospitality

Accountant Executive (CHAE), Certified Hospitality Technology Professional (CHTP), Certified Hotel Administrator (CHA), and a Certified Food Service Manager (CFSM).

He has several published articles in leading hospitality management journals, such as *The International Journal of Contemporary Hospitality Management* and *The Bottom Line: The Journal of Hospitality Financial and Technology Professionals*.

When Professor Willie is not teaching, writing, researching, or consulting, he can be found in a local gym, on the tennis court, or enjoying a great Niagara wine.

Preface

Hospitality Financial Management, Canadian edition, is intended as a first finance course for hospitality and tourism students. It may also be useful to hospitality industry professionals who want to know more about the financial management function in the hospitality industry.

This book focuses primarily on long-term finance decisions, especially the hospitality firm's capital budgeting decision. Given the fixed asset–intensiveness of the industry, capital budgeting is an important process for hospitality and tourism students to understand. Additionally, a significant amount of background information is required to fully understand this process.

The text has a number of features to facilitate learning and understanding. Each chapter begins with a list of objectives and an introduction to the chapter content. Chapters conclude with discussion questions and problems that demonstrate key concepts. Problems that may be solved by using Excel spreadsheets are indicated with **EXCEL** in the margin, with spreadsheets accessible online at www.pearsoned.ca/chatfield. Key terms and concepts are identified and defined in the glossary.

Chapter 1 provides an introduction to the topic of Canadian hospitality financial management. Various types of business organization are discussed along with an introduction to agency problems and the concept of value creation.

Chapter 2 provides an introduction to the fundamental principles of financial management and speaks to the roles, responsibilities, and obligations of the prudent financial manager.

Chapter 3 provides an overview of the Canadian financial environment, with an in-depth look at the pillars of Canadian finance.

Chapter 4 explores various financial markets and financial instruments. Foreign exchange and commodity markets are also discussed.

Chapter 5 is a good review of the major financial statements and discusses some of the key ratios used in the hospitality industry. It also identifies the limitations of ratio analysis.

Chapter 6 introduces the student to the concept of risk and return. The important features of the chapter include the market portfolio and the capital asset pricing model.

Chapter 7 covers the time value of money. This includes discounting and compounding and demonstrates a wide variety of applications. (Appendices 1 and 2 at the end of the book demonstrate how to solve time value of money problems using two different financial calculators.)

Chapter 8 discusses bonds and preferred stock. This chapter explains the basic approach to both bond and preferred stock valuation. It also includes examples of bonds and preferred stocks issued by hospitality firms. Appendices 3 and 4 demonstrate how to solve bond value and yield to maturity problems using different financial calculators.

Chapter 9 covers common stock. It features common stock terminology as well as an introduction to basic common stock valuation.

Chapter 10 focuses on the cost of capital. This chapter elaborates on how the weighted cost of capital is derived.

Chapter 11 is an introduction to capital budgeting. This chapter covers the calculation of net investment and the subsequent cash flows.

Chapter 12 builds on the concepts of Chapter 11 by examining the different methods used to determine whether a capital budgeting project will create value. Such methods as net present value, internal rate of return, and payback are thoroughly explained. (Appendix 5 demonstrates how to calculate NPV and IRR problems using two different business calculators. Appendix 6 at the end of the book provides an example of a capital budgeting project.)

Chapter 13 introduces the student to hotel valuation. The chapter begins with hotel market studies and also discusses the hotel appraisal process. The income capitalization approach is emphasized.

Chapter 14 provides an introduction to capital structure. It shows the impact of capital structure on firm value and reviews some major capital structure theories.

Chapter 15 is a discussion on mergers and acquisitions, with an informative look at recent M&A transactions that have taken place in Canada.

The text concludes with a glossary to help students become familiar with key terms.

A variety of online tools and resources enhance the text's content for both instructors and students. An *Instructor's Manual with Test Bank and PowerPoint slides* is provided through Pearson Education Canada's password protected online catalogue (vig.pearsoned.ca). Navigate to your book's catalogue page to view a list of those supplements that are available. See your local sales representative for details and access.

A Text Enrichment Site, accessed at www.pearsoned.ca/chatfield, contains PowerPoint slides reinforcing the key points in each chapter as well as the Excel spreadsheet templates for solutions of chapter problems where applicable.

CourseSmart is a new way for instructors and students to access textbooks online anytime from anywhere. With thousands of titles across hundreds of courses, CourseSmart helps instructors choose the best textbooks for their class and give their students a new option for buying the assigned textbook as a lower cost eTextbook. For more information, visit www.coursesmart.com

ACKNOWLEDGMENTS

The authors wish to acknowledge helpful comments and suggestions made by the following professors: Robert Lebrun, Canadore College; Bryan Bessner, George Brown College; Joe Mariani, Algonquin College; Nicole Robinson, Nova Scotia Community College.

We would like to thank Joel Gladstone, who was our constant contact at Pearson Education Canada. We appreciate his prodding, reminders, and encouragement that were instrumental in providing the motivation we needed to finish this project. Kelli Howey's editing is much appreciated. Claire Horsnell was professional and a delight to work with in guiding us through the production process. These are the three professionals we dealt with directly in finishing this project. We are sure there are many others to whom we are also indebted and we wish to thank them as well.

Robert E. Chatfield extends a special thanks to his wife, Hyun Kyung Chatfield. Her many hours spent reading the manuscript, answering questions, testing the book in the classroom, and recommending many student-friendly improvements are greatly appreciated.

Michael C. Dalbor would like to thank his wife, Cindy, for her love and support. Her patience and understanding during this process facilitated the project immensely.

Paul A. Willie thanks his wife, Lesley, for her love, understanding, and support with this project and in life overall. Her dependable and loyal encouragement throughout the task at hand was greatly appreciated.

Chapter 1

Introduction to Canadian Hospitality Financial Management

Chapter Objectives

This chapter covers the following topics:

1   The scope of hospitality financial management

2   The relationships between finance and other functional areas of business management

3   The different forms of business organization

4   The three main decisions in financial management

5   The goal of wealth maximization

6   The different types of agency relationships

7   The ways managers act to increase value

8   How projects are undertaken to create value

9   A brief introduction to the remainder of the text

1.1 Introduction

The world of hospitality financial management is an important and exciting place to be. The financial decisions made by hospitality managers have important implications for not only the managers and owners of the company, but also the overall industry. Some of the more exciting developments related to hospitality finance in Canada include the following recent transactions:

■   In 1995, Wendy's International acquired Tim Hortons; in 2007, the two companies were separated once again by spinning off Tim Hortons as a separate company

■   In 2005, the premium craft beer maker Creemore Springs was purchased by Molson Canada

■   In 2006, the initial public common stock offering (IPO) of Tim Hortons on both the Toronto Stock Exchange and the New York Stock Exchange saw investors who purchased the stock at the beginning of trading almost double their earnings on their investment by the end of the first day

- In 2006, Fairmont Hotels and Resorts was purchased by Saudi Prince Alwaleed bin Talal's Kingdom Hotels International and Colony Capital
- In 2007, Four Seasons Hotels and Resorts was acquired by Kingdom Hotels International and Bill Gates's Cascade Investments

There are many other examples of financial decisions that have had an impact on the hospitality industry. It is important to understand the thought processes behind these and other types of financial decisions. For example, how does Swiss Chalet decide where to open a new restaurant? How does Delta Hotels decide the best way to finance its next hotel project? How does Boston Pizza (a Canadian company that originated in Edmonton) know whether or not to pay dividends to its investors? These are just a few of the types of questions that the study of financial management can help answer.

The purpose of this textbook is to introduce the hospitality student to the field of financial management. The authors hope that after completing your course in conjunction with this textbook you will be better informed about how important financial decisions are made within hospitality firms. An understanding of how financial decisions are made is important because financial management continues to be recognized as an important component of the hospitality curriculum by many hospitality company recruiters. Additionally, the concepts discussed herein can often apply directly to your own personal financial circumstances.

Some hospitality students may fail to grasp the significance of financial management because it seems of little interest to them initially. However, as we discuss throughout the text, there are really no business decisions that do not affect the financial position of the hospitality organization. It does not matter whether you are in food and beverage operations, rooms division, sales and marketing, or human resources: you will be responsible for making decisions that will have an impact on the wealth of the owners (and possibly yourself). This text describes how we can determine whether a decision or project creates value. **Value creation** is an integral part of financial management.

So what, specifically, is financial management? Financial management is the process of making decisions about assets, financing those assets, and distributing any potential cash flows generated by the assets. Financial management therefore involves these three major decisions, all of which have an impact on the different departments of a hospitality organization.

1.2 The Relationship of Financial Management to Other Functional Areas of Management

Hospitality students often take a sequence of quantitative courses, usually beginning with financial accounting. Many of them subsequently take managerial accounting, followed by a financial management course. It is important to understand that although all these courses are quantitative, accounting and finance are separate academic fields—more like cousins, as opposed to being twin siblings.

One major difference is that there are many different types of accounting. Financial accounting, for example, is recording and classifying financial information for use by others. Other types of accounting include asset, managerial, tax, and cost accounting. Another branch of accounting that has become very significant to the welfare of the hospitality enterprise is auditing. Auditing—the attest function—involves statistical approaches in reviewing and verifying the accuracy and validity of the accounting system and its output, the financial statement, and other records and documentation. On the other hand, financial management uses accounting information (an income statement, for example) to help make value-maximizing decisions. Accordingly, students are often required to take both accounting and finance courses, because they help to evaluate the financial condition of a firm and assist in the decision-making process as to which future projects should be undertaken.

Another important difference between accounting and finance is that financial and managerial accounting often focuses on earnings—accrual-based earnings. You may recall from your accounting courses that accrual-based financial statements (such as the income statement) show revenues when they are earned and expenses when they are incurred. This may or may not be the same time period in which cash is received or paid. Another example is depreciation—an expense that reduces taxable income but is not an actual cash outlay. Financial managers and investors are generally more concerned with cash flow, because hospitality firms pay employees and suppliers with cash, lenders are repaid with cash, and owners are often paid cash dividends. Therefore, the value of a project or a firm is much more dependent on cash flows than on accounting-type earnings.

Financial management and the field of economics are also closely related. Many hospitality students are required to take at least one course in economics. Macroeconomics is important to financial management because of key factors such as inflation values, interest rates, unemployment numbers, and foreign exchange rates. Microeconomics is related to finance because financial managers must understand how individual investors behave. Marginal analysis (such as the concept of declining marginal utility) is an important concept in microeconomics. Additionally, marginal analysis is commonly used in financial management to determine whether a project's incremental benefits exceed its incremental costs.

Another important area of financial management is marketing. Marketing is related to financial management in at least two ways. First, marketing projects often involve capital expenditures that require a complete analysis before implementation. Second, changes in the marketing plan can affect the cash flows of a potential project and therefore require careful consideration during the evaluation stage.

Other management functions are related to finance, including strategic management, operations management, revenue management, human resources management, management information systems, and even property maintenance and security. Nevertheless, to be effective, managers should have a fundamental understanding of financial management principles.

1.3 Organization of the Firm

In this section, we briefly review the different types of business organization and discuss the important differences among them.

The most common type of business in Canada is the *sole proprietorship,* in which individuals are in business for themselves. Although this form of business is easy and inexpensive to establish, the owner assumes unlimited liability for the business. Another problem for this type of organization is the relative difficulty in raising capital. On the other hand, the business itself is not subject to tax; any profits are simply part of the individual owner's personal income and are taxed accordingly.

A *partnership* exists when two or more people form a legally registered business. Like the sole proprietorship, it is easy and inexpensive to organize. Similarly, it can be difficult to raise capital, and the partners share unlimited liability for the business. In a *limited partnership*, a general partner has unlimited liability for the business and limited partners are responsible only for their investment in the business. However, the general partner has more control over decisions affecting the business and usually receives extra compensation for these management duties.

The focus of this textbook is on the *corporate* form of business organization, although much of the discussion and analysis can be applied to other forms of business. A corporation must first have a charter and be incorporated within a specific province or territory. The corporation must use the Canada Incorporation Act to operate in more than one province or territory. If the corporation plan is to operate exclusively in one province or territory, then the entity executes only the provincial or territorial Act. Once the charter is established, the owners (shareholders) of the corporation elect a board of directors to make decisions regarding corporate policy. The board of directors does not typically handle day-to-day operations but instead makes policy decisions such as the hiring of executives and the corporation's auditors.

A corporation has some advantages over other types of business organization, including unlimited life and a lack of dependency on any one individual. Another advantage is the limited liability for its owners. In other words, investors can lose the value of their investment, but they are not responsible for the liabilities of the business. Finally, it is generally easier for a corporation to raise either debt or equity capital than it is for a sole proprietor or partnership to do so.

On the other hand, corporations are more difficult to organize and are generally subject to more stringent regulation by federal and provincial or territorial governments. Additionally, corporations suffer from double taxation. The corporate entities themselves pay tax, and any dividends paid to shareholders are also subject to tax; the Canada Revenue Agency treats the dividend payments as additional personal income to the shareholders. Fortunately there is a dividend tax credit that helps mitigate the shareholders' tax burden to some degree.

Another potential issue facing a corporation is control over the direction of the company. A person or group of persons can effectively take control of the company with 51 percent of the outstanding common shares. Another issue is the relationship between the owners and the management of the corporation. Problems can develop when management takes actions to benefit themselves at the expense of the owners. Problems between owners and lenders can also arise in the corporation. These potential challenges are discussed later in this chapter.

In addition to the pure form of the corporation, other hybrid forms of business organization exist. One is the *limited liability company*, or LLC. This type of organization uses the limited liability features of a corporation while being taxed in a manner similar to that of a partnership, thus avoiding double taxation. However, the LLC must specify a date of dissolution, and one cannot join the company without approval from the other members. A variety of firms such as those in the legal and accounting professions are organized as a *limited liability partnership*, or LLP. In these organizations, the personal liability of the partners is limited.

Another advantage of the corporation is the prospective ability to raise large amounts of capital through the public exchange markets. In order to raise equity capital through

Exhibit 1-1 Comparison of Business Organizations

Type	Advantages	Disadvantages
Sole proprietorship	Relatively low startup costs Greatest freedom from regulation Owner in direct control of decision making Minimal working capital required Tax advantages to owner All profits to owner	Unlimited liability Lack of continuity in business organization in absence of owner Difficulty raising capital
Partnership	Ease of formation Relatively low startup costs Additional sources of investment capital Possible tax advantages Limited regulation Broader management base	Unlimited liability Lack of continuity Divided authority Difficulty raising additional capital Hard to find suitable partners Possible development of conflict between partners
Corporation	Limited liability Specialized management Ownership is transferable Continuous existence Separate legal entity Possible tax advantage Easier to raise capital	Closely regulated Most expensive form to organize Charter restrictions Extensive recordkeeping necessary Double taxation of dividends Possible development of conflict between shareholders and executives
Cooperative	Owned and controlled by members Democratic control (one member, one vote) Limited liability Profit distribution (surplus earnings) to members in proportion to use of service; surplus may be allocated in shares or cash	Possible conflict between members Longer decision-making process Participation of members required for success Extensive recordkeeping necessary Less incentive to invest additional capital

Canadian public exchange markets (stock exchanges/markets), the corporation must meet certain conditions and requirements of the province or territory in which the entity plans to go public. In addition, self-regulatory organizations such as the exchanges themselves, the Investment Dealers Association of Canada, and Market Regulation Services Inc. play an important regulatory role.

Once these conditions and requirements are met, the corporation can issue either common stock or preferred stock. Common stock is the most prevalent type of stock issued. Common shareholders are considered to have a residual claim on the cash flows of the firm; in other words, all other parties receive payment before common shareholders. They bear the most risk of any supplier of capital to a corporation.

On the other hand, preferred shareholders are paid before the common shareholders. They have a dividend that is based on the par value of the stock. However, preferred shareholders generally do not have the right to vote as the common shareholders do. Additionally, preferred stock is not issued nearly as often as common stock. For example, each day the closing stock prices from the previous day are listed in the

Exhibit 1-2 Comparison of Preferred Stocks and Bonds

Security	Features
Preferred stock	Shown in equity section of balance sheet
	Shareholder paid a fixed dividend
	Shareholder paid after bondholders, before common shareholders
	Shareholder cannot vote for board of directors
	Dividends not tax deductible for issuing corporation
	Often convertible to common stock
	Sometimes callable by the issuing corporation
Bonds	Shown as a corporate liability
	Bondholder receives a fixed interest payment
	Bondholder paid before shareholders
	Bondholders have very limited influence on corporation
	Interest payments are tax deductible for issuing corporation

Financial Post—the common stock prices take up approximately seven pages of the paper, whereas preferred stock listings take up less than one-half of one page.

Preferred stock, with its fixed dividend, is similar to a bond. Bonds are a form of debt capital issued by a corporation to investors, who receive interest payments and a repayment of their loan at the end of a specific term. Corporate bonds, just like common and preferred stock, can be traded on exchanges. Exhibit 1-2 shows a comparison of preferred stock and bonds. These financial instruments are discussed in greater detail in Chapter 2.

A *cooperative* is a type of business that is owned and controlled on an equity basis. The daily operational management of the cooperative is determined by the individuals who contribute to it in terms of both an investment interest and labour economics. Housing, lodging, retail, and utilities are common types of cooperatives.

Exhibit 1-1 summarizes the advantages and disadvantages of the four major types of business organization.

Armed with an understanding of the organization of the firm, we can proceed to develop a basic understanding of financial management in the hospitality industry.

1.4 A Basic Understanding of Financial Management

As previously discussed, financial management involves the firm's three major decisions: the **investment decision, the financing decision,** and the **dividend decision**. We discuss these decisions briefly using Exhibit 1-3.

Beginning with a simplified balance sheet, we can start to examine the three major financial decisions of the firm. The balance sheet, of course, is based on the fundamental accounting equation that states assets must equal liabilities plus owners' equity. You may recall from your accounting courses that current assets include items such as cash, accounts receivable, and inventory. Fixed assets are items such as land, building, and equipment. We have shown only two major categories to simplify the presentation.

Exhibit 1-3 SHC Balance Sheet, December 31, 200X

Assets		Liabilities	
Cash	$ 50,000	Accounts payable	$ 150,000
Accounts receivable	$ 40,000	Notes payable	$ 50,000
Inventory	$ 110,000		
Total current assets	$ 200,000	Total current liabilities	$ 200,000
		Long-term debt	$ 300,000
Fixed assets	$ 800,000		
		Total liabilities	$ 500,000
		Owners' equity	
		Preferred stock	$ 50,000
		Common stock	$ 150,000
		Retained earnings	$ 300,000
		Total equity	$ 500,000
		Total liabilities and	
Total assets	$1,000,000	owners' equity	$1,000,000

Assets are things of value that are controlled by the firm. In this example, the Sample Hotel has only 20 percent of its total assets in current assets. This is not unusual for a hotel company that owns real estate, because the assets with the highest costs are land, building, and equipment. These assets typically produce the greatest amount of revenue for the firm. The selection of which assets to hold is called the **investment decision**. The investment decision for firms is parallel to that of an individual on a microeconomic level: Because resources are limited, which assets are the best for us to own? A significant portion of this textbook involves how to determine whether an asset is worth the investment.

Moving to the right side of the balance sheet, we can see that we have liabilities (both current and long-term from lenders) and owners' equity. Current liabilities are debts owed to others (such as accounts payable and notes payable), and should be paid within one fiscal year. Long-term liabilities are debts that take longer than a year to pay (such as bonds). Owners' equity includes preferred stock, common stock, and retained earnings. Both lenders and owners have claims on the assets. The lenders have a priority claim.

How should we pay for the assets we decide to acquire? Should we borrow money, issue stock, or use retained earnings (or some combination of all three)? This decision is called the **financing decision**. In our example, the corporation has decided to finance the $1,000,000 worth of assets using equal amounts of debt and equity. The proportion of debt used versus equity varies across segments of the hospitality industry, and even across firms within one segment of the same industry. It remains an ongoing debate among analysts on how firm managers should decide how much debt or equity to have on their balance sheets.

Finally, we know that people invest in firms to make money. If they purchase common stock, they are hoping not only that the price of their stock will increase, but also that they will receive dividends. Firms have a choice regarding dividend payments.

They may choose to pay dividends to their shareholders, or they can retain these earnings and use them to finance new assets. Many firms do a combination—pay out some earnings as dividends, and retain the rest for future growth. This decision is the **dividend decision** and it is influenced by the firm's dividend policy. The intended and consistent outcome of all three financial decisions is to create or maximize the value of the owners' investment, more commonly known as wealth maximization.

1.5 Wealth Maximization

The goal of financial management is to maximize the wealth of the owners. When a firm has common stock that is publicly traded, its ultimate goal is to maximize the stock price. Wealth maximization means raising the stock price to its highest possible level.

Although it is sometimes emphasized in certain contexts, revenue maximization is not the only financial goal of a hospitality organization. Profits are a function of revenues and expenses. Therefore, if expenses increase at the same rate as or a greater rate than revenues, profits will not increase or could even decline. We can say that maximizing revenues is a necessary but insufficient condition to increase cash flows and, thus, the stock price—another reason why hospitality managers must be effective in managing both revenues and expenses.

Given the goal of financial management, it is important to know how stock prices are determined. In very general terms, the price of a share of stock is the sum of all cash flows received from the ownership in the stock. Although we cannot yet specifically determine the price of a share of stock, we can introduce the three major factors that affect the value of these dividends.

1. *The size of the dividends:* All else being equal, larger dollar-value dividends yield a higher stock price.

2. *The timing of the dividends:* All else being equal, more frequent dividend payments raise the stock price.

3. *The risk associated with the dividends:* People generally prefer less risk to more risk. Accordingly, the lower the risk associated with the dividends, the higher the stock price.

Now that we have some understanding of the determinants of the wealth of the owners, we can address the goal of wealth maximization. Why should this be the financial goal of the firm? Thinking of the income statement in reverse—looking at it from the bottom to the top—can help us understand the logic of this goal.

In terms of the priority claim on the firm's cash flow, the owners have the lowest priority and are paid last. This can be understood by visualizing the flow of a vertical income statement from top to bottom. Revenues are generated and are usually shown first. In general, direct operating expenses such as labour, benefits, supplies, and cost of goods sold are shown next. Subsequent to these expenses are the undistributed expenses such as marketing, maintenance, and energy. Last but not least are fixed expenses, such as administration and general management, insurance, and interest paid to lenders. Income taxes are paid to governmental authorities, with the owners accruing the post-tax earnings.

The owners are paid after taxes because the government is paid beforehand through taxes. However, before the government is paid, lenders are paid with principal and interest. Before the lenders the other current liabilities, such as suppliers and employees, are paid. Thus, we have covered most of the typical expenses of a hospitality operation: costs of employees, suppliers, various administrative costs (marketing, for example), costs of borrowing, and taxes to the government. Accordingly, if we have made the owners happy (remember, they get paid last), then we probably have satisfied the requirements of the other parties. It is important to remember throughout this textbook the importance of satisfying the needs of the suppliers of financial capital.

Additionally, it is important for students to understand that the goal of wealth maximization is not achieved at the expense of other departments in a hospitality organization. Hospitality financial management should be considered in conjunction with other functional areas. Basically, a good financial decision is a good business decision, and vice versa. For example, good relations with employees should help increase productivity, employee retention, and future dividends. Likewise, we cannot expect to maximize the wealth of the owners without an effective marketing program. Like other goals in the hospitality operation, wealth maximization can be viewed as a long-term goal. Arguably, all managerial decisions made within the hospitality firm have implications for the owners.

1.5.1 DIFFERENT INDIVIDUALS, DIFFERING OBJECTIVES

Hotel investments often involve numerous parties: a developer/owner, a management company, and usually a franchise company (such as Choice Hotels or Travelodge). A common way for hotel companies to operate is through the use of hotel management companies. Courtyard by Marriott is largely developed through the use of management contracts. Marriott Corporation constructs the property and sells it to a group of owners on completion. Once the sale is completed, Marriott Corporation manages the property for a fee. The advantage to Marriott Corporation is it does not have to own the real estate and can maintain the image of Courtyard through effective and consistent management. On the other hand, the owners pay management fees knowing their property is being managed by a large, experienced hospitality company.

Accordingly, when a management company signs an agreement to work for the owners, an **agency relationship** is established. The term *agency* originated from the practice of corporations delegating decision making to their hired agents (management), who theoretically act in the best interest of the principals (outside financiers). **Agency problems** are caused by the conflicting interests among a corporation's various stakeholders. Stakeholders include management, owners, creditors, employees, suppliers, and government.

The design of the contract between the two parties is crucial to the success of the enterprise. Given that each individual in the relationship is attempting to maximize his or her own welfare, different ideas about what is the best course of action can arise. Because most corporations have numerous stakeholders, the corporation is actually a complex web of relationships among them. The following is a discussion of some of the typical agency problems arising from these agency relationships.

Agency problems frequently occur between managers and owners. For example, one type of problem is shirking, which can occur if a manager receives only a high, fixed salary that is guaranteed. With no positive incentive to increase profits, the manager may choose simply to work as few hours as possible (without incurring the risk of termination). One way to solve this problem is to offer the manager stock in the company or a portion of the profits. The basic strategy here is to align the incentives for the manager with those of the owners.

Another classic agency problem between managers and owners relates to excessive consumption of perquisites, such as the use of corporate jets, fancy offices, and other executive privileges. The incentive–compensation method for solving this problem has already been mentioned. Other methods include threat of termination and/or takeover of the company. Finally, another way to solve this problem is through the use of increased monitoring of management actions. To better control this type of problem the board of directors of the company can hire auditors, who will discover and reveal any excessive spending by management that decreases the value of the firm.

Other agency relationships exist in the hospitality industry. One of these is the owner–lender relationship. The ability to raise debt capital is important to the hospitality industry. However, the primary task of managers is to maximize the wealth of the shareholders, not necessarily to increase the price of the company bonds. Accordingly, agency problems can also occur between bondholders (lenders) and shareholders. There are circumstances in which managers can invest in risky ventures whose benefits, if the project pays off, largely accrue to the shareholders. On the other hand, if the project fails, the loss is greater to the bondholders. The splitting of Marriott Corporation into two separate companies in October 1992 is an example. On the day of the announcement, the value of Marriott bonds decreased by approximately 30 percent, while the value of Marriott common stock increased approximately 12 percent. Although controversial at the time, the action taken by Marriott was intended to increase the wealth of the shareholders. Since then, Marriott International has operated very successfully as a hotel management company. Host Marriott began operating as a real estate investment trust (REIT) in 1999 and leases hotels and resorts to subsidiaries. Overall, one could certainly argue that the decision to split into separate companies led to a successful outcome.

1.5.2 TAKING ACTIONS TO INCREASE VALUE

The goal of wealth maximization may seem distant to a hospitality operations manager. However, by thinking about the elements of an income statement once again, we can easily give astute consideration to a host of actions managers can take to help increase the overall value of the enterprise.

One example is controlling expenses. Labour expense is usually the largest expense for most hotels and the second largest for most restaurants. If managers can increase employee efficiency and decrease labour costs, cash flow will increase. Controlling food and beverage costs (usually the largest expense category for food and beverage operations) also increases cash flow.

From a sales perspective, increasing revenues also help increase cash flow, assuming costs remain the same. Discounting room rates or prices can, in the proper context, perform this function. Another way to increase value is opening an existing restaurant at different hours. This was the idea McDonald's had many years ago about opening for breakfast. Using existing locations that previously had served only lunch and dinner, McDonald's developed a new menu and had to incur only some incremental labour costs to develop and later dominate the fast-food breakfast market.

It is important for students to understand that, in reality, most of the everyday tasks completed by managers are done for the financial well-being of the firm. Specifically, most hospitality managers increase shareholder value by decreasing expenses, increasing revenue, or some combination of the two. In a general sense, managers take actions to address the three factors affecting the stock price discussed earlier.

1.5.3 UNDERTAKING PROJECTS TO CREATE VALUE

Successful companies often use good ideas to create value for their shareholders. These ideas can turn into significant opportunities that change not only the financial position of the company but also the industry in which the company operates. Many hospitality examples exist; we discuss a few here.

Kemmons Wilson, the founder of Holiday Inn, built his hotel chain on good ideas. He got many of his ideas after travelling with his family to Washington, D.C. Along the way, he found roadside accommodations to be of only minimal and inconsistent quality. He was upset by many motels charging extra fees for children staying in the same room with their parents and not offering any food and beverage service.

Recognizing the needs of travelling families like his own, he developed a chain of hotels that offered his guests swimming pools, food and beverage service, and the opportunity for children under the age of 12 to stay with their parents for no extra charge. Although common today, these simple ideas were revolutionary when first implemented.

Other innovations by Wilson had a larger impact on the hotel business as we know it. Holiday Inn had the first nationwide reservation system, known as Holidex. Furthermore, the chain was the first to partner with a gas company and accept its credit cards for payment at Holiday Inn hotels (Holiday Inns at one time accepted the Gulf credit card).

Another lodging giant, Marriott Corporation, pioneered the guest rewards program in the hotel industry and was the first to offer in-room video checkout. Additionally, many good ideas are thought of not by the company but instead by its customers. For example, Marriott conducted extensive consumer research before it designed the Courtyard by Marriott prototype. After listening to customers, Marriott designed rooms tailored for the business traveller, offering two telephones, high-speed Internet access, in-room coffee, exercise facilities, and other amenities frequently requested by this market segment. Accordingly, good ideas helped Marriott create value for its shareholders and spur its tremendous growth.

So far we have given examples of good ideas that created value for shareholders. However, we have looked at these ideas in hindsight. How do we know in advance whether or not we have a good idea? In other words, how do we know our potential project will create value? The project could be a new hotel, a new wing of rooms, a new gaming boat, or any number of different projects undertaken nearly every day in the hospitality industry. Can we be certain about the outcome?

Unfortunately, we do not live in a world with perfect information, nor can we predict the future with certainty. Nevertheless, managers must make decisions about which assets to invest in. We call this situation "decision making under uncertainty." Uncertainty can also be

Exhibit 1-4 New Hotel Project Summary	
Projected incremental benefits	$5,000,000
Projected incremental costs	($4,000,000)
Projected net incremental benefits	$1,000,000

defined as risk. **Risk** really should not be thought of as taking a chance but instead as the potential for outcomes to be different from our expectations—whereby the greater the difference between the outcome and our expectations, the greater the risk (for better or for worse).

Therefore, knowing that nearly every undertaking has some risk associated with it, we can incorporate this into our calculations regarding **value creation.** In Chapter 6, we discuss the different types of risk and how they are measured. But for now, we take a preliminary look at the big picture of value creation.

Consider the proposed hotel project shown in Exhibit 1-4. We see the project generates incremental benefits of $5,000,000. The term *incremental* refers to the additional benefits or costs attributable to this project alone. By subtracting the costs from the benefits, we obtain the net incremental benefits of $1,000,000.

Should we invest in the proposed project? In the absence of other information, it appears we should. Why? If we invest in the new hotel, the shareholders will be wealthier. How much wealthier will they become? The project summary indicates the owners will become $1,000,000 wealthier. Thus, the new hotel project *creates value*. On the other hand, suppose the costs were *greater* than the benefits. We would then have a value-destroying project, and it would be rejected.

Thus far, we have discussed the investment decision. If the aforementioned project were undertaken, the financing decision also would have to be involved. Finally, after the project began to generate economic benefits, the managers would be involved in the dividend decision. Thus, all three financial decisions made by managers either affect or are affected by the process of value creation.

1.6 A General Outline of the Textbook

This book deals in detail mainly with the process of value creation. Each chapter contains chapter objectives provided as an informal benchmark against which students can measure their progress. In addition to the text itself, each of the following chapters contains a chapter summary and a list of key terms used in the chapter; a glossary defining the key terms is provided at the end of the book. Finally, the chapters contain a number of discussion questions and problems.

Chapter 2 provides the student with an introduction to the three principal sources of financing: internally generated funds, debt, and equity.

Chapter 3 speaks to the Canadian financial environment and provides the student with an overview of Canadian financial intermediaries. In particular, a discussion on the Canadian banking system, legal scope, compliance, and regulations is provided, along with a look at pension funds and insurance companies as a potential source of project capital.

Chapter 4 introduces the financial world at large, specifically in the form of capital markets and financial instruments. Included in this chapter is a discussion of stock and bond exchanges, hospitality lenders, and the importance of hedging risk by using forward and futures markets.

Chapter 5 reviews the major financial statements and the uniform system of accounts. The chapter also examines the relationship between the financial statements and various ratios used by financial managers.

Chapter 6 introduces students to the concept of risk and the different types of risk. Moreover, it develops in detail the relationship between risk and return. Chapter 7 gets to the heart of the textbook, the time value of money. This concept is key to determining whether or not a project creates value for the owners. Chapters 8 and 9 discuss the procedures for the valuation of bonds, preferred stock, and common stock. This helps the student become familiar with the financing decision. Chapter 10 discusses the important concept of cost of capital.

Chapter 11 begins a two-chapter introduction to the concept of capital budgeting, and Chapter 12 provides an applied example of deciding whether to invest in a new hospitality project. These chapters relate to the first of the major financial decisions, the investment decision.

Chapter 13 builds on the capital budgeting concepts from Chapters 11 and 12 to discuss in detail the valuation of hospitality investments such as hotels. Chapter 14 discusses the concept of capital structure management. Although this involves the financing decision, it shows how firms must not only find value-creating projects but also try to minimize the cost of capital for those who supply funds for the project. Finally, Chapter 15 looks at the current and popular topic of mergers and acquisitions (M&A).

In summary, the first 12 chapters cover the time value of money, risk and return, the cost of capital, and investment in long-term assets (an example of which we discussed in the previous section). The last three chapters involve more specific topics in hospitality finance: valuation/appraisal, capital structure, and M&A activity and concepts. Building on the basic knowledge of the time value of money and risk and return, these later chapters provide more detail regarding the important decisions financial managers make.

1.7 SUMMARY

This chapter

- Introduced the scope of hospitality financial management
- Explained the relationships between finance and other functional areas of business management
- Explained the different forms of business organization
- Introduced the three main decisions in financial management
- Explained the goal of wealth maximization
- Introduced the different types of agency relationships
- Explained the ways managers act to increase value
- Explained how projects are undertaken to create value
- Provided a brief introduction to the remainder of the text

Key Terms

Agency problem

Agency relationship

Dividend decision

Financing decision

Investment decision

Risk

Value creation

Discussion Questions

1. What is financial management?

2. How is financial management different from accounting?

3. What are the advantages of a corporation? The disadvantages?

4. What are the three fundamental decisions of financial management?

5. What three factors affect the present worth of future dividends?

6. What is the difference between wealth maximization and value creation?

7. How do hospitality managers increase (maximize) value for their shareholders? Give some examples from your own experience.

8. Define an agency relationship. Who are the most typical parties involved in agency relationships in financial management?

9. Why do agency problems exist in financial management?

10. How do we know if a proposed project creates value for the shareholders?

11. How can a good decision in one functional area of hospitality management affect the financial position of the owners? Give some examples.

12. Describe some recent developments in hospitality financial management that have been in the news but are not discussed in this chapter.

Chapter 2
Fundamental Principles of Financial Management

Chapter Objectives

This chapter covers the following topics:

1   The three principal sources of financing

2   A definition of internally generated funds

3   How a hospitality firm can increase internally generated funds

4   How internally generated funds can be used as a source of financing

5   A definition of equity financing

6   How a hospitality firm can secure equity financing

7   An explanation of debt financing

8   How a hospitality firm can secure debt financing

9   How internally generated funds, equity, and debt financing work together

2.1 Introduction to the Fundamental Principles of Financial Management

All hospitality enterprises require financial, human, and physical resources in order to plan, establish, commence, and conduct day-to-day operations. In particular, financial resources must be secured so that many of the required assets and resources can be acquired as needed. Both initial and future **capital outlays** continue throughout the life of the hospitality business and therefore a need for financing always exists. In the beginning—sometimes even before any physical assets have been secured—the identified aggregate financial requirement is often referred to as **startup capital**, **venture capital** (private equity), or **seed money**. Further, as the hospitality business conducts operations on a day-to-day basis, it also requires **working capital** (current assets minus current liabilities) so that short-term maturing financial obligations are satisfied along with any immediate expenditures that arise during the normal course of business. Three theoretical examples that speak to the concepts identified above are provided below.

■   Canadian Restaurants Inc. plans to open 20 stores across Canada by 2014. It has identified the need for $400,000 today to cover the costs of setting up an office and hiring graduates of a hotel and restaurant management program to assist in the strategic planning process.

- Canadian Casinos Ltd. needs to build an on-site massive electronic marquee that will help advertise the entertainment venues to be hosted at its new resort property. Company officials believe $1,000,000 will be required for this project.
- McDonald's Canada intends to introduce new Olympic-themed staff uniforms to all of its British Columbia stores in time for the 2010 Winter Olympics at an estimated cost of $200,000.

In the examples provided above, Canadian Restaurants requires startup capital or seed money, Canadian Casinos needs additional capital funds, and the McDonald's Canada plan calls for more working capital. With Canadian Restaurants the seed money may come from equity financing, debt financing, or both. Canadian Casinos can use internally generated funds, debt or equity financing, or some combination of all three. Finally, McDonald's Canada in all likelihood would make use of internally generated funds. This leads us to our first topic, an introduction to what comprises internally generated funds.

2.2 Internally Generated Funds

In an ideal world, the objective to make a profit should be easily found within the strategic master plan as well as in the basic operating agenda for all hospitality enterprises. Preferably, what constitutes a profit for the business is much more tangible than just a theoretical positive dollar value identified on paper. Instead, profit should to some degree represent actual money that is placed in the owner's pocket as an outcome of successful business operations. This, for the most part, is the concept of internally generated funds. Any and all money produced as a result of profitable operations qualifies to be labelled as **internally generated funds**: funds created as a result of revenues exceeding expenses. It does not represent money raised or provided as a result of any external transaction, such as securing a bank loan or selling shares on a public stock exchange. Those are balance sheet transactions and have no impact on the overall financial performance of the hospitality enterprise. There are also some practical treatments that can be applied to enhance and improve the value of a firm's internally generated funds; we explain and demonstrate these for you in this chapter.

We first look at the effect of depreciation and its impact on a firm's value of internally generated funds. A quick overview of depreciation is appropriate here. Remember that **depreciation, amortization**, and **capitalization** are all methods of cost allocation whereby specific charges are consistently appropriated over a long period (more than one operating cycle or one fiscal year, whichever is greater). With depreciation in particular, this accounting procedure of cost allocation continues until there is no remaining book value for the relevant asset(s) as identified on the balance sheet. These cost allocation treatments are necessary to facilitate the reduction of the firm's book values of assets as found on the balance sheet. This accounting treatment helps to provide a more accurate assessment of the hospitality enterprise's true total assets value and, consequently, net worth. Further, these types of charges—whether depreciation, amortization, or capitalization—do not represent true out-of-pocket expenses; they are only a method to appropriate and match a measured portion of use, value, benefit, and/or utility of a particular element within and for a defined period of time. In layman's terms, no actual "real" money leaves the general chequing account when depreciation, amortization, and/or capitalization charges occur.

Exhibit 2-1 Depreciation As a Tax Shield

	Niagara Hotel & Resorts Ltd.	
	(without depreciation)	(with depreciation)
Revenue	$1,000,000	$1,000,000
Operating expenses	300,000	300,000
Gross operating profit	700,000	700,000
Fixed expenses	100,000	100,000
Depreciation	0	**80,000**
EBIT	600,000	520,000
Interest	40,000	40,000
EBT	560,000	480,000
Tax expense (40%)	224,000	192,000
Net income	$ 324,000	$ 288,000

Remember that in the case of depreciation the capital outlay already occurred when the assets were first acquired by the firm. Also remember from your financial accounting course that whenever depreciation, amortization, and/or capitalization charges are incurred they automatically provide the hospitality enterprise with a **tax shield**. Accordingly, depreciation, amortization, and capitalization can be positive contributors to the hospitality enterprise's value of internally generated funds (see Exhibit 2-1).

As you can see from Exhibit 2-1, the depreciation charge of $80,000 results in a reduction of $32,000 ($224,000 − $192,000) in tax expense for Niagara Hotel and Resorts Ltd. This $32,000 in tax savings represents the provision of an additional $24,000 in internally generated funds.

It is worthwhile to recognize not only that depreciation assists in reducing a firm's tax expense, but also that as a result of lowering the firm's net income value a publicly traded hospitality enterprise would have fewer funds available to reward shareholders on record for their investment in the firm. Continuing with the Niagara Hotel and Resorts example, the financial templates provided in Exhibit 2-2 illustrate the impact of depreciation on earnings per share (EPS).

Exhibit 2-2 shows there would be approximately $0.48 less in EPS to be paid out by the hospitality enterprise as a result of the $80,000 depreciation charge. Therefore, one should objectively as well as intuitively recognize that more internally generated funds would be provided as a result of any depreciation, amortization, and/or capitalization charges incurred by the firm that intends to reward its shareholders by paying out **dividends**.

A hospitality enterprise can be successful in creating internally generated funds as a result of profitable operations, the effective use of tax shields, and prudent dividend policy. Therefore, if the hospitality manager can embrace and leverage the concept of internally generated funds, they can be used as a consistent and dependable monetary stream as well as a source of financing for current working projects or ambitious capital endeavours. This concept of internally generated funds is commonly referred to within the accounting and finance community as "plowing back profits."

Exhibit 2-2 Depreciation Impact on EPS Value

	Niagara Hotel & Resorts Ltd. Dividends to Shareholders Payout 100,000 Shareholders on Record	
	(without depreciation)	(with depreciation)
Revenue	$1,000,000	$1,000,000
Operating expenses	300,000	300,000
Gross operating profit	700,000	700,000
Fixed expenses	100,000	100,000
Depreciation	**0**	**80,000**
EBIT	600,000	520,000
Interest	40,000	40,000
EBT	560,000	480,000
Tax expense (40%)	224,000	192,000
Net income	$ 336,000	$ 288,000
Earnings per share	$ 3.366	$ 2.88

2.3 Equity Financing

Another source of financing for the hospitality enterprise is the use of equity. **Equity financing** represents financial resources secured as a result of the business owner investing his or her own money, selling company stock, having other investors make a financial commitment to the firm, or some combination of the above.

Within the hospitality industry, and in particular among small business owners, most first-time entrepreneurs use their own money or funds provided by family members and close friends. The entrepreneur commonly and diligently cobbles together equity financing by dipping into a personal savings account, selling personal assets, and/or refinancing existing assets such as a house. Sometimes the entrepreneur is fortunate enough to secure angel investors. **Angel investors** are typically affluent, commerce-minded individuals who see potential and promise in the proposed hospitality enterprise and are willing to provide the required startup capital. The funds provided by the angel investors are exchanged for shares in the company. This transaction can prove to be quite lucrative in some cases; however, sometimes the angel investor ends up with nothing. In some situations the hospitality enterprise has successfully secured human resources or intellectual capital in exchange for an "equity kicker." An **equity kicker** is an arrangement in which an individual agrees to provide services to a hospitality enterprise in exchange for little or no pay but a significant portion of the company's shares. The hope for the person participating in an equity kicker scheme is that eventually those company shares will be worth something. A recent example is provided by Teresa Cascioli, the former CEO of Lakeport Breweries. Cascioli joined the Hamilton, Ontario–based brewery in 1999 for very little pay and a 21 percent stake in the company. As a result of her expertise in guiding Lakeport to become a highly successful beverage operation, in 2007 the brewery was purchased by Labatt Brewing Co. For Cascioli, letting go of her 21 percent ownership in Lakeport to the purchaser (Labatt) earned her more than $43 million. With no guarantees but lots of optimism and the skill set to get the job done, agreeing to an equity kicker was a smart move for Teresa Cascioli.

For well-established hospitality enterprises with a proven track record regarding financial performance and position, the stock market is a viable option for equity financing. In Canada the general public can invest in publicly traded Canadian hospitality corporations on public stock markets including the Toronto Stock Exchange and the Toronto Venture Exchange. (See Chapters 4 and 9 for more in-depth discussion of equity financing.)

2.4 Debt Financing

The third source of financing for the hospitality enterprise is debt. Debt financing can take on a variety of forms and provides an opportunity for the hospitality manager to be discerning with respect to choosing the best possible debt instrument for the firm's financial requirements. However, if the hospitality enterprise is struggling financially, it is a great challenge to find a willing provider of debt financing.

For small-business owners and first-time entrepreneurs, secured equity financing usually opens the door to obtain some degree of debt financing. Under most circumstances, lenders are not willing to provide debt financing unless the hospitality enterprise has some equity already in place. Therefore, entrenched equity represents the fact that a financial commitment to the hospitality enterprise has been made and for that reason lowers the amount of risk incurred by a lender who may provide most of the required financing. Thus, the attractiveness and viability of providing debt financing increases in direct proportion to the amount of equity financing already secured for hospitality startups and relatively new businesses.

The two principal types of debt financing are loans and bonds. Loans may be obtained from any financial institution. It is imperative the hospitality manager has a complete understanding of the terms and conditions of the loan agreement to mitigate any possibility of paying too much in interest or service charges, or of defaulting on the loan itself.

Floating (bringing to market) a bond issue is much more complex than obtaining a loan and is a viable source of financing only for the hospitality enterprise that has an established significant asset base and a successful financial record to date. A more detailed discussion on bonds is provided in Chapter 8, "Fixed Income Securities: Bonds and Preferred Stock."

One of the best possible resources for professional assistance in securing debt financing for small and medium-sized hospitality businesses is the Business Development Bank of Canada, more commonly known as the BDC (www.bdc.ca). The BDC, a financial institution owned entirely by the Canadian federal government, is an excellent resource whether the business is in a startup scenario or already up and running. It can provide flexible financing solution sets, consulting services at reasonable prices, and the possibility of access to venture capital. BDC branches are strategically located in every province and territory across the country. The BDC also offers the convenience of online financing applications for those businesses that have at least one year of financial data and history.

Hospitality managers also can apply at other financial institutions to secure debt financing in the form of a loan, although it is important to note that obtaining a bank loan is often difficult and is not an absolute. Many applicants are denied the opportunity to borrow money for a new or existing hospitality-related business. Accordingly, debt financing has a very high barrier to entry for most hospitality enterprises. One of the most influential reasons why hospitality-related businesses have such a challenge in obtaining debt financing in the form of a bank loan is the high business failure rate within the industry. Most lending organizations want the applicant to provide a business plan, evidence that personal assets can be pledged as collateral, and proof of professional management qualifications, such as postsecondary education in hospitality management and relevant work experience. (Herein lies another valid reason why your education is so important!) In those rare circumstances when a financial institution is willing to lend money, the standard relationship is that the greater the amount of identified risk (as calculated and determined by the lender), the higher the interest rate the borrower pays on the outstanding principal amount. Additionally, the loan agreement might also stipulate a compensating balance requirement. Clearly, debt financing can become a very expensive source of funds for the hospitality enterprise. Chapter 6, "The Relationship between Risk and Return," and Chapter 10, "Cost of Capital," provide additional information and greater depth on the important topic of debt financing.

2.5 How Internally Generated Funds, Equity, and Debt Work Together

In this chapter we have discussed the three main sources of financing for the hospitality enterprise: internally generated funds, equity, and debt. As previously identified, internally generated funds are not an option for a new hospitality enterprise. In all likelihood, equity and debt will be the principal sources of financing for a new business startup. However, once the business proves itself a success any one of the three sources of financing, or any combination of the three, will become available to the hospitality manager in need of additional funding.

It is important to recognize that the cost of financing a hospitality enterprise depends upon the type of financing secured by the business. If the business is using only internally generated funds as a source of financing for current operations, what is the cost associated with this financial management choice? An easy way to determine what internally generated funds cost is to use a current bank savings rate, which represents the economic opportunity cost incurred by the hospitality enterprise. For example, assume the Canadian "Best in the West" Burger Company generates $200,000 in net income for fiscal year-end 2007. Instead of parking this money in a savings account to earn 4.25 percent interest per annum, the company's executives decide to reinvest the $200,000 into store operations (and, more specifically, product quality) by spending the money on staff training and development. Therefore, the decision to use internally generated funds to pay for staff training and development has cost the hospitality enterprise approximately $8,500 ($200,000 × 4.25%) for the year.

The calculations that can be applied to determine the cost of equity are a little more involved and are discussed in Chapter 9, "Common Stock," as are other formulas employed to determine the cost of debt, which will be illustrated in Chapter 10, "Cost of Capital."

It is important to recognize here that the duty and obligation of the hospitality financial manager is to find the optimal mix of internally generated funds, equity, and debt. When this objective is achieved, the business has access to the required funds when they are needed and at the lowest possible cost to the hospitality enterprise. This is what financial managers refer to as the **optimal capital structure**, and is discussed in greater detail and scope in Chapter 14, "Capital Structure." When the right blend of internally generated funds, equity, and debt has been identified and secured by using a strategic approach to financing the hospitality enterprise, the business entity reaps the financial rewards of an effective and efficient capital structure.

2.6 SUMMARY

This chapter:

- Introduced the three principal sources of financing
- Defined internally generated funds
- Explained how a hospitality firm can increase internally generated funds
- Explained how internally generated funds can be used as a source of financing
- Defined equity financing
- Explained how a hospitality firm can secure equity financing
- Explained debt financing
- Explained how a hospitality firm can secure debt financing
- Outlined how internally generated funds, equity, and debt financing work together

Key Terms

Amortization

Angel investors

Capital outlays

Capitalization

Depreciation

Dividends

Equity financing

Equity kicker

Internally generated funds

Optimal capital structure

Seed money

Startup capital

Tax shield

Venture capital

Working capital

Discussion Questions

1. What are the three principal sources of financing for the hospitality enterprise?
2. What are internally generated funds?
3. How can the value of internally generated funds be maximized?
4. Can a new hospitality business use internally generated funds? Why or why not?
5. What is equity?
6. What is a common form of equity financing for entrepreneurs starting a new hospitality enterprise?
7. What is debt?
8. Is it easy to secure debt financing for the hospitality enterprise?
9. What is optimal capital structure?

Chapter 3
The Canadian Financial Environment

Chapter Objectives

This chapter covers the following topics:

1 An introduction to Canadian financial intermediaries

2 An outline of the Canadian financial system

3 An introduction to Canadian banking

4 The role of the Bank of Canada

5 Canadian legal reporting and compliance requirements

6 An introduction to trust companies, insurance firms, and pension funds

3.1 Introduction

This chapter introduces the student to the how, what, and why of Canadian financial intermediaries and the important role they play in contributing to the Canadian financial system. A brief overview of Canadian banking is provided with some articulation of the different types of banks that conduct business on Canadian soil. An examination of the functions performed by the Bank of Canada as well as a brief discussion on Canadian legal reporting and compliance requirements for banks is provided. Finally, the student will gain an insight as to how trust companies, insurance firms, and pension funds can be potential sources of financing for the hospitality enterprise.

3.2 Canadian Financial Intermediaries

The Canadian financial system is perhaps one of the most efficient and effective exchange processes in the world. Many options are available to consumers and corporations alike regarding where and how their money can be borrowed, deposited, channelled, invested, and redistributed. Investors have some assurance that their invested money, held in account, is safe—and, perhaps more importantly, that their investments are legitimate.

Financial intermediary corporations including chartered banks, trust companies, life insurance firms, pension funds, finance companies, credit unions, and other financial intermediary specialist entities such as brokerage houses encourage consumers to invest their surplus cash into the financial instruments they promote. The prospect of being financially rewarded for participating in such investments is presented and identified to the investing consumer via advertising and a variety of promotional written literature, including **prospectuses**. Upon successfully securing the consumer's or investor's funds—as the result of a combination of an attractive prospectus, solid marketing and promotion, productive meetings, positive financial analysis, and artful negotiation—the financial intermediary may shuttle the consumer's surplus cash into a capital market, where the funds become available to entrepreneurs and other business entities requiring a capital infusion either in a startup or expansion scenario. Alternatively, the financial intermediary may provide the capital to the hospitality enterprise directly; this method of financing represents an indirect approach and is a departure from more conventional or traditional financing practices, such as going to the bank for a loan.

Clearly, financial intermediaries can be a friendly and valuable resource to the hospitality financial manager in search of additional or required capital for a hospitality enterprise. Within the hospitality industry, as in other business sectors, the financial intermediary fundamentally acts as a broker on behalf of the hospitality enterprise, actively seeking an investor to provide required capital and facilitating the actions required for the capital provider and capital searcher to eventually end up working together, either directly or indirectly. In short, the financial buyer (the one who needs the capital) is put in touch with the financial seller (the provider of capital).

In Canada, professional firms such as PKF Consulting, BLG, Integrated Hospitality Management, HVS International, and others act as agents on behalf of their clients in procuring and securing required capital. This service is provided for a professional fee. Hospitality financial managers should explore the possibility of using the services of a financial intermediary to assess whether the financial benefits exceed the financial costs.

3.3 The Canadian Financial System

In Canada the most important financial system players are the chartered banks, trust and insurance companies, and investment firms. As identified earlier in this chapter, Canada's financial system is very reliable and secure. To this end, you can think of the Canadian financial system as a big sturdy work table. If you were to look underneath the table, you would find four strong legs providing the required support. These four legs represent the chartered banks, trust companies, insurance firms, and investment entities. All of these organizations qualify as financial intermediaries. To this end, they can assist the hospitality enterprise in securing required capital.

3.4 Canadian Banking

The first Canadian chartered bank was the Bank of Montreal, from May 19, 1817. Since then, the number of banks has multiplied and under the direction of the Canadian Bank Act, there are now 22 domestic banks. Further, there are also 24 foreign bank subsidiaries, 20 full-service foreign banks, and 20 foreign bank lending branches conducting business operations in Canada. All together, these banks employ approximately 250,000 people and manage more than $2.5 trillion in assets (about the equivalent of China's current gross

Exhibit 3-1 Schedule I Banks in Canada	
BMO (Bank of Montreal)	Bank West
BCPBank Canada	Bridgewater Bank
CIBC	Canadian Tire Bank
Canadian Western Bank	Citizens Bank of Canada
CS Alterna Bank	Dundee Bank of Canada
First Nations Bank of Canada	General Bank of Canada
Laurentian Bank of Canada	Manulife Bank of Canada
National Bank of Canada	National Bank of Greece (Canada)
Pacific & Western Bank of Canada	President's Choice Bank
RBC Royal Bank	Scotiabank (Bank of Nova Scotia)
TD Bank Financial Group	Ubiquity Bank of Canada

domestic product—a very significant responsibility!). Canadian banks serve millions of customers each day both online via the Internet (about 42 percent of all transactions) and in person (approximately 58 percent of all transactions).

Most foreign banks have only a modest number of satellite operations in Canada and their range of services is limited. The exception is HSBC Canada, which is a full-service bank and has a significant presence right across the country.

The major Canadian domestic banks, known as **Schedule I banks**, are authorized under the Bank Act to accept deposits. They are able to retain a small portion of the depositor's money on hand while the rest goes outside the bank in some form of investment or debt instrument. Further, they embody Canada's chartered banks (see Exhibit 3-1). Foreign bank subsidiaries that are controlled and owned by foreign banks are called **Schedule II banks**, and they also have the legal authority to accept deposits. Therefore, they also provide other banking services and are able to leverage the depositor's money for additional financial gain. Finally, the **Schedule III banks** represent foreign bank lending branches that operate under precise restrictions and that do not have legal authority to accept deposits.

It is important to realize that Schedule I banks are insured by the **Canadian Deposit Insurance Corporation (CDIC)**, a federal government agency, up to $100,000 per account (this amount was raised from $60,000 in 2005). Some Schedule II banks may also qualify for the insurance services CDIC provides to account holders.

3.5 The Bank of Canada

All banks operating in Canada depend to some degree upon the services provided by Canada's central bank, the **Bank of Canada**. The Bank of Canada is Canada's counterpart to the **Federal Reserve**, a federal government institution in the United States. The Bank of Canada does not operate as other commercial banks do, and its banking services are for the most part not available to the general public.

The Bank, founded in 1934, is located in Ottawa and operated as a privately owned corporation until 1938, when it became a Crown corporation (managed by the Government of Canada). The Bank exists for the people of Canada and is owned by the people of Canada. The federal Minister of Finance is the principal steward of the Bank and holds all the issued share capital. Accordingly, the Minister of Finance can be held accountable for any misconduct by the Bank.

The Bank is a significant piece of Canada's financial system and performs many important roles. First, it provides expert guidance, governance, and direction with respect to monetary policy. Herein, **monetary policy** is primarily concerned with the health of the economy and what the Bank can do to improve the likelihood that Canadians will enjoy a robust and productive economy—which hopefully includes a low unemployment rate, low interest rates, and strong purchasing power from the Canadian dollar. These positive aims are accomplished in part by focusing both on the money supply (i.e., how much money is in circulation) and on the value of the Canadian dollar in terms of domestic purchasing power and foreign exchange. Accordingly, the Bank controls how much money is in circulation by releasing additional bank notes or retiring bank notes from Canada's financial system as deemed necessary. Remember from your economics course that when there is a greater amount of money in circulation there is also a greater possibility that the value of the dollar will decline. So if the value of the Canadian dollar starts to decline, more bank notes can be retired without replacement by the Bank to shore up the value of the dollar. Alternatively, if the value of the Canadian dollar is high, then the Bank can increase the money supply into Canada's financial system, although this action may also cause unwanted inflationary pressure in the long run.

Additionally, as part of prudent monetary policy management the Bank monitors inflation and sets short-term interest rates in an appropriate and justified manner. Once again, remember from your economics course that interest rates are an effective inflation fighter as well as an efficient demand stimulator. High interest rates can curtail inflation, and low interest rates can stimulate demand. The Bank's goal is to keep Canada's inflation around 2 percent. As at June 2007, Canada's inflation rate was 2.2 percent and the Bank of Canada's overnight lending rate (ONLR) was 4.5 percent. Within this framework, as inflation increases the Bank will respond appropriately by increasing short-term interest rates. When the Bank changes interest rates it usually does so in increments of 25 basis points. For example, on June 10, 2007, the Bank increased its ONLR from 4.25 percent to 4.50 percent—an increase of 25 basis points. As at April 21, 2008, the inflation rate was only 1.4 percent, and the ONLR was set at 3.5 percent. Given the low inflation rate, on April 22, 2008, the Bank of Canada slashed the ONLR by 50 basis points to 3.0 percent.

The Bank is managed by a Governor, currently Mark J. Carney. Born in Fort Smith, Northwest Territories, Carney received a bachelor's degree in economics from Harvard University in 1988. He received a master's degree in economics in 1993 and a doctorate in economics in 1995, both from Oxford University. The selection process for the Governor of the Bank of Canada is basically a political appointment. Carney was appointed on February 1, 2008, by Prime Minister Stephen Harper. Carney replaces outgoing Governor David Dodge, who held the position since February 1, 2001. A typical appointment as Governor is seven years in length. The Governor is appointed by a special committee of the Bank's Board of Directors, subject to approval by the Minister of Finance and the federal cabinet.

The Governor and his administrative staff meet regularly to examine and discuss the state of Canada's economy. Additionally, the Governor and his senior executive branch meet exactly eight times each year to specifically review inflationary pressure, the value of the Canadian dollar, the unemployment rate, gross domestic product, and Canada's balance of trade, and to make a decision as to whether the bank rate should be decreased, increased, or left unchanged. The outcome of these important and significant events becomes public knowledge on the same day the meetings are held, usually by late afternoon. These public broadcasts and subsequent press releases are referred to as Bank of Canada interest rate announcements. (In comparison, the U.S. Federal Reserve has a Chairman, currently Ben Bernanke, and it also makes use of eight fixed meeting dates a year, which result in Federal Reserve interest rate announcements.)

The second role of the Bank is to monitor and control bank notes, and to ensure that Canada has an adequate amount of secure bank notes in circulation to meet current levels of demand. It is also imperative that new bank notes with the latest anti-counterfeit features are constantly introduced. As such, the Bank retires old bank notes at every opportunity and injects new ones into the financial system. Further, the Bank is always involved in researching and developing new security features for Canada's bank notes. The Bank's principal objective in this regard is to make it as difficult as possible for counterfeiters to produce illegal, fraudulent bank notes. In Canada the RCMP works closely with the Bank to apprehend, deter, and charge those who produce, circulate, distribute, or use counterfeit bank notes. (In comparison, in the U.S. this task is performed largely by the Secret Service and the FBI.)

The third role performed by the Bank is to provide cash as required to those financial institutions that are actively engaged in Canada's financial system. This is done by electronically transferring money overnight to commercial banks so that Canada's **payments system** (the interexchange financial network that connects Canadian banks for the clearing and settlement of accounts) can continue to operate effectively and efficiently.

Finally, the Bank acts as the "fiscal agent" for the Government of Canada. This means that the Bank manages all of the federal government's accounts (i.e., pays the bills through Treasury operations), accepts responsibility for debt management, and provides stewardship over Canada's foreign-exchange reserves.

3.6 Canadian Legal Reporting and Compliance Requirements

The Government of Canada has the exclusive legal authority over how banks conduct business in Canada as per the Canadian Constitution Act of 1867. To this end, the banking sector is a heavily regulated industry with very tight operating parameters and pragmatic restrictions. In particular, financial institutions that provide monetary products and services across the country are subjected to regulatory policies and procedures by both federal and provincial authorities, which can create some cost redundancies, inefficiencies, and overlap. However, it is to the consumer's benefit to have an extra layer of protection in place, and this possible redundancy may also be to the bank's advantage. For example, if a bank is not satisfied with a judgment or ruling issued in a provincial or territorial court, it may appeal to the Supreme Court of Canada.

In Canada, the **Office of the Superintendent of Financial Institutions (OSFI)**, a federal government agency, performs the tasks of monitoring, evaluating, and policing all banks conducting business in Canada. The OSFI also provides the technical regulatory framework, guidance, and rules for all banks. As such, all banks are subject to periodical audits and have formal reporting obligations to the OSFI that must be satisfied. These compliance requirements represent a significant contributing factor to the reliability and safety of banking in Canada and help to protect the consumer.

3.7 Trust Companies, Insurance Firms, and Pension Funds

3.7.1 TRUST COMPANIES

Trust companies are significantly different from what they used to be. In the past, trust companies conducted business in a **fiduciary** capacity only—that is, they provided administrative services for estates, asset management, pension funds, living trusts, charitable trusts, and so on. As the name implies, the benefactor parties and donor entity placed their confidence, faith, and *trust* in the fiduciary agency, the trust company, to fulfill its duties and obligations when the need arose. Today's trust companies have the authority to accept deposits and operate in a fashion very similar to banks. However, the lending practices of trust companies are somewhat different from their bank counterparts in that the vast amount of their loans are related to long-term mortgages. In terms of the hospitality industry, a trust company would not be a likely choice for **bridge financing** (a type of short-term financing) but would be an alternative for a long-term debt instrument such as a building mortgage.

3.7.2 INSURANCE FIRMS

Insurance firms are typically very cash-rich, as a result of collecting and holding vast amounts of cash from policyholders making their regular premium payments. Accordingly, insurance firms are constantly looking for lucrative investments where they can safely park cash and make an adequate return on the investment over time, to ensure they have enough cash on hand when it is necessary to pay out a claim or policy. To this end, the larger insurance companies participate in *leaseback transactions* with hotel companies in property development.

The **leaseback transaction** has been around since the late 1940s, and when the right players come together for the right reasons it is an innovative and smart method of financing for new hotel construction. Basically, in this method of finance the insurance company works closely with a proven hotel company—one that is profitable and has a well-established positive history. The hotel company builds a new hotel property according to the insurance company's mandate and requests. Once the hotel property has been constructed, the hotel company sells the property to the insurance company. The insurance company, the new property owner, has successfully invested a large amount of capital and now leases the hotel property back to the hotel company. This "leaseback" is usually a long-term arrangement (10 to 20 years) whereby the hotel company secures 100 percent financing and still retains the use of the hotel property. Further, this frees up much-needed capital for the hotel company and provides an income stream for the insurance company. The insurance company not only has a constant flow of cash coming in from profitable hotel operations, but also carries a valuable piece of real estate in inventory. In an ideal scenario the hotel's property value will increase over time, and the leaseback transaction thereby provides a win–win scenario for both parties.

In addition, most life insurance firms offer incentives in order to attract new clients. These incentives include

- allowing the policyholder to borrow funds against the insurance policy,
- paying out cash dividends to the policyholder, and
- providing a type of policy with a market value that increases over time as a result of plowing cash dividends back into the policy's carrying market value; the accumulated dollar amount is not paid out until the policy is terminated.

In offering these attractive product amenities insurance companies provide some services that are similar to a bank and thereby qualify as financial intermediaries.

3.7.3 PENSION FUNDS

Like insurance companies, pension funds also are cash-rich and carry very significant assets. For example, the Ontario Teachers' Pension Plan (OTPP)—unique in its position as the largest single-profession pension fund in Canada—carries more than $106 billion in net assets. This fund also is notable for its 58-percent ownership stake (acquired through the Teacher's Merchant Bank, a subsidiary operation of the OTPP) in Maple Leaf Sports & Entertainment Ltd., which owns the Toronto Maple Leafs, the Toronto Raptors, Air Canada Centre, Leafs TV, and Raptors NBA TV. The OTPP also has about $157 million invested in the WestJet airline, approximately $62 million in Carnival Cruises, and $53 million in Disney. The OTPP is friendly to the hospitality industry indeed!

As is the case with insurance companies, pension funds also need to park their cash in safe and lucrative investments that provide an adequate return over time. Accordingly, it is quite common for pension funds to be invested in hotel companies and other hospitality-related business enterprises as exemplified by the OTPP. A recent example is provided by the pension fund *Caisse de dépôt et placement du Québec*, which, in partnership with Westmont Hospitality Group and InnVest Real Estate Investment Trust, purchased Legacy Hotels Real Estate Investment Trust for $2.5 billion in the summer of 2007. Under the guidance and tutelage of Fairmont Hotels and Resorts, Legacy Hotels operated 25 luxury hotel properties across Canada. Some of the properties included the world famous Fairmont Le Chateau Frontenac (Quebec City), the landmark hotel Fairmont Royal York (Toronto), the Fairmont Empress (Victoria), and the Fairmont Olympic Hotel (Seattle). The Legacy portfolio also included several Delta hotels.

3.8 SUMMARY

This chapter:

- Introduced Canadian financial intermediaries
- Outlined the Canadian financial system
- Introduced Canadian banking
- Discussed the role of the Bank of Canada
- Explained Canadian legal reporting and compliance requirements
- Introduced trust companies, insurance firms, and pension funds

Key Terms

Bank of Canada

Bridge financing

Canadian Deposit Insurance
  Corporation (CDIC)

Federal Reserve

Fiduciary

Leaseback transaction

Monetary policy

Office of the Superintendent of Financial
  Institutions (OSFI)

Payments system

Prospectus

Schedule I banks

Schedule II banks

Schedule III banks

Discussion Questions

1. What is a financial intermediary?
2. Can an insurance company qualify as a financial intermediary? Why or why not?
3. What is a Schedule I bank?
4. What is a Schedule II bank?
5. What is the role of the Bank of Canada?
6. What federal government agency monitors the activities and performance of banks operating in Canada?
7. What is the role of a trust company? Can you use a trust company to finance a hospitality enterprise? Why or why not?
8. How can insurance firms be a viable source of financing for the hospitality enterprise?
9. What is the name of the financial agreement used by hotel and insurance companies? How does the transaction work? Who does it benefit? Why?
10. Are pension funds an attractive option for financing a hospitality enterprise? Explain why or why not.

Chapter 4

Financial Markets and Financial Instruments

Chapter Objectives

This chapter covers the following topics:

1   The reasons why individuals invest

2   How to calculate a holding period return

3   Different capital markets and how trading takes place

4   The bond market

5   The money market and various money market instruments

6   Risk-hedging techniques such as forward and futures contracts

7   The potential financial impact of fluctuations in foreign exchange rates

8   Key financial intermediaries to the hospitality industry

9   Some common indicators of stock market performance

4.1 Introduction

Financial markets are places in which the suppliers of financial instruments (firms) meet the buyers of these instruments (investors) through financial intermediaries (such as brokers), as discussed in the previous chapter. A tremendous variety of financial instruments are available for investors to use at their discretion. This chapter discusses the different types of existing financial markets and their importance. Additionally, it discusses the functioning of these markets, the parties involved, and the financial instruments that are part of financial markets. Moreover, it introduces the student to a variety of topics such as foreign exchange, forward and futures contracts, and stocks and bonds.

4.2 Why People Invest

To some students, investing is something that *other people* do. Perhaps they think this because they do not have much disposable income to invest. However, they may not realize that—although different from stocks or bonds—their pursuit of a postsecondary education is really an investment. Many students defer full-time employment in hopes of working full-time later at a higher salary. The motivation to give something up today to earn something in the future is similar to that of Bay Street investors.

Investors are hoping to make money, of course, but they are also doing something else. They are deferring present consumption in hopes of increased future consumption. This would be much more difficult to do without relatively efficient capital markets and a tremendous variety of financial instruments from which to choose. However, this is only one side of the story. From the hospitality firm's perspective, firms need capital to fund their operations in the form of equity (common or preferred stock) and debt (bonds or other loans). We examine equity capital first.

4.2.1 DESCRIPTION OF STOCK

We briefly introduced the features of common and preferred stock in Chapter 1 in our discussion of corporations. As you may recall, shares of stock owned by investors are a source of equity financing for companies that issue them. Two types of equity are issued. Preferred shareholders receive a specified dividend that is expressed as a percentage of the price. On the other hand, common shareholders cannot receive dividends until preferred shareholders are paid. Moreover, although there is no guarantee of common shareholders receiving a dividend, prospective investors often examine a company's history to assess the likelihood of future dividend payments. Despite these disadvantages, common shareholders are allowed to vote on important issues at the annual shareholders' meeting, whereas preferred shareholders are not. The most important decision shareholders make involves voting for the board of directors, which in turn makes decisions about the management team, the auditing firm, and many other issues.

When investors purchase stock, they hope to increase their future purchasing power in two ways: by receiving a stream of dividend payments, and by eventually selling their stock at a higher price than what they paid, which is called a *capital gain*. Shareholders must pay income taxes on any dividends paid by the corporation in the year they are distributed. On the other hand, taxes on capital gains can be deferred until the share of stock is actually sold. Additionally, capital gains are currently taxed at a lower rate than ordinary dividends.

Investors are concerned with the return on their equity investments. One of these types of returns is called a **holding period return**, which is calculated as follows:

$$\frac{(\text{Price at sale} - \text{Purchase price}) + \text{Dividends received}}{\text{Purchase price}} \times 100$$

$$= \text{Holding period return } \%$$

For example, assume you purchased a share of stock one year ago for $10. During the year you received $1 in dividends, and today you sell the stock for $12. What is your holding period return? Using the preceding formula,

$$\frac{(\$12 - \$10) + \$1}{\$10} \times 100 = 30\%$$

This return, of course, is calculated before taxes. If dividend income is taxed at 27 percent and capital gains are taxed at 20 percent, you will receive $0.73 in after-tax dividends and $1.60 in after-tax capital gains. Therefore, your overall after-tax return is lowered to 23.3 percent ($2.33/$10).

Walt Disney Company

The Walt Disney Company, one of the hospitality industry's oldest companies, began in 1923 with a cartoon character called Mickey Mouse. The common stock of the company is part of the Dow Jones Industrial Average.

The company is involved in theme parks such as Disneyland in California, Disney World in Florida, Disneyland Resort Paris in France, and Disneyland in Tokyo. Additionally, the company owns Touchstone Motion Pictures along with the ABC television network and ESPN.

In 1992 Disney announced the issuance of $300 million in bonds that would mature in 100 years. Disney was the first company since 1954 to offer bonds with a 100-year maturity period. The Disney bonds were callable beginning July 15, 2023, at a price that declined to 100 percent of face value after July 15, 2043.

The issue was met with some skepticism, as investors thought Disney was only trying to lock in a lower interest rate. Additionally, if interest rates were to fall, the value of the bonds would rise, but of course Disney can eventually buy them back, perhaps at a lower price. This makes the bond issue less appealing to potential investors.

An important part of the holding period return calculation is the price of the stock. What affects the price of stocks? Although supply and demand definitely plays a key role, the price is largely dependent on the company's current and future prospective cash flows. As you may recall from Chapter 1, three factors affect the **present value** of these cash flows: size, timing, and risk. Each of these factors is discussed in greater detail later in this book.

4.2.2 DESCRIPTION OF BONDS

Bonds represent a method of debt financing for a company and are basically a promise to repay investors over a period of time. Unlike with common stock, bondholders do not have a true ownership claim on the assets of the firm. Nevertheless, they receive a return on their investment in the form of semiannual interest payments and the return of the face value of the bond (called the **principal**) at the end of the term. Much like dividends, this represents a series of cash payments that can be valued. Thus, bonds can be traded like stocks (although they are usually not traded in the same volume).

Bond prices are indexed relative to 100. Therefore, if a $1,000 bond is selling at 100, the price is $1,000. However, if its price increases to 102, the price is $1,020. If the price decreases to 98, it is selling for $980. Although the price of the bond often changes, the amount of interest it pays does not. For example, a $1,000 bond paying 8 percent interest yields $80 in interest each year for an investor, regardless of what happens to the price. Bond prices are also based on the present value of the cash flows of the bond. The same three factors that determine the present value of dividends for common stocks also affect principal and interest payments of bonds. Exhibit 4-1 shows how bond prices are typically presented in the financial press.

Exhibit 4-1 Bond Pricing

Bond	Current yield	Volume	Close	Net chg
Hilton 7¼ 14	7.23	40	101	+0.012

The exhibit contains a fictitious bond issued by Hilton Corporation. Reading from left to right, the name of the company is first, followed by two sets of numbers. The first set is the annual interest rate on the bond—in this case, $7\frac{1}{4}$ percent.

The second set of numbers is the last two numbers of the year the bond matures. The next column shows the current yield, which is simply the amount of annual interest earned divided by the current price. Note that this yield is *not* the return an investor will receive if she holds the bond until maturity. The yield to maturity calculation is shown in Chapter 8, on stock and bond valuation. The next column is the volume of bonds traded that day, expressed in thousands of dollars. In this example, Hilton bonds worth $40,000 were traded. The next column shows the closing price, with the principal value of the bond indexed to 100. Finally, the net change column measures the change in closing price from the last day of trading.

A number of differences between stocks and bonds exist. One of the most important relates to federal taxes. Under the current tax systems in Canada and the United States, debt financing has an inherent advantage over equity financing. This is because interest payments on bonds are tax-deductible expenses for the issuing firms, and the interest expense is included on the income statement. On the other hand, dividend payments to shareholders are not considered operating expenses and do not appear on a basic income statement, as they are essentially a balance sheet transaction. This is one of the reasons why firms often choose to finance their assets (in part) with debt instead of equity. It is important to note that most hospitality firms use some combination of debt and equity to finance their assets.

The remainder of this chapter focuses on capital markets and some of the most common financial instruments.

4.3 Capital Markets

Capital markets are those markets in which debt and equity issues are traded. Many people think primarily of the stock market when they hear the term *capital markets*. However, there are many other types of capital markets, including the bond market and the mortgage market. There is also more than one stock market. We begin with an examination of the various stock markets.

4.3.1 TORONTO STOCK EXCHANGE

The largest stock exchange in Canada is the Toronto Stock Exchange (TSX), formerly known as the TSE for Toronto Stock Exchange. It is Canada's only exchange market for the trading of senior equities. The TSX is the sixth largest equity exchange market in the world in terms of total market capitalization. It hosts a diverse listing of equities, income trusts, and investment funds representing corporations from Canada, the United States, and other nations from around the world. The TSX has corporate offices located in Vancouver, Calgary, Winnipeg, Toronto, and Montreal. The TSX is not a government institution; it is owned and operated for profit by the TSX Group.

Today's TSX has evolved significantly since its start in approximately 1852 by a group of Toronto businessmen. Though there are no official records to this effect, it is believed about 24 businessmen got together at the then Masonic Hall and formulated a set of guidelines and procedures to create the TSE. After much success, the TSE became officially recognized by the provincial government and was formally incorporated by an act of the Legislative Assembly of Ontario in 1878.

Since then the TSX has experienced tremendous growth in terms of total equity listings as well as the volume and dollar value of traded shares. In 1977 the TSX embraced a computer assisted trading system (CATS), which provided automated price quotations for equities that are considered to be less liquid.

In 1997 the TSX closed its trading floor and became one of the largest virtual (completely electronic) stock exchanges in North America. Today, investors can get price quotes electronically for any investment product that is traded on the TSX. The TSX is also the only stock exchange in North America that has had a female president and CEO, Barbara Stymiest. In 2004, she left the TSX to become the new CEO of RBC.

4.3.2 OTHER CANADIAN STOCK EXCHANGES

Other significant Canadian stock exchange markets exist. The Bourse de Montréal, or Montreal Exchange, has responsibility for derivative trading. The Vancouver Stock Exchange and the Alberta Stock Exchange, both financially sound and viable alternatives to the TSX, decided to collapse and consolidate for marketing purposes, becoming the Canadian Venture Exchange (CDNX), which facilitates junior equity trading. Further, the Canadian Dealing Network, the Winnipeg Stock Exchange, and the equities side of the Montreal Exchange have all merged with the CDNX. The Toronto Stock Exchange acquired the CDNX in 2001 and renamed it the TSX Venture Exchange in 2002.

4.3.3 NEW YORK STOCK EXCHANGE

The New York Stock Exchange (NYSE) is the oldest stock market in the United States. It was founded in 1792 and became designated as a national securities exchange by the Securities and Exchange Commission (SEC) in 1934. The NYSE is a physical location in which buyers and sellers conduct secondary trading of financial instruments, including bonds. (The difference between primary and secondary trading is discussed later in this chapter.)

In general, the NYSE lists most of the largest corporations in the United States. As of this writing, 2,800 different companies offer securities on the NYSE. These companies must meet certain standards to be listed on the NYSE. Additionally, the NYSE is not only for American companies—more than 470 non–U.S. companies are listed.

The NYSE offers membership to securities dealers and brokerage firms in the form of "seats" on the trading floor. Only member firms are allowed to deal in securities offered on the exchange. Each of the 1,336 seats carries a price and seats can be bought and sold among competing firms. However, although the NYSE is a major exchange, it is not the only place for firms to list their securities in the United States.

4.3.4 NASDAQ

NASDAQ is an acronym that stands for National Association of Securities Dealers and Automated Quotations. The growth of the economy and the interest by investors in smaller companies has contributed to the growth of NASDAQ, as evidenced by the increase in stock ownership by American households. In 1971, only 27 percent of American households owned stock, but by 1999 the number had grown to approximately 45 percent. NASDAQ serves an important function by allowing companies that are too small to be listed on the NYSE access to financial capital. However, NASDAQ is also home to many large companies such as Microsoft and Intel.

NASDAQ is known as an over-the-counter (OTC) market because it is not a physical location like the NYSE. It was created in 1971 as the first electronic stock market via a network of securities dealers. Although the NYSE lists the largest companies, NASDAQ is the fastest-growing securities market and in 1994 surpassed the NYSE in the number of shares traded. NASDAQ actually comprises two separate markets: the National market, which contains stocks of 4,400 companies, and the Small Cap market, which contains stocks of 1,800 companies. The key element in the system comprises the dealers who act as "market makers" and compete with each other for business. A **market maker** is someone who helps stabilize prices by helping to guarantee trades between buyers and sellers. If buyers or sellers cannot be found, market makers utilize securities from their own personal inventory to help ensure the liquidity of stock issues.

4.3.5 OTHER STOCK EXCHANGES

There are also smaller regional stock exchanges in the United States, which include the Pacific Stock Exchange as well as exchanges in Boston, Chicago, Cincinnati, and Philadelphia. In addition, the United States and Canada are not the only countries with stock markets. Many other countries also have stock markets on which both domestic and foreign companies are listed. Some of the largest include the Tokyo Stock Exchange and the London Stock Exchange. Given the increasing use of technology and globalization of information, many investors track the performance of other stock exchanges around the world. The financial crisis in East Asia in 1998 that affected the U.S. and other stock markets demonstrates the increasing links among the various exchanges and economies.

4.3.6 BOND MARKET

In Canada, corporate and government bonds, as well as Canada Treasury Bills, are traded on OTC (over-the-counter) markets. As previously discussed, bonds are financial instruments that are different from stocks. Although bonds represent a contractual agreement between lender and borrower, most bonds (with the exception of government bonds) are not guaranteed. Accordingly, the safety of bonds is scrutinized carefully by investors. Investment service firms such as Moody's and Standard & Poor's rate the safety of bonds in terms of the probability of company payments of interest and principal to investors. Companies that do not make interest or principal payments on their bond issues on time are said to be in **default**.

In terms of bond ratings, the closer the rating is to the beginning of the alphabet, the greater the quality of the bond. For example, a B bond is riskier than an A bond. Additionally, when more of the same letters are present in the rating, the quality of the bond is greater. Standard & Poor's rates bonds using all capital letters. For example, AAA bonds are higher quality than AA bonds. Moody's rates bonds with a capital letter followed by lowercase letters. For example, Aaa bonds are rated higher than Aa bonds. Companies with C-rated bonds are highly speculative and, therefore, are given the lowest rate.

Dominion Bond Rating Service (DBRS) is the primary bond rating company in Canada. It is an independent rating agency that assesses an entity's ability to make timely payments on interest accrued and principal owed. Like Standard & Poor's, DBRS assigns credit ratings based on an alphabetically ascending coded scale.

As previously mentioned, most bonds represent a series of interest payments and the repayment of principal. In addition to being affected by the size and timing of payments, the price of a bond is also affected by the current assessment of risk associated with those payments. When the risk value of the company is high and its ability to make payments is in doubt, the present value or price of the bond is lower. Think of it this way: if you are holding a bond from McDonald's Corporation, which is paying you 8 percent interest, and a comparable bond is issued and pays 10 percent, your bond would not be as desirable (because of the lower interest payments), and the price of your bond should decline (all else being equal). The price declines because the interest and principal payments are discounted at a higher rate. This discounting is discussed in later chapters.

Some bonds are *callable*, which means that the issuer has the right to buy back the bonds at a certain price within a certain period of time prior to the maturity date of the bond. This feature is used by the issuing company to protect its interests in the event that market interest rates start to decrease. The call price has to be high enough to entice investors to want to purchase the bonds despite this feature. Therefore, the investor must be convinced that the potential call price is an additional benefit, or the call feature of the bond simply will not function. Other aspects of bonds are discussed in Chapter 8.

4.3.7 MORTGAGE MARKET

The mortgage market refers to the pooling of home mortgages by government-sponsored agencies. The **Canada Mortgage and Housing Corporation (CMHC)** is Canada's national housing agency. It was originally created as a federal government institution in 1946 to assist in alleviating Canada's postwar housing shortage. Since then, the CMHC has evolved and grown to become Canada's principal provider of mortgage insurance, mortgage-backed securities, housing policy and programs, and housing research.

The CMHC works closely with consumers and financial institutions alike to provide alternative and complementary finance options to Canadians who may be financially challenged to purchase their own home. The CMHC can assist the consumer in this regard and accomplishes this in part by providing security to at-risk borrowers and through the facilitation of mortgage-backed securities.

Mortgage-backed securities, or **pass-through securities,** are financial instruments issued by financial institutions that represent participation in a pool of NHA-insured mortgage loans, which they resell to investors in the form of securities. The investors receive income from those making the mortgage payments. These securities are primarily sold to institutional investors such as insurance companies and pension funds and can be traded like bonds. The NHA mortgage-backed securities are totally guaranteed by the CMHC through the National Housing Act (NHA). Consequently, they are generally considered to be very low risk and earn lower returns than commercial paper.

4.4 Money Market

The money market represents the market for debt instruments that are short term, meaning they will mature in one year or less. The most common money market instruments are certificates of deposit (CDs), commercial paper, guaranteed investment certificates (GICs), and Treasury bills. CDs are debt securities issued through commercial banks. They are available not only to institutional investors in large denominations but also to small investors in denominations of only $100. The maturities and interest rates vary. Commercial paper is a short-term debt instrument with maturities ranging up to 270 days. It is typically issued by well-known, quality companies to investors who are looking for safety yet want a return on their investment. Commercial paper is rated much like corporate bonds.

Guaranteed investment certificates (GICs) are popular in Canada and can be used by financial institutions to set up the product offering of CDs and commercial paper. The financial institution borrows money from the consumer for an agreed-upon period of time and interest rate. The GIC interest rate offered is always more attractive in comparison to an entry-level interest rate (that is, a standard savings account). The GIC as an alternative savings instrument provides the consumer with an incentive to commit funds to a GIC for a specific period of time at a slightly higher interest rate than a savings account. The financial institution uses these funds to meet its own short-term maturing financial obligations and to channel funds into business entities in the form of a CD or commercial paper. Most financial institutions require a minimum deposit of $1,000 for 30 days before a GIC is executed.

Treasury bills (T-bills) are short-term debt instruments issued by the federal government and most provincial governments. T-bills are usually issued in terms of 30, 90, 182, and 365 days. They are sold by governments to financial institutions and investment dealers in large denominations. Once received, the financial institutions and investment dealers carve the large block of T-bills into smaller digestible pieces. The end result is that T-bills of $1,000, $5,000, $10,000, or sometimes larger are available for purchase by the investing public. It is important to recognize that T-bills do not actually pay interest. They are **zero-coupon securities,** meaning that investors buy them at a discount and that no interest payments are made. The return is paid to the investors in the **spread,** which represents the difference between the actual purchase price for the T-bill and the redemption value (that is, the face value) of the T-bill on the maturity date.

All of the treasury issues are backed by the credit of the government; therefore, their return is essentially guaranteed. Additionally, the instruments can be sold rather easily if needed. The rate of return on these instruments has an important implication in finance. Investors consider the return on these securities to be the market **risk-free rate of return.** The return on Treasury bills, for example, is often quite low for short maturities. However, the risk associated with them is virtually nonexistent. This direct relationship between risk and return is discussed later in this book.

The Canadian federal government also sells **Canada Savings Bonds (CSBs).** CSBs can be purchased at almost any financial institution, and most corporations offer their employees a payroll deduction purchase program to acquire CSBs. CSBs are on sale from October to April each year and they can be redeemed by the holder at any time. Unlike a T-bill, a CSB pays interest. Purchasers who have held on to the CSB for at least three months are entitled to the accrued interest as well as the face value of the CSB at the time of redemption.

4.5 Raising Financial Capital and Security Trading

We noted above that firms finance assets with debt and equity issues. A new common stock issue by a firm is called an initial public offering (IPO). The firm first establishes a relationship with an investment banker, who effectively acts as an intermediary between the firm and potential investors. The investment banker provides consulting services to the firm regarding the price of the new issue and completes the necessary legal work required by the SEC. Investment bankers often work with bankers in other firms to help sell the new issue to the public. The investment banker purchases the issue from the firm and then reissues the stock to the public through brokers. The initial sale of the stock is called the **primary market**.

In Canada the securities industry is regulated at the provincial and territorial level as well as by the exchanges themselves and the Investment Dealers Association of Canada. The Canadian regulatory framework is currently the subject of a hot political debate and has been under review by the Canadian federal government. At present, Finance Minister Jim Flaherty is in the process of trying to persuade all Canadian provinces and territories to get on board with supporting a single national securities regulator similar to the SEC in the United States.

Canada's largest coffee shop chain, Tim Hortons, is a recent example of a successful IPO. On March 24, 2006, Tim Hortons offered up its very own IPO in both Canada and the United States. Canadian shares were sold on the TSX, and American shares were sold on the New York Stock Exchange. By the end of the day, more than 17.5 million shares in Tim Hortons stock were sold worth an estimated C$6.6 billion—a greater market value than Air Canada.

Investment banking firms make a significant amount in fees when they help with an IPO. A recent scandal involving investment banking showed some firms were falsely touting certain stocks and enticing clients to buy them for the firm to get more investment banking business. In the spring of 2003 a number of investment firms settled a major case with the State of New York and were forced to pay large fines.

On the other hand, most trading of stocks occurs on the **secondary market**, which represents investors trading among themselves through brokers. Although the firm is usually concerned about the share price (because managers and employees may also own stock), no new funds are raised for the company in this process. We examine this process in more detail.

Say you would like to purchase 100 shares of Tim Hortons (which is listed on the TSX with the ticker symbol THI). You place a call to your broker, or you place an online order on your broker's website. The order is virtually communicated to the TSX, which returns an immediate quote. If you placed the order online, you receive the quote on your own computer; otherwise, your dealer informs you of the price quote. If you accept the price quoted, the trade is completed, and you receive an immediate confirmation (or it is sent to your broker). If the price is not acceptable, you can state the price you are ready to pay, and your offer to purchase will be left open until the TSX virtual system identifies a seller who accepts your price. The transaction will then be confirmed as above. Although you now own 100 common shares of Tim Hortons, you will not be sent the share certificate. Share certificates are generally kept by the brokers for their customers.

The pricing of shares is based on a "bid" price and an "ask" price. The bid price is what a prospective buyer is willing to pay for a share. The ask price is the amount for which a broker will sell it to you. The difference between the two is called the bid–ask spread and represents a small profit for the broker. Share prices were once expressed in dollars and eighths of a dollar. However, in late 2000, share prices changed to dollars and cents.

In Canada, the buying and selling process for shares is almost instantaneous, especially if the orders are placed online from the client's computer and the client is using high-end trading software. The speed of the process indicates the heavy reliance on computers by the stock exchanges. Although the system normally functions well, a software problem in June 2001 at the NYSE led to a trading halt of approximately 90 minutes. Trading was eventually restored, but the problem is indicative of the financial markets' significant reliance on advanced technology and the potential problems that sometimes occur.

4.6 Financial Markets and Hedging Risk

Are investments ever made to avoid losing money as opposed to making money? Consider the purchase of homeowners' insurance. Although mortgage companies require such insurance, prudent homeowners will on their own pay a monthly premium to insure their home and valuables. Hopefully nothing happens to the house and the value of the asset is maintained. Conversely, if the house burns down, a claim is filed, the house is rebuilt, and the valuables are replaced. Thus, the homeowners are effectively hedging risk. Either way, they have a home and personal property. Financial instruments are available so that hospitality financial managers can also hedge risk.

4.6.1 FORWARD AND FUTURES CONTRACTS

Some assets are purchased immediately, or "on the spot," such as a share of stock. Other examples could include the purchase of commodities, such as wheat or pork bellies. If we make the purchase today we would pay the spot price, or cash price. However, in some cases we may want to order assets for delivery (and payment) sometime in the future. One of the problems with this is that prices can change over time, which creates uncertainty for both the buyer and the seller of the asset. A good example is a farmer taking bushels of wheat to market. The price of wheat may change dramatically between the time of harvest and the time he or she gets to the market to make a sale. This circumstance created the need for financial instruments known as forward and futures contracts.

A **forward contract** is an agreement about a sale of an asset that will be delivered in the future. The price agreed on for future delivery is called the forward price. An important feature of a forward contract is that cash payment is not required until delivery is made. The details of the transaction, such as the quantity and purchase price of the asset to be delivered, are negotiated between the two parties. However, one problem with forward contracts is that both parties are locked into the agreement and must trust the other to perform. Moreover, because of the specific nature of forward contracts, they are very difficult to sell to a third party. Accordingly, the uncertainties and other difficulties associated with the forward contract led to the development of another type of financial instrument, the futures contract.

A **futures contract** is similar to a forward contract in that the contract involves a future delivery of an asset at a set price (called the forward price). However, the features of a futures contract are largely standardized, as opposed to being negotiated between the two parties. The contract is actually between a trader and a clearing-house that guarantees contract performance and the solvency of the two parties. Contract sizes and delivery dates are standardized, making them much easier to sell to a third party.

In Canada, commodity futures contracts for wheat, canola, and barley can be purchased through the services offered by the Winnipeg Commodity Exchange, a subsidiary of the Atlanta-based Intercontinental Exchange. Futures contracts are also traded on the Montreal Exchange. The value of the contract changes each day because the value of the underlying asset changes. The process of settling the value of the contract between the parties is called "marking to market."

If one party wants to exit from the contract, it can either sell the contract or take an opposite position (in other words, instead of buying bushels of wheat on a certain date, the party would sell bushels of wheat on a certain date). This effectively offsets the position in the contract. Taking a second and opposite position is quite common. It is estimated that only 5 percent of futures contracts are actually fulfilled. In addition to contracts on commodities, hospitality managers can employ forward and futures contracts on foreign currencies and interest rates to help hedge risk.

4.6.2 FOREIGN EXCHANGE MARKETS

As trade barriers between countries are removed, more Canadian and U.S. companies are doing business overseas. This means that revenues, and consequently profits, are generated in a variety of foreign currencies, making knowledge of exchange rate movements important. Comparing foreign currencies to a domestic currency can be done using either direct or indirect quotes. For companies based in Canada, a direct quote would indicate the cost of one unit of foreign currency in Canadian dollars. For example, on August 10, 2007, the spot exchange rate as a direct quote for the euro was C$1.44292. In other words, 1 euro would cost you approximately $1.44 Canadian. An indirect quote is simply the inverse of the direct quote. Using the previous example, the indirect quote would indicate that C$1.00 was equal to 0.69304 of a euro on that date. In other words, it would cost an individual in Europe on August 10, 2007, a little more than two-thirds of a euro to purchase one Canadian dollar. Or, for approximately 69 euros, that person could purchase 100 Canadian dollars.

Foreign exchange rates are important to hospitality companies. McDonald's, for example, generated approximately 65 percent of its revenues from locations outside the

United States in 2006. Nevertheless, the SEC requires that profits from overseas must be "repatriated" and converted to U.S. dollars before they are reported to investors. This also holds true for Canadian companies that have international operations. All foreign currency must be repatriated and reported in Canadian dollars in compliance with trading regulations and the Canada Revenue Agency. Because exchange rates between currencies frequently change, this means that reported profits could also change. We look at an example.

Say you manage a hospitality company in France and have earned profits of 100,000 euros. When you started the year, the exchange rate was 1 euro per $1. However, by the end of the year, the exchange rate is 2 euros per $1. Have your profits as stated in Canadian dollars increased or decreased? We look at the calculations.

$$\text{January 1: } 100{,}000 \text{ euros} \times \frac{\$1}{1 \text{ euro}} = \$100{,}000$$

After rate change:

$$\text{December 31: } 100{,}000 \text{ euros} \times \frac{\$1}{2 \text{ euro}} = \$50{,}000$$

As shown by these calculations, you have experienced a foreign exchange loss. Remember, we are interested in the value of the profits in terms of dollars. The number of euros has not changed—but their value in terms of Canadian dollars has. Think of it this way: At the beginning of the year, it took 1 euro to purchase $1 worth of goods. At the end of the year, however, it took 2 euros to buy the same amount of Canadian goods. You are then worse off holding euros than you were before the change in the exchange rate. A good exercise would be to calculate the effect on dollar profits if the exchange rate changed from 1 euro per $1 to 0.50 euro per $1.

The previous example shows how devaluation of currency can affect profits. Although a number of factors affect exchange rates, one of the primary ones is the difference between the expected rates of inflation for the two countries. At this time, we provide a brief discussion on how foreign exchange rates change. Later, an overview focuses on how hospitality managers can hedge this foreign exchange rate risk.

4.6.3 THE GREAT CANADIAN DOLLAR

On July 24, 2007, the Canadian dollar soared to 96.72 cents U.S., its highest level since 1977. Then, on November 7, 2007, it surpassed US$1.10 during intraday trading. That was the strongest the Canadian dollar had been against the U.S. greenback since 1959. As at April 2008, the Canadian dollar traded slightly under par with the U.S. dollar. Think back to January 21, 2002, when the Canadian dollar was worth only 61.79 cents U.S. and it would have cost you approximately C$1.6184 to purchase one U.S. dollar. What happened? Why the significant increase in the Canadian dollar's value?

Several important factors influence foreign exchange rates and the perceived value of domestic currency. Upon reviewing the last five years, we note the following inputs that have lifted the Canadian dollar to higher ground in the world of foreign exchanges.

1. Canada participates in what is called a **floating currency exchange** system, which means the Canadian dollar is subject to change dependent largely upon supply and demand factors for the Canadian dollar.

2. Canada's political and economic landscape strongly influences the value of the Canadian dollar. When a country's political system is seen as being stable and safe, that in general has a positive impact on the value of the domestic currency. Think back to October 1995, when Canada was facing the prospect of Quebec separation. During that troubled time the dollar was trading around 70 cents U.S. However, once it became clear that Quebec would not separate, the Canadian dollar climbed its way back up to about 75 cents U.S. This is an example of the political stability effect on the dollar. Also, when the economy is strong and inflation is absent the dollar too will be relatively strong. A robust economy means dollars are in demand to purchase and spend as wanted and required. Therefore, with a greater level of demand placed on the dollar its value will rise accordingly.

3. The movement of international businesses and their degree of foreign investment has an impact on the value of the Canadian dollar. If companies wish to build or acquire factories, warehouses, or offices on Canadian soil they need to do so in Canadian dollars. Thus, greater upward pressure is made on the demand for the Canadian dollar and therefore the dollar increases in value.

4. Immigration and the arrival of new Canadians causes the dollar to increase. Canada has one of the most liberal immigration policies in the world. To this end, Canada welcomes more than 250,000 new Canadians each year. These newcomers purchase Canadian dollars prior to and after arriving in their new country. This also places upward pressure on the Canadian dollar.

5. Canada has an excellent international credit rating. In fact, Standard & Poor's rates Canada's ability to manage debt at the highest level (AAA). This translates into a strong message that Canada has a robust economy as well as healthy prospects for sustained economic growth in the years ahead. This is attributed in large part to the federal government's financial prudence in using large tax surpluses to pay down the federal debt load.

6. Interest rates and inflationary pressure influence the value of the Canadian dollar. In general, when interest rates are high the Canadian dollar has a higher value as well. This is because foreign investors would rather park their money in a Canadian bank paying, say, 4 percent interest in comparison to a U.S. bank that is paying only 3 percent interest. So once again the movement and conversion of U.S. dollars into Canadian dollars causes the Canadian dollar to increase in value. Inflation can cause a downward spiral effect on the value of the Canadian dollar. When inflation is present, the purchasing power of the dollar is eroded in that it now takes more dollars to buy the same bundle of goods. Eventually consumers get smart and either hold off on making purchases or make purchases internationally. That is why interest rates and the purchasing power of the dollar work together almost in tandem. As inflation increases interest rates also increase, and this to some effect stabilizes the purchasing power of the dollar.

7. Canada has what other countries need. Canada is rich with oil, gas, lumber, coal, iron ore, gold, uranium, sulphur, water, technology, wheat, pharmaceuticals, and so on. Therefore, foreign companies are purchasing these commodities and goods in Canadian dollars. Once again, this creates greater demand for the Canadian dollar and causes it to rise in value.

During 2007–2008, the Canadian dollar was often referred to as a "petrodollar" or "petrocurrency." This is because the strength of the Canadian dollar has increased in direct relationship with the price of crude oil.

4.6.4 HEDGING

If, in the example in section 4.6.2 you calculated the exchange rate change to 0.50 euro per $1, you have doubled your profits in terms of dollars. As the example shows, however, the possibility of cutting your profits in half also exists. Therefore, one can understand the uncertainty (and risk) involved if you choose to do nothing.

On the other hand, a hospitality manager could hedge the risk by using a forward or futures contract to sell euros for Canadian dollars at an agreed rate of exchange. This way, the exchange rate would be locked in and the uncertainty would be eliminated. Who would be interested in selling dollars to your firm? A likely candidate would be a European company operating in Canada that needed to sell Canadian dollars and buy euros.

The use of the euro as currency was not agreed to until 1991, and it was finally coined and distributed in 2002. The introduction of the currency was expected to help unify the European area and increase the flow of goods and services across countries. The single currency was formally issued in Austria, Belgium, Finland, France, Germany, Greece, Ireland, Italy, Luxembourg, Netherlands, Portugal, and Spain.

4.6.5 COMMODITY MARKETS

Hospitality managers must worry not only about repatriating and converting profits to Canadian dollars for reporting purposes, but also about costs. Consider a restaurant operation that sells large quantities of orange juice. If poor weather occurs and the orange crop is damaged, prices will probably increase. This can put a hospitality manager in a bind because it is unlikely that prices can be raised substantially in the short term without adversely affecting revenues. What options are available to the hospitality manager?

The first option would be to do nothing and hope for the best. Depending on the crop damage, the price increase may be modest. Additionally, a hospitality manager could try substituting a less-expensive juice for orange juice on the menu. Another option would be to buy a forward or futures contract. Although no cash payment is required up front, futures contracts deal in large quantities. For example, orange juice contracts are traded in 15,000-pound units (approximately 6,818 kg). Only a major restaurant company could handle such a large delivery of orange juice on the date the contract is executed. How could a smaller company deal with a contract of this size?

Say you have a futures contract to purchase orange juice for $1.00 per 10 litres. If the spot price of orange juice increases to $1.25 per 10 litres, your contract has increased in value. You could then sell your contract at a profit and use the profits to pay for the price increase from a local orange juice purveyor in the quantity desired. Thus, even small restaurateurs can utilize the futures market to help them hedge price risk.

4.7 Key Financial Intermediaries: Lenders to the Hospitality Industry

In the beginning of the chapter we mentioned the idea of financial intermediaries that help make capital markets function. Although brokers definitely play a key role in the overall financial marketplace, lenders are of critical importance to the hospitality industry. Although most hospitality firms use common stock to finance assets, many finance only a percentage of assets this way. The remaining financing must come from debt instruments. Bonds, which are a type of debt, were previously discussed. However, hospitality firms often use loans instead. This section discusses the different types of lenders to the hospitality industry.

4.7.1 COMMERCIAL BANKS

Commercial banks, traditionally the largest lender to the hospitality industry, take in capital from depositors to whom they provide a return on their money in the form of interest. To be able to pay this interest, banks lend out money to businesses and individuals. The interest rate on the loan is the bank's rate of return. Because banks are willing to bear this risk, the banks earn the difference between the interest rate charged on loans and the interest rate paid to depositors, called the spread. The larger the spread, the greater the income-generating potential for the bank. In addition to the interest spread, commercial banks also generate revenue by charging fees for making loans. Given the importance of interest expense to lenders and borrowers alike, it is important to understand how it is calculated. Interest expense is calculated as follows:

$$\text{Interest} = \text{Principal} \times \text{Rate} \times \text{Time}$$

Commercial banks offer many types of loans. One type is a fully amortized loan. This means each payment contains a portion that is interest and a portion that is principal. As stated in the bond discussion, principal is the amount of money that was originally borrowed. Most commercial mortgage loans are fully amortized, and the interest portion is tax deductible. On the other hand, some commercial loans are interest only, with the principal being repaid only at the end of the loan term—called a balloon payment.

Banks have also become more involved in investments for individuals; they also offer Treasury instruments, certificates of deposit, individual retirement accounts, and other instruments. For many years banks had been prevented from underwriting securities, although this is now allowed for certain issues. However, banks still cannot sell insurance directly; banks in Canada are allowed to sell insurance products through insurance subsidiaries of banks, but not through bank branches themselves. For example, TD Canada Trust has an insurance subsidiary called TD Insurance, Home and Auto. In Ontario, the TD Insurance products are underwritten by TD General Insurance Company; for the rest of Canada, the insurance products are managed by Primmum Insurance Company and TD Home and Auto Insurance Company. At this time, the auto insurance program is not offered in B.C., Manitoba, or Saskatchewan.

4.7.2 REAL ESTATE INVESTMENT TRUSTS (REITs)

These companies manage real estate portfolios for shareholders. The stock of the REIT is traded on one of the stock markets. Equity REITs are those that actually own real estate and pass income from the real estate on to the owners. Mortgage REITs lend money to the industry and provide interest income to the owners. REITs are exempt from corporate income taxes if they distribute at least 95 percent of their earnings to shareholders. They have become a popular method of financing hotels over the past decade, but their popularity can be affected by changes in tax laws; for example, on October 31, 2006, the Canadian federal government announced changes to the existing tax laws that were expected to have a negative impact on the attractiveness of REITs to investors. One of the more prominent REITs in the Canadian hospitality industry is CHIP REIT. CHIP manages more than 30 hotels and resorts across Canada and in the United States. Its shares/units are sold on the TSX with the trading symbols HOT.un, HOT.db, and HOT.db.a. In the United States, one of the better-known REITs is Host Marriott Corporation. After its creation along with Marriott International in 1992, Host Marriott became a REIT in January 1999.

4.8 Stock Market Performance

When people talk about the "performance" of the stock market, it is not always clear what they are referring to. Instead of tracking the performance of the entire listing of stocks traded on the different exchanges, investors examine certain stock market indicators or indices. We discuss two of the more popular indicators in the following sections.

4.8.1 DOW JONES INDUSTRIAL AVERAGE

Dow Jones & Company is a corporation that has been tracking the performance of American shares on American exchanges for many years. It established a way of tracking the general performance of the stock market by creating a price-weighted index of the common stock of 30 large companies that are considered industry leaders—blue chip corporations. The index is often referred to simply as "the Dow." A list of the current 30 companies is provided in Exhibit 4-2.

This index is the oldest stock market index in use and is widely reported in the financial press. The index is a weighted average of the stock prices, based on the value of each stock. It should be noted that although the Dow industrial stocks are probably reported the most, Dow Jones also tracks an index of 20 transportation companies and 15 utility companies. The three indices are combined into the Dow Jones Composite Average.

4.8.2 STANDARD & POOR'S 500

Standard & Poor's (S&P) is a financial services corporation that rates stocks, bonds, and commercial paper. Additionally, the company tracks the performance of the American stock markets and creates an index of 500 stocks, primarily those listed on the New York

Exhibit 4-2 Dow Jones Industrial Average as at February 2008

Company	Symbol	Industry
3M	(NYSE: MMM)	Diversified industrials
Alcoa	(NYSE: AA)	Aluminum
American Express	(NYSE: AXP)	Consumer finance
American International Group	(NYSE: AIG)	Full line insurance
AT&T	(NYSE: T)	Telecoms
Bank of America Corp.	(NYSE: BAC)	Banks
Boeing	(NYSE: BA)	Aerospace/defence
Caterpillar	(NYSE: CAT)	Commercial vehicles & trucks
Chevron Group	(NYSE: CUX)	Integrated oil and gas
Citigroup	(NYSE: C)	Banks
Coca-Cola	(NYSE: KO)	Beverages
DuPont	(NYSE: DD)	Commodity chemicals
ExxonMobil	(NYSE: XOM)	Integrated oil & gas
General Electric	(NYSE: GE)	Diversified industrials
General Motors	(NYSE: GM)	Automobiles
Hewlett-Packard	(NYSE: HPQ)	Diversified computer systems
Home Depot	(NYSE: HD)	Home improvement retailers
Intel	(NASDAQ: INTC)	Semiconductors
IBM	(NYSE: IBM)	Computer services
Johnson & Johnson	(NYSE: JNJ)	Pharmaceuticals
JP Morgan Chase	(NYSE: JPM)	Banks
McDonald's	(NYSE: MCD)	Restaurants & bars
Merck	(NYSE: MRK)	Pharmaceuticals
Microsoft	(NASDAQ: MSFT)	Software
Pfizer	(NYSE: PFE)	Pharmaceuticals
Procter & Gamble	(NYSE: PG)	Non-durable household products
United Technologies Corporation	(NYSE: UTX)	Aerospace
Verizon Communications	(NYSE: VZ)	Telecoms
Wal-Mart	(NYSE: WMT)	Broadline retailers
Walt Disney	(NYSE: DIS)	Broadcasting & entertainment

Source: www.dowjones.com

Stock Exchange. The index, commonly known as the S&P 500, is often reported in conjunction with the performance of the Dow. It is calculated using a weighted average based on the value of the 500 individual stocks. A comparison of the annual returns of the two stock market indices from 1950 to 2001 is shown in Exhibit 4-3.

Exhibit 4-3 Annual Performance of S&P 500 and DJIA

Year	S&P 500 % gain (loss)	Dow % gain (loss)	Year	S&P 500 % gain (loss)	Dow % gain (loss)	Year	S&P 500 % gain (loss)	Dow % gain (loss)
1950	22.51	17.64	1968	7.66	4.28	1986	14.62	23.49
1951	14.44	14.36	1969	(11.36)	(15.19)	1987	2.03	1.34
1952	11.64	8.43	1970	0.10	4.81	1988	12.39	8.83
1953	(6.52)	(3.77)	1971	10.79	6.12	1989	27.25	27.79
1954	44.21	43.97	1972	15.63	14.58	1990	(6.56)	(4.86)
1955	23.76	20.77	1973	(17.37)	(16.81)	1991	26.31	20.23
1956	3.34	2.27	1974	(29.72)	(27.58)	1992	4.48	4.93
1957	(13.44)	(12.77)	1975	31.38	37.68	1993	7.06	13.47
1958	36.90	33.97	1976	19.15	17.87	1994	(1.55)	2.15
1959	8.03	16.40	1977	(11.50)	(17.10)	1995	34.13	33.36
1960	(3.00)	(9.35)	1978	1.06	(2.38)	1996	20.26	25.04
1961	24.28	20.62	1979	12.31	4.47	1997	31.00	23.94
1962	(11.81)	(10.81)	1980	25.77	15.37	1998	26.67	15.95
1963	18.89	17.01	1981	(9.73)	(9.36)	1999	19.53	24.80
1964	12.97	14.56	1982	14.76	19.37	2000	(10.14)	(6.18)
1965	9.06	10.89	1983	17.26	19.99	2001	(13.04)	(7.10)
1966	(13.09)	(18.94)	1984	1.40	(3.72)			
1967	20.09	15.20	1985	26.36	28.63			

Sources: Yahoo! Finance Web site (1950–1999) and *Wall Street Journal* (2000–2001).

4.8.3 MARKET PERFORMANCE IN TERMS OF RETURN

As shown in Exhibit 4-3, the two indices have overall average returns that are fairly close together. The average, or mean return, of the S&P 500 is 9.63 percent, whereas the mean return for the Dow is 9.01 percent. The mean will change, of course, depending on the time period examined. The market has recently had two consecutive years of negative returns, something that has not occurred since 1973–1974. The market has not had three consecutive years of negative returns since the 1939–1941 period.

Another important aspect of returns is their standard deviation. As the student is aware, a return on the stock market is not guaranteed. An interesting feature of stock market performance is the variation of returns. Although the mean return for the S&P 500 for the past 52 years is 9.63 percent, the returns have ranged from nearly negative 30 percent to more than 44 percent.

One of the reasons why the stock market is considered risky is the inability to obtain a mean return on a consistent basis. How can we assess the risk of the stock market? There are ways of quantifying the differences between the actual returns in any given year and the overall average. One quantifiable measure of this uncertainty is called **variance**.

Another way is the square root of the variance, called the **standard deviation**. The standard deviations for the two market indicators are nearly identical, with the standard deviation of returns for the S&P 500 being 16.2 percent as compared to 16.1 percent for the Dow. Standard deviation calculations are shown in greater detail in Chapter 9.

By examining the rate of return patterns of the two indices, we can see that they generally follow each other fairly consistently. A measure of how returns move together over time is called the **correlation coefficient,** which is a number that ranges from −1.0 to +1.0. Returns that move together perfectly have a correlation coefficient of +1.0, whereas those that move in exact opposite directions have a correlation coefficient of −1.0. In reality, most assets have returns that move somewhere between 0 and +1.0. Correlation coefficients are important when calculating the risk of groups of assets called portfolios, which are discussed later in the book.

4.8.4 S&P/TSX COMPOSITE INDEX

As we saw earlier, the Dow Jones Industrial Average and Standard & Poor's 500 concentrate on the American stock markets. Administered by Standard & Poor's, the S&P/TSX Composite Index is their equivalent for the Canadian equity markets. It includes common shares and income trust units and serves as the benchmark for the majority of Canadian pension funds and mutual market funds.

The S&P/TSX Composite is the basis for numerous sub-indices, which break down the Canadian market by different factors including size, Global Industry Classification Standard (GICS), and income trust inclusion versus non-inclusion. At December 31, 2007, it included 258 companies for an adjusted market cap of $1,435.48 billion. Exhibit 4-4 lists the top ten companies in the S&P/TSX Composite at that date.

Exhibit 4-4 S&P/TSX Composite Top 10 Companies as at December 31, 2007

Company	Float adjusted market cap (C$ million)	Index weight	GICS® sector
Royal Bank of Canada	64,757.4	4.51%	Financials
Manulife Financial Corporation	60,861.2	4.24%	Financials
Research in Motion Limited	53,040.0	3.69%	Information technology
Encana Corporation	50,702.3	3.53%	Energy
Toronto-Dominion Bank (The)	49,956.6	3.48%	Financials
Suncor Energy Inc.	49,876.1	3.47%	Energy
Bank of Nova Scotia (The)	49,469.4	3.45%	Financials
Potash Corporation of Saskatchawan Inc.	45,366.7	3.16%	Materials
Canadian Natural Resources Limited	39,165.0	2.73%	Energy
Barrick Gold Corporation	36,296.7	2.53%	Materials

4.9 SUMMARY

This chapter:

- Explained why individuals invest
- Explained how to calculate a holding period return
- Examined different capital markets and how trading takes place
- Examined the bond market
- Discussed the money market and various money market instruments
- Considered risk-hedging techniques such as forward and futures contracts
- Examined the potential financial impact of fluctuations in foreign exchange rates
- Reviewed key financial intermediaries to the hospitality industry
- Introduced some common indicators of stock market performance

Key Terms

Canada Mortgage and Housing
    Corporation (CMHC)

Canada Savings Bonds (CSBs)

Correlation coefficient

Default

Floating currency exchange

Forward contract

Futures contract

Holding period return

Market maker

Mortgage-backed securities

Pass-through securities

Present value

Primary market

Principal

Risk-free rate of return

Secondary market

Spread

Standard deviation

Variance

Zero-coupon securities

Discussion Questions

1. Why do people invest?
2. What are the key differences between common shares and preferred shares?
3. How is a holding period return calculated?
4. Describe the two largest stock markets.
5. What is a bond? How does it differ from common shares?
6. In general, what happens to the value of a bond when interest rates rise? Why?
7. Describe the process companies use to raise equity capital.
8. What is the difference between a futures contract and a forward contract?
9. Assume you are a restaurant manager facing a potential price increase for orange juice. What options are available to you to deal with this problem?
10. What causes the value of the Canadian dollar to rise or fall?
11. What is the role of the CMHC?

12. Describe the major lenders to the hospitality industry.

13. Describe three of the most common stock market indicators.

14. How can we measure the total risk of an investment?

15. What is a spread and what relevance does it have to the investor?

Problems

Problems designated with EXCEL can be solved using Excel spreadsheets accessible at www.pearsoned.ca/chatfield.

1. Assume you own a share of stock that has achieved the following historical returns.

Year	Return percentage
1	10%
2	(4%)
3	25%
4	13%
5	0.5%

Calculate the average return for the share of stock over the past five years.

2. Assume you own a portfolio of five separate stocks. Each yields a different return and represents a different proportion of your portfolio. The stocks and their returns are as follows.

Stock	Percentage of portfolio	Return percentage
1	15%	10%
2	25%	8%
3	40%	6%
4	10%	12%
5	10%	5%

What is the weighted average return for your portfolio?

3. Joe Smith purchased a share of stock for $58. During the year, he received $2.40 in dividends. At the end of the year he sold the stock for $64. Calculate the holding period return for his investment (excluding taxes).

4. Sally Jones purchased a share of stock for $42. During the year, she received $1.80 in dividends. At the end of the year she sold her stock for $40.50. Calculate the holding period return for her investment (excluding taxes).

5. You would like to purchase five 8.5 percent $10,000 bonds that are currently selling for 102.

   a. How much will it cost you to purchase these bonds?

   b. How much interest will you earn in one year from these five bonds?

6. Assume a $10,000 bond paying 12 percent interest is currently selling at 104.

   a. What is the current selling price of the bond in dollars?

   b. What is the current yield of this bond?

7. A $100,000 bond is currently selling at 98, and the current yield on the bond is 6.2 percent. What is the interest rate on the bond?

8. Hans Stern is a manager of a McDonald's in Germany, and he is interested in the indirect quote for Canadian dollars and euros. The direct quote of the euro per Canadian dollar is 1.75 euro/$1. What is the indirect quote?

9. Assume you are a manager of a Canadian hospitality firm in France. You forecast a net income of 200,000 euros. Also assume that the exchange rate has changed from $1/1 euro to $0.50/1 euro. When you repatriate your profits to dollars, has your net income increased or decreased from the change in the exchange rate?

EXCEL 10. Examine the return data from the S&P 500 Index and the Dow Jones Industrial Average. Using a spreadsheet program such as Excel, calculate the correlation coefficient of their returns between 1996 and 2006.

11. You purchase a German sports car for 117,000 euros. At the time of your purchase, the exchange rate was 1.72 euro/$1. Now the exchange rate has changed to 1.67 euro/$1. Does your sports car cost more or less in Canadian dollars now than when you purchased it? By how much?

12. Jennifer Annisette purchased two hectares of land for $50,000 and received 50 percent financing of the purchase price from the seller (the loan is interest-free). A home developer is interested in developing houses on Jennifer's land and is offering her $30,000 per hectare. What is Jennifer's net holding period return on her investment?

Chapter 5
Review of Financial Statements and Selected Ratios

Chapter Objectives

This chapter covers the following topics:

1 The income statement

2 The Uniform System of Accounts format

3 The balance sheet

4 The relationship between the income statement and the balance sheet

5 The statement of retained earnings

6 The statement of cash flows

7 The validity of financial statements

8 Ratios of particular importance to the hospitality industry and the limitations of ratio analysis

5.1 Introduction

This chapter provides a review of the major financial statements that students should have worked with in earlier courses, such as financial and/or managerial accounting. The *income statement* indicates the performance of an operation over a period of time. The *balance sheet* indicates the financial position of the operation at a particular point in time. The *statement of retained earnings* shows changes in the owners' position during an operating cycle. And, finally, the *statement of cash flows* explains the changes in the cash account for an operating cycle. Each of these financial statements is reviewed in this chapter.

Once the statements are completed, new information can be generated by utilizing ratio analysis. Although many ratios can be calculated, Chapter 5 focuses on the ratios used most commonly by managers, owners, and lenders. Additionally, this chapter discusses the limitations of ratio analysis.

5.2 Review of the Income Statement

The **income statement** provides details on the revenues and expenses of a hospitality operation for a period of time. Students need to be very familiar with the construction of the income statement because it is frequently used as the major tool to assess management's capabilities. Furthermore, income statements can be compiled for individual departments, divisions, and properties and reported to outsiders.

Most "line items" shown on the income statement represent expenses. Typically, the largest expense category for hotels is labour cost, whereas the largest for food service operations is cost of goods sold (with labour cost usually second largest). Accordingly, the importance of the income statement and its frequent use led to a special construction for the hospitality industry.

5.2.1 UNIFORM SYSTEM OF ACCOUNTS FOR HOTELS

The **Uniform System of Accounts** for hotels is a standardized income statement that provides numerous advantages to the hospitality industry. It allows new properties to understand immediately the proper format of their income statements. It also allows easier comparison between properties, and can be used for properties of different sizes. Finally, it is a system that has been time tested since its design in 1925. Although the Uniform System has been updated since that time, the changes in recent years have been relatively minor.

The Uniform System of Accounts for hotels is unique to the hotel industry. Instead of focusing on one particular area of expense (such as labour cost or cost of goods sold), as retail or manufacturing concerns do, it allows management to focus on different functional areas of a full-service hotel. Thus, labour expense can be appropriately attributed to an individual department to help determine that department's profitability, as opposed to examining a single good or service. This chapter discusses primarily the income statements for multidepartment hotel properties.

5.2.2 HOTEL INCOME STATEMENT

Before examining a detailed income statement for an individual hotel property, we will examine a consolidated income statement from InnVest Real Estate Investment Trust. This Canadian investment trust operates its hotel properties under fifteen internationally recognized franchise brands: Comfort Inn®, Quality Suites®, Quality Hotels®, Holiday Inn®, Radisson Hotels®, Radisson Suites®, Delta®, Hilton Hotels®, Fairmont Hotels®, Sheraton Suites®, Hilton Garden Inn®, Hilton Homewood Suites®, Travelodge®, Staybridge Suites®, and Best Western®.

The income statement shown in Exhibit 5-1 is somewhat short and general, grouping all hotel revenues under one line, followed by hotel expenses and other income and expenses. However, this is a corporate-level income statement that is a summary of operations typically shown to investors, who are usually not concerned with the statistics of an individual property. The statistics provided on the statement are for an entire system of properties and would be of little value to a department manager at the property level or other internal users. Accordingly, department managers would be more interested in results at the property level. The level of detail in the statement varies depending on the needs of the user. An income statement for a sample hotel property is shown in Exhibit 5-2.

The focus of the income statement for use at the property level is on the operated departments—primarily rooms, food and beverage, and telephone. However, there may be other important departments such as casino operations or a golf course that are treated in a similar manner. The operated department income of each department represents the profit that each department contributes to the rest of the property. It is also important to

Exhibit 5-1 Hotel Consolidated Income Statement

InnVest Real Estate Investment Trust

**Consolidated statements of net income
and comprehensive income**

(in thousands of dollars)	Year ended December 31, 2007	Year ended December 31, 2006
Total revenues (reference only)	$ 505,753	$ 388,191
Hotel revenues	$ 495,955	$ 380,470
Hotel expenses		
Operating expenses	297,454	217,768
Property taxes, rent, and insurance	41,964	34,353
Management fees	17,729	12,784
	357,147	264,905
Hotel operating income	138,808	115,565
Other (income) and expenses		
Interest on mortagages and other debt	36,814	28,802
Interest on operating and bridge loans	5,262	638
Convertible debentures interest and accretion	11,047	9,445
Corporate and administrative	6,883	5,384
Capital tax	75	1,523
Other business income, net	(5,916)	(4,850)
Other income	(1,614)	(310)
Depreciation and amortization	63,583	50,803
	116,134	91,435
Income before income tax recovery	22,674	24,130
Income tax recovery		
Current	(4)	(392)
Future	(25,869)	(15,473)
	(25,873)	(15,865)
Net income from continuing operations	48,547	39,995
Loss from discontinued operations	(1,003)	(399)
Write down on assets held for sale, net of gain on sales of assets	(6,322)	(1,000)
Net loss from discontinued operations	(7,325)	(1,399)
Net income and comprehensive income	$ 41,222	$ 38,596

Source: InnVest Real Estate Investment Trust 2007 Annual Report, www.innvestreit.com

note that each department has a supporting schedule that provides more details on both revenue and expenses for each department. The total operated department income for the property is also called its contribution margin.

Exhibit 5-2 Sample Hotel Income Statement for the Year Ended December 31, 2006

	Net revenue	Cost of sales	Payroll expense	Other expense	Operated dept income (loss)
Operating department					
Rooms	$5,000,000		$1,000,000	$200,000	$3,800,000
Food and beverage	2,500,000	$1,000,000	1,000,000	200,000	300,000
Telephone	500,000	150,000	50,000	20,000	280,000
Rentals and other income	20,000				20,000
Total operated departments	8,020,000	1,150,000	2,050,000	420,000	4,400,000
Undistributed operating expenses					
Administrative and general			500,000	600,000	1,100,000
Marketing			200,000	100,000	300,000
Franchise fees				250,000	250,000
Energy				300,000	300,000
Property maintenance			150,000	250,000	400,000
Total undistributed expenses			850,000	1,500,000	2,350,000
Income before fixed charges	8,020,000	1,150,000	2,900,000	1,920,000	2,050,000
Real estate taxes				160,000	160,000
Property insurance				80,000	80,000
Interest				450,000	450,000
Management fees				305,000	305,000
Depreciation and amortization				100,000	100,000
Income before income taxes					955,000
Income taxes					257,000
Net income					$ 698,000

The remainder of the income statement comprises undistributed operating expenses—expenses that are not directly attributable to any one department. These include expenses such as administrative and general, marketing, maintenance, and utilities. The final section of the statement includes fixed expenses such as real estate taxes, property insurance, interest, depreciation, amortization, rent, and management fees. The last item is income taxes, and it is based on a percentage of the income before income taxes.

5.2.3 RESTAURANT INCOME STATEMENT

Just as the hotel industry has a uniform income statement, so too does the restaurant industry. However, the corporate income statements for restaurant companies are also generalized and abbreviated. Similar to hotel income statements, more detailed income statements can be produced for internal users. The income statement for The Great Canadian Pancake House is shown in Exhibit 5-3.

Exhibit 5-3 Sample Restaurant Income Statement

The Great Canadian Pancake House
for the year ended December 31, 2008

	Amount ($)	Percentage (%)
Revenue		
Food	$1,500,000	71.4
Beverage	500,000	23.8
Merchandise	100,000	4.8
Total revenue	2,100,000	100.0
Cost of sales		
Food	555,000	37.0
Beverage	115,000	23.0
Merchandise	30,000	30.0
Total cost of sales	700,000	33.3
Gross profit	1,400,000	66.7
Controllable expenses		
Salaries and wages	580,000	27.6
Employee benefits	90,000	4.3
Direct operating expenses	50,000	2.4
Marketing and promotion	36,000	1.7
Heat, light, and power	54,000	2.6
Engineering and maintenance	28,000	1.3
Total controllable expenses	838,000	39.9
Earnings before occupation cost	562,000	26.8
Occupation cost	90,000	4.3
Amortization	45,000	2.1
Earnings before interest and taxes	427,000	20.4
Interest expense	37,000	1.8
Earnings before taxes	390,000	18.6
Taxes	156,000	7.5
Net income	234,000	11.1

The major difference between this statement and the hotel income statement shown in Exhibit 5.2 is the lack of segmentation of payroll costs across departments. Additionally, other income, which could include items such as vending and pay phone commissions, is either shown as a minor revenue (after food and beverage) or as a reduction of uncontrollable expenses. Furthermore, all items are expressed as a percentage of total revenue with the exception of food, beverage, and merchandise cost of sales, which are shown as a percentage of food, beverage, and merchandise revenue, respectively.

5.3 Review of the Balance Sheet

The **balance sheet** is used to represent the financial position of the firm for a specific point in time. There are really no significant differences in the balance sheets used internally (by management) as compared to those seen by external users (creditors, government). Moreover, there is no uniform system for the balance sheet because all balance sheets follow a specific format.

The balance sheet comprises three major sections: assets, liabilities, and owners' equity. Assets are items that are owned or in possession by the firm; liabilities are claims on the assets by creditors or lenders to the firm. Owners' equity represents the claims to the assets by the owners or the financial commitment that has been made to the firm by the owners/investors. All of the assets are essentially claimed by someone—in other words, the total of all assets must equal the total of all liabilities plus owners' equity; this is known as the fundamental accounting equation or the conventional balance sheet formula (Assets = Liabilities + Owners' Equity). To continue the example started with Exhibit 5-1, consolidated balance sheets for InnVest Real Estate Investment Trust are shown in Exhibit 5-4.

A simpler balance sheet is also provided for our sample hotel from Exhibit 5-2; it is presented in Exhibit 5-5. These balance sheets show that the assets of a firm are listed in order of liquidity. The most liquid assets are always listed first. Therefore an account such as cash would always be presented first since there is no asset more liquid than cash itself.

Cash and cash equivalents include such items as cash on hand, chequing accounts, certificates of deposit, and commercial paper. Accounts receivable is presented net of allowance for doubtful accounts. Inventories are also considered a current asset and are recorded at the lower of cost or market value, that is, whichever is the lower of the two.

Deferred income taxes result from differences between reporting to investors and reporting to the Canada Revenue Agency. In other words, the differences between income taxes payable and actual income tax expense, produced by accrual accounting, result in deferred income taxes. Furthermore, the federal government allows firms with an operating loss to use either a **tax carryback** against previous years or a **tax carryforward** for future years. This represents an asset to the firm, called "income tax receivable." A subtotal for current assets is always presented to analyze the firm's current financial position. This is discussed in greater detail in the ratio analysis section of the chapter.

Investments are items such as stocks and bonds of other companies that the firm intends to hold for more than one fiscal year. Property and equipment are shown at cost less accumulated depreciation. Note that for our sample hotel, as well as for InnVest (where it appears on the line "Hotel properties"), the greatest concentration of assets is in property and equipment; this is quite typical for hotels, restaurants, resorts, and casino firms. Other long-term assets include items such as goodwill and other intangibles. Goodwill is an intangible asset obtained when the price paid for an asset exceeds the value of the asset. Patents and franchise fees could represent other assets. InnVest shows assets held for sale under both current and long-term assets. This represents and signals its intention to sell some properties within one year, thus these particular properties are currently being inventoried, and the rest of its property holdings will be up for sale at some point in time in the future; at the very least a time window that is more than one fiscal year from now.

The firm's liabilities are also divided between "current" (due within one fiscal year) and "long term" (due date or payment period greater than one fiscal year). Current maturity of long-term debt is the portion of the long-term debt that is due within one

Exhibit 5-4 Hotel Balance Sheet

InnVest Real Estate Investment Trust

Consolidated balance sheets

(in thousands of dollars)	December 31, 2007	December 31, 2006
Assets		
Current assets		
Cash	$ 22,271	$ 4,531
Accounts receivable	28,677	13,354
Prepaid expenses and other assets	9,487	5,569
Assets held for sale	301	407
	60,736	23,861
Restricted cash	2,995	4,693
Hotel properties	1,884,765	1,105,384
Other real estate properties	16,428	16,933
License contracts	19,169	20,485
Intangible and deferred assets	55,101	19,984
Assets held for sale	23,085	37,012
	$2,062,279	$1,228,352
Liabilities		
Current liabilities		
Bank indebtedness	$ 223,200	$ 3,300
Accounts payable and accrued liabilities	73,682	40,405
Acquisition related liabilities	17,569	957
Distributions payable	6,844	5,161
Current portion of long-term debt	12,725	11,141
Liabilities related to assets held for sale	610	711
	334,630	61,675
Long-term debt	698,892	476,520
Other long-term obligations	6,692	4,145
Convertible debentures	177,387	126,339
Future income tax liabillty	225,503	124,759
Long-term liabilities related to assets held for sale	14,509	17,297
	1,457,613	810,735
Unitholders' Equity	604,666	417,617
	$2,062,279	$1,228,352

Source: InnVest Real Estate Invest Trust 2007 Annual Report, www.innvestreit.com

year of the balance sheet date. For example, if a firm borrows $5,000,000 and $500,000 is due within six months, the firm presents $500,000 as a current maturity of long-term debt and $4,500,000 as a long-term liability.

Exhibit 5-5 Sample Hotel Balance Sheet (in thousands of dollars)

	December 31, 2008	December 31, 2007
Assets		
Cash and cash equivalents	$ 200	$ 134
Accounts receivable, net	120	110
Inventories, prepaids, and other	50	50
Income taxes receivable	25	25
Future income tax asset	3	3
Total current assets	398	322
Investments	500	—
Property and equipment, net	6,250	6,150
Goodwill	150	150
Other assets	20	20
Total assets	$7,318	$6,642
Liabilities and Shareholders' Equity		
Accounts payable and accrued expenses	$ 138	$ 130
Bank loan	150	—
Current maturities of long-term debt	100	100
Total current liabilities	385	230
Long-term debt, net of current portion	2,565	2,665
Other liabilities	20	20
Total liabilities	2,973	2,915
Shareholders' equity		
Common shares, no par value, 1 million shares authorized, 539,000 shares issued	1,617	1,617
Retained earnings	2,728	2,110
Total shareholders' equity	4,345	3,727
Total liabilities and shareholders' equity	$7,318	$6,642

Owners' equity shows common stock, additional paid-in capital, and retained earnings. The retained earnings account is reduced immediately upon the declaration of dividends to be paid out to shareholders on record. However, it does not represent an immediate cash outlay. The cash outlay will not take place until the dividends have actually been paid.

Therefore at this time, the retained earnings account and the statement of retained earnings represents the accumulation of net income earned by the firm in previous periods less any dividends declared. A firm must have positive retained earnings to declare a dividend. Also included in this section is treasury stock, representing the repurchase of the firm's stock and shown as a reduction in owners' equity. Firms may from time to time believe it is necessary to purchase their own stock. They may do this as part of a "defensive strategy" in a hostile takeover scenario. This was the case when American billionaire Carl Icahn threatened to buy Fairmont Hotels and Resorts in 2006. Fairmont CEO William Fatt immediately coordinated an effort to acquire as much Fairmont stock as possible thus causing the market value of the stock to increase significantly and hopefully making the purchase of stock by Icahn more difficult and much more expensive.

In our sample hotel, the owner's section of the InnVest balance sheet is represented by a single line item called "Unitholders Equity." This is because InnVest is not a corporation per se; it is an *investment trust* of which units are sold to investors. Once the investors have purchased said units the investors become "unitholders." Also, instead of dividends, cash distributions are made on a quarterly basis to the unitholders. This explains the different presentation of the owner's section of the balance sheet.

As discussed in the previous chapter, many companies do business around the world. Accordingly, all assets and liabilities of their foreign operations must be presented in an average of exchange rates during the year or in the exchange rate in effect on the balance sheet date or via historical rates. The actual approach/methodology used by the hospitality firm will be dependent upon the appropriate jurisdictional accounting rules and requirements. Any gains or losses from translations are reported in the owners' equity section as "Other comprehensive income (loss)." For many hospitality firms, this line item can be significant. With respect to our two sample balance sheets this particular financial concern/element is absent.

5.4 Relationship between the Income Statement and the Balance Sheet

It is important for hospitality students to learn the differences between the income statement and the balance sheet because the two statements are reported separately and serve very different functions. However, the two statements are presented together, and it is also important to understand how the statements relate to one another. The relationships are explained in Exhibit 5-6.

As shown in Exhibit 5-6, assets are utilized to generate revenue (and also cash flow). The majority of assets are fixed—land, building, and equipment are necessary to produce a wide variety of revenues. There is one key exception to the usage of assets to produce revenue: depreciation is related to building and equipment and is shown on the income statement. Nevertheless, depreciation expense is a "paper expense" that is used to lower taxable income and thereby generate tax savings.

Liabilities are associated with expenses on the income statement. Accounts payable is related to food and beverage cost, whereas wages payable is affiliated with labour expense. The last major balance sheet category is owners' equity. The major link with the income statement is the retained earnings account. Net income increases retained earnings, and a net loss reduces retained earnings (along with dividends declared). Dividends, however, are not an operations expense and do not appear on the income statement.

The bottom portion of the figure displays the relationship between the two statements over time. The purpose of the balance sheet is to reveal the financial position of the firm for a specific point in time, often the end of the month or a quarter. The income statement is

Exhibit 5-6 Relationship between the Income Statement and the Balance Sheet

Balance sheet accounts	Income statement line items
Assets	**Revenues**
Examples:	Examples:
Inventory	Rooms
Land	Food
Building	Beverage
Equipment	Casino
Liabilities	**Expenses**
Examples:	Examples:
Accounts payable	Cost of goods sold
Wages payable	Labour expense
Income taxes payable	Income tax expense
Owner's equity	**Net income**
Example:	
Retained earnings	
Balance sheet	
Report assets, liabilities, and owner's equity on December 31, 2007	
	Income statement
	Report revenue and expenses for the month of December 2008
Balance sheet	
Report assets, liabilities, and owner's equity on December 31, 2008	

then compiled to demonstrate the firm's performance for a period of time—often a month, three months, or a year. After the firm's performance is shown on the income statement, another balance sheet is completed that incorporates the earnings or losses of the period.

5.5 Statement of Retained Earnings

The **statement of retained earnings** is now often included in a consolidated statement of shareholders' equity. However, given the importance of retained earnings and its link to the income statement, we focus on the calculation of the ending balance in retained earnings. A statement of retained earnings for our sample hotel is shown in Exhibit 5-7. See how it integrates the balances in retained earnings shown in the sample hotel balance sheets

Exhibit 5-7 Sample Statement of Retained Earnings for the Year Ended December 31, 2008

Retained earnings, beginning of year	$40,000
Net income	$50,000
Dividends declared	$10,000
Retained earnings, end of year	$80,000

(Exhibit 5-5), the net income shown in the income statement (Exhibit 5-2), and the payment of dividends shown in the statement of cash flows (Exhibit 5-8).

The calculation of the ending balance of retained earnings is straightforward. Net income is added to the beginning balance, and any dividend declarations are subtracted to obtain the final balance. Occasionally, unusual adjustments must be made to retained earnings. Adjustments would include errors made in a prior period or a change in an accounting principle.

Retained earnings is only a small portion of the shareholders' equity account that is usually presented by corporations. Items that can affect shareholders' equity in a given period include issuance or repurchase of stock, unrealized gains or losses on investments, and foreign exchange contracts. However, further in-depth analysis of these items is beyond the scope of this text.

5.6 Statement of Cash Flows

The **statement of cash flows** is important because cash is considered the lifeblood of the business. Suppliers are paid in cash, lenders are paid in cash, and dividends are paid in cash. Additionally, as you may recall from your accounting courses, earnings from the income statement are accrual-based and do not represent cash flows into the business.

Recent accounting scandals involving Enron, WorldCom, Tyco International, and other companies have revolved largely around the ability of the average investor to assess the current and future cash flows of the company. Many investors have argued that cash flows are more readily observable than are accrual-based earnings (either dividends are paid or they are not). Therefore, the statement of cash flows receives greater scrutiny than ever before.

A hospitality firm may derive cash inflows (or outflows) from three basic sources: operating, investing activities, or financing activities. Operating activities are those for which the firm is primarily in business (selling rooms or food, for example). A successful and vibrant firm should be able to generate most of its cash flows from operating activities. The other two activities are those related to investing (primarily securities and equipment) and financing (loans and dividend payments).

One difficulty for students in compiling the statement of cash flows is the conversion of accrual-based figures to cash flows. For example, although depreciation is an expense shown on the income statement, it is a noncash expense that is shown to reduce taxable income. Therefore, because we never spent the cash to begin with, we must add it back to net income. Other items that require adjustments are accrual items. Increases in current assets (inventory, for example) represent decreases to cash flows and must be subtracted. Liabilities act in an opposite fashion to cash. An increase in accounts payable, for

Exhibit 5-8 Sample Hotel Statement of Cash Flows for the Year Ended December 31, 2008

Net cash flow from operating activities:	
Net income	$698,000
Depreciation and amortization	100,000
Increase in accounts receivable	(10,000)
Increase in accounts payable	8,000
Net cash flow from operating activities	$796,000
Net cash flow from investing activities:	
Purchase of investments	($500,000)
Purchase of equipment	(200,000)
Net cash flow from investing activities	($700,000)
Net cash flow from financing activities:	
Proceeds from bank loan	$150,000
Payments of long-term debt	(100,000)
Payment of dividends	(80,000)
Net cash flow from financing activities:	$ 70,000
Total net cash flow:	$166,000
Cash balance 1/1/2008	$ 34,000
Cash balance 12/31/2008	$200,000

example, means that we bought inventory on credit (as opposed to cash). Therefore, this cash "saved" means an increase to cash. Exhibit 5-8 shows a statement of cash flows for the year 2008 for our sample hotel.

Take a look back at Exhibit 5.5, the balance sheet for the sample hotel, and you will notice that the "Cash and cash equivalent" balances for 2007 and 2008 are the "plug in" values for the "Cash balance" account values as at January 1, 2008, and December 31, 2008. In this example, these extracted or "exogenous variables" are required to generate or "build" the **statement of cash flows** for the sample hotel. When constructing a statement of cash flows, the beginning and ending cash balances will be required to complete the generation of said financial statement.

As stated previously, most investors are concerned with the statement of cash flows from operating activities. A very rough estimate of this number is found by taking net income from the income statement and adding back depreciation. Although this is not exact, many of the accrual items tend to balance out, leaving depreciation and perhaps amortization as the largest noncash expenses that need to be added back to derive a rough estimate of cash flow. Cash flows become more important later in valuation because value is primarily related to cash flows, not accrual-based earnings.

Students should also note the importance of cash flow relative to accrual-based earnings and the survivability of the business. It is possible for firms to have a negative net income and a positive cash flow. The opposite can also occur: a positive net income and a negative cash flow. However, the latter situation can cause business failure if it occurs over a long period of time.

5.7 Validity of Financial Statements

In early 2002, investors on Bay Street and Wall Street became concerned about the accuracy of financial statements of some major corporations. The major (although not the only) focus was on Enron Corporation. Enron was at one time the seventh-largest corporation in the United States and aspired to eventually become the largest. In early 2001, the company's common stock was selling for approximately $80 per share; however, by October the accounting of some of the company's transactions had fallen under intense scrutiny. On December 3, the company filed for bankruptcy, and the stock price in early 2002 was less than $1.00 per share. Employees were outraged because many of them had been encouraged to purchase large amounts of Enron stock to hold in their retirement plans. What went wrong for Enron?

Although many of the transactions were complex, some involved the establishment of various partnerships that were separate from but related to Enron. Enron would obtain loans for the partnerships while not disclosing the loans on Enron's balance sheet, along with declaring "earnings" on Enron's income statements that were not really there. The investigation is ongoing as of this writing, and more detailed information is forthcoming. Nevertheless, the practice that produced bogus financial statements is falling under increased scrutiny.

The effects of the Enron case were immediate and widespread. The public began to ask questions about the accounting practices that were essentially approved by Enron's auditor, Arthur Andersen. Partners and employees of Arthur Andersen were called before the U.S. Congress to testify about their knowledge of these transactions. In addition, the way auditors were engaged by companies came into question along with the issue of federal regulation of the accounting profession and tougher accounting standards. Finally, investors became concerned that there were more companies like Enron using questionable accounting practices when compiling their financial statements.

One of the fundamental principles of an efficient market is the lack of information asymmetry and the accessibility of accurate and timely information. Without it, investors lose confidence in capital markets, and the impact on the economy can be devastating. If breaches of ethical standards are discovered in the investigation the wrongdoers will be prosecuted, and the accounting profession can be improved to detect such actions. Hopefully, such a circumstance is a rarity and not an established practice.

Nevertheless, a significant amount of responsibility lies with investors as well. In financial management, one of our tasks is to conduct some analysis to help make better-informed decisions. It is not the task of the financial manager to compile the financial statements; he or she usually assumes the information supplied to make a decision is reasonably accurate and correct. We also make this assumption as we analyze financial information. However, it is important for the student to understand that when financial managers utilize analytical tools such as ratio analysis, the results often raise more questions than answers and usually require further investigation. This is true even with the relatively simple financial statement examples we display in this chapter. It is one of the functions of this text to make the student a more critical reviewer of financial statements—even those that are compiled correctly.

5.8 Ratio Analysis

One major tool used by financial managers and financial analysts is ratio analysis. Ratios are important because they are used by various individuals to help evaluate a firm's financial position or performance. However, ratios can be misleading if not used properly because a ratio is simply one number placed over another.

Therefore, ratios become more meaningful when they are used appropriately as the beginning of a detailed investigation into a particular portion of a hospitality operation. One appropriate use is to compare ratios to industry standards when measuring performance. Ratios for different industries are compiled by sources such as the Risk Management Association as well as a variety of sources on the World Wide Web. Industry comparisons are primarily used by lenders and investors to assess performance.

However, when utilizing industry comparisons, one must be careful in consideration of the benchmark used. For example, although it could be done, it would not be logical to compare a hotel or restaurant operation to the overall hospitality industry. This is because the hospitality industry is not homogeneous and contains many different segments such as hotels, motels, restaurants, cruise ships, amusement parks, and many others. Moreover, it is also important to understand that even within a particular industry segment there are many subsegments. For example, if you want to compare the ratios of McDonald's to the overall restaurant industry, this comparison could be misleading because McDonald's is a fast-food chain, and the "industry average" that is calculated could be heavily weighted by other types of restaurants.

This brings us to our final caveat regarding comparisons to industry averages. Despite the plethora of sources of financial information on the World Wide Web, the information is not necessarily appropriate for the purpose of your analysis. There are a number of potential pitfalls in utilizing industry averages. For example, how many firms are included in the average? The size and type of firms can have a significant impact on the overall average. Certain firms may be included in an industry average one year but not the next because of takeovers and bankruptcies. Additionally, large firms can dominate a sample of an industry and distort the overall picture.

Moreover, not all firms use the same accounting methods (such as depreciation and inventory valuation methods). Furthermore, firms compile their statements over different periods of time—some use the calendar year and others use the fiscal year. These are all important considerations when making comparisons.

Hospitality operations managers frequently compare common hotel operation ratios, such as average daily rate, occupancy rate, and revenue per available room, to a prior period or goal. However, caveats similar to those used in comparing ratios to industry averages also need to be considered here. For example, the events of September 11, 2001, adversely affected the occupancy of many hotels that month. Therefore, comparisons with previous September months may not be meaningful. Additionally, changes such as renovations and revised advertising strategies can make comparisons difficult even for the same property.

5.8.1 CLASSES OF RATIOS

A large number of ratios can be utilized for purposes of financial analysis, and we do not intend to list them all. Instead, we discuss the most popular ratios using surveys of

The key information needed to calculate the preceding ratios is listed in the supplementary schedule shown in Exhibit 5-11. The P/E ratio for the Jamestown Hotel is calculated in the following manner.

$$\frac{\text{Market price of common shares}}{\text{Earnings per share}} = \text{Price-to-earnings ratio}$$

$$\frac{\$92.00}{\$7.28} = 12.64 \text{ times}$$

In the case of the Jamestown Hotel, the market price is more than 12 times its earnings. Although there is no theoretical evidence that a P/E ratio is either "too low" or "too high," investors examine this ratio (among many others) to help them make decisions about buying or selling stocks. Additionally, some generalizations can be made in a relative sense about this ratio. Firms with very high P/E ratios are generally considered companies with good prospects for strong growth in future earnings. Companies with lower P/E ratios are generally considered to have lower prospects for future earnings growth. It is also important to remember that although investors look for future earnings growth, they also recognize that *value is based on future cash flows, not accrual-basis earnings*.

The next two ratios relate to the dividend policy of the firm. The dividend payout ratio measures the percentage of earnings paid to the owners in the form of dividends. The calculation is as follows.

$$\frac{\text{Dividend per common share}}{\text{Earnings per share}} = \text{Dividend payout ratio}$$

$$\frac{\$1.67}{\$7.28} = 0.2294 \text{ or } 22.94\%$$

In general, more stable and well-established firms pay out a larger proportion of their earnings as dividends. On the other hand, high-growth companies tend to retain their earnings to reinvest in assets. Outback Steakhouse is a fast-growing restaurant company, with three locations in Edmonton, Alberta, and nine throughout Ontario. As of this writing it has yet to declare a dividend for shareholders, preferring to retain those earnings to finance growth. Additionally, once firms begin to pay a dividend, they do not want to decrease it because of the potential impact on the stock price in the financial markets.

The final investor ratio is the dividend yield, which is the expected dividend for the coming year divided by the current stock price. The calculation for the Jamestown Hotel is

$$\frac{\text{Annual dividend per common share}}{\text{Market price per share}} = \text{Dividend yield}$$

$$\frac{\$1.67}{\$92.00} = 0.0182 \text{ or } 1.82\%$$

In general, dividend yields are inversely related to the firm's prospects for future growth. Therefore, a relatively low dividend yield implies high growth prospects.

This appears to be the case for the Jamestown Hotel. It is important to remember that the dividend yield is not a true rate of return for holding the stock, which would be based on the dividends received plus any increase in the stock price.

5.9 Perspectives on and Limitations of Ratio Analysis

Now that we have reviewed a significant number of the important ratios used in the hospitality industry, we need to understand some of the differing viewpoints regarding the ratios. As previously discussed, the major parties interested in ratios are lenders, owners, and managers. Given that the ratio is calculated correctly, can these parties disagree about what makes a "good" ratio versus a "bad" one? We look at an example.

One of the most commonly used liquidity ratios is the current ratio, which measures a firm's ability to meet its current debt obligations. All else being the same, most lenders would prefer a high ratio to a low one. Lenders, often commercial banks, have investors who are concerned about receiving interest income and the repayment of principal. Accordingly, lenders hope that borrowers such as hotels will maintain a relatively high cash position to ensure repayment.

On the other hand, consider the perspective of the owners. Given the relatively fixed-asset-intensive nature of a hotel company, it is these assets that produce the earnings and the cash flow—land, buildings, and equipment. Owners generally do not want their investment tied up in current assets like cash, accounts receivable, and inventory because these assets do not produce the return on equity desired by the owners. Therefore, all else being the same, the owners would prefer a low current ratio. Given that the lenders want a higher current ratio and the owners want a lower current ratio, what can management do?

In general, management must strike a balance. Although management works for the owners of the firm, they cannot ignore the needs of the lenders because of their importance to the hotel industry. Overall, management must work to satisfy the suppliers of both debt and equity capital. Although it may seem that lenders and owners have totally opposing viewpoints regarding this ratio, there is a reasonable range for management to work toward. Additionally, a number of ratios are available (such as the number of times interest earned) when both lenders and owners are looking for a higher ratio.

It is important to understand that it is very difficult to say precisely what a particular ratio "should" be. We discussed earlier in the chapter that ratios are much more meaningful when they are compared to a standard, such as an industry average, actual performance from a prior period, or budgeted figure. Careful consideration must be given to each of these situations.

Moreover, even when a ratio is calculated correctly and a proper comparison is made, it doesn't tell you what the problem is. As an example, suppose our restaurant achieved a cost-of-food-sold percentage of 45 percent for 2008. This figure is higher than 2007, higher than our budgeted amount of 42 percent, and higher than other comparable firms within our industry segment. So what's the problem?

This exemplifies the fact that ratio analysis is really just the beginning. Experience, judgment, and managerial skill must come into play to investigate the reasons for the high

Proper Ratios

Most introductory accounting courses teach basic ratios. Some of them try to teach students what an "acceptable" current ratio is. The current ratio is one of the first ratios students learn, and it is generally considered to be one of the easiest to remember. Additionally, it is one of the more important ratios from the lender's perspective.

However, it is important to remember that industries are not homogenous. As an example, one accounting text mentions that a "normal" ratio for most companies in most industries is between 1.6 and 1.9. Moreover, a current ratio of 2.0 is considered "good." Can we assume, then, that the higher the current ratio, the better? Some current ratios for different companies are shown in the table opposite.

The last two current ratios are those of two large and successful hospitality companies. Both have current ratios below the "acceptable" range. How can this be?

We have to remember that we cannot simply assume ratio "rules" are the same for each company. Industries are

Company	2006 current ratio
International Paper	1.90
Microsoft	2.18
3M Corporation	1.22
Marriott Corporation	1.31
McDonald's	1.21

not all alike, and companies within the same industry can differ significantly. It may be such that the shareholders of the hospitality companies shown do not want management tying up their investment in current assets. They want management to invest in long-term assets because they are more effective in producing cash flows to maximize the wealth of the owners.

food cost. Some of the questions that could be asked include, Have we accounted for our employee and complimentary meals properly? Are our menu prices too low? Are we paying too much for our food? Is our sales mix too heavily weighted toward high-cost buffets? The overall point in this example is that ratios raise more questions than answers. Moreover, ratios don't solve problems—that's what hospitality managers are supposed to do!

A final caveat is also useful here. Some accounting textbooks and courses attempt to instruct about minimums and maximums for ratios. As an example, a current ratio is "good" only if it is greater than 1.0, with current assets exceeding liabilities. However, the student should ask whether this rule is true for all firms across all industries. As an example, Marriott International is considered to be a very successful company by almost any standard. At the end of 1999, Marriott had current assets of $1.6 billion. On the other hand, it had current liabilities of $1.743 billion, indicating a current ratio of only 0.92. It appeared that Marriott had violated the "rule" that current assets must exceed current liabilities. Does this mean Marriott was in trouble with its creditors? In all likelihood, Marriott was not in financial difficulty and was not in trouble with its creditors. At the end of 2006, Marriott had improved its current ratio to approximately 1.31.

As previously discussed, the hotel business is fixed-asset-intensive, and owners prefer firms to invest in assets that produce cash flows. Therefore, we cannot effectively compare current ratios of retail firms and hospitality firms. Moreover, some particular corporate policy may be affecting that ratio at that particular time. Ratio analysis can be more effective if the ratios are examined over a period of time. It is important to remember that ratios are more valuable when appropriate comparisons are made. In general, ratios do not solve problems, and they raise more questions than answers. They are intended to help managers and other users begin a path of investigation (see Exhibit 5-12 for a recap of this chapter's ratios).

Exhibit 5-12 List of Ratios Discussed in the Chapter

$$\frac{\text{Current assets}}{\text{Current liabilities}} = \text{Current ratio}$$

$$\frac{\text{Current assets} - \text{Inventories} - \text{Prepaid expenses}}{\text{Current liabilities}} = \text{Quick ratio}$$

$$\text{Current assets} - \text{Current liabilities} = \text{Working capital}$$

$$\frac{\text{Cost of sales}}{\text{Average inventory}} = \text{Inventory turnover}$$

$$\frac{\text{Sales}}{\text{Total assets}} = \text{Asset turnover}$$

$$\frac{\text{Sales}}{\text{Fixed assets}} = \text{Fixed-asset turnover}$$ *No*

$$\frac{\text{Total debt}}{\text{Total assets}} = \text{Debt-to-assets ratio}$$ *Equity Ratio*

$$\frac{\text{Total debt}}{\text{Total equity}} = \text{Debt-to-equity ratio}$$ *No*

$$\frac{\text{Earnings before interest and taxes}}{\text{Interest expense}} = \text{Times interest earned ratio}$$

$$\frac{\text{Net income}}{\text{Total revenue}} = \text{Net profit margin}$$

$$\frac{\text{Net income}}{\text{Total assets}} = \text{Return on investment (return on assets)}$$

$$\frac{\text{Net income}}{\text{Total revenue}} \times \frac{\text{Total revenue}}{\text{Total assets}} = \text{Return on investment (return on assets)}$$ *No*
$$- \text{Output ratio}$$

$$\frac{\text{Net income}}{\text{Shareholders' equity}} = \text{Return on equity}$$ *No*

$$\frac{\text{Occupied room nights}}{\text{Available room nights}} = \text{Occupancy percentage}$$

$$\frac{\text{Rooms revenue}}{\text{Occupied room nights}} = \text{Average daily rate (ADR)}$$ *No*

$$\frac{\text{Rooms revenue}}{\text{Available room nights}} = \text{RevPAR}$$ *No*

or

$$\text{Occupancy percentage} \times \text{Average room rate} = \text{RevPAR}$$

$$\text{Average food cheque} = \frac{\text{Food revenue}}{\text{Number of customers}}$$

$$\text{Average beverage cheque} = \frac{\text{Beverage revenue}}{\text{Number of customers}}$$

$$\frac{\text{Food cost of sales}}{\text{Food revenue}} = \text{Food cost percentage}$$

(continued)

Exhibit 5-12 (continued)

$$\frac{\text{Beverage cost of sales}}{\text{Beverage revenue}} = \text{Beverage cost percentage}$$

$$\frac{\text{Market price of common shares}}{\text{Earnings per share}} = \text{Price-to-earnings ratio}$$

$$\frac{\text{Dividend per common share}}{\text{Earnings per share}} = \text{Dividend payout ratio}$$

$$\frac{\text{Annual dividend per common share}}{\text{Market price per share}} = \text{Dividend yield}$$

5.10 SUMMARY

This chapter:

- Introduced the income statement
- Introduced the Uniform System of Accounts format
- Introduced the balance sheet
- Explained the relationship between the income statement and the balance sheet
- Introduced the statement of retained earnings
- Introduced the statement of cash flows
- Examined the validity of financial statements
- Introduced ratios of particular importance to the hospitality industry and explained the limitations of ratio analysis

Key Terms

Activity ratios	Statement of cash flows
Balance sheet	Statement of retained earnings
Income statement	Tax carryback
Investor ratio	Tax carryforward
Liquidity ratios	Turnover ratios
Profitability ratio	Uniform System of Accounts
Solvency ratios	

Discussion Questions

1. What are the four major types of financial statements?
2. What is the Uniform System of Accounts? What are the advantages of its use?
3. How is the income statement related to the balance sheet?

4. In general, are investors more concerned with earnings (i.e., net income) or cash flows? Why?

5. Discuss the Enron situation. Why did it have such a widespread impact?

6. Why must an analyst be careful when comparing ratios to industry averages?

7. What is the major difference between liquidity ratios and solvency ratios?

8. What is working capital? Where is it listed on the balance sheet?

9. What are the three major ratios used by investors? What does each of them measure?

10. Can parties disagree about the same ratio? Why? Give an example.

Problems

1. You have been provided with the current assets and current liabilities section of the Pacifica Hotel.

PACIFICA HOTEL Partial Balance Sheet December 31, 2007			
Current assets		**Current liabilities**	
Cash	$ 20,000	Wages payable	$ 10,000
Marketable securities	25,000	Accounts payable	20,000
Accounts receivable	35,000	Notes payable	70,000
Inventory	20,000		
Prepaid expenses	5,000		
Total	$105,000	Total	$100,000

   a. Calculate the current ratio for the Pacifica Hotel.

   b. Calculate the acid-test ratio for the Pacifica Hotel.

   c. Comment on these ratios from a lender's perspective and a shareholder's perspective.

2. Describe the effect on working capital under the following scenarios.

   a. A company decides to issue common shares.

   b. A company generates revenue on account.

   c. A company goes to a bank and gets a loan.

3. John Q. Public is the Director of Sales for the Harbour Lights Hotel. In 2006, the hotel obtained an occupancy percentage of 70 percent and an average daily rate of $80. In 2007, he lowered rates in order to boost occupancy—the hotel had an occupancy percentage of 73 percent and an average daily rate of $76. Describe the effect of this strategy using a key ratio(s). Should Public lower rates further in 2008?

4. Jones Restaurant Corporation has reported the following financial information as of December 31, 2007.

Total revenue	$4,000,000
Cost of goods sold	2,300,000
Gross profit	1,700,000
Operating expenses	1,200,000
Fixed charges	150,000
Income taxes	100,000
Net income	250,000
Total assets as of 12/31/07	$1,000,000

   a. Calculate the return on assets for Jones Restaurant Corporation using the DuPont ratio.

   b. What can we conclude about the two ratios comprising the return on assets?

5. Starbucks, a major seller of roasted coffees, currently has a market price of $22.15 per common share and a P/E ratio of 43. Diedrich Coffee, a competitor to Starbucks, has a market price of $3.84 per share and a P/E ratio of 6.

   a. Calculate the earnings of both companies.

   b. Compare the earnings growth prospects of the two companies.

Current Ratio	1.2
Current liabilities	$100,000
Debt/equity ratio	2.0
Acid-test ratio	.8
Inventory turnover ratio	4 times
Cost of goods sold	$160,000
Accounts receivable	$ 40,000
Net income	$ 90,000
Return on assets	10%

6. You are provided with the following information about the Heartland Hotel Corporation. Calculate the balance sheet for the end of the year for Heartland Hotel Corporation.
Notes: **a.** Assume average inventory is the same as end of year inventory.
      b. "Quick" assets include only cash and accounts receivable.

7. Dawn's Fruitcake Factory specializes in making Christmas fruitcakes. During the year, it had $3 million in food sales with a 40 percent food cost. Dawn takes inventory every quarter. The inventories for the past year are shown as follows.

End of 1st quarter	$300,000
End of 2nd quarter	$400,000
End of 3rd quarter	$600,000
End of 4th quarter	$200,000

   a. Which quarter is Dawn using for her inventory turnover calculation?

   b. Do you think this is the appropriate approach to calculate inventory turnover?

8. The following is the balance sheet for Sullivan Hotels Corporation as of December 31, 2006. In 2006, the corporation generated a net income of $430,000.

SULLIVAN HOTELS CORPORATION
Balance Sheet
December 31, 2006

Current assets		Current liabilities	
Cash	$ 50,000	Wages payable	$ 30,000
Marketable securities	30,000	Accounts payable	25,000
Accounts receivable	40,000	Notes payable	50,000
Inventory	60,000		
Prepaid expenses	15,000		
Total current assets	195,000	Total current liabilities	105,000
Fixed assets, net	7,000,000	Long-term debt	2,500,000
		Owner's equity	
		Common shares, 3,000,000 shares outstanding ($1 par)	3,000,000
		Paid in capital	500,000
		Retained earnings	1,090,000
		Total liabilities and	
Total assets	$7,195,000	owner's equity	$7,195,000

a. Calculate the earnings per share in 2006.

b. Assume that in 2007 Sullivan Corporation issued 300,000 more shares of $1 par value common stock for a market price of $10 per share. Fifty percent of the proceeds will be used to pay down the long-term debt, 25 percent of the proceeds will be used to buy fixed assets, and the remainder will be deposited in the corporate bank account. Compile the balance sheet after the new stock issue.

c. Assume that Sullivan Corporation generates a net income of $450,000 in 2007 (after the new share issue). Calculate the new earnings per share. How might the shareholders feel about the results of the new share issue?

9. The following information pertains to the performance of the Williams Hotel for 2007, along with some pertinent industry averages.

Total revenue	$4,500,000
Net income	$ 256,000
Total assets, net	$3,000,000
Industry average profit margin	10%
Industry average return on investment (return on assets)	6.5%

a. Calculate the profit margin and return-on-investment ratios for the Williams Hotel. Is the hotel being managed effectively?

b. What could explain the conflicting information from the two ratios?

Chapter 6
The Relationship between Risk and Return

Chapter Objectives

This chapter covers the following topics:

1   The concept of risk from a financial standpoint

2   The risk preferences of typical investors

3   A definition of risk aversion

4   How to calculate expected return, variance, and standard deviation

5   The concept of the market portfolio

6   The differences between systematic and unsystematic risk

7   How to calculate the beta of a hospitality company

8   How to use the capital asset pricing model to estimate the required rate of return

6.1 Introduction

This chapter introduces students to the concepts of risk and return. We begin by developing an understanding of risk and basic human behaviour. From there, we discuss how returns on investments are calculated, along with how risk can be measured. Additionally, we discuss the components of risk and their importance.

Once we develop a measure of the risk relevant to the investor, we discuss how combinations of assets can be used to reduce risk, as shown by the concept of the market portfolio. Furthermore, risk is broken down into components. Finally, we use a measure of risk to help determine our return from an asset.

6.2 How Typical Investors Feel about Risk

Before we discuss how the typical investor feels about risk, we must define the term. **Risk** is uncertainty about whether future outcomes will differ from our expectations. In terms of investments, it translates into the notion that cash flows or percentage returns will be different from what we expect. Although it is true that the outcome could always be better than we expect, it could also be significantly worse. Typical investors do not merely look at the upside potential of an investment but the downside as well, considering all the possible outcomes. As the range of potential outcomes increases (widens), so does the risk.

We can examine how people feel about risk by watching the popular television show *Who Wants to Be a Millionaire*. The show features contestants who must answer a series of increasingly difficult questions for cash prizes. The first questions are fairly easy, and the money prizes are relatively small. However, the contestants usually get increasingly nervous as they approach the million-dollar question. The reason for this is because if they answer a question incorrectly, they will lose a substantial portion of their winnings up to that point. Many opt to quit and keep their winnings rather than risk them by giving an incorrect answer.

So why don't most contestants take a chance and risk their existing winnings for bigger cash prizes? This decision relates to the declining marginal utility for money. The concept is best illustrated using Exhibit 6-1.

Assume you are a rational investor and you are participating in a similar game show. You already have $1,000 and are preparing to answer the next question. The host informs you that if you answer the question correctly, you will win another $500. However, if you answer the question incorrectly, you will lose what you have and go back down to a total of $500. The horizontal axis measures the amount of money you have, and the vertical axis measures the happiness, or utility, you receive from winning the money. As shown in the graph, an increase from $1,000 to $1,500 gives you an extra 30 units of happiness. On the other hand, if you answer the question incorrectly and give up $500, you lose 50 units of happiness. As a rational investor, you forgo the opportunity to answer the next question, and keep the money.

Are you just acting scared in this situation? You might be nervous, but you are actually exhibiting risk-averse behaviour. Being risk averse does not mean you do not take risks. Millions of investors take risks every day. Being risk averse simply means that for us to take risks, we must be compensated. Investors who take large risks must be compensated with large returns, or they would not take them.

Does this example also apply to hospitality companies? Absolutely. McDonald's took a risk in opening a new restaurant in Russia after the collapse of the Soviet Union.

Exhibit 6-1 Declining Marginal Utility for Money

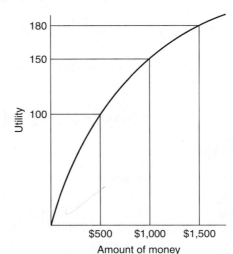

Numerous risks involving political stability, currency translation, and even factors such as the ability to procure appropriate inventory presented significant challenges to the company. However, George Cohon, former CEO of McDonald's Canada, carefully weighed the various risks against the potential benefits of bringing the first major North American fast-food restaurant chain into Russia and came to the decision that the venture created value for the owners of the company. Today, the McDonald's store in Pushkin Square is the largest (700 seats) and has the highest customer count for McDonald's in the world. This successful international hospitality expansion was driven by a team of dedicated and hardworking individuals from McDonald's Canada in 1990.

6.3 Returns and Distributions

Returns on investments can be expressed in monetary units as well as percentages. We begin our discussion using monetary units of an investment in a hypothetical restaurant company in which we own a share of common stock.

6.3.1 EXPECTED RETURN

Probably the most familiar situation for students regarding **expected return**, or **mean value**, is with exam scores. Many professors announce the mean or class average on exams. In most situations, the class average is known as a simple average. A simple average is calculated as

The sum of all observations / The number of observations

This is the easiest type of average to calculate and is appropriate for test scores because each student represents the same proportion of the total class (one divided by the total number of students in the class). However, when we deal with prospective outcomes that have different probabilities, the calculation of expected value will change. We examine a financial example for a hospitality company.

Assume you purchase a share of stock in Joe's I Am Canadian Restaurant Company, which is expected to pay a dividend at the end of the year. As you well know, the payment of dividends is not guaranteed, nor is the amount of the dividend a certainty. Accordingly, we can say there is risk associated with the payment of the dividend. The potential payoffs and their associated probabilities are shown in Exhibit 6-2.

Exhibit 6-2	Potential Dividend Distribution for Joe's I Am Canadian Restaurant Company Ltd.
Dividend	**Probability of dividend**
$10	10%
$ 7	20%
$ 5	40%
$ 3	20%
$ 1	10%

If you calculate a simple average of the potential dividends, you take $10 + $7 + $5 + $3 + $1 and divide that by 5 to get $5.20. However, that approach is incorrect. Why? This calculation assumes that each potential dividend has the same associated probability or likelihood of occurrence. This is clearly not the case. The appropriate calculation is a weighted average, or expected value of the dividends. The expected value calculation involves each outcome being multiplied (or weighted) by the associated probability. This is done for each dividend, and then those products are added together. The proper calculation is as follows.

$$($10 \times 0.10) + ($7 \times 0.20) + ($5 \times 0.40) + ($3 \times 0.20) + ($1 \times 0.10) = $5.10$$

This is the weighted average amount of what we should expect our investment to generate. Notice the difference between this answer and the result using the simple average. Accordingly, the weighted average generates the correct value for the expected dividend.

6.3.2 THE NORMAL DISTRIBUTION

Although we now know what to expect from our investment, it is, after all, only an average—there is a range of potential outcomes. As shown in Exhibit 6-2, the different dividends are each associated with different probabilities. The probability is the "chance" of occurrence for each outcome. What the exhibit is really showing is a **probability distribution**, or a series of outcomes and the probabilities associated with each one. We can graph the dividend outcomes against each of the probabilities in a block diagram or histogram to get a visual depiction of this probability distribution, as shown in Exhibit 6-3.

Exhibit 6-3 shows boxes that are shorter on the axis ends and taller in the middle. If we draw a line connecting the corners of the tops of the boxes and remove the boxes, we have the graphical representation shown in Exhibit 6-4. This exhibit should be familiar to you. It is the famous bell-shaped curve, also known as the normal probability distribution. This is the "curve" that students may hear professors talk about before they adjust exam scores. The curve is normal because it indicates that half of the observations are to the right of the midpoint of the curve and half of the observations are to the left of the

Exhibit 6-3 Probability Distribution of Dividends—Histogram

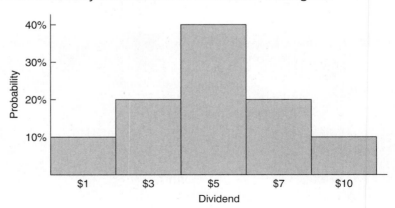

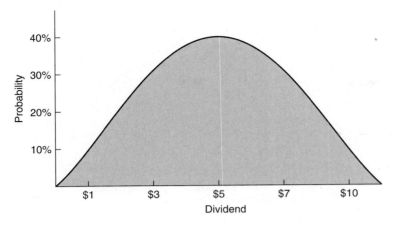

Exhibit 6-4 Probability Distribution of Dividends—Bell Curve

midpoint of the curve. However, not all distributions are normal. Some are "skewed" distributions in which one tail is larger than the other. This can be problematic when making inferences about the outcomes. Accordingly, if a distribution of exam scores is skewed, then professors may change scores to make the distribution more normal, so that any statistical tests conducted on the scores are more useful.

6.3.3 VARIANCE AND STANDARD DEVIATION

We have calculated the expected value of the potential dividend distribution from Joe's I Am Canadian Restaurant. Although we know the average dividend, is there any way we can assess the risk associated with investment? By examining how each potential outcome differs or varies from the expected value, we can arrive at some conclusion about the risk of this investment. One measure is the variance. The **variance** represents the sum of the squared, weighted differences between each outcome and the expected value. The calculation in general form is

The sum of $[(\text{outcome } 1 - \text{expected value})^2 \times \text{probability of outcome } 1]$
$+ [(\text{outcome } 2 - \text{expected value})^2 \times \text{probability of outcome } 2]$
$+ \cdots [(\text{outcome } n - \text{expected value})^2 \times \text{probability of outcome } n]$

The variance is a measure of the total risk of an investment. It is a positive number that can be expressed as a percentage or in currency values. It is also an absolute measure (as opposed to a relative measure, which is discussed later). In the Joe's I Am Canadian Restaurant example, the variance is calculated as follows.

The sum of $[(\$10 - \$5.10)^2 \times 0.10] + [(\$7 - \$5.10)^2 \times 0.20] + [(\$5.00 - \$5.10)^2$
$\times 0.40] + [(\$3 - \$5.10)^{20} \times 0.20] + [(\$1 - 5.10)^2 \times 0.10]$. This reduces to
$$\$2.40 + \$0.72 + \$0.00 + \$0.88 + \$1.68 = \$5.68$$

Thus, the variance of the distribution of dividends for Joe's I Am Canadian Restaurant is $5.68. However, in order to have the correct interpretation relative to the

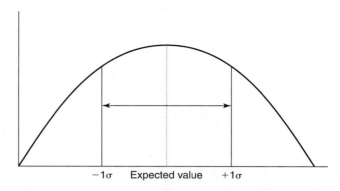

-1σ   Expected value   +1σ

Exhibit 6-5 Bell Curve and Standard Deviation

normal probability distribution, we need to find the **standard deviation** of the dividends. This is found by taking the square root of the variance, which is abbreviated with the lowercase of the Greek letter sigma (σ). The square root of $5.68 is $2.38. We can now further discuss the risk of this investment using standard deviation, as in Exhibit 6-5.

Exhibit 6-5 shows the expected value under the centre of the normal distribution curve. The portion of the arrow to the right of the expected value represents one standard deviation added to the expected value. The portion of the arrow to the left of the expected value is one standard deviation subtracted from the expected value. In terms of our example, one standard deviation added to the expected value represents $5.10 + $2.38, or $7.48. One standard deviation subtracted from the expected value indicates $5.10 − $2.38, or $2.72. The characteristics of the normal probability distribution are shown in Exhibit 6-6.

We can see that approximately 68 percent of the time we can expect an outcome to be within plus one and minus one standard deviation from the expected value. In our example, Joe's I Am Canadian Restaurant should generate a dividend between $2.72 and $7.48 about two-thirds of the time. We now have developed some level of confidence regarding the payoff of this investment. Note that nearly all outcomes will be within plus or minus three standard deviations from the expected value.

6.3.4 STANDARD DEVIATION AND RISK AVERSION

The concept of **risk aversion** refers to how financial managers, consumers, and investors alike behave when presented with an investment decision that has a high degree of uncertainty. Financial managers, consumers, and investors are reluctant to make a financial investment

Exhibit 6-6 Percentage of Observations within Range of Standard Deviations	
Number of standard deviations from expected value	**% of observations within range**
−1σ and +1σ	68.3
−2σ and +2σ	95.4
−3σ and +3σ	99.7

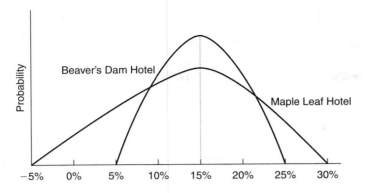

Exhibit 6-7 Comparison of Two Return Distributions

without some knowledge of the risk value and projected calculated return—in other words, an unknown payoff. Therefore, financial managers, consumers, and investors are more willing to make an investment commitment when there is at least some knowledge of the risk and return values—a known payoff.

To this end, given an understanding of the risk of an investment, we consider choosing between two different hotel investments. The Maple Leaf Hotel and the Beaver's Dam Hotel each have the potential for generating a wide variety of returns. Each of them, however, has the same expected return with normal return distributions. The distribution of each of their returns is shown in Exhibit 6-7.

As shown in Exhibit 6-7, each hotel investment has the same expected return of 15 percent. However, the distribution of their returns is quite different. Although both return distributions are approximately normal, the Maple Leaf Hotel has a much wider and flatter distribution of returns. On the other hand, the Beaver's Dam Hotel has a much narrower distribution. Which do we prefer? Given that most people are risk averse, the Beaver's Dam Hotel would be a better investment. Why?

The reason is because of the greater level of certainty (or lower level of uncertainty) associated with the Beaver's Dam Hotel. As you may have guessed, the Beaver's Dam Hotel has a smaller deviation associated with its return distribution. Given that both hotel investments have the same expected value, we feel much more comfortable with a tighter distribution than a wider one. Some students will focus on the fact that the Maple Leaf Hotel has some potentially high returns. However, it also has potential for some disastrous returns as well. Remember the declining marginal utility of money illustrated in Exhibit 6-1 to understand how people feel about uncertainty and gaining extra wealth.

Additionally, it is important to note that if the standard deviations are different, then we cannot compare them without standardizing them by their returns. The standard deviation is an absolute measure of total risk of an investment. To better evaluate the potential of two or more investments, we can use a relative measure—the ratio of standard deviation to return. This ratio is called the **coefficient of variation** and is shown in Exhibit 6-8.

Which hotel is the better investment from a risk–return perspective? Calculate the coefficient of variation as follows.

$$\text{ABC Hotel} = .12/.18 = .67$$
$$\text{Benson Hotel} = .15/.16 = .94$$

Exhibit 6-8	Standard Deviations and Expected Returns of Two Investments	
Investment	**Standard deviation**	**Expected return**
ABC Hotel	12%	18%
Benson Hotel	15%	16%

In this ratio, we seek the lowest amount of risk for the largest return. In this case, ABC Hotel has the highest return (18%) and the lowest total risk. This would lead us to choose the ABC Hotel from the two hotels listed.

As we consider the risk and return profiles of different investments, it is a good time to reconsider some information from Chapter 3. Is there any investment that gives you a return without any standard deviation? Indeed there is: a risk-free investment such as a Canada Savings Bond, which is guaranteed by the Canadian government. Because the return is always provided as advertised, there is no variety of returns and the standard deviation of this investment is zero.

6.4 Diversification

Up to this point, we have discussed the case where investors choose which asset to hold. We have also shown how to decide between two assets when you know the risk and return profile of these assets using the coefficient of variation. However, rational investors rarely hold only a single asset. In this section, we discuss why investors want to hold more than one asset, known as **diversification**.

6.4.1 BENEFITS OF A PORTFOLIO

When we use the term *portfolio,* we mean a group of investments (at least two) that investors choose to own. Why own more than one asset? You may have heard the expression "Don't put all your eggs in one basket." If you put all your money (and your hopes) in one plan, idea, or investment, you could easily be disappointed if something bad happens. Accordingly, most wise investors own more than one type of asset.

The reason for this is quite simple. Investors want to guard against the possibility of a single asset declining in value. The idea is that even if one asset declines, another asset will gain in value to balance against the lower return on the first asset. This principle remains the same whether investors have two assets or hundreds of assets. This is the main idea of diversification, or holding what is known as a diversified portfolio. This type of portfolio attempts to maximize the return and minimize the risk (or standard deviation of returns) by being constructed based on how the assets within it relate to one another over time.

6.4.2 CORRELATION COEFFICIENT

The **correlation coefficient**, called *rho*, is abbreviated as ρ. Although it has a wide variety of applications, it is often used in finance to measure how returns of assets are related to one another. A nonfinancial example would be to compare the amount of rainfall to umbrella sales in cities around the world. We would expect to find a positive relationship between rainfall and umbrella sales. Therefore, we could say these two variables are positively correlated. On the other hand, we could measure days of sunshine and umbrella sales in cities around the world. We would expect to find these two variables to be negatively correlated.

The correlation coefficient is also handy because of its limited range. The coefficient ranges from negative 1 to positive 1. These are the extremes, of course, meaning that two variables moving exactly opposite to each other all the time are perfectly negatively correlated and have a *rho* of −1.0. Two variables moving together in perfect lockstep have a *rho* of +1.0. Note that these two situations are fairly rare, particularly in a financial context. If no relationship exists between the two variables, the correlation coefficient between them is zero.

Let's return to our portfolio example. Investors hold more than one asset in a portfolio to maximize return and minimize risk. However, as we have learned, most assets (excluding risk-free assets) have a standard deviation of return. Additionally, if we put two or more assets into a portfolio, the portfolio itself will have a standard deviation of return (similar to the standard deviation of an individual asset). The return on a portfolio is relatively easy to calculate: it is the return of each asset multiplied by its weight in the portfolio. Let's look at the return profile of Restaurant A and Restaurant B shown in Exhibit 6-9.

As shown in Exhibit 6-9, the overall return in the portfolio is the weighted average of the returns of the assets within the portfolio. Therefore, if we hold two-thirds of our money in Restaurant A shares and one-third in Restaurant B shares, the average return on our portfolio is 10.67 percent (rounded). It is important to remember that this is only an expected value; there is a distribution of returns around this expected value, and our actual return could be higher or lower and vary from period to period. Now we can examine how to measure the risk of a portfolio.

The formula for the standard deviation of a two-asset portfolio is as follows.

$$\sigma_p = \sqrt{W_A^2 \times \sigma_A^2 + W_B^2 \times \sigma_B^2 + 2W_A W_B \rho_{AB} \sigma_A \sigma_B}$$

where W_A represents the proportion of asset A in the portfolio, W_B represents the proportion of asset B in the portfolio, and ρ_{AB} is the correlation coefficient for the returns of asset A and asset B. Let's add some risk to the example so we can calculate the standard deviation of a portfolio of Restaurant A and Restaurant B.

Given the information in Exhibit 6-10, we can calculate the standard deviation of the portfolio of these two assets. Assume the returns are perfectly correlated. The calculation is shown as:

$$\sigma_p = \sqrt{(0.6667^2 \times 4^2) + (0.3333^2 \times 8^2) + 2(0.6667)(0.3333)(1.0)(4)(8)}$$
$$= \sqrt{7.11 + 7.11 + 14.22} = 5.333 \text{ or } 5.333\%$$

Exhibit 6-9 Risk of Two Restaurants When Held in a Portfolio

Asset	Return	% in portfolio (weight)	Weighted return
Restaurant A	12%	66.67	8%
Restaurant B	8%	33.33	2.67%
Total	—	100	10.67%

Exhibit 6-10 Risk Profile of Two Restaurants

Asset	Weight in portfolio	Standard deviation of return
Restaurant A	66.67%	4%
Restaurant B	33.33%	8%

As shown in the preceding example, the correlation coefficient between the two assets is +1.0—which, as previously discussed, is perfect positive correlation. The 5.333 percent (rounded) standard deviation is merely the weighted average of the standard deviations of the two assets in the portfolio. Are we better off by combining these two assets into a portfolio? No. When two assets are perfectly positively correlated, we can reduce the risk only by weighting the portfolio with a greater percentage of the asset with the lower standard deviation. But this does not give us the benefits of diversification. We would like to be able to combine two assets and have the risk of the combined assets be less than either of the two individually.

Let's look at another example, which assumes the returns of the two restaurant assets have a correlation coefficient of −1.0, or perfect negative correlation (we assume the same weights of the assets in the portfolio). Let's recalculate the standard deviation of the portfolio.

$$\sigma_p = \sqrt{(0.6667^2 \times 4^2) + (0.3333^2 \times 8^2) + 2(0.6667)(0.3333)(-1.0)(4)(8)}$$
$$= \sqrt{7.11 + 7.11 - 14.22} = 0.000 \text{ or } 0\%$$

Notice that the standard deviation is now zero, and risk is eliminated. This shows that if we can find two assets that are perfectly negatively correlated, we can create a portfolio that has no risk. Note that we have used the appropriate proportion (two-thirds of asset A and one-third of asset B in this example) to completely eliminate risk. If we alter the weights of these assets in the portfolio, the standard deviation is not zero. However, as long as the two assets of interest have returns with a correlation coefficient of less than +1.0, we can find numerous combinations that have the same return with lower risk than when we combined the two perfectly positively correlated assets.

We now look at one more example. Assume we wish to combine the same two assets in the same proportion into a portfolio. The only parameter we change is the correlation coefficient of their returns. We assume there is no correlation between them—in other words, the correlation coefficient is zero. Here is the calculation for the standard deviation of such a portfolio.

$$\sigma_p = \sqrt{(0.6667^2 \times 4^2) + (0.3333^2 \times 8^2) + 2(0.6667)(0.3333)(0)(4)(8)}$$
$$= \sqrt{7.11 + 7.11 + 0} = 3.77 \text{ or } 3.77\%$$

We can summarize the risk profiles of the different portfolios we have examined showing their different correlation coefficients as in Exhibit 6-11.

There are two important considerations here before we consider which portfolio is best. First, the return of each portfolio is the same. Recall the discussion on risk aversion and declining marginal utility for money: we know we would like to have the greatest return for a given level of risk. Accordingly, the ideal portfolio would be the one with the negative correlation coefficient between the assets (and with the assets in the right proportion) such that standard deviation (and risk) is zero.

Exhibit 6-11 Standard Deviation of Portfolios with Different Correlation Coefficients between Assets

Correlation coefficient	Standard deviation of portfolio	Return on portfolio
+1.0	5.33%	10.67%
0	3.77%	10.67%
−1.0	0.00%	10.67%

Unfortunately, finding two assets that are perfectly negatively correlated is practically impossible. Therefore, the potential to eliminate *all* risk is extremely rare. However, this does not mean we do not obtain benefits from diversification. As Exhibit 6-11 shows, if we can just find two assets that are *less than perfectly positively correlated,* we can reduce risk and obtain some benefits of diversification through the construction of a portfolio.

6.5 The Market Portfolio

After the discussion on the construction of portfolios, you may be wondering how investors decide which assets to hold in their portfolios. As we learned in Chapter 2, there are a number of financial assets to invest in and more are being developed every year. In addition to deciding which assets to include in a portfolio, is it possible to afford all the assets necessary to construct such a portfolio?

Investors have a number of choices about the construction of their portfolios. If we want to invest in a portfolio of three or more assets, we can calculate the expected return of the portfolio as well as its total risk (it is more complicated than a two-asset portfolio, so we do not show the formula here). After we calculate these statistics for a number of hypothetical portfolios, we plot risk and return as shown in Exhibit 6-12.

Exhibit 6-12 shows the risk–return profile of a sample of 10 different portfolios. All of them have different levels of return for a given level of risk. Which one do we choose? Given the previous discussion about correlation coefficients, we know that most people are risk averse and want the highest level of return for a given level of risk. This means

Exhibit 6-12 Set of Hypothetical Portfolios

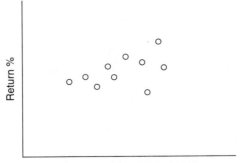

people are seeking a portfolio that is efficient, which in a general sense means the most output for a given input. In a financial context, the most efficient portfolio is the one that provides the highest level of return for a given level of risk. At this point, we don't quite have enough information to decide which portfolio is best.

An important factor to consider is that although most people are risk averse, they do have different risk preferences. Some investors may want to invest only in a risk-free asset, whereas others are willing to invest in portfolios of risky assets as long as they are compensated with a higher return. An important assumption in portfolio selection is the notion that investors can borrow or lend money at the risk-free rate of interest. If you choose to do so, you can invest only in Canada Savings Bonds and thus lend money to the Canadian government. On the other hand, you can borrow money from a broker (called "trading on margin") and invest in a variety of assets. If we add the risk-free asset to our set of hypothetical portfolios, we can perhaps select the best portfolio. This is shown in Exhibit 6-13.

Now that we have placed the risk-free asset on our graph (designated r_f), we can draw a line connecting the risk-free asset and a few of the hypothetical portfolios. Recall that a line is an infinite series of points; therefore, the lines we have drawn indicate an infinite variety of combinations of the risk-free asset and a portfolio of assets. These lines are called borrowing–lending lines because investors can put some of their money into a portfolio and lend the rest to the government; on the other hand, they can use borrowed money to invest in a portfolio to increase their return (but bear more risk).

You may recall from math classes that the equation for a straight line involves slope. The slope of the line is the rise (increase in y-axis) over the run (increase in x-axis). In our case, the rise indicates the return above the risk-free rate of return, or a return premium. The run is the total risk of the investment. A risk-averse investor would prefer to hold the portfolio with the greatest level of return for a given level of risk—the portfolio that is tangent to the line with the steepest slope connecting it with the risk-free asset. In Exhibit 6-13, this line is labelled Portfolio M.

You will notice the portion of the line between Portfolio M and the risk-free asset is labelled the lending line. The portion of the line beyond Portfolio M is called the borrowing line. Earlier, we mentioned that people have different risk preferences. How does this affect our portfolio selection? Interestingly enough, it doesn't here. If you compare the top line

Exhibit 6-13 Capital Market Line

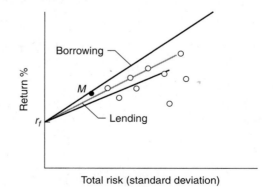

with the other two lines, you can see it has a higher slope. Therefore, no matter what our risk preferences are, every point along the top line that intersects point M dominates the points on the other two lines. In other words, no matter which combination of Portfolio M and the risk-free asset you hold, it is superior to the combinations used to comprise the other two lines.

Portfolio M has a special name—it is called the **market portfolio**, which is a theoretical portfolio of all the assets of value in the world held in the appropriate proportions to yield the highest level of return for the least amount of risk. Therefore, it is the most efficient portfolio to hold. Additionally, the borrowing–lending line that connects the risk-free asset with the market portfolio is called the **capital market line**. The equation for the capital market line, which can be used to predict a required level of return, is discussed in greater detail later in this chapter.

6.5.1 WHAT MAKES THE MARKET PORTFOLIO UNIQUE?

We have shown that the market portfolio is the best in terms of yielding a return for a given level of risk. Who, then, wouldn't want to hold this portfolio? Nobody! Rational investors who are placing their capital at risk want to get the highest level of return possible. Therefore, we assume every investor holds the market portfolio.

Investors want not only the highest return, but also the lowest level of risk. The risk becomes lowered as more and more assets (with less-than-perfect correlation) are added to the portfolio. Therefore, adding all the assets in existence to the portfolio provides the ultimate diversified portfolio. And, most important, if everyone wants to hold the market portfolio then we must assume investors are diversified.

6.5.2 THE MARKET PORTFOLIO AND RISK COMPOSITION

The problem is that holding every asset in existence would be impossible. Even the richest people in the world could not have every type of tradeable asset—including commodities, real estate, stocks, bonds, and many other investments. However, the good news is that holding *all* the assets is not necessary to obtain the benefits of the market portfolio.

We have discussed only the concept of total risk—the standard deviation of return. However, total risk is actually divided into two separate components:

$$\text{Systematic risk} + \text{Unsystematic risk} = \text{Total risk}$$

Systematic risk is the type of risk involved in all assets that do not have a guaranteed return. These involve characteristics of the general economy such as interest rates and inflation rates. This type of risk cannot be diversified away even as more assets are added to a portfolio. **Unsystematic risk** is the component of total risk related to a specific business or industry. This type of event may be a work stoppage or a new piece of legislation that affects only a particular industry. These circumstances do not impact the economy as a whole, and thus this type of risk can be diversified away by adding assets to a portfolio.

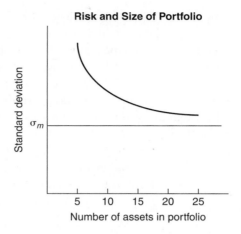

Risk and Size of Portfolio

Standard deviation

σ_m

Number of assets in portfolio

Exhibit 6-14 Risk Reduction through the Inclusion of Assets

The story of diversification has good news and bad news for investors. The good news is that investors do not actually need to hold every type of asset to obtain the same benefits of diversification as the market portfolio. We can see the benefits of risk reduction in Exhibit 6-14. Notice what happens to the standard deviation of the portfolio as we add more assets to it. The initial reduction of risk is very great. However, as we add more assets to a portfolio, the amount of risk reduction begins to decrease. Research has shown that as we accumulate approximately 25 to 50 assets in a portfolio, no further risk reduction is achieved.

In other words, we can emulate the benefits of the market portfolio by having only about 25 or 30 assets in a portfolio. Thus, we do not have to hold every asset in the world. However, have we completely eliminated risk at this point? Certainly not. We have eliminated the unsystematic risk but cannot eliminate the systematic risk. Of interest is the fact that the portfolio size used for the Dow Jones Industrial Average is exactly 30 companies from a diverse company and sector mix. Going back to the discussion on market portfolio, note that the curve flattens out at the level of systematic risk designated as σ_m in the graph. This is the level of risk contained in the market portfolio or other similar portfolios we can construct or purchase.

What investments are available for investors to gain the benefits of holding the market portfolio? Investors have many choices. Some will buy a group of individual stocks. However, long ago the market recognized the benefits of holding a diversified portfolio. Therefore, many mutual funds invest in a wide variety of assets to maintain a diversified portfolio for investors, offering investments in stock indices such as the Standard & Poor's 500 index or the Dow Jones Industrial Average (there are other indices as well). The mutual fund invests in these 500 different companies in the same proportion as they are held in the index itself. This yields two advantages to the investor: (1) the portfolio is well diversified, which means that (2) the mutual fund manager does not actively buy or sell stocks too often, thereby reducing the cost of fund management to the investor. Although some criticize this approach because returns can be reduced by taxes and fees, these are some of the largest and most popular mutual funds in existence. Furthermore, it is relatively inexpensive to hold this diversified portfolio; some mutual fund companies, banks, and investment dealers allow an individual to open an RRSP (registered retirement savings plan) account for as little as $100.

Overall, investors should hold a diversified portfolio not only because it is efficient, but also because it is relatively inexpensive to obtain the benefits of diversification. This conclusion has important implications for how investors examine the risk and return of assets. It also affects how hospitality managers select capital improvement projects for their owners.

6.6 The Market Portfolio and Beta

Now that we understand why investors want to hold (and can hold) a portfolio of assets similar to the market portfolio, we now must assume the shareholders of the hospitality firm we work for are diversified. If investors are diversified, they are no longer concerned with an investment's unsystematic risk; once the investment is added to the investors' well-diversified portfolio, unsystematic risk is removed because of the effects of diversification. Therefore, analyzing investments from a total risk standpoint (standard deviation) is inappropriate.

A better measure would be one that measures the relevant risk to the diversified investor. The tool to do this is called *beta*. **Beta** measures the risk of an investment relative to the market portfolio. Because it is a relative measure, it makes use of a correlation coefficient as follows.

$$\text{Beta} = \frac{\rho_{xm}\sigma_x}{\sigma_m}$$

The formula shows *rho*, the correlation coefficient of the returns from any asset (asset *x* in this example) and the market portfolio. This is multiplied by the standard deviation of the returns of asset *x*. This product is then divided by the standard deviation of the returns of the market portfolio.

One of the features of beta is that it measures risk relative to a unit of one. The market portfolio, for example, has a beta of 1.0. This means, basically, the overall market is as risky as itself. If an asset has a beta of 2.0, then that asset is twice as risky as the market. If an asset has a beta of 0.5, then the asset is only half as risky as the market.

Betas for hospitality companies can be obtained in a number of ways. One way is to get historical stock returns (usually daily) for the company of interest and an asset representing the market portfolio (the S&P 500 index, for example); regressing the two sets of returns yields a beta. Beta calculations are also available on the World Wide Web. One source is Reuters.com; other sources include various brokerage firms. The betas of a sample of hospitality companies are shown in Exhibit 6-15.

As shown in Exhibit 6-15, betas can vary significantly from company to company. Most of the betas of these randomly selected hospitality companies are relatively low. A word of caution about using betas from sources on the Web: it is not always clear how the betas were calculated. There is no magic number in terms of the number of years of returns to be used in the calculation, and this could have a significant impact on the beta. Some betas are calculated using three years of returns; some may use five years. Which years are chosen could also have an impact on the calculation. Additionally, some betas don't make a lot of sense—they may be unusually large or unusually small. Sometimes they may even be negative—which does not make much economic sense, as we discuss in the next section.

Exhibit 6-15 Betas for Selected Hospitality Firms

Company name	Ticker	Beta
Boston Pizza Royalties Fund	TSX: BPF.UN	0.17
California Pizza Kitchen	CPKI	0.29
CHIP REIT	TSX: HOT.UN	0.36
Harrah's Entertainment	HET	1.26
Intercontinental Hotels	IHG	1.63
Marriott Hotels	MAR	1.09
McDonald's	MCD	1.51
Starbucks	SBUX	0.63
Starwood Hotels	HOT	1.06
The Keg	TSX:KEG.UN	0.35
Tim Hortons Inc	TSX: THI	1.06
Wendy's	WEN	0.93
Yum Brands	YUM	0.96

Source: www.reuters.com

6.7 Beta, Expected Return, and the Security Market Line

This is a good time to be reminded of a basic principle in finance: Risk and return go together. In other words, a higher return is coupled with higher risk. Until our discussion on beta, we measured this risk in terms of total risk and standard deviation. However, once we introduced the concept of the diversified investor, the total risk measure was no longer the best measure to use. We can use beta as a predictive measure to understand the relationship between the risk investors bear and the return they expect.

In a previous section we discussed a special borrowing–lending line called the capital market line. It measured the return on a portfolio against the risk of the portfolio, as measured by standard deviation. We now introduce another special borrowing–lending line called the security market line (SML), shown in Exhibit 6-16.

As shown in Exhibit 6-16, the SML is drawn from the risk-free rate of return through point M, which represents the market portfolio. The graph is measuring the systematic risk of an investment (beta) against the expected return. The beta of the market portfolio is 1.0, whereas the beta of the risk-free asset is 0. The return on the market portfolio is designated R_m. Notice that the slope of the line is positive; in other words, the higher the relevant (systematic) risk of an asset, the higher its expected return. This has important implications for value creation and decision criteria in capital budgeting.

The SML actually represents a *minimum standard of return* given the relevant risk of a project. Once again, we assume investors are diversified and want to hold (and do hold) a well-diversified portfolio. Therefore, investors can lend to the government or borrow

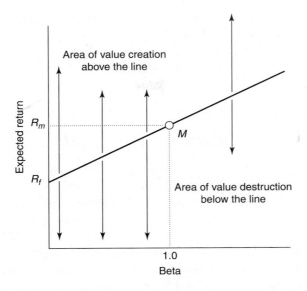

Exhibit 6-16 Security Market Line

against their portfolio and move up and down the line depending on their risk preferences. However, at every level of risk a minimum return should be generated. This is the standard by which we can measure asset returns. In other words, if a stock investment or a new capital asset does not at least generate a return as predicted by the SML, it is a value-destroying project and should be rejected.

Although we have discussed the SML in general graphic terms, we can calculate the specific rate of return an asset should generate. The equation for the SML is

$$\text{Expected return} = R_f + (R_m - R_f) \times \beta$$

where R_f is the rate of return on the risk-free asset, R_m is the rate of return on the market portfolio, and β is the beta of the asset. This equation is also known as the **capital asset pricing model (CAPM)** and is used to predict the expected rate of return on an equity investment. Basically, the equation states that shareholders putting their capital at risk should get the risk-free rate of return plus a risk premium. The risk premium is the difference between the return on the market portfolio and the risk-free rate of return (this is also the slope of the SML shown in the graph). The risk premium is then adjusted by the systematic risk profile of the asset as compared to the market portfolio. In other words, if an asset is twice as risky as the market, the investor should be rewarded with twice the risk premium in terms of return.

Assume the risk-free rate of return is 4 percent, and the return on the market portfolio is 12 percent. Additionally, the beta of an investment is 1.5. What return should the investment generate? The calculation is shown as:

$$4\% + [(12\% - 4\%) \times 1.5] = 16\%$$

The investment should generate a return of 16 percent.

The SML can help us determine whether or not a project creates value. We can plot the return on equity (ROE) of a project against its systematic risk. If the ROE exceeds the required rate of return as shown by the SML, then the project is value creating and would plot above the line, as noted in Exhibit 6-16. If the ROE of the project is below the minimum as shown by the SML, the project destroys value and would be below the line in Exhibit 6-16. We discuss this in the context of criteria for value creation in Chapters 11 and 12.

6.7.1 THE LIMITATIONS OF THE CAPM

The CAPM is arguably one of the most significant developments in finance in the last 50 years. It is a frequently used tool to help assess the viability of a capital budgeting project. Nevertheless, the ability of the CAPM to effectively predict expected returns has been questioned in recent years. Therefore, we discuss a few limitations of the model here.

First, the market portfolio is a theoretical concept. Although many proxies for this portfolio exist, there is no consensus on which one is best. A number of indices (S&P/TSX, Dow Jones Industrial, and S&P 500, to name a few) are frequently used. However, none of these indices is an exact replica of the market portfolio. Second, betas are calculated based on *historical* returns. These betas are then used to forecast *future* returns. Research has shown that betas are more useful for predicting returns for certain time periods, but not for all. The time period that encompasses the analyzed returns can have a significant impact on the accuracy of the predicted returns.

A significant amount of academic research has been conducted in an attempt to find other variables (other than systematic risk) to forecast expected returns. During certain periods, firm size has been more useful in predicting returns. Nevertheless, a definitive set of significant variables that accurately predicts all the variance in stock returns has yet to be established. The search continues for important variables that can consistently and accurately predict stock returns over time.

In the final analysis, the CAPM and beta have been shown to have some limitations. On the other hand, CAPM remains popular today because of the fundamental intuition of the model: The return of an asset is positively related to its relevant risk. It also was largely responsible for getting average investors to consider risk and its components and to begin thinking of risk in a different way than they did before.

6.7.2 BETAS FOR HOSPITALITY ASSETS

It is a relatively simple task to use the CAPM to predict returns on companies' common stock investments. Risk-free rates of return are published in newspapers, and betas can be found on the World Wide Web. Information on proxies for the market portfolio (such as the S&P 500 index) can also be found on the Web. But what should be the expected return for a new restaurant investment?

We know that because it can produce a cash flow and is not guaranteed, it must yield a return greater than the risk-free rate. We could use the CAPM if we could calculate a beta; however, because it is a prospective project with no historical returns, this cannot be done. How should we proceed?

This is a fairly common problem for new hospitality ventures. One of the simplest methods is to find betas of publicly traded corporations similar to the project under consideration. If you are building a gourmet coffee store, you might consider using the beta of Starbucks. If you are considering a steak house, examining the beta of The Keg might be helpful. Remember that the beta is an estimate based on past returns and is being used to predict future equity returns. Although it is an important component in the assessment of a capital budgeting project, the process of estimating the shareholder return is not an exact science and needs to be considered with other important components in the analysis such as cash flows, the return expected by lenders, tax rates, and other considerations discussed in Chapters 11 and 12.

Is the Restaurant Business Risky?

In this chapter we have learned about the systematic risk of an investment, called beta. Exhibit 6-15 shows the betas for a small sample of hospitality companies. One of the companies, The Keg, has a beta of only 0.35, the second-lowest beta in the sample. This means that an investment in the Keg has about one-third of the risk of the overall market. The Keg is a well established steakhouse and bar operation founded more than 35 years ago in Vancouver. The company has grown and prospered over the years and now has more than 90 locations across North America. Only recently has a new heavyweight competitor shown up to challenge The Keg's supremacy within the Canadian steak concept market: Canyon Creek Chophouse, which is owned and operated by SIR Corp., now has seven locations throughout Ontario. SIR Corp. has seven different restaurant concepts currently in operation, with a total of 40 units located in Canada and the United States.

Traditionally, the restaurant business has been thought to be risky. Why, then, does The Keg have such a low beta? Does this mean the restaurant business is not risky after all? Not necessarily. Remember, the beta is only an indication of systematic or market-related risk. This is only a portion of the risk of an investment. It may be such that the risk of the restaurant business is unrelated to the market and more specific to the local operations. However, these unsystematic factors can be reduced substantially when investors move toward and commit to a well-diversified portfolio. That is why many restaurant stocks such as The Keg, McDonald's, Tim Hortons, and others are logical choices for many investors.

6.8 SUMMARY

This chapter:

- Considered the concept of risk from a financial standpoint
- Examined the risk preferences of typical investors
- Defined risk aversion
- Explained how to calculate expected return, variance, and standard deviation
- Introduced the concept of the market portfolio
- Considered the differences between systematic and unsystematic risk
- Explained how to calculate the beta of a hospitality company
- Explained how to use the capital asset pricing model to estimate the required rate of return

Key Terms

Beta

Capital asset pricing model (CAPM)

Capital market line

Coefficient of variation

Correlation coefficient

Diversification

Expected return

Market portfolio

Mean value

Probability distribution

Risk

Risk aversion

Standard deviation

Systematic risk

Unsystematic risk

Variance

Discussion Questions

1. Why are rational investors risk averse?
2. Define risk aversion.
3. Define expected value.
4. Why is a simple average calculation usually not appropriate when calculating expected values?
5. Define variance and standard deviation.
6. If two assets have the same expected return but different standard deviations, which one would we prefer?
7. What is the coefficient of variation?
8. What would you expect the correlation coefficient between a university football team's winning percentage and the following year's home game ticket sales to be?
9. What is the main objective of diversification?
10. What is the market portfolio? What makes it unique?
11. Define the components of total risk, and describe how they differ.
12. Define beta.
13. How do we know if a project creates value for its owners?

Problems

Problems designated with EXCEL can be solved using Excel spreadsheets accessible at www.pearsoned.ca/chatfield.

1. The Clayton Hotel is expected to generate different returns based on the state of the economy. These are shown in the following table.

State of the economy	Probability of each state	Return
Recession	10%	–5%
Moderate growth	60%	6%
Boom	30%	18%

a. Calculate the expected return for the Clayton Hotel using a *simple* average.

b. Calculate the expected return for the Clayton Hotel using a *weighted* average.

2. Based on the information from Problem 1, complete the following for the Clayton Hotel.

    a. Calculate the variance.

    b. Calculate the standard deviation.

    c. Interpret the standard deviation relative to the normal distribution.

3. You are given the following information about three potential hotel investments.

Hotel	Return	Risk (standard deviation)
Hotel X	12%	7%
Hotel Y	20%	19%
Hotel Z	14%	10%

If you could choose only one, which of these investments would you choose?

4. You are given the following information.

Hotel	Return	Weight (proportion of portfolio)	Risk (standard deviation of return)
Hotel X	10%	75%	3%
Hotel Y	20%	25%	9%

    a. Calculate the expected return of the portfolio.

    b. Calculate the standard deviation of the portfolio with a ρ of +1.0.

    c. Calculate the standard deviation of the portfolio with a ρ of 0.

    d. Calculate the standard deviation of the portfolio with a ρ of −1.0.

5. Given that the standard deviation of returns on the market is 10 percent, the standard deviation of the Hotel Lockhart is 20 percent, and the correlation coefficient of their returns is 0.5, calculate the beta for the Hotel Lockhart.

6. If the standard deviation of returns for the Lafayette Restaurant is 15 percent, the standard deviation of returns for the market portfolio is 12 percent, and the beta of the Lafayette Restaurant is 0.75, what is the correlation coefficient for the returns of the Lafayette Restaurant and the market portfolio?

7. If the risk-free rate of return is 4 percent, the return on the market portfolio is 12 percent, and the beta of the Hotel Norwood is 1.5, calculate the expected rate of return for the Hotel Norwood.

8. If the expected return for the Park Hotel is 20 percent, the risk-free rate of return is 6 percent, and the return on the market portfolio is 16 percent, what is the beta of the Park Hotel?

Chapter 7
Time Value of Money

Chapter Objectives

This chapter covers the following topics:

1   The future value and present value computations of a single lump sum

2   Annuities and the difference between an ordinary annuity and an annuity due

3   The future value and present value computations of an annuity

4   The present value computations for a perpetuity, a deferred annuity, and a series of non-constant cash flows

5   Annual compounding and compounding other than annual

6   Effective annual rates

7   Amortization tables

7.1 Introduction

This chapter introduces the topic of financial mathematics, which we also call the time value of money (TVM). Although the topic may seem intimidating, many students are surprised by how much they enjoy solving financial problems—after all, the topic is based on common sense and is very logical. Learning financial mathematics enables students to perform important functions, such as calculating mortgage payments on a home loan, monthly payments on an automobile loan, or how much to save for retirement.

The TVM is a foundation topic in hospitality finance because it is relevant to many decisions in the hospitality industry, such as capital budgeting, cost of capital estimating, and bond issuance pricing. We discuss these topics in later chapters as we introduce the related information. For now, we focus on developing our ability to use TVM analytical procedures. The orientation of this chapter is personal finance, as this is a rich and interesting context for presenting TVM concepts. Building on this foundation, we apply TVM concepts in a hospitality industry framework in forthcoming chapters.

The **time value of money** is the concept that a set amount of money has different values at different points in time. In other words, $1 today is not worth $1 one year from now. A simple example to illustrate this concept is to think in terms of how the value of something changes over time. For example, whereas your parents could purchase the nicest house in the neighbourhood in 1970 for $42,000, you may have to pay $200,000 or $300,000 for that same house today. In the early 1970s a basic economy car could be purchased for less than $8,000. Today very few new cars are available for less than $20,000. Of course, when you consider the salaries of 1970 compared to today, proportionally your cost of purchasing a house or car may be relatively the same.

Financial mathematics requires the use of **interest rates**, which reflect the change in the value of money from time period to time period. For example, if you deposit $10,000 into a bank account today, you expect to have more than $10,000 one year later. How much more? It depends on the interest rate. If the interest rate is 5.5 percent annually, then you expect to have $550 more ($10,000 times 5.5%), for a total of $10,550.

This is the time value of money. The preceding example is simple, with limited usefulness. However, as you go through this chapter you will learn more complex ways to find the value of money at different points in time. After you have mastered this chapter, you will be able to apply your newfound skills to all sorts of situations. In fact, many future chapters rely on the TVM concept. If you do not understand the TVM concept, chances are you will not be able to successfully complete your study of financial management.

As we move through this chapter, you will learn how to find the value of a sum of money in the future at a given rate of interest. We refer to this as calculating the **future value** of a lump sum. You will also be able to calculate how much money must be invested today at a given interest rate to provide a given future amount. This is called calculating the **present value** of a lump sum. In addition, you will learn how to calculate the present and future values of a series of payments, known as annuity payments. All other concepts follow from these four basic concepts.

7.2 Future Value—Compounding

The first TVM concept we present is how to calculate the future value of a lump sum. In other words, what is a certain sum of money worth in the future at a particular rate of interest? The term **compounding** refers to the process of a present value earning interest and growing to a future value.

For example, say you deposit $1,000 into a bank account today. The account pays interest at a rate of 5 percent annually. An example of this type of account is a certificate of deposit (CD). We now calculate the future value of this lump sum of $1,000 one year from now at the 5 percent annual interest rate.

We start by modelling this problem on a timeline. Timelines are a useful way to keep your numbers organized to avoid making mistakes and to help visualize the problem more clearly. We strongly suggest you draw a timeline when solving financial mathematics problems—timelines greatly assist in learning the time value of money concept and can help to avoid errors. A properly labelled timeline helps you visualize the problem and helps keep everything organized.

$$0 \qquad\qquad\qquad\qquad\qquad\qquad 1$$
$$PV = \$1{,}000 \qquad\qquad\qquad\qquad FV_1 = ?$$

Before formally solving the problem, we consider the logic. One year from today your bank account will have a balance of $1,000 plus any interest earned. At an interest rate of 5 percent, your interest earned amounts to $50. Therefore, the balance in your account one year from today will be $1,050.

$$FV_1 = PV + \text{Interest}$$
$$= \$1,000 + \$1,000 \times 0.05 \ (5\% = 0.05)$$
$$= \$1,000 + \$50 = \$1,050$$

Now, what if we leave this money in the bank account for a second year, and it earns the same 5 percent rate of interest over this second year? Again, model this problem on a timeline.

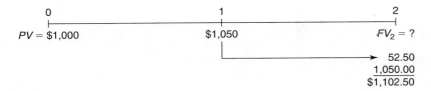

As you can see, your balance will increase to $1,102.50 by the end of the second year. You have earned interest of $52.50 during this second year. Fifty dollars of this interest is earned on the original deposit of $1,000, and the other $2.50 is earned on the first year's interest of $50. In other words, the amount of interest earned in year two can be calculated as $1,050 times 5 percent, which is $52.50. We refer to this concept of earning interest on interest as **compound interest**. To calculate the future value of any sum for any interest rate over any period of time, we use the following equation.

$$FV_n = PV \times (1 + i)^n = \$1,000 \times (1.05)^2 = \$1,102.50$$

FV_n is the future value of a lump sum at time n
PV is the present value
i is the interest rate
n is the number of compounding periods between the future value and the present value

There are three ways to solve the preceding equation and find the future value of $1,102.50. The first method is to work through the math. The second method is to use a business calculator programmed to perform financial mathematics. If you are using a calculator to perform the financial mathematics calculation, be sure the calculator is properly set up (see Appendix 1, which provides some guidance for using two of the more popular business calculators to solve TVM problems). Then enter the three known variables.

$$PV = \$1,000 \quad n = 2 \quad i = 5\% \quad \text{then compute } FV = \$1,102.50$$

The third method is to use financial mathematics tables that are designed to save the user from working through the mathematics (Exhibit 7-1). For this type of problem, the table provides a factor that we multiply by the known present value to solve for the future value. In this case, because we are solving for a future value, the factor is called a *future value interest factor (FVIF)*. $FVIF_{i,n}$ is equal to $(1 + i)^n$ so that the equation

$$FV_n = PV \times (1 + i)^n \text{ can also be written as } FV_n = PV \times (FVIF_{i,n})$$

where the $(FVIF_{i,n})$ is the FVIF for a given interest rate (i) and a given number of periods (n).

To solve the preceding problem, we can write the equation as

$$FV_n = \$1,000 \times (FVIF_{5\%,2})$$

where $(FVIF_{5\%,2}) = 1.1025$ from Exhibit 7-1. Thus, the answer is

$$FV_n = \$1,000 \times 1.1025 = \$1,102.50$$

Now, practise what you have just learned. Suppose you deposit \$12,000 into an account paying 7 percent annual interest. How much will you have in this account 14 years from now? Calculate the future value in this example using each of the three methods: (1) working through the mathematics of the equation, (2) using a business

Exhibit 7-1 Future Value Interest Factor

Value of \$1 Earning *i*% per Period for *n* Periods

Periods	1%	2%	3%	4%	5%	6%	7%	8%	9%	10%
1	1.0100	1.0200	1.0300	1.0400	1.0500	1.0600	1.0700	1.0800	1.0900	1.1000
2	1.0201	1.0404	1.0609	1.0816	1.1025	1.1236	1.1449	1.1664	1.1881	1.2100
3	1.0303	1.0612	1.0927	1.1249	1.1576	1.1910	1.2250	1.2597	1.2950	1.3310
4	1.0406	1.0824	1.1255	1.1699	1.2155	1.2625	1.3108	1.3605	1.4116	1.4641
5	1.0510	1.1041	1.1593	1.2167	1.2763	1.3382	1.4026	1.4693	1.5386	1.6105
6	1.0615	1.1262	1.1941	1.2653	1.3401	1.4185	1.5007	1.5869	1.6771	1.7716
7	1.0721	1.1487	1.2299	1.3159	1.4071	1.5036	1.6058	1.7138	1.8280	1.9487
8	1.0829	1.1717	1.2668	1.3686	1.4775	1.5938	1.7182	1.8509	1.9926	2.1436
9	1.0937	1.1951	1.3048	1.4233	1.5513	1.6895	1.8385	1.9990	2.1719	2.3579
10	1.1046	1.2190	1.3439	1.4802	1.6289	1.7908	1.9672	2.1589	2.3674	2.5937
11	1.1157	1.2434	1.3842	1.5395	1.7103	1.8983	2.1049	2.3316	2.5804	2.8531
12	1.1268	1.2682	1.4258	1.6010	1.7959	2.0122	2.2522	2.5182	2.8127	3.1384
13	1.1381	1.2936	1.4685	1.6651	1.8856	2.1329	2.4098	2.7196	3.0658	3.4523
14	1.1495	1.3195	1.5126	1.7317	1.9799	2.2609	2.5785	2.9372	3.3417	3.7975
15	1.1610	1.3459	1.5580	1.8009	2.0789	2.3966	2.7590	3.1722	3.6425	4.1772
16	1.1726	1.3728	1.6047	1.8730	2.1829	2.5404	2.9522	3.4259	3.9703	4.5950
17	1.1843	1.4002	1.6528	1.9479	2.2920	2.6928	3.1588	3.7000	4.3276	5.0545
18	1.1961	1.4282	1.7024	2.0258	2.4066	2.8543	3.3799	3.9960	4.7171	5.5599
19	1.2081	1.4568	1.7535	2.1068	2.5270	3.0256	3.6165	4.3157	5.1417	6.1159
20	1.2202	1.4859	1.8061	2.1911	2.6533	3.2071	3.8697	4.6610	5.6044	6.7275
25	1.2824	1.6406	2.0938	2.6658	3.3864	4.2919	5.4274	6.8485	8.6231	10.8347
30	1.3478	1.8114	2.4273	3.2434	4.3219	5.7435	7.6123	10.0627	13.2677	17.4494
40	1.4889	2.2080	3.2620	4.8010	7.0400	10.2857	14.9745	21.7245	31.4094	45.2593
50	1.6446	2.6916	4.3839	7.1067	11.4674	18.4202	29.4570	46.9016	74.3575	117.3909

(continued)

Exhibit 7-1 (continued)

Value of $1 Earning *i*% per Period for *n* Periods

Periods	11%	12%	13%	14%	15%	16%	17%	18%	19%	20%
1	1.1100	1.1200	1.1300	1.1400	1.1500	1.1600	1.1700	1.1800	1.1900	1.2000
2	1.2321	1.2544	1.2769	1.2996	1.3225	1.3456	1.3689	1.3924	1.4161	1.4400
3	1.3676	1.4049	1.4429	1.4815	1.5209	1.5609	1.6016	1.6430	1.6852	1.7280
4	1.5181	1.5735	1.6305	1.6890	1.7490	1.8106	1.8739	1.9388	2.0053	2.0736
5	1.6851	1.7623	1.8424	1.9254	2.0114	2.1003	2.1924	2.2878	2.3864	2.4883
6	1.8704	1.9738	2.0820	2.1950	2.3131	2.4364	2.5652	2.6996	2.8398	2.9860
7	2.0762	2.2107	2.3526	2.5023	2.6600	2.8262	3.0012	3.1855	3.3793	3.5832
8	2.3045	2.4760	2.6584	2.8526	3.0590	3.2784	3.5115	3.7589	4.0214	4.2998
9	2.5580	2.7731	3.0040	3.2519	3.5179	3.8030	4.1084	4.4355	4.7854	5.1598
10	2.8394	3.1058	3.3946	3.7072	4.0456	4.4114	4.8068	5.2338	5.6947	6.1917
11	3.1518	3.4785	3.8359	4.2262	4.6524	5.1173	5.6240	6.1759	6.7767	7.4301
12	3.4985	3.8960	4.3345	4.8179	5.3503	5.9360	6.5801	7.2876	8.0642	8.9161
13	3.8833	4.3635	4.8980	5.4924	6.1528	6.8858	7.6987	8.5994	9.5964	10.6993
14	4.3104	4.8871	5.5348	6.2613	7.0757	7.9875	9.0075	10.1472	11.4198	12.8392
15	4.7846	5.4736	6.2543	7.1379	8.1371	9.2655	10.5387	11.9737	13.5895	15.4070
16	5.3109	6.1304	7.0673	8.1372	9.3576	10.7480	12.3303	14.1290	16.1715	18.4884
17	5.8951	6.8660	7.9861	9.2765	10.7613	12.4677	14.4265	16.6722	19.2441	22.1861
18	6.5436	7.6900	9.0243	10.5752	12.3755	14.4625	16.8790	19.6733	22.9005	26.6233
19	7.2633	8.6128	10.1974	12.0557	14.2318	16.7765	19.7484	23.2144	27.2516	31.9480
20	8.0623	9.6463	11.5231	13.7435	16.3665	19.4608	23.1056	27.3930	32.4294	38.3376
25	13.5855	17.0001	21.2305	26.4619	32.9190	40.8742	50.6578	62.6686	77.3881	95.3962
30	22.8923	29.9599	39.1159	50.9502	66.2118	85.8499	111.0647	143.3706	184.6753	237.3763
40	65.0009	93.0510	132.7816	188.8835	267.8635	378.7212	533.8687	750.3783	1051.6675	1469.7716
50	184.5648	289.0022	450.7359	700.2330	1083.6574	1670.7038	2566.2153	3927.3569	5988.9139	9100.4382

calculator programmed for financial mathematics, and (3) using the financial mathematics tables.

Now, solve the problem using each of the three methods. You get the same answer regardless of the method used. Do you understand why?

Equation: $FV_{14} = \$12{,}000 \times (1.07)^{14} = \$30{,}942.41$

Calculator: $PV = \$12{,}000 \quad n = 14 \quad i = 7\%$ then compute $FV = \$30{,}942.41$

Exhibit 7-1: $FV_{14} = \$12,000 \times (FVIF_{7\%,14}) = \$12,000 \times (2.5785) = \$30,942.00$

Notice when you look up the $FVIF_{7\%,14}$ you find the factor of 2.5785. Thus $FVIF_{7\%,14}$ is calculated as $(1 + i)^n$, or $(1.07)^{14}$, which is 2.5785. In other words, $FVIF_{i,n} = (1 + i)^n$ for a given interest rate, i, over a specified period of time, n. Therefore, using the factor is the same as working through the mathematical equation, except the tables round the factors to four decimal places.

Next, consider your calculator. If you enter $PV = 1$, $n = 14$, $i = 7\%$, and then solve for FV, you get the same answer you calculated for the $FVIF_{7\%,14}$ or $(1.07)^{14}$, which is 2.5785. Thus the calculator is just a shortcut—an efficient method for working through the mathematical equation. Note that all three methods really use the same mathematical equation, whether you work through the mathematical equation yourself, use a business calculator programmed for financial mathematics, or use the tables; these are all alternative methods to solve for the same answer. You should obtain an FV equal to $\$30,942.41$ solving the mathematical equation or using the calculator. Using Exhibit 7-1 you should obtain an FV equal to $\$30,942.00$, because Exhibit 7-1 rounds off the factors at four decimal places (2.5785).

7.3 Present Value—Discounting

What if we know the value of a lump sum of money at some point in the future and want instead to calculate the appropriate present value today at some specified rate of interest? In other words, what is a future sum of money worth today? For example, what is $\$1,320$ worth today at a 10 percent annual rate? How much do you have to invest today at 10 percent to end up with $\$1,320$ in one year? **Discounting** is the process of computing the present value of a future value.

Just as with the previous future value problem, this problem can be solved in three different ways. We can work through the math, use a business calculator, or use financial mathematics tables. First, we will work through the math.

$$(2)\ PV = \frac{FV_n}{(1 + i)^n} = \frac{\$1,320}{(1 + 10\%)^1} = \$1,200$$

Using a business calculator, enter the three known variables:

$$FV = 1,320 \quad n = 1 \quad i = 10\% \quad \text{then compute } PV = \$1,200$$

Financial mathematics tables provide a factor that we multiply by the known future value to solve for the present value. Because we are solving for the present value, the factor in this case is called a *present value interest factor (PVIF)*. $PVIF_{i,n}$ is equal to $1/(1 + i)^n$ so that the equation

$$PV = \frac{FV_n}{(1 + i)^n}$$

can also be written as $PV = FV_n \times (PVIF_{i,n})$.

To solve the preceding problem, we can write the equation as

$$PV = \$1{,}320 \times (PVIF_{10\%,1})$$

where $(PVIF_{10\%,1}) = 0.9091$ from Exhibit 7-2. Thus, the answer is

$$PV = \$1{,}320 \times 0.9091 = \$1{,}200.01$$

Notice once again that the answer obtained from the financial mathematics tables is slightly different from the answer obtained by working through the mathematics or by

Exhibit 7-2 Present Value Interest Factor

Value of $1 Discounted at *i*% per Period for *n* Periods

Periods	1%	2%	3%	4%	5%	6%	7%	8%	9%	10%
1	0.9901	0.9804	0.9709	0.9615	0.9524	0.9434	0.9346	0.9259	0.9174	0.9091
2	0.9803	0.9612	0.9426	0.9246	0.9070	0.8900	0.8734	0.8573	0.8417	0.8264
3	0.9706	0.9423	0.9151	0.8890	0.8638	0.8396	0.8163	0.7938	0.7722	0.7513
4	0.9610	0.9238	0.8885	0.8548	0.8227	0.7921	0.7629	0.7350	0.7084	0.6830
5	0.9515	0.9057	0.8626	0.8219	0.7835	0.7473	0.7130	0.6806	0.6499	0.6209
6	0.9420	0.8880	0.8375	0.7903	0.7462	0.7050	0.6663	0.6302	0.5963	0.5645
7	0.9327	0.8706	0.8131	0.7599	0.7107	0.6651	0.6227	0.5835	0.5470	0.5132
8	0.9235	0.8535	0.7894	0.7307	0.6768	0.6274	0.5820	0.5403	0.5019	0.4665
9	0.9143	0.8368	0.7664	0.7026	0.6446	0.5919	0.5439	0.5002	0.4604	0.4241
10	0.9053	0.8203	0.7441	0.6756	0.6139	0.5584	0.5083	0.4632	0.4224	0.3855
11	0.8963	0.8043	0.7224	0.6496	0.5847	0.5268	0.4751	0.4289	0.3875	0.3505
12	0.8874	0.7885	0.7014	0.6246	0.5568	0.4970	0.4440	0.3971	0.3555	0.3186
13	0.8787	0.7730	0.6810	0.6006	0.5303	0.4688	0.4150	0.3677	0.3262	0.2897
14	0.8700	0.7579	0.6611	0.5775	0.5051	0.4423	0.3878	0.3405	0.2992	0.2633
15	0.8613	0.7430	0.6419	0.5553	0.4810	0.4173	0.3624	0.3152	0.2745	0.2394
16	0.8528	0.7284	0.6232	0.5339	0.4581	0.3936	0.3387	0.2919	0.2519	0.2176
17	0.8444	0.7142	0.6050	0.5134	0.4363	0.3714	0.3166	0.2703	0.2311	0.1978
18	0.8360	0.7002	0.5874	0.4936	0.4155	0.3503	0.2959	0.2502	0.2120	0.1799
19	0.8277	0.6864	0.5703	0.4746	0.3957	0.3305	0.2765	0.2317	0.1945	0.1635
20	0.8195	0.6730	0.5537	0.4564	0.3769	0.3118	0.2584	0.2145	0.1784	0.1486
25	0.7798	0.6095	0.4776	0.3751	0.2953	0.2330	0.1842	0.1460	0.1160	0.0923
30	0.7419	0.5521	0.4120	0.3083	0.2314	0.1741	0.1314	0.0994	0.0754	0.0573
40	0.6717	0.4529	0.3066	0.2083	0.1420	0.0972	0.0668	0.0460	0.0318	0.0221
50	0.6080	0.3715	0.2281	0.1407	0.0872	0.0543	0.0339	0.0213	0.0134	0.0085

(continued)

Exhibit 7-2 (continued)

Value of $1 Discounted at *i*% per Period for *n* Periods

Periods	11%	12%	13%	14%	15%	16%	17%	18%	19%	20%
1	0.9009	0.8929	0.8850	0.8772	0.8696	0.8621	0.8547	0.8475	0.8403	0.8333
2	0.8116	0.7972	0.7831	0.7695	0.7561	0.7432	0.7305	0.7182	0.7062	0.6944
3	0.7312	0.7118	0.6931	0.6750	0.6575	0.6407	0.6244	0.6086	0.5934	0.5787
4	0.6587	0.6355	0.6133	0.5921	0.5718	0.5523	0.5337	0.5158	0.4987	0.4823
5	0.5935	0.5674	0.5428	0.5194	0.4972	0.4761	0.4561	0.4371	0.4190	0.4019
6	0.5346	0.5066	0.4803	0.4556	0.4323	0.4104	0.3898	0.3704	0.3521	0.3349
7	0.4817	0.4523	0.4251	0.3996	0.3759	0.3538	0.3332	0.3139	0.2959	0.2791
8	0.4339	0.4039	0.3762	0.3506	0.3269	0.3050	0.2848	0.2660	0.2487	0.2326
9	0.3909	0.3606	0.3329	0.3075	0.2843	0.2630	0.2434	0.2255	0.2090	0.1938
10	0.3522	0.3220	0.2946	0.2697	0.2472	0.2267	0.2080	0.1911	0.1756	0.1615
11	0.3173	0.2875	0.2607	0.2366	0.2149	0.1954	0.1778	0.1619	0.1476	0.1346
12	0.2858	0.2567	0.2307	0.2076	0.1869	0.1685	0.1520	0.1372	0.1240	0.1122
13	0.2575	0.2292	0.2042	0.1821	0.1625	0.1452	0.1299	0.1163	0.1042	0.0935
14	0.2320	0.2046	0.1807	0.1597	0.1413	0.1252	0.1110	0.0985	0.0876	0.0779
15	0.2090	0.1827	0.1599	0.1401	0.1229	0.1079	0.0949	0.0835	0.0736	0.0649
16	0.1883	0.1631	0.1415	0.1229	0.1069	0.0930	0.0811	0.0708	0.0618	0.0541
17	0.1696	0.1456	0.1252	0.1078	0.0929	0.0802	0.0693	0.0600	0.0520	0.0451
18	0.1528	0.1300	0.1108	0.0946	0.0808	0.0691	0.0592	0.0508	0.0437	0.0376
19	0.1377	0.1161	0.0981	0.0829	0.0703	0.0596	0.0506	0.0431	0.0367	0.0313
20	0.1240	0.1037	0.0868	0.0728	0.0611	0.0514	0.0433	0.0365	0.0308	0.0261
25	0.0736	0.0588	0.0471	0.0378	0.0304	0.0245	0.0197	0.0160	0.0129	0.0105
30	0.0437	0.0334	0.0256	0.0196	0.0151	0.0116	0.0090	0.0070	0.0054	0.0042
40	0.0154	0.0107	0.0075	0.0053	0.0037	0.0026	0.0019	0.0013	0.0010	0.0007
50	0.0054	0.0035	0.0022	0.0014	0.0009	0.0006	0.0004	0.0003	0.0002	0.0001

using the calculator. This is again because the factors in the financial mathematics tables are rounded to four decimal places.

Now, practise what you have just learned. Calculate the present value in the following problem using each of the three methods. Your grandmother promises to deposit a lump sum into an account today to pay for your newborn child's first year of postsecondary education. Assume your child's first year of tuition will have to be paid 18 years from now and will be in the amount of $30,000. How much will your grandmother have to deposit into the account, which promises to pay 8 percent annual interest?

Start out with a timeline to help organize and visualize the problem:

```
0                                                    18
├────────────────────────────────────────────────────┤
PV = ? ◄─────────────────────────────── FV₁₈ = $30,000
              8% interest for 18 years
```

Now solve the problem using each of the three methods.

Equation: $PV = \dfrac{\$30{,}000}{(1 + 8\%)^{18}} = \$7{,}507.47$

Calculator: $FV = \$30{,}000 \quad n = 18 \quad i = 8\% \quad$ then compute $PV = \$7{,}507.47$

Exhibit 7-2: $PV = \$30{,}000 \times (PVIF_{8\%,18}) = \$30{,}000 \times 0.2502 = \$7{,}506.00$

All three methods arrive at the same answer (the answer from Exhibit 7-2 is slightly lower due to rounding).

Captain Canada Mulberry Pie Ltd. (CCMP), a fictitious Canadian company, issues two money multiplier notes. The first is sold for $250 and promises to return $1,000 12 years from now. The second is sold for $500 and promises to return $1,000 six years from now. When CCMP sells these notes, it is essentially borrowing money from the investors who are willing to purchase them.

What is CCMP's cost of borrowing $250 for 12 years or the return to the investor lending CCMP $250 for 12 years? Financial mathematics can be used to answer this question. The $250 selling price of the first money multiplier note is a present value (PV) and the $1,000 paid back at the end of 12 years is a future value (FV). The interest cost to CCMP or the interest return to the investor is computed as follows.

$PV = \dfrac{FV}{(1 + i)^n}$ where the $PV = \$250$, $FV = \$1{,}000$, and $n = 12$, so we have

$\$250 = \dfrac{\$1{,}000}{(1 + i)^{12}}$ where $i = 12.25\%$

We can also compute CCMP's cost of borrowing the $500 for six years or the return to the investor lending CCMP $500 for six years in a similar manner using financial mathematics. The $500 selling price of the second money multiplier note is a present value (PV), and the $1,000 paid back at the end of six years is a future value (FV). The interest cost to CCMP or the interest return to the investor is computed as follows.

$PV = \dfrac{FV}{(1 + i)^n}$ where the $PV = \$500$, $FV = \$1{,}000$, and $n = 6$, so we have

$\$500 = \dfrac{\$1{,}000}{(1 + i)^{6}}$ where $i = 12.25\%$

So, the interest cost to CCMP or the interest return to the investor is the same on both money multiplier notes.

7.4 Future Value of an Annuity

An **annuity** is a series of payments of a fixed amount for a specified number of periods of equal length. We often encounter annuities in our everyday life. Examples include payments toward a car loan or home mortgage, or even monthly pension plan receipts. These examples generally call for monthly payments, but for now we focus on solving problems that have annual payments. Later we explain how to solve problems with monthly or other periodic payments.

All annuities consist of a series of equal, periodic payments and a single lump sum. If the single lump sum follows the payments, it is a **future value** of an annuity. For example, suppose you plan to deposit $1,000 into an account at the end of each of the next five years. If the account pays 12 percent annually, what is the value of the account after five years? This is shown on a timeline as follows.

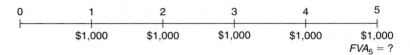

The timeline shows five annual payments of $1,000 each, and "$FVA_5$ = ?" indicates we are looking for the future value of the five payments at the end of five years. The FVA_5, the future value of the annuity, is the single lump sum associated with the annuity. Because the lump sum follows the payments in time, this is a future value of an annuity problem. There are four ways to solve this problem:

1. Compute the future value of each payment individually and then add them up. In other words, view the problem as the sum of the future value of five lump sums.

2. Work through the mathematics of the future value of an annuity equation.

3. Use a calculator programmed for financial mathematics.

4. Use Exhibit 7-3.

Each of these four methods generates the same answer to the problem.

First, we will compute the future value of each payment and then add. We revisit the timeline with some additional detail to help explain this method.

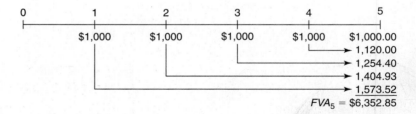

The timeline shows the first, second, third, and fourth $1,000 payments earning 12 percent interest for 4, 3, 2, and 1 years, respectively. The fifth payment is already a future value in five years and thus earns no interest. We would have the following:

$$FVA_5 = \$1,000 \times (1.12)^4 + 1,000 \times (1.12)^3 + 1,000 \times (1.12)^2$$
$$+ 1,000 \times (1.12) + 1,000$$
$$= \$1,573.52 + 1,404.93 + 1,254.40 + 1,120.00 + 1,000 = \$6,352.85$$

The preceding equation summing the future value of five lump sum payments to obtain the future value of an annuity can be simplified to the following equation.

$$FVA_5 = \$1,000 \times \left[\frac{(1 + 12\%)^5 - 1}{12\%} \right] = \$6,352.85$$

Exhibit 7-3 Future Value Interest Factor for an Annuity

Future Value of $1 per Period for n Periods Earning at i% Interest per Period

Periods	1%	2%	3%	4%	5%	6%	7%	8%	9%	10%
1	1.0000	1.0000	1.0000	1.0000	1.0000	1.0000	1.0000	1.0000	1.0000	1.0000
2	2.0100	2.0200	2.0300	2.0400	2.0500	2.0600	2.0700	2.0800	2.0900	2.1000
3	3.0301	3.0604	3.0909	3.1216	3.1525	3.1836	3.2149	3.2464	3.2781	3.3100
4	4.0604	4.1216	4.1836	4.2465	4.3101	4.3746	4.4399	4.5061	4.5731	4.6410
5	5.1010	5.2040	5.3091	5.4163	5.5256	5.6371	5.7507	5.8666	5.9847	6.1051
6	6.1520	6.3081	6.4684	6.6330	6.8019	6.9753	7.1533	7.3359	7.5233	7.7156
7	7.2135	7.4343	7.6625	7.8983	8.1420	8.3938	8.6540	8.9228	9.2004	9.4872
8	8.2857	8.5830	8.8923	9.2142	9.5491	9.8975	10.2598	10.6366	11.0285	11.4359
9	9.3685	9.7546	10.1591	10.5828	11.0266	11.4913	11.9780	12.4876	13.0210	13.5795
10	10.4622	10.9497	11.4639	12.0061	12.5779	13.1808	13.8164	14.4866	15.1929	15.9374
11	11.5668	12.1687	12.8078	13.4864	14.2068	14.9716	15.7836	16.6455	17.5603	18.5312
12	12.6825	13.4121	14.1920	15.0258	15.9171	16.8699	17.8885	18.9771	20.1407	21.3843
13	13.8093	14.6803	15.6178	16.6268	17.7130	18.8821	20.1406	21.4953	22.9534	24.5227
14	14.9474	15.9739	17.0863	18.2919	19.5986	21.0151	22.5505	24.2149	26.0192	27.9750
15	16.0969	17.2934	18.5989	20.0236	21.5786	23.2760	25.1290	27.1521	29.3609	31.7725
16	17.2579	18.6393	20.1569	21.8245	23.6575	25.6725	27.8881	30.3243	33.0034	35.9497
17	18.4304	20.0121	21.7616	23.6975	25.8404	28.2129	30.8402	33.7502	36.9737	40.5447
18	19.6147	21.4123	23.4144	25.6454	28.1324	30.9057	33.9990	37.4502	41.3013	45.5992
19	20.8109	22.8406	25.1169	27.6712	30.5390	33.7600	37.3790	41.4463	46.0185	51.1591
20	22.0190	24.2974	26.8704	29.7781	33.0660	36.7856	40.9955	45.7620	51.1601	57.2750
25	28.2432	32.0303	36.4593	41.6459	47.7271	54.8645	63.2490	73.1059	84.7009	98.3471
30	34.7849	40.5681	47.5754	56.0849	66.4388	79.0582	94.4608	113.2832	136.3075	164.4940
40	48.8864	60.4020	75.4013	95.0255	120.7998	154.7620	199.6351	259.0565	337.8824	442.5926
50	64.4632	84.5794	112.7969	152.6671	209.3480	290.3359	406.5289	573.7702	815.0836	1163.9085

(continued)

Exhibit 7-3 (continued)

Future Value of $1 per Period for n Periods Earning at i% Interest per Period

Periods	11%	12%	13%	14%	15%	16%	17%	18%	19%	20%
1	1.0000	1.0000	1.0000	1.0000	1.0000	1.0000	1.0000	1.0000	1.0000	1.0000
2	2.1100	2.1200	2.1300	2.1400	2.1500	2.1600	2.1700	2.1800	2.1900	2.2000
3	3.3421	3.3744	3.4069	3.4396	3.4725	3.5056	3.5389	3.5724	3.6061	3.6400
4	4.7097	4.7793	4.8498	4.9211	4.9934	5.0665	5.1405	5.2154	5.2913	5.3680
5	6.2278	6.3528	6.4803	6.6101	6.7424	6.8771	7.0144	7.1542	7.2966	7.4416
6	7.9129	8.1152	8.3227	8.5355	8.7537	8.9775	9.2068	9.4420	9.6830	9.9299
7	9.7833	10.0890	10.4047	10.7305	11.0668	11.4139	11.7720	12.1415	12.5227	12.9159
8	11.8594	12.2997	12.7573	13.2328	13.7268	14.2401	14.7733	15.3270	15.9020	16.4991
9	14.1640	14.7757	15.4157	16.0853	16.7858	17.5185	18.2847	19.0859	19.9234	20.7989
10	16.7220	17.5487	18.4197	19.3373	20.3037	21.3215	22.3931	23.5213	24.7089	25.9587
11	19.5614	20.6546	21.8143	23.0445	24.3493	25.7329	27.1999	28.7551	30.4035	32.1504
12	22.7132	24.1331	25.6502	27.2707	29.0017	30.8502	32.8239	34.9311	37.1802	39.5805
13	26.2116	28.0291	29.9847	32.0887	34.3519	36.7862	39.4040	42.2187	45.2445	48.4966
14	30.0949	32.3926	34.8827	37.5811	40.5047	43.6720	47.1027	50.8180	54.8409	59.1959
15	34.4054	37.2797	40.4175	43.8424	47.5804	51.6595	56.1101	60.9653	66.2607	72.0351
16	39.1899	42.7533	46.6717	50.9804	55.7175	60.9250	66.6488	72.9390	79.8502	87.4421
17	44.5008	48.8837	53.7391	59.1176	65.0751	71.6730	78.9792	87.0680	96.0218	105.9306
18	50.3959	55.7497	61.7251	68.3941	75.8364	84.1407	93.4056	103.7403	115.2659	128.1167
19	56.9395	63.4397	70.7494	78.9692	88.2118	98.6032	110.2846	123.4135	138.1664	154.7400
20	64.2028	72.0524	80.9468	91.0249	102.4436	115.3797	130.0329	146.6280	165.4180	186.6880
25	114.4133	133.3339	155.6196	181.8708	212.7930	249.2140	292.1049	342.6035	402.0425	471.9811
30	199.0209	241.3327	293.1992	356.7868	434.7451	530.3117	647.4391	790.9480	966.7122	1181.8816
40	581.8261	767.0914	1013.7042	1342.0251	1779.0903	2360.7572	3134.5218	4163.2130	5529.8290	7343.8578
50	1668.7712	2400.0182	3459.5071	4994.5213	7217.7163	10435.6488	15089.5017	21813.0937	31515.3363	45497.1908

Thus, we have solved the future value of an annuity with the second method—we have worked through the mathematics of the future value of an annuity equation. This equation can be expressed more generally as

$$FVA_n = PMT \times \left[\frac{(1 + i)^n - 1}{i}\right]$$

We can also solve the problem using a business calculator. Enter the three variables we know:

$$PMT = \$1,000 \quad n = 5 \quad i = 12\% \quad \text{then compute } FV = \$6,352.85$$

Finally, we can solve the problem using Exhibit 7-3. The table provides a factor that we multiply by the known annuity payment to solve for the future value. Because we are solving for the future value of an annuity, the factor in this case is called a *future value interest factor for an annuity (FVIFA)*.

The $FVIFA_{i,n}$ is equal to

$$\left[\frac{(1 + i)^n - 1}{i}\right]$$

so that the equation

$$FVA_n = PMT \times \left[\frac{(1 + i)^n - 1}{i}\right] \quad \text{can also be written as } FVA_n = PMT \times (FVIFA_{i,n})$$

To solve the problem using Exhibit 7-3 we can write the equation as

$$FVA_5 = PMT \times (FVIFA_{12\%,5})$$

where $(FVIFA_{12\%,5}) = 6.3528$ from Exhibit 7-3. Thus the answer is

$$FVA_5 = \$1,000 \times 6.3528 = \$6,352.80$$

Again, notice the answer obtained from the financial mathematics tables is slightly different due to rounding.

Contracts calling for annuity payments can stipulate that the payment is made either at the end of each period (an **ordinary annuity**) or at the beginning of each period (an **annuity due**). The example we just worked through is an ordinary annuity. It can be quite tricky to properly identify an annuity as either an ordinary annuity or an annuity due. We naturally tend to look at when the first payment is paid. This works for present value of annuities, which we will consider later, but it doesn't always work for future value of annuities. To properly classify the future value of an annuity as an ordinary annuity or an annuity due, we need to consider whether the last payment is at the beginning of the period or the end of the period. If the *last* annuity payment is at the *end* of the *last* period, then it is a future value of an ordinary annuity. If the *last* annuity payment is at the *beginning* of the *last* period, then it is a future value of an annuity due. Consider the timeline for the preceding example.

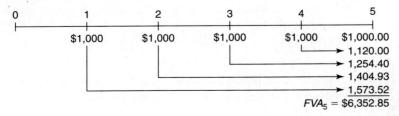

This is an ordinary annuity, because the last payment is at the end of the last year (not because the first payment is at the end of the first year). The following timeline should clearly show the difference.

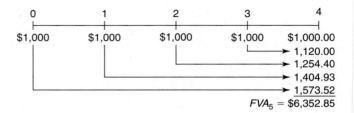

In the timeline, the first payment is at the beginning of the first year, but the first, second, third, and fourth payments still earn interest for 4, 3, 2, and 1 years respectively. The last payment is already a future value at the appropriate time and earns no interest. With a 12 percent annual interest rate, the future value of the annuity is the same as before. The distinguishing characteristic is that the last payment is still at the end of the last year. This is an ordinary annuity.

To change the example to the future value of an annuity due, we need to solve for the future value one period after the last payment. The timeline is as follows.

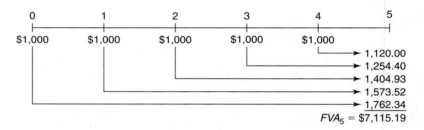

The timeline shows that the last payment comes at the beginning of the last year. The first payment at the beginning of the first year does not make this an annuity due. Instead, the last payment at the beginning of the last year distinguishes this as an annuity due. In this future value of an annuity due, each payment earns one more period of interest than in the otherwise equivalent ordinary annuity. If each payment earns an extra 12 percent for one period, then the entire future value of the annuity due will earn an extra 12 percent for one period. Thus, we can solve this problem using the following equation.

$$VAD_5 = \$1,000 \times \left[\frac{(1 + 12\%)^5 - 1}{12\%} \right] \times (1 + 12\%)$$
$$= \$6,352.85 \times (1 + 12\%) = \$7,115.19$$

We can express the equation for a future value of an annuity due more generally as

$$FVAD_n = PMT \times \left[\frac{(1 + i)^n - 1}{i} \right] \times (1 + i)$$

Thus, the future value of an annuity due is always greater than an otherwise equivalent ordinary annuity by the amount of the interest rate for one period.

Imagine you wisely decide to plan for your retirement when you graduate. You open a registered retirement savings plan (RRSP) and plan to deposit $2,000 into this account every year until you retire 40 years from now. Assume you make 40 deposits in the form of an ordinary annuity (deposits at the end of each year). If your RRSP earns 11 percent per year, how much will you have in your account when you retire in 40 years?

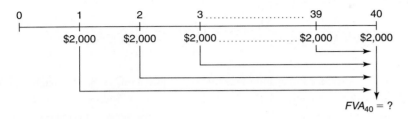

We can solve this problem by working through the mathematics of the future value of an annuity equation.

$$FVA_{40} = \$2,000 \times \left[\frac{(1 + 11\%)^{40} - 1}{11\%} \right] = \$1,163,652.13$$

When solving the problem using a business calculator, we need to enter the three known variables:

$$PMT = \$2,000 \quad n = 40 \quad i = 11\% \quad \text{then compute the } FV = \$1,163,652.13$$

We can also solve the problem using Exhibit 7-3.

$$FVA_{40} = \$2,000 \times FVIFA_{11\%,40}$$

where $(FVIFA_{11\%,40}) = 581.8261$ from Exhibit 7-3. Thus, the answer is

$$FVA_{40} = \$2,000 \times 581.8261 = \$1,163,652.20$$

(This answer is slightly different from the other two answers due to rounding in the tables.)

Are you surprised? After investing only $80,000 (40 times $2,000), you retire a millionaire! The power of compound interest can often surprise. Investing $2,000 annually and earning 11 percent interest over a long period of time can create immense wealth.

How much more will the investment be worth if you invest the $2,000 payments at the beginning of each year, changing the problem to an annuity due calculation? Remember, the future value of the annuity will be higher by the amount of the interest earned on the entire future value for one year.

$$FVAD_{40} = \$2,000 \times \left[\frac{(1 + 11\%)^{40} - 1}{11\%} \right] \times (1 + 11\%)$$
$$= \$1,163,652.13 \times (1 + 11\%)$$
$$FVAD_{40} = \$1,291,653.87$$

Now we consider an alternative investment in which instead of starting your RRSP now you wait for 20 years. In this case you plan to make only 20 deposits, so you will double the amount of these deposits to $4,000 annually at the end of each year. What is the future value of your retirement annuity at the end of the 20 years if you still earn 11 percent annually? Is the answer the same as we calculated previously? After all, you are depositing twice the amount of money in half the time—50 percent of the previous number of years. Wrong! It turns out to be far less.

$$FVA_{20} = \$4,000 \times \left[\frac{(1 + 11\%)^{20} - 1}{11\%} \right] = \$256,811.33$$

Why is there such a huge difference? With 40 payments of $2,000 each, you end up with a future value of $1,163,652.13. With 20 payments of $4,000 each you end up with less than one-fourth as much. This illustrates the immense power of compound interest. In one case you are earning interest on interest for 40 years and in the other case you are earning interest on interest for only 20 years. So do not delay. Start saving for retirement as soon as possible.

7.5 Present Value of an Annuity

Remember, all annuities consist of a series of equal, periodic payments and a single lump sum. If the single lump sum occurs before the payments, then it is a present value of an annuity. For example, suppose you plan to withdraw $1,000 annually from an account at the end of each of the next five years. If the account pays 12 percent annually, what must you deposit today to have just enough to cover the five withdrawals? This can be viewed on a timeline as follows.

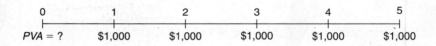

The timeline shows five annual payments of $1,000 each, and "PVA = ?" indicates we are looking for the present value of the five payments. The PVA, the present value of the annuity, is the single lump sum associated with the annuity.

Because this lump sum occurs before the payments, this is a present value of an annuity problem. There are four ways to solve this type of problem:

1. Compute the present value of each payment individually and then add them up. In other words, view the problem as the sum of the present value of five lump sums.

2. Work through the mathematics of the present value of an annuity equation.

3. Use a calculator programmed for financial mathematics.

4. Use Exhibit 7-4.

Each of these four methods generates the same answer to the problem.

First, we will compute the present value of each payment and then add. We revisit the timeline with some additional detail to help explain this method.

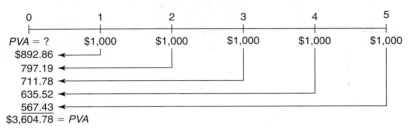

Exhibit 7-4 Present Value Interest Factor for an Annuity

Present Value of $1 per Period for *n* Periods Discounted at *i*% Interest per Period

Periods	1%	2%	3%	4%	5%	6%	7%	8%	9%	10%
1	0.9901	0.9804	0.9709	0.9615	0.9524	0.9434	0.9346	0.9259	0.9174	0.9091
2	1.9704	1.9416	1.9135	1.8861	1.8594	1.8334	1.8080	1.7833	1.7591	1.7355
3	2.9410	2.8839	2.8286	2.7751	2.7232	2.6730	2.6243	2.5771	2.5313	2.4869
4	3.9020	3.8077	3.7171	3.6299	3.5460	3.4651	3.3872	3.3121	3.2397	3.1699
5	4.8534	4.7135	4.5797	4.4518	4.3295	4.2124	4.1002	3.9927	3.8897	3.7908
6	5.7955	5.6014	5.4172	5.2421	5.0757	4.9173	4.7665	4.6229	4.4859	4.3553
7	6.7282	6.4720	6.2303	6.0021	5.7864	5.5824	5.3893	5.2064	5.0330	4.8684
8	7.6517	7.3255	7.0197	6.7327	6.4632	6.2098	5.9713	5.7466	5.5348	5.3349
9	8.5660	8.1622	7.7861	7.4353	7.1078	6.8017	6.5152	6.2469	5.9952	5.7590
10	9.4713	8.9826	8.5302	8.1109	7.7217	7.3601	7.0236	6.7101	6.4177	6.1446
11	10.3676	9.7868	9.2526	8.7605	8.3064	7.8869	7.4987	7.1390	6.8052	6.4951
12	11.2551	10.5753	9.9540	9.3851	8.8633	8.3838	7.9427	7.5361	7.1607	6.8137
13	12.1337	11.3484	10.6350	9.9856	9.3936	8.8527	8.3577	7.9038	7.4869	7.1034
14	13.0037	12.1062	11.2961	10.5631	9.8986	9.2950	8.7455	8.2442	7.7862	7.3667
15	13.8651	12.8493	11.9379	11.1184	10.3797	9.7122	9.1079	8.5595	8.0607	7.6061
16	14.7179	13.5777	12.5611	11.6523	10.8378	10.1059	9.4466	8.8514	8.3126	7.8237
17	15.5623	14.2919	13.1661	12.1657	11.2741	10.4773	9.7632	9.1216	8.5436	8.0216
18	16.3983	14.9920	13.7535	12.6593	11.6896	10.8276	10.0591	9.3719	8.7556	8.2014
19	17.2260	15.6785	14.3238	13.1339	12.0853	11.1581	10.3356	9.6036	8.9501	8.3649
20	18.0456	16.3514	14.8775	13.5903	12.4622	11.4699	10.5940	9.8181	9.1285	8.5136
25	22.0232	19.5235	17.4131	15.6221	14.0939	12.7834	11.6536	10.6748	9.8226	9.0770
30	25.8077	22.3965	19.6004	17.2920	15.3725	13.7648	12.4090	11.2578	10.2737	9.4269
40	32.8347	27.3555	23.1148	19.7928	17.1591	15.0463	13.3317	11.9246	10.7574	9.7791
50	39.1961	31.4236	25.7298	21.4822	18.2559	15.7619	13.8007	12.2335	10.9617	9.9148

(continued)

Exhibit 7-4 (continued)

Present Value of $1 per Period for *n* Periods Discounted at *i*% Interest per Period

Periods	11%	12%	13%	14%	15%	16%	17%	18%	19%	20%
1	0.9009	0.8929	0.8850	0.8772	0.8696	0.8621	0.8547	0.8475	0.8403	0.8333
2	1.7125	1.6901	1.6681	1.6467	1.6257	1.6052	1.5852	1.5656	1.5465	1.5278
3	2.4437	2.4018	2.3612	2.3216	2.2832	2.2459	2.2096	2.1743	2.1399	2.1065
4	3.1024	3.0373	2.9745	2.9137	2.8550	2.7982	2.7432	2.6901	2.6386	2.5887
5	3.6959	3.6048	3.5172	3.4331	3.3522	3.2743	3.1993	3.1272	3.0576	2.9906
6	4.2305	4.1114	3.9975	3.8887	3.7845	3.6847	3.5892	3.4976	3.4098	3.3255
7	4.7122	4.5638	4.4226	4.2883	4.1604	4.0386	3.9224	3.8115	3.7057	3.6046
8	5.1461	4.9676	4.7988	4.6389	4.4873	4.3436	4.2072	4.0776	3.9544	3.8372
9	5.5370	5.3282	5.1317	4.9464	4.7716	4.6065	4.4506	4.3030	4.1633	4.0310
10	5.8892	5.6502	5.4262	5.2161	5.0188	4.8332	4.6586	4.4941	4.3389	4.1925
11	6.2065	5.9377	5.6869	5.4527	5.2337	5.0286	4.8364	4.6560	4.4865	4.3271
12	6.4924	6.1944	5.9176	5.6603	5.4206	5.1971	4.9884	4.7932	4.6105	4.4392
13	6.7499	6.4235	6.1218	5.8424	5.5831	5.3423	5.1183	4.9095	4.7147	4.5327
14	6.9819	6.6282	6.3025	6.0021	5.7245	5.4675	5.2293	5.0081	4.8023	4.6106
15	7.1909	6.8109	6.4624	6.1422	5.8474	5.5755	5.3242	5.0916	4.8759	4.6755
16	7.3792	6.9740	6.6039	6.2651	5.9542	5.6685	5.4053	5.1624	4.9377	4.7296
17	7.5488	7.1196	6.7291	6.3729	6.0472	5.7487	5.4746	5.2223	4.9897	4.7746
18	7.7016	7.2497	6.8399	6.4674	6.1280	5.8178	5.5339	5.2732	5.0333	4.8122
19	7.8393	7.3658	6.9380	6.5504	6.1982	5.8775	5.5845	5.3162	5.0700	4.8435
20	7.9633	7.4694	7.0248	6.6231	6.2593	5.9288	5.6278	5.3527	5.1009	4.8696
25	8.4217	7.8431	7.3300	6.8729	6.4641	6.0971	5.7662	5.4669	5.1951	4.9476
30	8.6938	8.0552	7.4957	7.0027	6.5660	6.1772	5.8294	5.5168	5.2347	4.9789
40	8.9511	8.2438	7.6344	7.1050	6.6418	6.2335	5.8713	5.5482	5.2582	4.9966
50	9.0417	8.3045	7.6752	7.1327	6.6605	6.2463	5.8801	5.5541	5.2623	4.9995

The preceding timeline shows the first, second, third, fourth, and fifth $1,000 withdrawals discounted at a 12 percent interest rate for 1, 2, 3, 4, and 5 years respectively. This gives us the following present value of an annuity.

$$PVA = \frac{\$1,000}{(1 + 12\%)^1} + \frac{\$1,000}{(1 + 12\%)^2} + \frac{\$1,000}{(1 + 12\%)^3} + \frac{\$1,000}{(1 + 12\%)^4} + \frac{\$1,000}{(1 + 12\%)^5}$$

$$= \$892.86 + 797.19 + 711.78 + 635.52 + 567.43 = \$3,604.78$$

The preceding equation summing the present value of five lump sum payments to obtain the present value of an annuity can be simplified to the following equation.

$$PVA = \$1,000 \times \left[\frac{1 - \dfrac{1}{(1 + 12\%)^5}}{12\%} \right] = \$3,604.78$$

Thus, we have solved the present value of an annuity with the second method. We have worked through the mathematics of the present value of an annuity equation. This equation can be expressed more generally as

$$PVA = PMT \times \left[\frac{1 - \dfrac{1}{(1 + i)^n}}{i} \right]$$

We can also solve the problem using a business calculator. Enter the three variables we know:

$$PMT = \$1,000 \quad n = 5 \quad i = 12\% \quad \text{then compute } PV = \$3,604.78$$

We can also solve the problem using Exhibit 7-4, which provides a factor that we multiply by the known annuity payment to solve for the present value. Because we are solving for the present value of an annuity, the factor in this case is called a *present value interest factor for an annuity (PVIFA)*.

The $PVIFA_{i,n}$ is equal to

$$\left[\frac{1 - \dfrac{1}{(1 + i)^n}}{i} \right], \text{ so the equation}$$

$$PVA = PMT \times \left[\frac{1 - \dfrac{1}{(1 + i)^n}}{i} \right] \text{ can also be written as } PVA = PMT \times (PVIFA_{i,n})$$

To solve the problem using Exhibit 7-4, we can write the equation as

$$PVA = PMT \times (PVIFA_{12\%,5})$$

where

$$(PVIFA_{12\%,5}) = 3.6048$$

from Exhibit 7-4. Thus the answer is

$$PVA = \$1,000 \times 3.6048 = \$3,604.80$$

Again, notice the answer obtained from the financial mathematics tables is slightly different due to rounding.

We now consider annuities due in the context of the present value of an annuity. Remember that an annuity due occurs when the annuity payments are made at the beginning of each year. The example we just worked through is an ordinary annuity. When dealing with the present value of an annuity, it is generally easy to properly identify an annuity as an ordinary annuity or an annuity due. We naturally tend to look at when the first payment is paid. This works fine for present value of annuities. To properly classify the present value of an annuity as an ordinary annuity or an annuity due, we need to consider whether the first payment is at the beginning of the period or the end of the period. Consider the timeline for the preceding example.

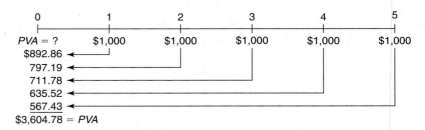

This is an ordinary annuity because the first payment is at the end of the first year. To change the example to the present value of an annuity due, we need to solve for the present value on the same date as the first payment. The timeline is as follows.

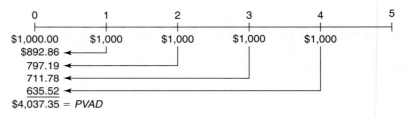

We can see in the preceding timeline that the first payment comes at the beginning of the first year. We can also see that the present value of the annuity due and the first payment coincide on the same date. In this present value of an annuity due, each payment is discounted one less period of time than in the otherwise equivalent ordinary annuity. If each payment is discounted for one less period at a 12 percent interest rate, then the entire present value of the annuity due will be 12 percent higher. Thus, we can solve this problem using the following equation.

$$PVAD = \$1,000 \times \left[\frac{1 - \dfrac{1}{(1 + 12\%)^5}}{12\%} \right] \times (1.12)$$

$$= \$3,604.78 \times (1.12) = \$4,037.35$$

We can express the equation for the present value of an annuity due more generally as

$$PVAD = PMT \times \left[\frac{1 - \dfrac{1}{(1 + i)^n}}{i} \right] \times (1 + i)$$

Thus, the present value of an annuity due is always greater than an otherwise equivalent ordinary annuity by the amount of the interest for one period.

payment. This is year 14. Then we discount the lump sum of $82,803.17 back 14 years to arrive at the present value of $28,191.25 today. The computation is as follows.

$$PV = \$25,000 \times \left[\frac{1 - \dfrac{1}{(1 + 8\%)^4}}{8\%} \right] \times \frac{1}{(1 + 8\%)^{14}}$$

$$= \$82,803.17 \times \frac{1}{(1 + 8\%)^{14}} = \$28,191.25$$

We can now answer the question of the present value of a deferred annuity in several different ways, which should offer more insight into solving for the present value of a deferred annuity and better explain ordinary annuities and annuities due. First, solve the problem by computing the present value of an annuity due and then discounting this lump sum back 15 years to arrive at a present value today.

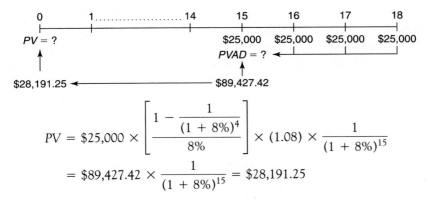

$$PV = \$25,000 \times \left[\frac{1 - \dfrac{1}{(1 + 8\%)^4}}{8\%} \right] \times (1.08) \times \frac{1}{(1 + 8\%)^{15}}$$

$$= \$89,427.42 \times \frac{1}{(1 + 8\%)^{15}} = \$28,191.25$$

We can also solve the problem by computing the future value of an ordinary annuity and then discounting this lump sum back 18 years to arrive at a present value today.

```
  0      1.................... 14      15       16       17       18
  ├──────┼──────────────────────┼──────┼────────┼────────┼────────┤
PV = ?                               $25,000  $25,000  $25,000  $25,000
                                       └────────┴────────┴────────→ FVA = ?
                                                                      ↑
$28,191.25 ◄─────────────────────────────────────────── $112,652.80
```

$$PV = \$25,000 \times \left[\frac{(1 + 8\%)^4 - 1}{8\%} \right] \times \frac{1}{(1 + 8\%)^{18}}$$

$$= \$112,652.80 \times \frac{1}{(1 + 8\%)^{18}} = \$28,191.25$$

Finally, we will solve the problem by computing the future value of an annuity due and then discounting this lump sum back 19 years to arrive at a present value today.

```
  0      1.................... 15      16       17       18       19
  ├──────┼──────────────────────┼──────┼────────┼────────┼────────┤
PV = ?                        $25,000  $25,000  $25,000  $25,000
                                 └────────┴────────┴────────┴──────→ FVAD = ?
                                                                       ↑
$28,191.25 ◄──────────────────────────────────────────── $121,665.02
```

$$PV = \$25{,}000 \times \left[\frac{(1 + 8\%)^4 - 1}{8\%}\right] \times \frac{(1.08) \times 1}{(1 + 8\%)^9}$$

$$= \$121{,}665.02 \times \frac{1}{(1 + 8\%)^9} = \$28{,}191.25$$

There is always more than one way to solve a time value of money problem. Understanding the preceding four methods for solving the present value of a deferred annuity leads to a much firmer grasp of the nature of annuities and how to work with them in time value of money problems.

7.8 Present Value of a Series of Non-constant Cash Flows

Now it is time to investigate how to value a complex stream of cash flows. Obviously not all cash flow streams meet the definition of an annuity. In this section, we show you how to value a stream of cash flows that are not constant.

We start with an example. Say you are considering new kitchen equipment for your restaurant that is expected to save you $1,000 the first year, $500 a year for years 2 through 5, and $750 in the sixth year. If you believe 10 percent is a fair discount rate, what is the present value of this non-constant stream of cash flow savings? We start by visualizing the problem on a timeline.

0	1	2	3	4	5	6
PV = ?	$1,000	$500	$500	$500	$500	$750

Solving this problem using the skills we have learned in this chapter, we first break the problem into separate parts.

Step 1—Find the present value of the $1,000 lump sum to be received one year from now.

0	1
PV = ?	$1,000

$$PV_0 = \frac{\$1{,}000}{(1 + 10\%)^1} = \$909.09$$

Step 2—Find the present value of the four-payment, $500-a-year deferred annuity.

0	1	2	3	4	5
PV = ?		$500	$500	$500	$500

$$PVA = \$500 \times \left[\frac{1 - \dfrac{1}{(1 + 10\%)^4}}{10\%}\right] \times \frac{1}{(1 + 10\%)^1} = \$1{,}440.85$$

Step 3—Find the present value of the $750 lump sum to be received six years from now.

$$PV_0 = \frac{\$750}{(1 + 10\%)^6} = \$423.36$$

Step 4—Next, because all cash flows are now restated in present value terms, we can add these present values together.

$$Total\ PV_0 = \$909.09 + 1{,}440.85 + 423.36 = \$2{,}773.30$$

7.9 Compounding Periods Other Than Annual

Now we can relax the assumption we have been using regarding the length of the compounding period. Remember, to this point we have assumed annual compounding and annual payments. However, many real-world applications use compounding and payments that are not annual.

Say you have $100 to invest for a year and have narrowed your choices to two banks. Saint John Bank pays 10 percent annually, compounded annually, and Yellowknife Bank pays 10 percent annually, compounded semiannually (every six months). Is there really a difference between these two banks if you deposit your money for one year? The timelines show what will happen and the difference between the two.

0	1
$100 ——————→ $110	

0	6 months	1
$100 ——→ $105 ——→ $110.25		

On the first timeline, $100 earns 10 percent interest for one year:

$$FV_1 = \$100 \times (1.10) = \$110$$

On the second timeline, $100 first earns 5 percent (half of 10 percent) for six months:

$$FV_{0.5} = \$100 \times (1.05) = \$105$$

And then $105 earns another 5 percent for the second six months:

$$FV_1 = \$105 \times (1.05) = \$110.25$$

In the second six months, 5 percent interest was earned not only on the original $100 invested but also on the $5 interest earned in the first six months. The interest earned on interest in the second six months has contributed an extra $0.25 to the future value. The $110.25 answer could have been computed in one equation. The general equation for computing the future value when compounding is not annual is as follows.

$$FV_n = PV \times \left(1 + \frac{i_{nom}}{m}\right)^{m \times n}$$

where i_{nom} is the **nominal annual interest rate** (an interest rate that does not factor in inflationary pressure or make any adjustments for the actual purchasing power of the dollar), m is the number of compounding periods in one year, and n is the number of years. Applying this equation to this example, we obtain

$$FV_1 = \$100 \times \left(1 + \frac{10\%}{2} \right)^{2 \times 1} = \$100 \times (1.05)^2 = \$110.25$$

Practise with an example you may find useful in your personal financial life. Say you are interested in a new car and venture down to your local car dealership to consider what it has to offer. Salespeople often quickly move the negotiation away from the total price you will pay to discuss the monthly payment that will "put you behind the wheel." They might be trying to take the intimidation out of buying the car, and they also might be trying to enhance the total price they can charge by masking the price through small monthly payments.

A good tactic is to negotiate price first before you discuss financing. So, when you go to buy a car, bring your financial calculator along. Once you have settled on a price, use the financial calculator to be sure you obtain the best financing deal. We work through some numbers to illustrate.

You have found a car with a value of $22,800. You have checked with your local bank and know you can obtain a five-year, 60-payment car loan at a 9 percent annual rate. You proceed to the dealership and are offered your dream car for less than $500 a month (by the dealership, not the bank). Actually the offer is for $498 a month for five years. To make the deal even more attractive, the salesperson says you can drive the car off the lot for no money down and the first payment is not due for one month. What do you think?

We now analyze this deal. We can calculate the present value of this 60-month, ordinary annuity of $498 per month to obtain the implied price. Because we can obtain a car loan at a 9 percent annual rate, this should be our discount rate. Remember, the annuity payments are monthly. The interest rate and number of payments must be consistent with a monthly payment. The interest rate will be 0.75 percent, or 0.0075 per month (9% divided by 12), and the number of payments will be 60 monthly payments in five years. With this information, we can obtain the present value of our payments and thus the price we are really paying for the car.

$$PVA_0 = \$498 \times \left[\frac{1 - \dfrac{1}{(1 + 0.75\%)^{60}}}{0.75\%} \right] = \$23{,}990.34$$

Surprised? Do not be. If the car should be priced at $22,800 or less, then the salesperson is trying to hide the higher price behind the monthly payments. If you bought the car for $22,800 and financed the purchase through the bank at 9 percent, then each of your 60 monthly payments would be as follows.

$$\$22{,}800 = PMT \times \left[\frac{1 - \dfrac{1}{(1 + 0.75\%)^{60}}}{0.75\%} \right] \qquad PMT = \$473.29$$

Learn time value of money concepts, and this is one area where you can save some money.

7.10 Effective Annual Rates

When compounding periods are not annual, the actual annual interest rate paid or received is referred to as the **effective annual rate**. Go back and consider the first example in the previous section. Remember, if you deposit $100.00 in an account earning 10 percent annually, compounded annually, then you will have a future value of $110.00 after one year. However, when the compounding is changed to 10 percent annually, compounded semiannually, then you will have a slightly greater future value of $110.25 after one year. We already know this greater future value is due to earning interest on interest during the year. So instead of earning 10 percent interest over one year, when the compounding is semiannual, 10.25 percent interest is earned over one year ($10.25/$100.00 = 10.25%). In other words, 10 percent annual, compounded semiannually, provides an effective annual interest rate of 10.25 percent. A general equation for calculating an effective rate is

$$\text{Effective annual rate} = \left(1 + \frac{i_{nom}}{m}\right)^m - 1$$

where i_{nom} is the nominal annual rate, and m is the number of compounding periods in one year. Applying the equation to this example we obtain

$$\text{Effective annual rate} = \left(1 + \frac{10\%}{2}\right)^2 - 1 = (1 + 5\%)^2 - 1$$
$$= (1.05)^2 - 1 = 0.1025 = 10.25\%$$

Appendix 2 shows an alternate way to compute effective annual rates using a business calculator.

When comparing interest rates that are compounded differently, convert the interest rates to effective annual rates and compare to determine which rate is effectively the lowest or highest.

7.11 Amortized Loans

Amortized loans are paid off in equal payments over a set period of time. In other words, an amortized loan is just an ordinary annuity in which the original amount borrowed is the present value of the future contracted payments. The terms of amortized loans are defined as follows.

PV = loan amount
PMT = contracted payment per period
n = number of payments
i = contracted interest rate
$FV = 0$

The future value is zero, because you pay off the entire loan amount with the contracted payments over the life of the loan.

An example is a home mortgage with the following contract terms: borrowing $120,000 for 30 years with a contract interest rate of 9 percent annually ($\frac{9\%}{12} = 0.75\%$ monthly), and payments due monthly with the first payment at the end of the first month. What is the monthly payment?

$$\$120{,}000 = PMT \times \left[\frac{1 - \dfrac{1}{(1 + 0.75\%)^{360}}}{0.75\%} \right] \qquad PMT = \$965.55$$

Notice that if you work out annual payments, they are more than 12 times the monthly payment.

$$\$120{,}000 = PMT \times \left[\frac{1 - \dfrac{1}{(1 + 9\%)^{30}}}{9\%} \right] \qquad PMT = \$11{,}680.36$$

Twelve times the monthly payment: $12 \times \$965.55 = \$11{,}586.60$. The actual monthly payment will be $93.76 less on an annual basis than paying once a year. Why is this? Earlier we showed that compounding interest more frequently in the course of a year equates to a higher future value due to interest being earned on interest. The opposite holds true for discounting. More frequent compounding periods reduce the total interest paid as the loan balance is paid down more frequently, and thus less interest is owed.

An **amortization table** is shown in Exhibit 7-5. When you finance a home with a mortgage, an amortization table for your loan is often provided. It shows the amount of each payment, how much of each payment is allocated to interest and how much is allocated to repayment of the principal balance, and your remaining principal balance owed at the end of each month assuming you make your payments on time.

Look at the first month of the amortization table. You see that at the beginning you owe $120,000. At the end of the first month, you will make your first payment in the amount of $965.55. First, calculate how much of this payment is allocated to interest. Remember, to this point you owe interest for one month at the rate of 9 percent annually, or 0.75 percent monthly on $120,000. Take the beginning balance of $120,000 times the monthly interest rate of 0.75 percent to obtain $900.00 owed in interest at the end of the

Exhibit 7-5 Amortization Table

Month	Payment	Interest	Principal	Balance
0				$120,000.00
1	$ 965.55	$900.00	$ 65.55	119,934.45
2	965.55	899.51	66.04	119,868.41
3	965.55	899.01	66.53	119,801.88
4	965.55	898.51	67.03	119,734.85
357	965.55	28.43	937.12	2,853.73
358	965.55	21.40	944.14	1,909.58
359	965.55	14.32	951.23	958.36
360	965.55	7.19	958.36	0.00

first month. The remainder of your first month's payment is allocated to repayment of the principal balance ($965.55 − 900.00 = $65.55).

That is correct! You are making a payment of $965.55, and only $65.55 is allocated to repayment of the principal balance from the first payment. After paying $965.55, you owe $65.55 less. You still owe $119,934.45 at the end after making your first payment. The good news is that each subsequent month less of your payment is allocated to paying interest, and more of your payment is allocated to the repayment of the principal balance.

To be sure you understand the logic of an amortization table, consider what happens with the second monthly payment. During the second month, interest is accruing at the 0.75 percent monthly rate on the end of the first month's balance of $119,934.45. So interest from the second monthly payment is $119,934.45 × 0.75% = $899.51. The remainder of the second monthly payment is allocated to repayment of the principal balance ($965.55 − 899.51 = $66.04). Thus, the principal balance owed after the second monthly payment is $119,868.41. This is $66.04 less than the balance at the end of the first month ($119,934.45 − 66.04 = $119,868.41).

Notice what happens by the last payment. Only $7.19 of the $965.55 payment is allocated to interest, and the remaining $958.36 is allocated to principal to finish off the loan. So at the beginning of a typical 30-year monthly mortgage loan, most of each monthly payment is allocated to interest. But with each payment made the principal balance continues to decline, and thus the interest allocation from each payment decreases and the repayment of principal allocation increases. By the time you reach the last year of the loan, most of each payment is allocated to principal with just a small portion allocated to interest.

Now, consider how the preceding mortgage example would change if you still borrow $120,000 at 9 percent but repay the loan with monthly payments over 15 years instead of 30 years.

$$\$120,000 = PMT \times \left[\frac{1 - \dfrac{1}{(1 + 0.75)^{180}}}{0.75\%} \right] \qquad PMT = \$1,217.12$$

It may surprise you to see that the monthly payment does not double in size but increases only by a little more than $250. Actually, 15-year mortgages usually have a slightly lower interest rate than 30-year mortgages. This would cause the 15-year mortgage payment to be slightly less than calculated here. This does not mean the 15-year mortgage is necessarily the better deal. The preferred mortgage maturity depends on your financial situation, your willingness to accept risk, and available investment opportunities. Now you have the ability to compare the myriad mortgage options.

7.12 SUMMARY

This chapter:

- Explained the future value and present value computations of a single lump sum
- Introduced annuities and explained the difference between an ordinary annuity and an annuity due
- Explained the future value and present value computations of an annuity
- Explained the present value computations for a perpetuity, a deferred annuity, and a series of non-constant cash flows
- Explained annual compounding and compounding other than annual
- Introduced effective annual rates
- Introduced amortization tables

Key Terms

Amortization table	Future value
Annuity	Interest rates
Annuity due	Nominal annual interest rate
Compound interest	Ordinary annuity
Compounding	Perpetuity
Deferred annuity	Present value
Discounting	Time value of money
Effective annual rate	

Discussion Questions

1. You are investing money at a 7 percent nominal annual interest rate. Would you prefer the rate be compounded more frequently or less frequently?
2. You are borrowing money at a 9 percent nominal annual interest rate. Would you prefer the rate be compounded more frequently or less frequently?
3. What happens to the future value of a single cash amount as the interest rate increases?
4. What happens to the future value of an annuity as the interest rate increases?
5. What happens to the present value of a single cash amount as the interest rate increases?
6. What happens to the present value of an annuity as the interest rate increases?
7. What are some examples of ordinary annuities?
8. What are some examples of annuities due?
9. Why are effective annual rates generally greater than equivalent nominal annual rates?
10. What does a loan amortization table show?

Problems

Problems designated with EXCEL can be solved using Excel spreadsheets accessible at www.pearsoned.ca/chatfield.

1. What is the future value of $1,000 invested for five years at the following interest rates?
   a. 5%
   b. 8%
   c. 10%

2. What is the future value of $1,000 invested at a 7 percent rate for the following length of time?
   a. 2 years
   b. 5 years
   c. 10 years

3. What is the present value of $10,000 to be received in four years at the following interest rates?
   a. 4%
   b. 7%
   c. 12%

4. Using an 8 percent interest rate, what is the present value of $10,000 to be received in the following number of years?
   a. 3 years
   b. 6 years
   c. 12 years

5. A bond issued by Fried's Restaurants pays no interest but will return $1,000 in 15 years. If you buy the bond for $326.39 today, what will be your interest rate of return on the investment?

6. If you invest $4,000 in a GIC today, a bank promises the GIC will be worth $5,000 in five years. What is your interest rate return on this investment?

7. Brewer Resorts is considering the purchase of a piece of real estate for the future site of a new project. The real estate costs $5 million. A bank has offered to finance the purchase at a 7 percent interest rate with a 10 percent down payment. The loan would be repaid with 15 equal, annual, end-of-year payments. If Brewer borrows the $4.5 million (90 percent of $5 million), what is the amount of each payment?

8. Grace turned 25 years old today and would like to retire by the time of her 60th birthday. In addition to the Canada Pension Plan and her company pension plan, she plans to invest $3,000 annually into an investment that promises to return 9 percent annually. If her first $3,000 payment is on her 26th birthday and her last $3,000 payment is on her 60th birthday, what will be the value of this investment on her 60th birthday?

9. Andy wants to take out a loan to purchase a new home. He is willing to pay up to $10,000 at the end of each of the next 30 years to repay the loan. If the loan interest rate is 6 percent, what is the most he can borrow?

10. An investment costs $20,000 today and will return $3,000 at the end of each of the next 10 years. What is the interest rate of return on this investment?

11. Carl would like to save $100,000 by his 40th birthday to pay for a special midlife crisis vacation. He plans to achieve this by investing equal annual amounts each year beginning on his 24th birthday and ending with a payment on his 40th birthday. If the investment pays an 11 percent interest rate, what is the size of each annual payment Carl needs to invest?

12. An investment of $1,000 annually at the end of each year for the next 15 years will be worth $30,000 at the end of 15 years. What is the interest rate of return on this investment?

EXCEL 13. A $20,000 loan requires equal annual end-of-year payments for four years. The interest rate is 10 percent.

    a. What is the amount of each loan payment?

    b. Construct a loan amortization table to include the amount of interest and principal paid each year as well as the remaining balance at the end of each year.

EXCEL 14. A $100,000 loan requires equal annual end-of-year payments of $38,803.35 for three years.

    a. What is the annual interest rate?

    b. Construct a loan amortization table to include the amount of interest and principal paid each year as well as the remaining balance at the end of each year.

15. An investment promises to return $2,000 at the end of each of the next 10 years and then $5,000 at the end of each of the next five years (years 11 through 15). What is the value of this investment today at a 7 percent interest rate?

16. An investment promises to return $8,000 at the end of each of the next eight years and then $3,000 at the end of each of the remaining seven years (years 9 through 15). What is the value of this investment today at a 9 percent interest rate?

17. You plan to invest $10,000 into a bank GIC for three years. The GIC pays a 12 percent nominal rate. What is the value of your investment in three years if the 12 percent rate is compounded at the following periods?

    a. annually

    b. semiannually (every six months)

    c. quarterly (every three months)

    d. monthly

18. You plan to invest $5,000 into a bank GIC for five years. The GIC pays a 6 percent nominal annual rate. What is the value of your investment in five years if the 6 percent rate is compounded at the following periods?

    a. annually

    b. semiannually (every six months)

    c. quarterly (every three months)

    d. monthly

19. An investment promises to return $1,000 annually with the first $1,000 to be received at the end of 10 years and the last $1,000 to be received at the end of 25 years. What is the value of this investment today at a 7 percent rate of return?

20. An investment promises to return $1,500 annually with the first $1,500 to be received at the end of 5 years and the last $1,500 to be received at the end of 12 years. What is the value of this investment today at a 5 percent rate of return?

21. Andy just won a lottery. The prize is 20 annual payments of $100,000 each with the first payment to be today. What is the value of this prize (the 20 payments of $100,000 each) today at an 8 percent interest rate?

22. You are celebrating your 25th birthday today. You plan to invest $1,000 annually, with the first $1,000 invested today and the last invested on your 59th birthday.

   a. What is the value of this investment on your 60th birthday if all invested funds earn 6 percent annually?

   b. What interest rate do you need to earn for the investment to be worth $150,000 on your 60th birthday?

23. You are celebrating your 25th birthday today. You plan to invest $2,000 annually, with the first $2,000 invested on your 26th birthday and the last invested on your 60th birthday.

   a. What is the value of this investment on your 61st birthday if all invested funds earn 6 percent annually?

   b. What interest rate do you need to earn for the investment to be worth $300,000 on your 61st birthday?

24: Mike is planning to provide for his son's future postsecondary education. He expects to need $40,000 in 15 years, $42,000 in 16 years, $45,000 in 17 years, and $50,000 in 18 years for this purpose. If he can earn 10 percent annually, what single amount does he need to invest today to provide for his son's education?

25. Mike is planning to provide for his son's future postsecondary education. He expects to need $40,000 in 15 years, $42,000 in 16 years, $45,000 in 17 years, and $50,000 in 18 years for this purpose. He plans to provide for this by investing equal annual end-of-year payments for the next 15 years. If he can earn 10 percent annually, what is the required amount of each payment?

26. Ted and Carol are planning to provide for their two daughters' future postsecondary education. The older daughter is expected to need $8,000 in 8 years, $9,000 in 9 years, $10,000 in 10 years, and $11,000 in 11 years. The younger daughter is expected to need $14,000 in 14 years, $15,000 in 15 years, $16,000 in 16 years, and $17,000 in 17 years. If Ted and Carol can earn 8 percent annually, what single amount do they need to invest today to provide for their daughters' future education?

27. Ted and Carol are planning to provide for their two daughters' future postsecondary education. The older daughter is expected to need $8,000 in 8 years, $9,000 in 9 years, $10,000 in 10 years, and $11,000 in 11 years. The younger daughter is expected to need $14,000 in 14 years, $15,000 in 15 years, $16,000 in 16 years, and $17,000 in 17 years. Ted and Carol plan to provide for this by investing equal annual end-of-year payments for the next 8 years. If they can earn 8 percent annually, what is the required amount of each payment?

28. Larry plans to retire in his 60s. Since both his company pension plan and his RRSP are maximized, he has started a new savings plan. All funds invested in this plan will earn 12 percent annually. From this investment plan he hopes to make 20 annual withdrawals of $100,000, with the first withdrawal on his 66th birthday and the last on his 85th birthday.

   a. What single amount does Larry need to invest on his 30th birthday to provide for the 20 withdrawals of $100,000 each?

   b. What equal annual payment does Larry need to invest in order to provide for the 20 withdrawals? The first payment will be on his 31st birthday, and the last payment will be on his 65th birthday.

29. Larry plans to retire in his 60s. Since both his company pension plan and his RRSP are maximized, he has started a new savings plan. All funds invested in this RRSP will earn 12 percent annually. From this investment plan he hopes to withdraw $500,000 on his

66th birthday and also make 20 annual withdrawals of $100,000, with the first withdrawal on his 66th birthday and the last on his 85th birthday.

a. What single amount does Larry need to invest on his 30th birthday to provide for these withdrawals?

b. What equal annual payment does Larry need to invest to provide for these withdrawals? The first payment will be on his 31st birthday, and the last payment will be on his 65th birthday.

30. Larry plans to retire in his 60s. Since both his company pension plan and his RRSP are maximized, he has started a new savings investment plan. All funds invested in this plan will earn 12 percent annually. Currently (assume today is Larry's 30th birthday), Larry has $15,000 invested in this plan. From this investment plan he hopes to withdraw $500,000 on his 66th birthday and also make 20 annual withdrawals of $100,000, with the first withdrawal on his 66th birthday and the last on his 85th birthday.

a. To provide for these withdrawals, what single amount does Larry need to invest on his 30th birthday in addition to the $15,000 already there?

b. To provide for these withdrawals, what equal annual payment does Larry need to invest in addition to the $15,000 already there? The first payment will be on his 31st birthday, and the last payment will be on his 65th birthday.

Chapter 8

Fixed-Income Securities: Bonds and Preferred Stock

Chapter Objectives

This chapter covers the following topics:

1   Why bonds and preferred stock are generally classified as fixed-income securities

2   Basic bond terminology

3   Basic bond features as detailed in a bond indenture

4   Bond ratings

5   How to compute the value and yield to maturity on a bond

6   Basic preferred stock terminology and basic preferred stock features

7   How to compute the value and yield to maturity on a preferred stock

8.1 Introduction

Corporations issue securities as a means of raising money. Investors buy securities with the hope that they will receive more money in the future than they pay for the securities today. Securities are generally classified as bonds, preferred stock, or common stock. We consider bonds and preferred stock together in this chapter because they are both considered fixed-income securities. In other words, if you invest in bonds or preferred stock, the cash you hope to receive in the future is fixed and is not expected to vary. Investor return on bonds and preferred stock generally does not depend on the financial success of the corporation. Of course, if a corporation is a failure and has cash flow difficulties, this is likely to reduce your return on bonds and preferred stock. But if a bond promises to pay interest of $80 annually or preferred stock promises to pay a dividend of $5 per share annually, the success of the corporation is not relevant. The most the bond will pay is $80 annually, and the most the preferred stock will pay is $5 per share annually. Thus, the upside return on bonds and preferred stock is limited to the fixed return contractually agreed on, and the return on the downside, in times of financial difficulty, could be as little as zero. Common stock is quite different from bonds and preferred stock in that the upside and downside returns very much depend on the corporation's financial success. Common stock is discussed in detail in Chapter 9.

Bonds and preferred stock are both considered fixed-income securities but differ from each other in several ways. The bond interest owed to an investor is a legally binding contractual obligation, whereas preferred dividends owed to an investor are not. As a result,

Exhibit 8-1 Bonds in the Hospitality and Tourism Industry

Since 1990, firms in the hospitality and tourism* industry have issued more than 1,800 debt securities. These debt issues raised more than $370 billion to be invested in the hospitality and tourism industry by these firms. Numerous well-known firms have issued debt securities over this period of time, including

- CHIP REIT, a Canadian hotel investment corporation
- BC Ferries, Canada's largest independent ferry service provider and one of the largest in the world
- Carnival Corporation
- Hilton Hotels Corporation
- Fairmont Hotels and Resorts
- Harrah's Entertainment Inc.
- Marriott International Incorporated
- Four Seasons Hotels and Resorts

Some examples of bonds issued recently (since 2005) include 250 million by BC Ferries Corporation; 43 million by CHIP REIT; and 600 million by West Edmonton Mall, one of the largest entertainment venues in Canada and the world.

As you can see, debt securities provide a significant amount of capital for firms in the hospitality and tourism industry.

*The phrase *hospitality and tourism industry* is used as defined by John R. Walker in *Introduction to Hospitality Management,* 4th ed. (Prentice Hall, 2005).

the ramifications for failure to pay bond interest are more serious than for failure to pay preferred dividends. Also, bond interest is a tax-deductible cost to the paying corporation, whereas preferred dividends are paid out of after-tax income and thus have no tax-shelter value. Corporate bonds have a specific maturity; preferred stock is generally considered perpetual. In fact, these differences between corporate bonds and preferred stock show that preferred stock is a hybrid security. Preferred stock shares some of the characteristics of bonds and also shares some of the characteristics of common stock. The fixed-income characteristic shared by both bonds and preferred stock is why we consider these two securities in the same chapter, and it makes the valuation methodology for these two securities similar. The first part of this chapter focuses on bonds and the second part focuses on preferred stock. Exhibit 8-1 provides an example of some bonds within the hospitality and tourism industry.

8.2 Bond Terminology

When an investor buys a corporate bond, the investor is essentially lending money to the corporation. The investor is the creditor, and the corporation is the borrower. Bonds generally promise to pay back the principal at maturity, and interest every six months until maturity. The principal is usually called the **par value** or the **face value**. Par values are usually $1,000, and bond prices are quoted as a percentage of par value. Thus, a bond selling for $970 would be quoted at a price of "97" (97% of $1,000 is $970). The interest rate on a bond is usually called the **coupon rate**, and the interest payment is called the **coupon payment**. The coupon rate is an annual rate multiplied by the par value to obtain the annual coupon payment. Most coupon payments are paid every six months. Divide the annual coupon payment by two to obtain the actual six-month coupon payment. Thus, a bond with a 9 percent coupon rate will pay $90 annually (9% times the $1,000 par value), but the actual payments will be $45 every six months.

The term **bond** generally denotes any type of long-term debt security. If the bond is collateralized by specific physical assets, such as equipment or real estate, it is called a **mortgage bond**. If a bond is not secured by collateral, it is called a **debenture**. Both mortgage bonds and debentures are backed by the cash flow of the issuing company, but mortgage bonds are safer because specific physical assets also back them.

Bonds also differ by seniority. **Seniority** refers to the order in which a corporation would pay off its obligations in case of financial difficulty. A senior obligation is paid before an obligation lacking seniority. Seniority among a corporation's bonds is often denoted by the terms *senior, junior, unsubordinated,* and *subordinated*. A senior debenture is paid before a junior debenture, and an unsubordinated debenture before a subordinated debenture. A senior, unsubordinated debenture would have the highest seniority ranking and be paid first, whereas a junior, subordinated debenture would have the lowest seniority ranking.

8.3 Bond Features

An investor in a corporate bond is essentially acting as a lender to the corporate bond issuer—the investor and issuing corporation have essentially entered into a credit agreement that is covered by a credit contract, called an **indenture**. The bond indenture is usually an extensive contract and often can be hundreds of pages long. It describes the characteristics of the bond and also includes a number of restrictions on the issuing corporation. These are called **restrictive covenants** and often include dividend payment limits, additional debt limitations, and restrictions on firm activities that might increase risk to the bond investors.

Bond characteristics are specifically explained by the indenture. Details include the nature of the interest rate and maturity. The interest rate on corporate bonds is usually fixed over the life of the bond, but sometimes bonds have an adjustable or floating interest rate. In this case, the rate adjusts to a predetermined market interest rate.

The maturity on most corporate bonds is fixed, but some features can cause a bond to be paid off before maturity. One is the **call feature**. If a bond is callable, the corporation can repay the bond early if it so wishes. The repayment amount is usually the bond's par value. Call features often come with a call deferment. For instance, a 20-year-maturity, callable bond with a five-year call deferment cannot be called in the first five years of its life. Over the remaining 15 years, the corporation can pay it off early. Many callable bonds also have a call premium that requires the corporation to pay an extra premium to an investor, in addition to the par value, if the bond is called prior to maturity. Call premiums usually start out at one year's worth of interest and then decline with time. For example, suppose the preceding bond had a 7.5 percent coupon rate and initially a 7.5 percent call premium. If the bond is called immediately at the end of the five-year deferment, the corporation would pay the $1,000 par value plus $75 (7.5% times $1,000 par value) to the investor for every $1,000 denomination owned. If the bond is called later, the call premium will decline 0.5 percent (7.5% call premium divided by the remaining 15 years to maturity) for each year after five years. So if the bond is called after six years, the call premium will be 7.0 percent, or $70.

A corporation might call a bond prior to maturity for two basic reasons. The first is to save on interest expense if market interest rates decline. The coupon rates on corporate bonds are generally fixed over the life of the bond. If market interest rates have declined, the only way to save interest expense is to call a fixed-rate bond early and refund with a new, lower-interest-rate bond. A second reason is to escape the restrictive covenants included in the bond indenture. For example, a large restaurant chain may want to acquire a smaller chain of restaurants, but restrictive covenants in a bond indenture may prevent this. The large restaurant chain could call the bond early and release itself from compliance with the indenture's restrictive covenants.

Another feature that can cause a bond to be repaid prior to maturity is the **put feature**. This is somewhat opposite to the call feature. A put feature allows an investor to demand the corporation repay the bond prior to maturity. This provides a measure of protection to the investor. Should the investor want repayment prior to maturity and the bond's market value has declined, a put feature allows the investor to require repayment from the issuing corporation. Repayment is usually at par value. This protects the investor against an increase in the general level of interest rates and also against other events that would negatively affect the value of the particular bond.

A **sinking fund feature** may also cause early repayment of a bond. Without a sinking fund, a corporation would pay only bond interest each year and no principal. At maturity, the entire principal would then be due. This is similar to taking out a five-year car loan for $25,000 and paying only interest each month for 60 months, then having to pay $25,000 all at once at the end of five years. This is sometimes called a "crisis at maturity," due to the possible difficulty of repaying a large sum of money. A sinking fund eliminates the crisis at maturity by requiring the corporation to "sink" a certain sum of money into a fund for the partial early retirement of the bond. In the preceding example, suppose the 20-year bond had a total par value of $100 million. The sinking fund might require the corporation to redeem $6 million per year beginning at the end of year 5. After 15 years of early redemptions, only $10 million of bonds are left to retire at maturity ($100 million − 15 × $6 million). The redemption can usually be through open market purchases or through the use of a call feature. If the call feature is used, a lottery generally determines which bonds are called each year.

Bonds can have many other features in addition to those just discussed. For example, a bond can be linked to the corporation's common stock through a conversion feature or the issuance of warrants with a bond. Bonds can also have "poison-pill" features to discourage a takeover attempt. We have discussed some of the basic features affecting the return and redemption of corporate bonds and do not try to cover all possible bond features.

8.4 Bond Ratings

Several **bond rating** companies rate bonds for default risk. These include Canadian bond rating company Dominion Bond Rating Service, more commonly known as DBRS, as well as the U.S.–based bond raters Moody's Investors Service and Standard & Poor's. Another significant Canadian bond rating company was Canadian Bond Rating Services; however, it was acquired by Standard & Poor's Corporation in 2000.

With respect to the rating process, bonds that are rated high, for low default risk, inherently have lower interest expense. Conversely, those bonds that are rated low, for high default risk, pay higher interest rates. The bond ratings and definitions are given in Exhibit 8-2 for Moody's Investors Service and in Exhibit 8-3 for Standard & Poor's Corporation. Exhibit 8-4 illustrates bond ratings as provided by Dominion Bond Rating Service. Exhibit 8-5 provides some current ratings for a few hospitality firms.

Exhibit 8-2
Moody's Investors Service Bond Ratings

Aaa

The best quality bonds and preferred stock with the smallest amount of risk.

Aa

High-quality bonds and preferred stock. Their long-term risk is a little higher than Aaa-rated securities. Aa- and Aaa-rated bonds are generally known as high-grade bonds.

A

Upper-medium-grade bonds and preferred stock. Considered to have adequate safety but with possible problems in the future.

Baa

Medium-grade bonds and preferred stock. Currently considered to have adequate safety but with possible problems in the future. These securities have speculative characteristics.

Ba

Bonds and preferred stock with only moderate safety and having speculative characteristics. Their future is uncertain.

B

Bonds and preferred stock with only small safety and lacking desirable investment characteristics.

Caa

Bonds and preferred stock of poor standing. The level of safety may be dangerous.

Ca

Bonds and preferred stock that are highly speculative and may be in default.

C

Bonds and preferred stock in the lowest rating class with poor prospects.

Note: Moody's applies qualifiers "1," "2," and "3" in each rating classification from Aa through Caa. The qualifier "1" indicates the higher end of its rating category, the qualifier "2" indicates the midrange, and the qualifier "3" indicates the low range.

Exhibit 8-3
Standard & Poor's Corporation Bond Ratings

AAA

Securities with the highest rating and considered extremely strong.

AA

Securities just slightly riskier than those rated AAA and considered very strong.

A

Securities with moderately more risk than those rated AAA and AA but still considered strong securities.

BBB

Securities with adequate safety, but more susceptible to changing conditions than those securities rated more highly.

All securities rated lower than BBB are considered to have speculative characteristics.

BB

The strongest of the speculative securities but still with speculative elements.

B

These securities are more risky than those rated BB but currently are likely to pay their obligations.

CCC

These securities have current safety problems, and continued success is dependent on favourable conditions.

CC

These securities have large current safety problems.

C

These securities are currently making payments, but this is likely to change soon. Issuing firm may have already filed for bankruptcy.

D

Indicates a default has already occurred.

Note: Standard & Poor's applies qualifiers "1" and "2" in each rating classification from AA through CCC to show a security's position with a rating classification.

Exhibit 8-4
Dominion Bond Rating Service Bond Ratings

AAA
Highest credit quality

AA
Superior credit quality

A
Satisfactory credit quality

BBB
Adequate credit quality

BB
Speculative credit quality

B
Highly speculative credit quality

CCC
Very highly speculative credit quality

CC
Extremely speculative

C
Extremely speculative and in danger to default

D
In default on interest, principal, or both. High risk value of financial stability

Source: Dominion Bond Rating Service, www.dbrs.com/intnlweb/jsp/common/infoPage.faces

Exhibit 8-5 Standard & Poor's Rating as at December 30, 2007	
Hilton Hotels	AAA
Marriott Hotels	BBB
Royal Caribbean Cruises	BBB
MGM Mirage	BB
Disney Enterprises Inc.	A
McDonald's	A

Source: Standard & Poor's, www2.standardandpoors.com/portal/site/sp/en/ca/page.article/2,1,3,0,1204834067208.html

8.5 Valuing Corporate Bonds

Remember, corporate bonds pay interest semiannually. The annual interest amount is equal to the coupon rate times the par value, which is the principal amount repaid at maturity. Bond par values are usually $1,000, and we use this for the remainder of the chapter. To determine the value of a corporate bond, we simply find the present value of the future cash flows an investor expects to receive. Again, there are two separate cash flows to value: (1) the coupon payments, and (2) the principal amount or par value. Although coupon payments are usually paid semiannually, for introduction purposes we assume coupon payments are paid annually.

To illustrate how to value a corporate bond, we consider an example. Suppose Gretzky Resorts Incorporated is looking to issue a 15-year corporate bond. The bond contractually promises to pay a 10 percent coupon rate and pay a par value of $1,000 at maturity. Assume that a fair market rate of return on bonds of this risk class is 10 percent annually. Investors consider the market rate of interest as their required rate of return and use this value as the discount rate to value these bonds. What is the value of one Gretzky Resorts corporate bond?

First, we define our terms.

C = Coupon payment = Coupon rate × Par value = 10% × $1,000 = $100 annually

M = Maturity value = Par value = $1,000

n = The number of payments to maturity = 15

i_b = The investor's required rate of return on corporate bonds = 10%

V_b = The value of the corporate bond

The following timeline illustrates the cash flows on the Gretzky Resorts bond.

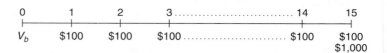

Notice there are two separate cash flows here. We want to find (1) the present value of an ordinary annuity (the $100 annually), and (2) the present value of a future lump sum (the $1,000 at maturity). Once we find the present value of each part in today's dollars, we can add these together. The sum of the two present values is the value of the corporate bond today.

$$V_b = PV \text{ of coupon payments annuity} + PV \text{ of lump sum maturity value}$$

Using our equations from Chapter 7, we can express this as follows.

$$V_b = C \times \left[\frac{1 - \dfrac{1}{(1 + i_b)^n}}{i_b} \right] + \frac{FV_n}{(1 + i_b)^n}$$

We use $1,000 for the maturity value (future value) in this generalized equation since the maturity value is usually $1,000 for corporate bonds. The equation for the above example is

$$V_b = \$100 \times \left[\frac{1 - \dfrac{1}{(1 + 10\%)^{15}}}{10\%} \right] + \frac{\$1,000}{(1 + 10\%)^{15}}$$

$$V_b = \$760.61 + 239.39 = \$1,000.00$$

Now think of the logic of this valuation. Our answer suggests it is fair to pay $1,000 for a contract that promises to pay us $100, or 10 percent per year, and give us our $1,000 back at maturity. Is this fair? Yes, if our required rate of return is 10 percent. We receive the 10 percent rate of return per year, and we get our investment back at the end of the contract. (See Appendix 3 for tips on using a business calculator to solve for the value of a corporate bond.)

Note in the preceding example that the value of the corporate bond equals the par value. This happens because the coupon rate equals the investor's required rate of return. Whenever the coupon rate equals the investor's required rate of return, the bond value and par value will be equal. Bond investors say these types of corporate bonds sell "at par." Many corporations try to issue bonds at par value, but not all do. In addition, market interest rates change through time, so even those bonds issued at par will change in value over time as market rates of interest change. Therefore, we explore the valuation of corporate bonds when the market rate of interest does not equal the coupon rate.

First, we consider how to value a corporate bond when the market rate of interest is less than the coupon rate. We will use the same example of the Gretzky Resorts corporate bond. Remember, the coupon rate is 10 percent, the maturity value is $1,000, and there are 15 years to maturity. Again, for simplicity, assume the coupon payments are annual. However, now assume the market rate of interest is 8 percent. What is the value of this corporate bond?

$$V_b = \$100 \times \left[\frac{1 - \dfrac{1}{(1 + 8\%)^{15}}}{8\%} \right] + \frac{\$1,000}{(1 + 8\%)^{15}}$$

$$V_b = \$855.95 + 315.24 = \$1,171.19$$

Does this make sense? Could the corporate bond sell for $1,171.19? Explore the logic: the bond is paying 10 percent interest per year, but you require only 8 percent. This is a good thing, right? Well, other investors will also see the advantageous coupon rate that is paid by this bond. Therefore, investors will bid the price up to $1,171.19, which is the price at which investors will get back exactly 8 percent if they hold the bond to maturity. Therefore, as in this case, when the market rate of interest is less than the contracted coupon rate, the value of the bond is greater than the par value. When the value of the bond is greater than the par value, we say the bond is selling at a premium. The premium in this example is the $171.19 over and above the $1,000 par value.

Now, alternatively, let's look at the case of how to value a corporate bond when the market rate of interest is greater than the coupon rate. We use the same example of the Gretzky Resorts corporate bond. Remember, the coupon rate is 10 percent, the coupon is paid annually, the maturity value is $1,000, and the bond matures in 15 years. If we assume the market rate of interest is 12 percent, what is the fair value of this corporate bond?

$$V_b = \$100 \times \left[\frac{1 - \frac{1}{(1 + 12\%)^{15}}}{12\%} \right] + \frac{\$1,000}{(1 + 12\%)^{15}}$$

$$V_b = \$681.09 + 182.70 = \$863.79$$

Does this make sense? Could the corporate bond sell for $863.79? Explore the logic: the bond is paying 10 percent interest per year, but you require 12 percent. This does not look good initially. Other investors will also see the disadvantageous coupon rate that is paid by this bond. Therefore, investors will bid the price down to $863.79, which is the price at which investors will get back exactly 12 percent if they hold the bond to maturity. Therefore, as in this case, when the market rate of interest is more than the contracted coupon rate, the value of the bond is less than the par value. When the value of the bond is less than the par value, we say the bond is selling at a discount. The discount in this example is the $136.21 under the $1,000 par value ($1,000 − $863.79).

The following are some rules about corporate bonds to keep in mind:

1. If i_b = coupon rate, then the bond sells for par value.
2. If i_b > coupon rate, then the bond sells for a discount (less than par value).
3. If i_b < coupon rate, then the bond sells for a premium (more than par value).
4. If i_b increases, then the bond value decreases (inverse relationship between i and PV).
5. If i_b decreases, then the bond value increases (inverse relationship between i and PV).

8.6 Computing Yield to Maturity on Corporate Bonds

We can also compute the investor's yield to maturity for a given bond price with our valuation equation. **Yield to maturity** is the investor's rate of return if the investor buys the bond and holds it to maturity. Let us use the same example. Remember, Gretzky Resorts' corporate bond has a 10 percent coupon rate, a $1,000 par value, and 15 years to maturity. Compute the yield to maturity for an investor buying this bond for $900. The following timeline illustrates the cash flows on this Gretzky Resorts bond:

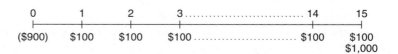

We can use the bond valuation equation to solve for the investor's *yield to maturity*.

$$V_b = \text{PV of coupon payments annuity} + \text{PV of lump sum maturity value}$$

$$V_b = C \times \left[\frac{1 - \dfrac{1}{(1 + i_b)^n}}{i_b} \right] + \frac{\$1,000}{(1 + i_b)^n}$$

In this case we are not solving for the bond's value. We know the bond can be purchased for $900, so we use this for the bond value and solve for the interest return.

$$\$900 = \$100 \times \left[\frac{1 - \dfrac{1}{(1 + i_b)^{15}}}{i_b} \right] + \frac{\$1,000}{(1 + i_b)^{15}}$$

$$i_b = 11.42\%$$

If the investor buys the bond for $900 and holds the bond until maturity, the rate of return is 11.42 percent. Solving for the interest rate in the preceding equation is more difficult than solving for the bond value. When solving for the bond value, the present value of the annuity (coupon payments) can be solved separately from the present value of the lump sum (maturity value), and then the two present values can be added together. But to solve for the interest rate that equates the two present values to the bond value of $900, you must solve the whole equation simultaneously. The easiest way to do this is with a business calculator. Appendix 3 shows that the easiest way to solve for the bond value is to solve the whole equation simultaneously on the business calculator. Similarly, Appendix 4 shows you how to solve for a bond's yield to maturity on a business calculator.

8.7 Bonds with Semiannual Coupon Payments

Most corporate bonds actually pay coupon payments semiannually, meaning every six months. We used an *annual* coupon payment to introduce the concept of bond valuation, but now we consider how things change when we allow the coupon payment to be paid semiannually. We once again use the Gretzky Resorts corporate bond with a 10 percent coupon rate, a $1,000 par value, and 15 years to maturity. The 10 percent coupon rate is expressed as an annual rate, but it is paid semiannually. What is the value of this bond to an investor requiring a 12 percent rate of return? The complete equation should look as follows.

$$V_b = \$50 \times \left[\frac{1 - \dfrac{1}{(1 + 6\%)^{30}}}{6\%} \right] + \frac{\$1,000}{(1 + 6\%)^{30}}$$

$$V_b = \$688.24 + 174.11 = \$862.35$$

Notice the coupon payment is $50, because the coupon is paid every six months. If the payment is a six-month payment, then i and n in the present value of an annuity equation must be consistent with the six-month payment. Thus, the interest rate must be a six-month rate (12%/2 = 6%), and the number of payments is 30 six-month payments in 15 years.

An implied assumption is that the 12 percent required rate of return is a nominal annual rate, compounded semiannually. This allows us to simply divide the 12 percent by 2 and use the resulting 6 percent as our six-month required rate of return. Because we are using a 12 percent nominal annual rate, compounded semiannually for the present value of the annuity, we must also use this for present value of the maturity value. So we have to use 6 percent for i and 30 for n in the entire equation. This simply implies the investor requires the same consistent rate of return for all bond cash flows, both the coupon payments and the maturity value. See Exhibit 8-6 for a snapshot look at some corporate bond quotations.

Exhibit 8-6 Corporate Bond Quotations

The following are typical quotations for bonds as listed on Yahoo Finance (http://reports.finance.yahoo.com) for Saturday, January 5, 2008.

(1) Issue	(2) Price	(3) Coupon (%)	(4) Maturity	(5) YTM (%)	(6) Current yield (%)	(7) Fitch ratings	(8) Callable
American Express Co	98.18	4.875	15-Jul-2013	5.229	4.965	A	No
Disney Walt CO	103.31	5.700	15-Jul-2011	4.788	5.517	A	No
Extended Stay America Inc	106.94	9.875	15-Jun-2011	7.803	9.234	Not rated	Yes
JetBlue AWYS CORP	101.50	3.75	15-Mar-2035	3.663	3.695	CCC	Yes
Hilton Hotels CORP	106.00	7.625	1-Dec-2012	6.300	7.193	BB	No

Notes: Column 1 provides the company name abbreviated or identified and the specific bond issue; one company may have several bond issues in circulation or outstanding at the same time. Column 2 shows the current market price of the bond. Column 3 is the coupon rate. The maturity date is found in Column 4. Column 5 is the yield-to-maturity (YTM) relative value; the YTM value calculation is based upon the anticipated rate of return on the bond while it is held until its maturity date. This calculation also takes into account the bond's current market price, par value, coupon rate, and time remaining to maturity date. Column 6 is the bond's current yield, calculated by dividing the bond's coupon payment by the closing price. The bond's current quality rating is identified in Column 7.

Look at the second bond identified in the table, Disney Walt CO. This bond has a current market price of $103.31. The coupon rate is 5.7 percent. Assuming a bond par value of $100, this translates into an annual coupon payment of $5.70 (5.7% × $100). Now, because the current market value of the bond is $103.31 with a coupon rate of 5.700, this provides us with a current yield of 5.517% ($5.70/$103.31), as identified in Column 6. This particular Disney bond will come to maturity (expire) on July 15, 2011, and is considered of high-quality grade given its current A rating. Notice also that this bond is not callable. This means Disney does not have any legal authority to call back the bonds from the current bondholders at any time prior to the maturity date.

(continued)

Exhibit 8-6 (continued)

However, look at the next bond in the table. The bond issuer is Extended Stay America. Notice that this particular bond does have a callable feature. This means the bond issuer (Extended Stay America) has the legal right to call in the bonds at any time subject to the terms and conditions as expressed during the issuance of the bond. Also notice that the coupon rate is greater than that provided by Hilton Hotels, which does not have a callable feature on its bond issue. In general, bond issuers will pay a higher coupon rate or provide some other financial incentive for investors to purchase bonds that have a callable feature. This is because it is quite likely the bond will never reach its maturity date and therefore the investor wants to be financially compensated for this possible outcome.

Bonds can also have a convertible feature. This means the bond issuer has the authority and ability to convert outstanding bonds into common shares as per the terms and conditions of the bond at the time of issue.

8.8 Preferred Stock Terminology

Preferred stock has seniority relative to common stock. A corporation must pay preferred stock dividends before paying common stock dividends—and, in the case of financial difficulty, preferred stock has a claim on the firm's assets prior to common stock's claim. It is called **preferred stock** because it holds a *preference* over and above common stock when it comes to the firm's cash flows and assets. See Exhibit 8-7 for an example of some hospitality companies that offer preferred stock.

Preferred stock usually has a par value of $25, $50, or $100. It pays a quarterly dividend, but the dividend is expressed as an annual amount. In fact, the annual preferred dividend amount is usually expressed as part of a corporation's preferred stock

Exhibit 8-7 Preferred Stock in the Hospitality and Tourism Industry

Since 1990, more than 140 firms in the hospitality and tourism* industry have issued preferred stock. These preferred stock issues raised more than $15 billion to be invested in the hospitality and tourism industry by these firms. Numerous well-known firms have issued preferred stock over this period, including

- McDonald's Corporation
- Royal Caribbean International
- MGM Grand Hotels Incorporated
- Wyndham International Incorporated
- Station Casinos Incorporated
- ACE Aviation (Air Canada)
- Marriott International Incorporated

In September 2004, ACE Aviation (Air Canada) sold 12,550 convertible preferred shares raising more than $3 million for Air Canada. These shares were eligible for conversion into common shares as at December 31, 2006.

*The phrase *hospitality and tourism industry* is used as defined by John R. Walker in *Introduction to Hospitality Management,* 4th ed. (Prentice Hall, 2005).

name. For example, "Six Flags $1.81 preferred" would most likely be the way investors would refer to Six Flags class B preferred stock that pays a $1.81 annual dividend.

We discussed in section 8.1 how preferred stock is a hybrid security. By that we mean it shares some of the characteristics of bonds and some of the characteristics of common stock. We discuss preferred stock in the same chapter with bonds because both securities are considered fixed-income securities. In other words, unless a firm has financial difficulty, the cash returns paid by bonds and preferred stock (coupon payments and dividends respectively) are known with certainty.

8.9 Preferred Stock Features

Preferred stock typically promises to pay a fixed dividend. In adjustable-rate preferred stock, the dividend adjusts along with market interest rates. In participating preferred stock, the preferred investors share, to a limited extent, in the firm's earnings. However, most preferred stock pays a fixed dividend. Although preferred stock has no stated maturity, it is often redeemed at some point in the future through the provisions of a sinking fund or a call feature. A sinking fund on preferred stock works much as it does on a bond. A preferred stock sinking fund generally requires that a certain percentage of the total preferred stock is redeemed each year. If the percentage redeemed each year is 2.5 percent, then the preferred stock will have a maximum maturity of 40 years (100%/2.5%). Some preferred stock is perpetual, meaning it will never be redeemed. In this case, the preferred stock is expected to pay dividends forever.

Most preferred stock has **cumulative dividends**. If a corporation misses a dividend on cumulative preferred stock, then the missed dividend accumulates. The corporation can never again pay a common stock dividend until all missed accumulated preferred dividends have been paid. This provides a powerful incentive for a successful firm to always pay its preferred dividends. Owners of preferred stock generally have no voting rights. However, most preferred stock provides voting rights if two or more quarterly preferred dividends are missed.

8.10 Valuing Preferred Stock

Preferred stock pays dividends quarterly, but for introductory purposes we will simplify this and assume preferred dividends are paid once a year. To determine the value of preferred stock, we simply find the present value of the future cash flows an investor expects to receive. If the preferred stock is perpetual, there is only one type of cash flow: the same fixed preferred dividend each year, forever. We call this cash flow a perpetuity, and we developed an equation for computing the present value of a perpetuity in Chapter 7. See Exhibit 8-8 for a small sample of preferred stock quotations.

To illustrate how to value preferred stock, we consider an example. Suppose Gretzky Resorts Incorporated has issued preferred stock. We will call it Gretzky Resorts $2.50 preferred. The preferred stock promises to pay a fixed dividend of $2.50 annually, forever. Assume that a fair market rate of return on preferred stock of this risk class is 11 percent annually. What is the value of one Gretzky Resorts $2.50 preferred share?

Exhibit 8-8 Preferred Stock Quotations

The following are typical quotations for preferred stock as listed in the online *Wall Street Journal* for Friday, January 4, 2008.

(1) Preferred stock	(2) Stock symbol	(3) Current dividend	(4) Yield	(5) Close	(6) Net change
Hosp Properties B	HPTB	2.22	9.1	24.37	−0.35
Host Hotels & Resorts	HSTE	2.22	8.9	25.05	−0.60
LaSalle Hotel Prop B	LHOB	2.09	9.3	22.48	0.49
Strat Hotel & Resorts B	BEEB	2.06	10.6	19.40	0.80

Under Column 1 we see the company name abbreviated. An A or B or C after the stock name or as the last letter of the stock symbol indicates the class of the preferred stock. Column 2 identifies the trading symbol of the preferred stock. Column 3 shows the annual dividend amount. Column 4 is the dividend yield; this is calculated by dividing the preferred stock dividend by the closing price (Column 3 divided by Column 5). The succeeding column is the closing price of the preferred stock at the end of the day. Column 6 is the net change in price from the previous trading day.

The first row shows a class B preferred stock issued by Hospitality Properties Trust. It pays a $2.22 annual dividend and has a 9.1 percent dividend yield ($2.22/24.37 = 9.1%). The closing price of this preferred stock at the end of the day is $24.37, and this is down $0.35 from the $24.72 closing price the day before.

First, we define our terms.

V_p = value of a share of preferred stock

d_p = preferred annual dividend per share = $2.50

i_p = required rate of return on preferred stock = 11%

The formula for the value of a share of preferred stock is the same as the formula for the present value of a perpetuity. The present value of the perpetuity is the value of the preferred stock (V_p), the perpetual payment is the preferred dividend payment (d_p), and the interest rate is the investor-required rate of return on the preferred stock (i_p).

$$V_p = \frac{d_p}{i_p} = \frac{\$2.50}{11\%} = \$22.73$$

The value of Gretzky Resorts $2.50 preferred at an 11 percent rate of return is $22.73.

The preceding equation can also be used to compute the investor's rate of return on preferred stock when purchased at a given price. For example, suppose Gretzky Resorts' $2.50 preferred is actually selling for $20 per share. What is your rate of return if you buy this preferred stock for $20? We can take the equation for the value of preferred stock and solve it for i_p.

$$i_p = \frac{d_p}{V_p} = \frac{\$2.50}{\$20} = 12.50\%$$

If you buy Gretzky Resorts' $2.50 preferred for $20 per share, your rate of return is expected to be 12.50 percent. This rate of return on preferred stock may be called the yield to maturity.

8.11 SUMMARY

This chapter:

- Explained why bonds and preferred stock are generally classified as fixed-income securities
- Introduced basic bond terminology
- Discussed basic bond features as detailed in a bond indenture
- Explained bond ratings
- Explained how to compute the value and yield to maturity on a bond
- Introduced basic preferred stock terminology and basic preferred stock features
- Explained how to compute the value and yield to maturity on a preferred stock

Key Terms

Bond	Mortgage bond
Bond rating	Par value
Call feature	Preferred stock
Coupon payment	Put feature
Coupon rate	Restrictive covenants
Cumulative dividends	Seniority
Debenture	Sinking fund feature
Face value	Yield to maturity
Indenture	

Discussion Questions

1. Why are bonds and preferred stocks considered fixed-income securities?
2. Why is preferred stock considered a hybrid security?
3. What is the difference between a mortgage bond and a debenture?
4. What is a bond indenture?
5. What is the difference between a call feature and a put feature?
6. How does a sinking fund feature reduce an investor's risk on a bond?
7. Why do corporations prefer a higher bond rating to a lower bond rating on their debt securities?
8. What is the difference between a bond's yield to maturity and its coupon rate?
9. Why is it important to an investor that preferred stock dividends be cumulative?
10. What is the general procedure for estimating the value of a security?

Problems

1. McDonald's Corporation's $1,000, par value zero-coupon notes mature in six years. What is the yield to maturity to an investor buying one of these notes for $250?
2. Mann Corporation's $1,000, par value zero-coupon debentures mature in 30 years. If they are priced to return 9 percent to the investor, what is the market price of one Mann Corporation zero-coupon debenture?

3. McDonald's Corporation has 8⅞ percent (8.875%) bonds that mature in 15 years. What is the value of a $1,000 par value McDonald's Corporation bond for each of the following required rates of return, assuming the investor holds the bond to maturity? Assume the coupon is paid annually.

   a. 10%

   b. 8.875%

   c. 6%

4. What is the yield to maturity on a $1,000 par value 8⅞ percent McDonald's Corporation bond if the investor buys the bonds at the following market prices? Assume the coupon is paid annually and the bond matures in 15 years.

   a. $1,175

   b. $1,000

   c. $850

5. What is the value of a $1,000 par value 8⅞ percent McDonald's Corporation bond for each of the following required rates of return, assuming the investor holds the bond to maturity? Assume the coupon is paid semiannually (every six months) and the bond matures in 15 years.

   a. 10%

   b. 6%

6. Marriott Corporation originally issued a 9⅞ percent (9.375%) bond in 1987. These $1,000 par value bonds mature in three years. What is the value of a Marriott Corporation bond at each of the following required rates of return, assuming the investor holds the bond to maturity? Assume the coupon is paid annually.

   a. 7%

   b. 9.375%

   c. 12%

7. What is the yield to maturity on a $1,000 par value 9⅞ percent Marriott Corporation bond if the investor buys the bonds at the following market prices? Assume the coupon is paid annually and the bond matures in three years.

   a. $1,025

   b. $1,000

   c. $950

8. What is the value of a $1,000 par value 9⅞ percent Marriott Corporation bond for each of the following required rates of return, assuming the investor holds the bond to maturity? Assume the coupon is paid semiannually (every six months) and the bond matures in three years.

   a. 7%

   b. 12%

9. What is the value of a share of Six Flags class B $1.81 preferred stock to an investor requiring the following rates of return? Assume dividends are paid annually.

   a. 12%

   b. 10%

   c. 9%

10. What is the yield to maturity on a share of Six Flags class B $1.81 preferred stock if an investor buys the stock at the following market prices? Assume dividends are paid annually.

   a. $30

   b. $25

   c. $19

11. What is the value of a share of Hospitality Properties Trust class B $2.22 preferred stock to an investor requiring the following rates of return? Assume dividends are paid annually.

   a. 11%

   b. 9%

   c. 7%

12. What is the yield to maturity on a share of Hospitality Properties Trust class B $2.22 preferred stock if an investor buys the stock at the following market prices? Assume dividends are paid annually.

   a. $35

   b. $25

   c. $17

Chapter 9
Common Stock

Chapter Objectives

This chapter covers the following topics:

1　How common stock represents a residual ownership claim on a corporation

2　Why it is more difficult to estimate the value of common stock than bonds

3　Basic common stock features

4　How to compute four basic dividend valuation models

5　How investor rate of return and a firm's earnings and dividends growth affect common stock value

9.1 Introduction

As we discussed in Chapter 8, corporations issue securities as a means of raising money. Investors buy securities because they hope to receive more back in the future for the securities than they pay today. Chapter 8 discussed the fixed-income securities—bonds and preferred stock. **Common stock**, another security that corporations may issue to raise funds, is quite different from bonds and preferred stock in that the upside and downside returns very much depend on the financial success of the corporation.

Common stock gives the investor ownership in the underlying corporation and provides a residual claim on both the firm's assets and the firm's cash flows. However, unlike the nature of corporate bonds, common stock does not represent a contractual obligation on the part of the corporation, nor does it have a stated maturity. The residual claim on assets implies the owners of common stock have a residual (leftover) claim on assets after other claimholders are paid. Common shareholders also have ownership rights to cash flows remaining after all other claimants are paid. For successful companies, this can be a very significant claim. The amount of this claim is typically equated with a company's earnings as shown on its income statement. Part of these earnings may be paid directly to the common shareholders in the form of a dividend. However, earnings not paid to common shareholders in the form of dividends still belong to the common shareholders. Therefore, we must consider both parts of the company's earnings stream when valuing common stock. The two parts of earnings are dividends and the addition to retained earnings.

The task of valuing common stock is not as clear-cut as valuing corporate bonds. The cash flows from corporate bonds, which consist of stated, periodic coupon payments and payment of a known par value at maturity, are generally easy to forecast. Common stock cash flows consist of dividend payments and a price should the investor sell the common stock at some point in the future. Future common stock dividends and future common stock price are generally difficult to forecast. Despite the difficulty, we introduce some basic models used to estimate the value of common stock.

9.2 Common Stock Features

When an investor buys common stock, the investor is buying ownership in the corporation. The defining features of common stock include (1) a residual claim on assets, (2) a residual claim on cash flows, (3) variable return, (4) voting rights, and (5) no set maturity.

The residual claim on assets implies the owners of common stock have a residual (leftover) claim on assets after other claimholders are paid. Other claimholders include employees, creditors, and the government. This residual claim can be worth a great deal if a successful company is sold. But in the case of bankruptcy, this residual claim is generally worth very little, if anything. Common shareholders also have ownership rights to cash flows remaining after all other claimants are paid. This is typically viewed as a claim on a company's earnings as shown on its income statement. Owners of common stock share equally in any payment of corporate dividends. Corporate dividends are generally paid quarterly.

A corporation's shareholders elect the corporation's board of directors, which has the ultimate control over the corporation. The board has the power to hire, fire, and set the compensation for the corporation's executives. The board also sets long-term policy and makes major corporate decisions. And, on occasion, the shareholders may also vote on other important corporate matters.

Sometimes a corporation has more than one class of stock, in which case a class A common stock typically has one vote per share or no votes per share. Class B common stock typically has superior voting power. An example would be class B stock with four votes per share. A corporation typically creates two classes of common stock when the controlling owners want to raise additional outside equity funding but not give up control of the company. Even though class B common stock typically has superior voting rights, dividend rights typically remain the same.

Common stock financing provides lower risk to the corporation than bond or preferred stock financing. Although corporations do not want to cut common stock dividends, the lack of a fixed dividend on common stock provides greater flexibility versus the use of bonds or preferred stock. Also, the use of debt financing places many restrictions on the firm as specified in the debt contract (an indenture, in the case of bond financing). Common stock financing does not come with restrictions on the firm, and by expanding the equity base of the corporation it is typically easier to increase debt financing. For example, if a firm typically has a debt to equity ratio of 2 to 1, then every one dollar of additional equity will allow the firm to borrow an additional two dollars of debt and still stay within its targets for debt financing.

Exhibit 9-1 Common Share Quotations

The following are typical quotations for common shares as listed on the TSX Web site for preferred shares trading on Friday, September 5, 2008.

(1) company	(2) Symbol	(3) Close	(4) $ Change	(5) % Change	(6) Volume	(7) 52-week high	(6) 52-week low
Ace Aviation Holdings Inc.	ACE.A-T	10.200	−0.380	−3.59	74,044	30.230	9.250
WestJet Airlines Ltd.	WJA-T	14.580	−0.650	−4.27	378,549	23.490	11.820
Great Canadian Gaming Corporation	GC-T	8.310	−0.150	−1.77	115,365	16.470	8.300
Tim Hortons Inc.	THI-T	32.750	−0.230	−0.70	287,509	40.410	26.750

In this table we see the company name provided in Column 1 followed by its trading symbol in Column 2. The letter "T" at the end of each symbol indicates that the shares trade on the Toronto Stock Exchange. In Column 3 is the latest, most current trading dollar value for these particular shares. Column 4 shows the latest dollar value change that has taken place from the current day's closing value in comparison to the previous day's closing value. Column 5 represents the relative value change (in percentage) that has occurred as a result of the most current day's closing price in comparison to the previous day's closing price. Column 6 shows the trading volume (trading activity) for the previous trading day. Finally, columns 7 and 8 show the 52-week high and low; that is, the highest and lowest price for the share during the last 52 weeks.

Look at Tim Hortons Inc., with trading symbol THI-T. The closing market value price for THI-T on Friday, September 5, 2008, was $32.75 per share. This represents a price change of $0.23 from its closing price of $32.98 on Thursday, September 4, 2008. In relative terms, THI-T shares have decreased by 0.70 percent on Friday, September 5, 2008. A total of 287,509 shares of THI-T were traded on Friday, September 5, 2008. Finally, the highest price for the shares over the last 52 weeks was $40.41, while the lowest price was $26.75.

Common stock financing comes with a downside as well as an upside. Investors view common stock as a riskier investment than bonds or preferred stock. As a result, investors in common stock require higher expected rates of return. This translates into a higher cost of common stock financing than bond or preferred stock financing for the corporation. Also, the costs involved with issuing common stock are much higher than the costs involved with issuing bonds and preferred stock. Exhibit 9-1 provides a quick perspective on some common stock quotations.

9.3 Valuing Common Stock

We now introduce four basic models that can be used to value common stock in some cases. These models are generally not used by analysts to value stocks in the simplified form presented here; analysts use more complex versions of these models or a type of earnings multiple methodology. Although the models presented apply only in simple situations, they illustrate the underlying principles of common stock valuation. These models provide insight into the determinants of common stock value. Also, these models provide the basis for a method for estimating the cost of equity, which is presented in Chapter 10. The four models are

1. General valuation model
2. Zero-growth model
3. Constant-growth model
4. Multiple growth rates ending in constant-growth model

First, we introduce the concept of growth of a company's earnings and a method that allows us to approximate this growth rate. Managers of a company have two choices of what to do with company earnings. Remember, these earnings belong to the common shareholders, who are the owners. Managers, acting as agents for the owners, decide whether to distribute earnings back to the owners or keep these earnings in the company. Earnings paid to owners are called *dividends*. Holders on record as at the date of dividend declaration are financially rewarded for their proportional investment in the company. Earnings as a result of profitable operations that are held within the company are called *retained earnings*.

In theory, managers pay out earnings as dividends when the company does not have profitable projects in which to invest earnings. Conversely, managers retain earnings when the company does have profitable projects in which to invest. Therefore, when earnings are retained and reinvested into profitable projects, the company and its earnings will grow in the future. This is known as using *internally generated funds* to finance the company's planned capital projects. The scale of this growth depends on the amount of earnings retained and on the return earned by the assets in which the retained earnings are invested. Therefore, to calculate the growth rate of a company's earnings, take the percentage of earnings retained (retention ratio) and multiply by the return on equity.

$$g = \text{Growth rate} = r \times ROE$$
$$r = \text{Retention ratio} = 1 - \text{Dividend payout ratio}$$
$$ROE = \text{Return on equity}$$

For example, say Feinstein's Microbrew Incorporated pays out 40 percent of earnings as dividends. Thus, the other 60 percent of earnings (one minus the portion of earnings paid out as dividends) must be reinvested in the firm and increase the firm's retained earnings. This 60 percent is the retention ratio. Suppose the earnings retained can be invested to earn 20 percent (return on equity). What is the growth rate (g)? In this example, the growth rate in the company's earnings is 60 percent multiplied by 20 percent, which equals 12 percent. We also use this as our best approximation of a company's growth rate in dividends.

$$g = 0.60 \times 0.20 = 0.12 = 12\%$$

We expect earnings and dividends to grow at a rate of 12 percent per year into the foreseeable future.

For companies that maintain consistency in their retention and payout ratios and earn a consistently stable return on equity, the growth rate approximates a constant. In these cases, we use the constant-growth model. If a company's retention and payout ratios are not consistent or its return on equity is not stable, then we must use a non–constant-growth model.

9.3.1 GENERAL DIVIDEND VALUATION MODEL

Remember that the value of a security is the present value of the future expected cash flows paid by the security. If an investor is considering the purchase of common stock and plans to hold the common stock for n years, then the value of the common stock can be expressed as follows.

$$P_0 = \frac{d_1}{(1 + k_e)} + \frac{d_2}{(1 + k_e)^2} + \cdots + \frac{d_n}{(1 + k_e)^n} + \frac{P_n}{(1 + k_e)^n}$$

where P_i = the value of common stock at the end of year i
d_i = the common stock dividend at the end of year i
k_e = the investor's required rate of return on equity or common stock

Because this is an introductory treatment of common stock valuation, we assume, for simplicity, that common stock pays dividends once a year. (If you continue to study finance, you will be able to advance to more realistic quarterly dividend models once you understand the annual dividend models.) We also assume the investor is buying common stock right after it pays a dividend, and therefore the investor has to wait for one year before receiving the first dividend.

The equation shows that the value of common stock is the present value of the expected dividends to be received plus the present value of the expected price you sell the stock for in the future. Thus, if an investor plans to buy common stock and hold it for three years and then sell it at the end of year 3 ($n = 3$), the valuation equation looks like

$$P_0 = \frac{d_1}{(1 + k_e)} + \frac{d_2}{(1 + k_e)^2} + \frac{d_3}{(1 + k_e)^3} + \frac{P_3}{(1 + k_e)^3}$$

Suppose the investor expects dividends to be $1.00, $1.05, and $1.10 at the end of years 1, 2, and 3, respectively, and expects to sell the stock for $15 at the end of three years. Also assume the investor requires a 15 percent rate of return.

$$P_0 = \frac{\$1.00}{(1 + 15\%)} + \frac{\$1.05}{(1 + 15\%)^2} + \frac{\$1.10}{(1 + 15\%)^3} + \frac{\$15.00}{(1 + 15\%)^3} = \$12.25$$

For ease of calculation, you can combine the last dividend with the selling price because they both occur in the last year.

$$P_0 = \frac{\$1.00}{(1 + 15\%)} + \frac{\$1.05}{(1 + 15\%)^2} + \frac{(\$1.10 + 15.00)}{(1 + 15\%)^3} = \$12.25$$

The common stock is worth $12.25 to the investor today. If the stock can be purchased for $12.25, then the investor expects to receive the 15 percent required rate of return. If the investor can buy the stock for less than $12.25, then the rate of return will be greater than 15 percent.

There are several obvious problems with using this model in practice. First, the investor must know how long he plans to hold the stock. Second, the investor needs to forecast the future expected dividends. And third, the investor needs to forecast the future expected selling price and the end of the holding period. However, as we consider other common stock valuation models, we discover that the investor's holding period does not affect the value of common stock today. Also, we consider how to use a company's expected growth rate in dividends and earnings to forecast a company's future expected dividends.

9.3.2 ZERO-GROWTH DIVIDEND VALUATION MODEL

Suppose a company's dividends are not growing; in other words, the company pays out a constant dividend every year. Investing in this type of company is similar to investing in a periodic, constant cash flow instrument known as a perpetuity. The present value of a perpetuity is

$$PV = \frac{PMT}{i}$$

We can readily adapt this to estimate the value of common stock with constant dividends. Again, remember that the value of common stock is the present value of the future expected cash flows from the common stock.

$$P_0 = \frac{d}{k_e}$$

where d = the constant common stock dividend.

Take as an example Atlantic Canada Hotels Incorporated, a hotel chain located in Nova Scotia that has older properties and does not expect to grow in the future. Atlantic Canada Hotels expects earnings per share of $5 over this coming year. Suppose investors believe a 10 percent required rate of return is appropriate. Because Atlantic Canada Hotels does not expect to grow in the future, its managers have decided not to retain any earnings. Note that because Atlantic Canada Hotels' management decides not to retain earnings, this company has a 100 percent payout. Therefore, we can best approximate the present value of a share of Atlantic Canada Hotels with the zero-growth dividend valuation model. Because Atlantic Canada Hotels' managers expect earnings of $5 per share and have decided to pay out 100 percent of earnings, the first annual dividend is also expected to be $5 per share. In addition, because the company is not expected to grow in the future, due to the absence of new retained earnings, all future dividends are also expected to be $5 per share.

$$d_1 = d_2 = d_3 = \cdots d_\infty = \$5.00$$

If we apply our zero-growth formula, we find the present value of a share of Atlantic Canada Hotels' common stock to be $50.

$$P_0 = \frac{\$5.00}{10\%} = \$50.00$$

Our zero-growth formula is based on the present value of a perpetuity and would seem to imply an investor plans to never sell the common stock, but to hold on to it forever. What if the investor has a finite holding period, or in other words plans to sell the stock in n years rather than hold it forever? Consider the implications by combining the general dividend valuation model with the zero-growth dividend valuation model.

Suppose an investor plans to hold the preceding constant-growth stock for just one year and then sell it. We know the investor's expected dividend in one year is $5. What is the expected selling price of the stock in one year? Assume the investor's required rate of return on the stock remains at 10 percent in the future. An investor considering the purchase of this stock in one year would expect to receive what future cash flows? Of course, the investor can expect a $5 annual dividend forever. Thus, the expected selling price of the stock one year from today is

$$P_1 = \frac{\$5.00}{10\%} = \$50.00$$

Therefore, an investor buying the stock today and planning to hold it for just one year expects to receive a $5 dividend in one year and also expects to sell the stock for $50 in one year. The value to this investor today is

$$P_0 = \frac{\$5.00}{(1 + 10\%)} + \frac{\$50.00}{(1 + 10\%)} = \$50.00$$

This is the same as the investor planning to hold the stock forever. What about an investor planning to buy the stock and hold it for two years? Again, we know expected dividends are $5 in each of year 1 and year 2. What is the expected selling price at the end of year 2? Again, just like for year 1, investors considering buying the stock in two years expect a $5 annual dividend. Thus, the expected selling price of the stock two years from today is

$$P_2 = \frac{\$5.00}{10\%} = \$50.00$$

In fact, for zero-growth common stock, the price will not change in the future as long as the required rate of return remains constant. In other words

$$P_0 = P_1 = P_2 = \cdots P_n$$

Therefore, an investor buying the stock today and planning to hold it for two years expects to receive a $5 dividend at the end of each of the first two years and also expects to sell the stock for $50 in two years. The value to this investor today is

$$P_0 = \frac{\$5.00}{(1 + 10\%)} + \frac{\$5.00}{(1 + 10\%)^2} + \frac{\$50.00}{(1 + 10\%)^2} = \$50.00$$

We could continue this pattern over and over and continue to get the same result. If the investor bought the stock and planned to hold it for three years, or four years, or more, the present value of the expected dividends and expected future stock price will still be $50. This illustrates that how long the investor plans to hold the stock should not affect the value of the stock to the investor. We show this result again when we present the constant-growth dividend valuation model.

9.3.3 CONSTANT-GROWTH DIVIDEND VALUATION MODEL

For our next example, we look at Western Canada Hotels Incorporated. This hotel company is in Alberta with an expanding portfolio of properties, and the managers expect significant growth in the future. Western Canada Hotels expects earnings per share of $5 in the coming year. Suppose investors believe a 10 percent required rate of return is appropriate. Because Western Canada Hotels expects to grow in the future, its managers have decided to retain 60 percent of future earnings. Based on this retention rate, the company will have a 40 percent dividend payout ratio. Also, Western Canada Hotels expects it can earn 12 percent on earnings reinvested in the firm (return on equity), and it expects this 12 percent return on equity and the 60 percent retention ratio to remain constant in the future. Therefore, we can best approximate the present value of a share of Western Canada Hotels with the constant-growth dividend valuation model.

First, what do you think will be the dividend paid to shareholders of Western Canada Hotels one year from now? Of course, the dividend will be $2.00 per share, because 40 percent of earnings are forecast to be paid out to shareholders (40% × $5.00 = $2.00).

Second, what will be the expected growth rate of Western Canada Hotels in the future? Assume the managers of Western Canada Hotels expect to keep a constant retention ratio of 60 percent to fund growth in projects that are expected to consistently earn a 12 percent return on equity. Given these assumptions, the future growth rate of Western Canada Hotels is

$$g = 12\% \times 0.60 = 7.2\%$$

The constant-growth dividend valuation model is

$$P_0 = \frac{d_1}{(k_e - g)}$$

Applying this to Western Canada Hotels common stock,

$$P_0 = \frac{\$2.00}{(10\% - 7.2\%)} = \frac{\$2.00}{2.8\%} = \$71.43$$

Stop for a minute and think about the valuation of these two companies—Atlantic Canada Hotels and Western Canada Hotels. Both expect earnings over the next year of $5.00 per share, and investors in each have a 10 percent required rate of return, so why do they have different stock prices? It is due to the assumption of growth. Because Western Canada Hotels expects earnings and dividends to grow, and Atlantic Canada Hotels does not, Western Canada Hotels is worth more. Our models let us determine a reasonable estimate of the relative values of the common stock for each company.

The constant-growth dividend valuation model provides good estimates of common stock value as long as a company's future earnings retention ratio and return on equity—and thus its growth rate—are roughly stable. If it is difficult to forecast these variables accurately, or if we expect large systematic differences year to year, then the model provides less accurate estimates and other procedures for estimating common stock value are more appropriate.

Notice in the preceding analysis of the constant-growth stock that we made no assumptions about the holding period. We now make some holding period assumptions and use the general dividend valuation model to estimate value based on different holding periods. First, assume an investor plans to buy the stock today and hold it for just one year. This investor expects to receive just two cash flows from an investment in this stock. One cash flow is the dividend in one year (d_1), and the other is the price the stock can be sold for in one year (P_1). Remember, we estimated a 7.2 percent growth rate in earnings and dividends for Western Canada Hotels. Also assume Western Canada Hotels' stock price will grow at 7.2 percent. This can be expected if the company's retention ratio remains at 60 percent, its return on equity at 12 percent, and investors' required rate of return at 10 percent. Therefore, if the company's stock price is currently $71.43 (from the preceding calculation) and is growing at 7.2 percent annually, the stock price in one year will be $76.57 ($71.43 × 1.072). The investor planning to buy and hold the stock for just one year can expect to receive a dividend of $2.00 ($d_1$) and sell the stock for $76.57 ($P_1$). The value to this investor is just the present value of these two cash flows at the 10 percent required rate of return:

$$P_0 = \frac{\$2.00}{(1 + 10\%)} + \frac{\$76.57}{(1 + 10\%)} = \$71.43$$

We can see the value to this investor is the same as from our constant-growth dividend valuation model with no assumption about holding period. Consider the value of Western Canada Hotels' common stock to an investor planning to buy the stock and hold it for just two years. In this case, two dividends are expected. The first is $2.00, and the second is $2.14 ($d_2$ = $2.00 × 1.072). Also, the investor expects to sell the stock in the second year for $82.08 ($P_2$). This is 7.2 percent higher than the expected stock price at the end of year 1 (P_2 = $76.57 × 1.072). The value to this investor is just the present value of these three cash flows at the 10 percent required rate of return:

$$P_0 = \frac{\$2.00}{(1 + 10\%)} + \frac{\$2.14}{(1 + 10\%)^2} + \frac{\$82.08}{(1 + 10\%)^2} = \$71.43$$

And, again, we see the value to the investor is the same as previously calculated (the preceding calculation actually comes out to $71.42, but if we do not round off d_2 and P_2 to two decimal places the calculation works out to $71.43). We could continue this pattern over and over and continue to get the same result. If the investor bought the stock and planned to hold it for three years, or four years—or more—the present value of the expected dividends and expected future stock price would still be $71.43. This illustrates once again that how long the investor plans to hold the stock should not affect the value of the stock to the investor.

9.3.4 VALUING COMMON STOCK WITH MULTIPLE GROWTH RATES

We have considered how to estimate the value of common stock in general and how to value when there is no growth and when there is constant growth. The general model is logical and provides insights into common stock valuation. But the general model is also difficult to apply in practice. The no-growth and constant-growth models work well when the assumptions of the models are met. In this section we consider how to estimate the value of common stock in which several different growth rates are expected and can be forecast with some degree of accuracy.

Reconsider the case of Central Canada Hotels Incorporated. This hotel chain is located in the high-growth areas of Toronto, Mississauga, and Niagara Falls, Ontario, with an expanding portfolio of properties that its managers expect to continue into the future. Suppose Central Canada Hotels expects a very high 15 percent growth rate for the next two years and thereafter expects a constant 7.2 percent growth rate. Because of the higher growth rate, Central Canada Hotels now expects higher earnings over the next year and thus a higher dividend of $2.15 to be paid in one year (d_1). The dividend in year 2 should grow 15 percent from year 1 and equal $2.47 [$d_2 = \$2.15 \times (1 + 15\%)$]. We can picture the cash flows and growth rates as follows.

0	$g = 15\%$	1	$\dot{g} = 15\%$	2	$\longrightarrow$	$g = 7.2\%$	$\longrightarrow$
		$2.15		$2.47			

What is the value of this common stock to an investor requiring a 10 percent rate of return? Remember, we showed in the last two sections that the investor's holding period does not affect the value of the common stock. We showed this by example in the case where growth was zero, and then growth was constant. The investor's holding period does not affect common stock value regardless of growth. This means that in the preceding example we can make any assumption we want about holding period, and we should obtain the same estimate of common stock value. In order to make the estimate calculation as easy as possible, we assume the investor will buy this stock and hold it for two years, expecting to receive three cash flows. The three cash flows are two dividends (d_1 and d_2) and the selling price of the common stock in two years (P_2). We have already estimated the two dividends. If we can obtain an estimate of the common stock selling price in two years, then we can estimate the value of the common stock today with the general dividend valuation model as follows:

$$P_0 = \frac{d_1}{(1 + 10\%)} + \frac{d_2}{(1 + 10\%)^2} + \frac{P_2}{(1 + 10\%)^2}$$

We estimate the common stock selling price in two years (P_2) by recognizing the growth rate after two years is constant at 7.2 percent. This allows us to adapt the constant-growth dividend valuation model to estimate P_2. The model as developed earlier is

$$P_0 = \frac{d_1}{(k_e - g)}$$

This can be written in a more general form as follows.

$$P_n = \frac{d_{n+1}}{(k_e - g)}$$

where the price of common stock at the end of any year n (P_n) is equal to the expected dividend one year later ($n + 1$) divided by the difference between the required rate of return and the growth rate. The growth rate used in this calculation must be the constant growth rate expected after n years. Adapting this to our example, we can estimate the selling price of Central Canada Hotels' common stock at the end of year 2 by

$$P_2 = \frac{d_3}{(k_e - g)}$$

We can estimate d_3 by letting d_2 grow at the 7.2 percent growth rate.

$$d_3 = \$2.47 \times (1 + 7.2\%) = \$2.65$$

We can now use this to estimate the expected selling price in two years. Be sure to use the growth rate expected after two years (7.2%, not 15%).

$$P_2 = \frac{\$2.65}{(10\% - 7.2\%)}$$

$$P_2 = \frac{\$2.65}{2.8\%} = \$94.64$$

Now we can use the expected selling price in year 2 along with the expected dividends in the first two years to estimate the value today.

$$P_0 = \frac{\$2.15}{(1 + 10\%)} + \frac{\$2.47}{(1 + 10\%)^2} + \frac{\$94.64}{(1 + 10\%)^2} = \$82.21$$

Therefore, the value of Central Canada Hotels' common stock in this case is \$82.21. We assumed a two-year holding period, but this was only to make the calculation easier. Assuming any other holding period would change not the answer but only how difficult and tedious the calculation is. For example, if we assume a three-year holding period we estimate value as follows.

$$P_0 = \frac{d_1}{(1 + 10\%)} + \frac{d_2}{(1 + 10\%)^2} + \frac{d_3}{(1 + 10\%)^3} + \frac{P_3}{(1 + 10\%)^3}$$

We already have an estimate for the first three dividends (d_1, d_2, and d_3). We need to estimate P_3 using the constant-dividend growth model.

$$P_3 = \frac{d_4}{(k_e - g)}$$

We can estimate d_4 by letting d_3 grow at the 7.2 percent growth rate.

$$d_3 = \$2.65 \times (1 + 7.2\%) = \$2.84$$

We can now use this to estimate the expected selling price in three years. Be sure to use the growth rate expected after three years (7.2%, not 15%).

$$P_3 = \frac{\$2.84}{(10\% - 7.2\%)}$$

$$P_3 = \frac{\$2.84}{2.8\%} = \$101.43$$

Now we can use the expected selling price in year 3 along with the expected dividends in the first three years to estimate the value today.

$$P_0 = \frac{\$2.15}{(1 + 10\%)} + \frac{\$2.47}{(1 + 10\%)^2} + \frac{\$2.65}{(1 + 10\%)^3} + \frac{\$101.43}{(1 + 10\%)^3} = \$82.21$$

Therefore, the value of Central Canada Hotels' common stock is still $82.21 (the preceding value actually comes out to $82.19, but this is due to rounding differences). The assumption of holding period does not affect the value. It affects only the amount of work involved in the estimation calculation. In a case such as this, the easiest computation is to assume the holding period is equal to the point at which the growth rate becomes constant. In our example of Central Canada Hotels, the growth rate is expected to become constant after two years. Therefore, using a two-year holding period makes for the easiest computation to estimate the value of the common stock.

Look at another example to be sure you know how to use the multiple-growth dividend valuation model. Consider the example of Great Big Canadian Casinos, Incorporated. Great Big Canadian Casinos operates in the same geographic region as Central Canada Hotels. Great Big Canadian Casinos expects a $2.24 dividend one year from now and a 20 percent growth rate for the second year, followed by a 12 percent growth rate in the third year and a 7.2 percent growth rate thereafter. Investors require a 10 percent rate of return once again. The dividend in years 2 and 3 should be as follows.

$$d_2 = \$2.24 \times (1 + 20\%) = \$2.69$$
$$d_3 = \$2.69 \times (1 + 12\%) = \$3.01$$

We can picture the cash flows and growth rates as follows.

What is the value of this common stock to an investor requiring a 10 percent rate of return? Remember, we can make any assumption we want about holding period and obtain the same estimate of common stock value. In order to make the estimate calculation as easy as possible, we assume the investor buys this stock and holds it until the growth rate becomes constant. This will be three years for this example. With a three-year holding period, the investor expects to receive four cash flows. The four cash flows are three dividends (d_1, d_2, and d_3) and the selling price of the common stock in three years (P_3). We have already estimated the three dividends. We need to obtain an estimate of the common stock selling price in three years; then we can estimate the value of the common stock today with the general dividend valuation model as follows.

$$P_0 = \frac{d_1}{(1 + 10\%)} + \frac{d_2}{(1 + 10\%)^2} + \frac{d_3}{(1 + 10\%)^3} + \frac{P_3}{(1 + 10\%)^3}$$

We estimate the common stock selling price in three years (P_3) by recognizing the growth rate after three years is constant at 7.2 percent. This allows us to adapt the constant-growth dividend valuation model to estimate P_3.

$$P_3 = \frac{d_4}{(k_e - g)}$$

We can estimate d_4 by letting d_3 grow at the 7.2 percent growth rate.

$$d_4 = \$3.01 \times (1 + 7.2\%) = \$3.23$$

We can now use this to estimate the expected selling price in three years. Be sure to use the growth rate expected after three years (7.2%, not 12% or 20%).

$$P_3 = \frac{\$3.23}{(10\% - 7.2\%)}$$

$$P_2 = \frac{\$3.23}{2.8\%} = \$115.36$$

Now we can use the expected selling price in year 3 along with the expected dividends in the first three years to estimate the value today.

$$P_0 = \frac{\$2.24}{(1 + 10\%)} + \frac{\$2.69}{(1 + 10\%)^2} + \frac{\$3.01}{(1 + 10\%)^3} + \frac{\$115.36}{(1 + 10\%)^3} = \$93.19$$

Therefore, the value of Great Big Canadian Casinos' common stock in this case is $93.19. We assumed a three-year holding period, but this was only to make the calculation easier. Assuming any other holding period would change not the answer but only how difficult and tedious the calculation is.

9.4 Common Stock Value, Investor's Rate of Return, and Growth

Consider the impact of a change in the investor's required rate of return or a change in a firm's expected future growth rate on common stock value. First, if the general level of interest rates increases, investors will require a higher rate of return because their opportunity cost will have increased. If a common stock's future expected cash flows (future dividend and future selling price) have not changed, then the stock value must decline to the investor. The only way for an investor to receive a higher rate of return if the future expected cash flows remain the same is to pay less for the stock. We illustrate this with the Western Canada Hotels example and the constant-growth dividend valuation model from section 9.3.3. Previously, we estimated Western Canada Hotels' common stock value at $71.43 using the following equation.

$$P_0 = \frac{\$2.00}{(10\% - 7.2\%)} = \frac{\$2.00}{2.8\%} = \$71.43$$

This is based on an expected dividend of $2 in one year, a 10 percent required rate of return, and a 7.2 percent growth rate in future dividends. We assume the general level of interest rates increases, and as a result investors require a 12 percent return on Western Canada Hotels common stock. The value of the common stock will decline as follows.

$$P_0 = \frac{\$2.00}{(12\% - 7.2\%)} = \frac{\$2.00}{4.8\%} = \$41.67$$

For ease of exposition, we have illustrated the inverse relationship between rates of return and stock value using the constant-growth dividend model. The same relationship holds for all the models of common stock valuation presented in this chapter.

Now consider the impact of a change in a firm's expected dividend growth rate on common stock value. If a firm's dividends are expected to increase more rapidly in the future, this means dividends are expected to be larger than the initial expectation. Of course, if the rate of return remains the same, the value of the common stock will increase. We once again illustrate this relationship with the Western Canada Hotels example and the constant-growth dividend valuation model. In section 9.3.3, we estimated Western Canada Hotels' common stock value at $71.43 using the following equation.

$$P_0 = \frac{\$2.00}{(10\% - 7.2\%)} = \frac{\$2.00}{2.8\%} = \$71.43$$

Now assume Western Canada Hotels' return on equity increases, causing the firm's expected dividend growth rate to increase to 8 percent. The value of Western Canada Hotels' common stock will increase as follows.

$$P_0 = \frac{\$2.00}{(10\% - 8\%)} = \frac{\$2.00}{2\%} = \$100.00$$

Actually, the stock value would go up to more than $100 because d_1 would increase to more than $2.00 with a higher growth rate (P_0 would equal $101; see the text box below). This illustrates the positive relationship between a firm's expected dividend growth rate and common stock value. Again, the same relationship holds for all the models of common stock valuation presented in this chapter, not just the constant-growth dividend valuation model.

In the example from section 9.3.3, we estimated Western Canada Hotels' common stock value at $71.43 using the following equation.

$$P_0 = \frac{\$2.00}{(10\% - 7.2\%)} = \frac{\$2.00}{2.8\%} = \$71.43$$

This implied a growth rate of 7.2 percent. We show what happens if growth increases to 8 percent. The dividend expected in one year (d_1) was previously expected to be $2.00. This implies the current dividend (d_0) was previously a bit less than $1.87 as follows.

$$d_1 = d_0 \times (1 + g)$$
$$\$2.00 = d_0 \times (1 + 7.2\%)$$
$$d_0 = \frac{\$2.00}{(1 + 7.2\%)} = \$1.87$$

But now we have an 8 percent growth rate, causing the dividend expected in one year (d_1) to be $2.02, as follows.

$$d_1 = \$1.87 \times (1 + 8\%) = \$2.02$$

The value of Western Canada Hotels' common stock increases as follows.

$$P_0 = \frac{\$2.02}{(10\% - 8\%)} = \frac{\$2.02}{2\%} = \$101.00$$

Chapter 10
Cost of Capital

Chapter Objectives

This chapter covers the following topics:

1   A firm's cost of capital

2   The reasons why a firm's cost of capital should be measured on a marginal, after-tax basis and should measure only the cost of long-term sources of funds

3   The relative risk of bonds, preferred stock, and common stock to an investor

4   How to estimate the cost of debt

5   How to estimate the cost of preferred stock

6   How to estimate the cost of common equity, both internal and external

7   The reasons why internal equity (new retained earnings) has a cost

8   How to compute the weighted average cost of capital

9   How to use the weighted average cost of capital, and the concept of separating the financing decision from the investment decision

10.1 Introduction

One of the key finance functions in a firm is to make investments and acquire assets. It is crucial to the firm's long-term success that investments earn a sufficient rate of return, called the **cost of capital**. It is the rate of return required to keep investors satisfied, and therefore the cost of capital is really an average rate of return reflecting the rates of return required by various investors in the firm. It takes into account the cost of funds for new investments raised from debt, preferred stock, retained earnings, and common stock.

It is well accepted not only that measuring a firm's cost of capital is often difficult, but also that estimating the cost of capital is crucial to a firm's decision making. This chapter offers an introduction to the concept of cost of capital as well as the basic means used to approximate a firm's cost of capital.

10.2 The Weighted Average Cost of Capital

A firm's **weighted average cost of capital** is essentially the firm's minimum **required rate of return** on investments. The cost of capital is measured as a percentage rate. As the name implies, the weighted average cost of capital is an average cost of the various sources of capital employed by a firm. We call these different sources of capital the "capital components." The capital components may include funds raised by debt, preferred stock, retained earnings, and common stock.

The weighted average cost of capital is a **marginal measurement**, meaning it is concerned with the cost of new funds used to finance new investments. We are not concerned with the cost of funds already raised and previously invested in the firm. The cost of funds previously raised is certainly important, but the weighted average cost of capital is to be used in the evaluation of new investment proposals. Therefore, we should measure the cost of new funds to be used to finance new investments.

The weighted average cost of capital is measured on an after-tax basis. Investors care about cash flows after all relevant costs have been paid. Taxes are certainly a real and relevant cost. If a firm is to maximize its value then the cost of capital should take taxes into account, and all costs should be measured on an after-tax basis.

In measuring the weighted average cost of capital, we consider only long-term sources of capital. Short-term sources of funds, such as a short-term bank loan, are generally not used to make long-term investments. As such, the weighted average cost of capital should consider short-term sources of funds only if they are used to finance long-term investments. An example would be a short-term bank loan that is refunded and rolled over every six months. Generally, the weighted average cost of capital measures the cost of long-term sources of funds to include long-term debt, preferred stock, retained earnings, and common stock.

The weighted average cost of capital is an average cost of a firm's various components of capital. The weights in the average cost of capital are a measurement of a firm's **target capital structure**, which is simply the proportion of various capital components a firm plans to use to fund investments. For example, gaming companies generally have a capital structure heavily weighted toward debt.

Great Canadian Gaming Corporation (GCGC) owns and operates six casinos in B.C. and two in Nova Scotia. It also owns and operates two horse tracks in Ontario. GCGC became listed on the Toronto Stock Exchange in 2005. As at December 31, 2006, the company had 50.2 percent of its capital from long-term debt and 41.9 percent from equity. This was GCGC's actual capital structure as of December 31, 2006, but may not be its target capital structure. The target might be to obtain 70 percent of capital from long-term debt and 30 percent from equity, in which case GCGC would plan to increase the proportion of debt and decrease the proportion of equity in the actual capital structure over time.

Another firm's target capital structure might be to obtain 40 percent of capital from long-term debt, 10 percent from preferred stock, and 50 percent from equity. The weights in the weighted average cost of capital are measures of a firm's target capital structure. Throughout this chapter we assume we know a firm's target capital structure. This topic is discussed again in Chapter 14.

The basic weighted average cost of capital (k_a) equation is as follows.

$$k_a = w_d \times k_d + w_p \times k_p + w_e \times k_e$$

where w represents the firm's target capital structure and is measured as a proportion. All the w's must add up to 100 percent.

$$w_d + w_p + w_e = 100\%$$

The terms of the equation are defined as follows.

w_d = the proportion of debt in the capital structure
w_p = the proportion of preferred stock in the capital structure
w_e = the proportion of equity in the capital structure
k_d = the after-tax cost of debt
k_p = the cost of funds raised from preferred stock
k_e = the cost of funds raised from equity

Many firms do not employ preferred stock, and for these firms the weighted average cost of capital equation breaks down more simply to the following.

$$k_a = w_d \times k_d + w_e \times k_e$$

If a firm does not use preferred stock, then the weighted average cost of capital is a weighted average of the cost of debt and the cost of equity.

Next, we consider how to estimate the cost of various capital components. This, along with a firm's target capital structure, allows us to approximate a firm's weighted average cost of capital and therefore have a measure of a firm's minimum required rate of return on new investments.

10.3 Estimating the Cost of Capital Components

The possible components of a firm's capital structure include long-term debt, preferred stock, retained earnings, and common stock. If short-term debt is used for long-term financing by continual refunding, then this is also a component of a firm's capital structure. For the remainder of this chapter we do not consider short-term debt as an element of a firm's capital structure.

Many firms do not use preferred stock as part of their capital structure. Like bonds, preferred stock generally pays a fixed return to investors. But unlike the interest cost of bonds, the dividend cost of preferred stock is not tax deductible for the issuing corporation. Thus, for most firms, the after-tax cost of debt is much less than the after-tax cost of preferred stock. This may explain why bonds are a much more popular fixed-income security than preferred stock.

The cost of a capital component is a reflection of the investor's required rate of return. For example, suppose Company A borrows $1,000 from you and pays you back $1,000 plus 10 percent interest in one year. What is your rate of return on the loan? Of course it is 10 percent. What is Company A's cost for borrowing $1,000 from you? Of course it is also 10 percent. But what if Company A had to pay $10 for a standard boilerplate legal contract to satisfy you with legal evidence of the loan? Then Company A's cost for borrowing $1,000 from you is 10 percent plus $10. This raises Company A's cost on the loan to 11 percent as follows.

$$
\begin{aligned}
\text{Interest} = 10\% \times \$1,000 &= \$100 \\
\text{Legal fee} &= \$\ 10 \\
\text{Total loan cost} &= \$110 \\
\text{Cost of borrowing } \$1,000 &= \frac{\$110}{\$1,000} = 11\%
\end{aligned}
$$

So we can see a component cost of capital is the investor's required rate of return plus an adjustment for any transaction costs the issuing corporation may have to pay. These transaction costs are called **issuance** or **flotation costs** because they are costs paid to issue or "float" securities to investors. Total issuance costs consist of professional fees paid to investment bankers and lawyers who assist a corporation in issuing bonds, preferred stock, or common stock.

The three possible types of securities issued by corporations differ in seniority and thus risk. Bonds have higher seniority than preferred stock and common stock and are first to be paid in the case of financial difficulty. Preferred stock has higher seniority than common stock and will be paid before common stock in case of financial difficulty. Common stock, which ranks last in terms of seniority, is the riskiest of the three securities from the investor's point of view because an investor in common stock has residual claims on the cash flows and assets of the corporation. Common stock dividends are paid from cash, only after interest on debt and dividends on preferred stock are paid. Thus, from the investor's point of view, common stock is the riskiest corporate security and bonds are the lowest-risk security, with preferred stock in between. As a result, investors demand the lowest returns on bonds and the highest returns on common stock. On top of this, the cost of bonds is tax deductible, but the cost of preferred stock and common stock is not. Therefore, there is a clear hierarchy of cost of capital components for a corporation. The cost of bonds is the lowest due to the relatively low risk of bonds and the tax deductibility of interest on bonds to the issuing corporation. The cost of common stock is the highest due to its relatively high risk to investors. And, of course, the cost of preferred stock falls between bonds and common stock.

Next, we consider how to estimate the components' cost of capital. In doing so, we build on the models for estimating investor returns from Chapters 8 and 9.

10.4 The Cost of Debt

The interest cost of debt is a tax-deductible cost, and we must take this into consideration. Therefore, the interest cost of debt expressed as a percentage rate is multiplied by one minus the firm's marginal tax rate to compute the firm's effective after-tax cost of debt.

$$
k_d = k_{dbt} \times (1 - t)
$$

where k_d is still the after-tax cost of debt,

k_{dbt} = the before-tax interest rate cost of debt, and

t = the firm's marginal tax rate

If a firm issues bonds to raise funds, then the before-tax interest rate can be calculated using the same basic equation from Chapter 8 for the calculation of yield to maturity on corporate bonds. There is one difference in the application of the equation here. In Chapter 8 we used the market value of the bond. Here we use the net proceeds to the company after issuance costs are paid. The equation used to calculate the before-tax interest cost on a bond is

$$V_{net} = C \times \left[\frac{1 - \frac{1}{(1 + k_{dbt})^n}}{k_{dbt}} \right] + \frac{M}{(1 + k_{dbt})^n}$$

where V_{net} is the net proceeds from the bond issuance after issuance costs are paid, and

C = Coupon payment
M = Maturity value or the par value = $1,000
n = Number of payments until maturity

Remember that once you obtain the before-tax interest rate on the bond (k_{dbt}) you still need to compute the after-tax interest cost as

$$k_d = k_{dbt} \times (1 - t)$$

We illustrate the computation of the cost of debt with an example. Suppose Yukon Dazzling Resorts Incorporated is considering the issuance of a bond in the near future. Investment bankers provide information about the likely selling price, coupon rate, and issuance costs. They believe a 20-year bond will sell at a market price of $1,000, with a 9 percent coupon rate, and issuance costs will be $5 for each $1,000 bond denomination. Assume Yukon's marginal tax rate is 40 percent. What is the after-tax cost of debt from this bond issue for Yukon Dazzling Resorts Incorporated? First we need to compute the net proceeds from the bond issuance—it is just the $1,000 market price minus the $5 issuance cost per bond.

$$V_{net} = \$1,000 - 5 = \$995$$

Then we need to compute the before-tax interest rate on the bond to Yukon.

$$\$995 = \$90 \times \left[\frac{1 - \frac{1}{(1 + k_{dbt})^{20}}}{k_{dbt}} \right] + \frac{\$1,000}{(1 + k_{dbt})^{20}}$$

The easiest way to solve the preceding equation is with a business calculator, as illustrated in Appendix 4. Using this procedure, we obtain

$$PV = V_{net} = -\$995$$
$$PMT = C = \$90$$
$$N = n = 20$$
$$FV = M = \$1,000$$

And then compute I/Y or I/YR to obtain the before-tax interest cost.

$$I/Y = I/YR = k_{dbt} = 9.05\%$$

Then we can compute the after-tax cost of funds raised by the bond issuance.

$$k_d = 9.05\% \times (1 - 0.40) = 5.43\%$$

You can see the issuance costs do not make a heavy impact on the before-tax interest rate. The before-tax return to an investor buying this bond at the $1,000 market price is the 9 percent coupon rate. The investor's before-tax rate of return and coupon rate are the same in this case because the bond is selling at par value. The $5 per bond issuance costs raise the cost only slightly, to 9.05 percent. The issuance costs on bonds are usually low, not having a large impact on the interest cost to the issuing corporation. As such, ignoring the issuance costs on bonds does not cause a large error and still provides a generally good approximate cost of debt. For instance, in our example here, ignoring the issuance costs gives us the following after-tax cost of debt.

$$k_d = 9\% \times (1 - 0.40) = 5.40\%$$

This is just 0.03 percent less than our calculation when considering issuance costs.

The preceding procedure works well when a corporation has just sold bonds or is currently in the process of selling bonds and all the information to use in the equation is readily available. If this is not the case, information can be used from bonds the firm currently has outstanding in the marketplace. By using the coupon rate, remaining maturity, and current market price on the outstanding bonds, the before-tax cost (k_{dbt}) can be computed and used as an estimate for the before-tax cost on new bonds to be issued by the firm. The only thing this method doesn't provide is an estimate of issuance costs. But issuance costs could be estimated independently or, as suggested earlier, a close estimate of before-tax cost can still be obtained while ignoring issuance costs.

Consider the following example for Yukon Dazzling Resorts Incorporated. Suppose Yukon does not have any information on a current bond issuance but has an outstanding 30-year bond with a 12 percent coupon rate issued 10 years ago. Currently this bond is selling for $1,280 and has 20 years remaining to maturity. We can estimate the before-tax interest rate on a new bond issued by Yukon by computing the before-tax yield on this bond.

$$\$1,280 = \$120 \times \left[\frac{1 - \dfrac{1}{(1 + k_{dbt})^{20}}}{k_{dbt}} \right] + \frac{\$1,000}{(1 + k_{dbt})^{20}}$$

$$PV = V_{net} = -\$1,280$$
$$PMT = C = \$120$$
$$N = n = 20$$
$$FV = M = \$1,000$$

And then compute I/Y or I/YR to obtain the before-tax interest cost.

$$I/Y = I/YR = k_{dbt} = 8.94\%$$

The estimate of after-tax interest cost on a new bond for Yukon is

$$k_d = 8.94\% \times (1 - 0.40) = 5.37\%$$

But what if Yukon has not recently sold any bonds, is not in the process of selling bonds, and has no bonds outstanding? Or, Yukon may have bonds outstanding but a good market price of the bonds cannot be obtained because they do not trade very often or trade privately. If Yukon has a relationship with an investment banker, that person can most likely provide good estimates of all the information needed to estimate the after-tax interest cost on a new bond. Even if this fails, Yukon can get a rough estimate of after-tax interest costs by considering the yields on bonds issued by companies with similar financial and risk characteristics.

10.5 The Cost of Preferred Stock

The use of preferred stock to raise funds is not nearly as common as the use of bonds. Nevertheless, a number of firms do use this method of raising capital. Some preferred stock is issued as a perpetuity, but many preferred stock issues have a call feature or a sinking fund, as described in Chapter 8. This complicates the valuation of preferred stock and also the computation of the true cost of the funds that have been raised with preferred stock. We show how to compute the cost of preferred stock funds assuming the preferred stock is a perpetuity, and also how to compute the cost in the case of a known ending date for the preferred stock.

Computing the cost of funds raised with preferred stock is similar to computing the investor's rate of return on preferred stock, as shown in Chapter 8. Instead of using the market price, we use the net proceeds from the preferred stock issuance after issuance costs are paid. The following equation is used when the preferred stock is a perpetuity.

$$k_p = \frac{d_p}{V_{net}}$$

where V_{net} is the net proceeds from the preferred stock issuance after issuance costs are paid and

d_p = the preferred annual dividend per share
k_p = the cost of funds raised by the issuance of preferred stock

Note that k_p is the final cost of funds raised by the issuance of preferred stock because preferred dividends are not a tax-deductible cost, as is interest expense.

We illustrate the computation of the cost of preferred stock with an example. Suppose Yukon Dazzling Resorts Incorporated is considering the issuance of preferred stock in the near future. Investment bankers provide information about the likely selling price, dividend rate, and issuance costs. They believe a perpetual preferred stock issue will sell at a market price of $100, the same as the par value. They expect a 10 percent dividend rate, and issuance costs will be $3 per share. What is the cost of preferred stock to Yukon Dazzling Resorts for this issue? First we need to compute the net proceeds from the preferred stock issuance. It is just the $100 market price minus the $3 issuance cost per share.

$$V_{net} = \$100 - 3 = \$97$$

The cost of funds raised by issuing preferred stock is

$$k_p = \frac{\$10}{\$97} = 10.31\%$$

You can see that issuance costs do make a more significant impact on the before-tax cost for this preferred stock example than for our earlier bond example. The before-tax return to an investor buying this preferred stock at the $100 market price is the 10 percent dividend rate. The $3 per share issuance cost raises the cost slightly to 10.31 percent. The issuance costs are usually a greater percentage of the market price for preferred stock than for bonds. As such, the issuance costs on preferred stock are usually taken into account because ignoring them generates a larger error than ignoring issuance costs for bonds.

Also notice we do not make any adjustments to our computation for taxes. Preferred stock dividends are not tax deductible, and therefore the issuing firm's marginal tax rate does not affect the firm's cost of raising funds with preferred stock.

Now suppose Yukon Dazzling Resorts Incorporated decided to issue preferred stock with an ending date in 10 years. In other words, Yukon will call all the preferred stock back in 10 years, paying each investor the par value of $100 at that time. We assume Yukon's preferred stock is still expected to sell at a $100 market price with a 10 percent dividend rate and $3 issuance costs per share. How do we figure out the cost of raising funds with this particular preferred stock issue? We compute the cost similar to how we did for bonds, except taxes do not affect this cost. The net proceeds from the preferred stock are still $97 per share. The dividends are still $10 per share. But now the $10 dividends are a 10-payment annuity instead of a perpetuity without end. And, in addition to the dividends, investors will receive $100 (par value) in 10 years. The preferred dividends are treated as coupon payments on a bond, and the $100 par value is treated just as the $1,000 par value on a bond.

$$\$97 = \$10 \times \left[\frac{1 - \dfrac{1}{(1 + k_p)^{10}}}{k_p} \right] + \frac{\$100}{(1 + k_p)^{10}}$$

$$PV = V_{net} = -\$97$$
$$PMT = d_p = \$10$$
$$N = n = 10$$
$$FV = \text{Par value} = \$100$$

And then compute I/Y or I/YR to obtain the cost for this preferred stock.

$$I/Y = I/YR = k_p = 10.50\%$$

Thus, in this example the cost for Yukon Dazzling Resorts Incorporated to raise funds with preferred stock is 10.50 percent.

10.6 Internal Common Equity—New Retained Earnings

Capital provided from a firm's common equity actually has two possible sources. New capital provided by the reinvestment of a firm's profits is called *additions to retained earnings* or *new retained earnings*. In the cost of capital context, this is called *internal equity* or *internally generated funds (IGF)* because the firm itself, through reinvestment of profits, provides these funds internally. The other source of common equity capital is from the sale of new common stock shares to investors. The proceeds of these sales (after issuance costs) are available for investment by the firm. We call this *external equity* because these funds come from outside the firm from external investors.

The cost of internal equity may at first appear to be zero, because internal equity is just the firm's own profits reinvested in the firm. But nothing could be further from the truth. Investors in a firm's bonds are paid by interest payments. Investors in a firm's preferred stock are paid by dividends. The remaining profit belongs to investors in common stock. This profit can be paid out as dividends to common shareholders or can be reinvested in the firm. If part of the profit is reinvested, there is an opportunity cost to the common shareholders. The shareholders could have used this money to make further investments on their own. Therefore, profits should be reinvested only if the firm can earn as much as common shareholders could earn on their own. How much is this? We propose that a minimum expected rate of return on reinvested profits is the rate of return that investors expect when they buy the firm's common stock at its current price. If the firm does not expect to earn this rate of return on reinvested profits, then the profits should be paid out as dividends to the common shareholders. We use this rate of return as the cost of using internal equity.

How do we measure the rate of return investors expect when they buy a firm's common stock? Measuring investor return on bonds and preferred stock is fairly straightforward because all the expected cash flows are stated. But the expected cash flows on common stock are not stated, and thus investor return on common stock is difficult to estimate. In the next three sections we present three different methods for estimating the cost of using internal equity. These are (1) the dividend valuation model method, (2) the capital asset pricing model method, and (3) the bond yield plus risk premium method. None of these methods is perfectly or necessarily superior to the other methods. They all provide an estimate subject to error of the cost of using internal equity. A company's final estimate for the cost of internal equity could be based on any one of these three methods or it could be an average of the three methods. No one method dominates the others.

10.6.1 DIVIDEND VALUATION MODEL METHOD

One of the commonly used procedures to estimate the cost of internal equity is the dividend valuation model. In Chapter 9, we showed that the value of common stock can be expressed as follows.

$$P_0 = \frac{d_1}{(1 + k_e)} + \frac{d_2}{(1 + k_e)^2} + \cdots + \frac{d_n}{(1 + k_e)^n} + \frac{P_n}{(1 + k_e)^n}$$

where P_i = the value of common stock at the end of year i
d_i = the common stock dividend at the end of year i
k_e = the investor's required rate of return on equity or common stock

Given the current market price of the common stock (P_0) and forecasts for future dividends (d_i) and future stock price (P_n), we could solve for the investors' required rate of return on equity (k_e) and thus the cost of using funds generated from internal equity. The problem is that future common dividends and future common stock price cannot be estimated with the same accuracy as bond coupon payments and preferred stock dividends. But, if the company's future dividends are expected to grow at a stable rate in the future, the constant-growth version of the dividend valuation model provides good estimates of either the stock value or the investor's required rate of return.

We used the constant-growth dividend valuation model in Chapter 9 to estimate the value of common stock (P_0) given a known investor's required rate of return (k_e), growth rate (g), and expected dividend in one year

$$P_0 = \frac{d_1}{(k_e - g)}$$

But now we want to use this model to estimate the investor's required rate of return for a given market value, growth rate, and expected dividend in one year. So we need to rearrange the terms algebraically to solve for investor's required rate of return (k_e).

$$k_e = \frac{d_1}{P_0} + g$$

It is much easier to see the intuition behind the constant-growth dividend valuation equation in this form than in the form used in Chapter 9. Basically, the preceding equation shows that the return to an investor in common stock is equal to the dividend yield (d_1/P_0) plus stock price appreciation (g).

We illustrate this model with an example. Suppose Yukon Dazzling Resorts Incorporated common stock is selling for $40 per share, pays a current dividend (d_0) of $3.50 per share, and is expected to grow at a 4 percent rate into the foreseeable future. The cost of internal equity estimate is

$$k_e = \frac{\$3.64}{\$40.00} + 4\%$$

$$= 9.10\% + 4\%$$

$$= 13.10\%$$

where we calculated $d_1 = d_0 \times (1 + g) = \$3.50 \times (1.04) = \$3.64$.

The investor's required rate of return on Yukon Dazzling Resorts common stock is estimated at 13.10 percent. This would also be the dividend valuation model estimate of the cost of internal equity for Yukon Dazzling Resorts Incorporated.

The difficulty in applying this model is in obtaining an estimate of the future growth rate (g). The actual market price of the common stock (P_0) can be obtained easily enough, as can next year's expected dividend (d_1). Research supports the use of analysts' forecasts of growth as the most accurate forecasts; analysts' forecasts also work best to explain market prices of common stock. Analysts' forecasts can be obtained from Value Line (www.valueline.com), TD Waterhouse (www.tdwaterhouse.ca), RBC Financial (www.rbc.com), ScotiaMcLeod (www.scotiabank.com), or other investment advisory services and brokerage houses.

10.6.2 CAPITAL ASSET PRICING MODEL METHOD

We presented the capital asset pricing model (CAPM) in Chapter 7 as a way to relate a firm's risk to the investor's required rate of return on the firm's common stock. And, of course, once we have a measure of investor's required rate of return on common stock then we also have a measure of the cost of using funds generated from internal equity.

The CAPM defines investor's required rate of return as a risk-free rate (k_r) plus a risk premium that increases with the amount of the firm's systematic risk as measured by beta (β_j). The risk premium is compensation to the investor for bearing systematic risk.

Higher systematic risk increases the risk premium and increases the required rate of return, and lower systematic risk decreases the risk premium and decreases the required rate of return. This relationship is expressed mathematically by the security market equation

$$k_j = R_f + (R_m - R_f) \times \beta_j$$

where
k_j = the investor-required rate of return on firm j's common stock
R_f = the expected risk-free rate of return
β_j = the beta or measure of systematic risk for company j's common stock
R_m = the expected market return
$(R_m - R_f) \times \beta_j$ = the risk premium for firm j's common stock
$(R_m - R_f)$ = expected risk premium on an average-risk ($\beta_j = 1.0$) firm's common stock

The security market line equation is explained throughly in Chapter 6; for convenience we do a brief recap here. The preceding equation shows the investor's required rate of return (k_j) is equal to a risk-free rate of return (R_f) plus a risk premium $[(R_m - R_f) \times \beta_j]$ for firm j's common stock. The risk premium is equal to an expected risk premium on an average-risk common stock $[(R_m - R_f)]$ multiplied by firm j's measure of systematic risk (β_j). So firm j's risk premium is essentially the average risk premium scaled up or down according to the level of firm j's systematic risk. If firm j is riskier than average, then we scale up the average risk premium for firm j. If firm j is less risky than average, then we scale down the average risk premium for firm j.

The expected risk-free rate of return (R_f) is usually measured by a Bank of Canada or U.S. Treasury bill rate. Beta (β_j) can be estimated on your own if you have the proper data and statistical ability, but Value Line and major brokerage firms also regularly compute the beta for major corporations. The expected market return (R_m) is the average return investors expect to receive on common stocks in the future. It should be the expected return on an average-risk ($\beta_j = 1.0$) common stock. Measuring the expected market return can be quite complex. Ibbotson Associates study market returns over long periods of time and provide information on past market returns that can be used to estimate future market returns. Also, financial service companies provide estimates of future market returns that can be used as an estimate of the expected market return in the CAPM.

We illustrate the use of the CAPM to estimate a firm's cost of internal equity with an example. Suppose Yukon Dazzling Resorts Incorporated has a beta (β_M) estimated at 1.20, the expected risk-free rate of return (R_f) is 5 percent, and the expected market return (R_m) is 12 percent. Use the security market line equation to compute the investor's required rate of return for Yukon Dazzling Resorts (k_M).

$$
\begin{aligned}
k_M &= R_f + (R_m - R_f) \times \beta_M \\
&= 5\% + 1.20 \times (12\% - 5\%) \\
&= 5\% + 1.20 \times 7\% \\
&= 5\% + 8.4\% \\
&= 13.4\%
\end{aligned}
$$

Notice in the preceding equation that the expected risk premium on an average-risk common stock is 7 percent $[(R_m - R_f)]$, and the risk premium for Yukon Dazzling Resorts is 8.4 percent $[\beta_M \times (R_m - R_f)]$. The investor-required rate of return for Yukon Dazzling

Resorts common stock is 13.4 percent, and this is also an estimate for the cost of using funds from internal equity. Notice the required rate of return for Yukon (13.4%) is higher than the expected market rate of return (12.0%) because the Yukon beta (1.2) is higher than the average beta (1.0).

10.6.3 BOND YIELD PLUS RISK PREMIUM METHOD

The bond yield plus risk premium method is probably the easiest of the three methods used to estimate the cost of internal equity. Its application requires an estimate of a firm's own bond yield on a before-tax basis—generally easy to find. Then you add a risk premium to the bond yield to estimate the cost of internal equity. The difficulty in applying this method is to estimate an appropriate risk premium. There is evidence supporting risk premiums as low as 2 percent and in some cases in excess of 7 percent, depending on the general level of interest rates and the riskiness of the firm. There is also evidence that the risk premium over and above the bond yield is larger when the general level of interest rates is low and smaller when the general level interest rates is high. Also companies with low systematic risk ($\beta_j < 1.0$) tend to have a smaller risk premium, and companies with a high systematic risk ($\beta_j > 1.0$) tend to have a larger risk premium.

We illustrate the use of the bond yield plus risk premium method for estimating the cost of internal equity with an example. Yukon Dazzling Resorts Incorporated has bonds trading at an 8.5 percent yield. Suppose the typical risk premium over bond yield for an average company ($\beta_j = 1.0$) is 4 percent. But remember from our previous example that Yukon Dazzling Resorts Incorporated has a beta of 1.20. As such, we use a higher-risk premium of 5 percent. So Yukon Dazzling Resorts' cost of internal equity using the bond yield plus risk premium method is

$$k_e = 8.5\% + 5.0\% = 13.5\%$$

10.7 External Common Equity—New Issues of Common Stock

When common equity funds are provided by growth in retained earnings, the cost of internal equity as estimated in the previous sections is the correct cost to use. But if retained earnings growth is not sufficient to meet a firm's need for equity funding, then new shares of common stock may be sold to raise capital. Capital generated by the sale of new common stock is called **external equity**. External equity has issuance costs as do bonds and preferred stock. Because internal equity is just the investment of the firm's own profits back into the firm, it involves no issuance costs. The issuance costs with external equity raise its cost above that for internal equity. The issuance costs on common stock involve several different cost items. They include investment banker and legal costs as well as the negative impact on the firm's common stock price usually caused by a new issuance of common stock.

The same general approach to handling issuance costs with bonds and preferred stock is used to adjust the cost of equity. We simply reduce the market price of the common stock by the amount of the issuance costs per share. But only one method is used to estimate the cost of equity that uses the market price of common stock in the equation.

The market price per share of common stock can be adjusted for issuance costs in the dividend valuation model, using the equation from section 10.6.1,

$$k_{ne} = \frac{d_1}{P_0} + g$$

where k_{ne} = the cost of new equity or the cost of external equity.

Replace the common stock market price (P_0) with the per share net proceeds from the sale of common stock after issuance costs are paid.

$$k_{ne} = \frac{d_1}{P_{net}} + g$$

We use the same example of Yukon Dazzling Resorts Incorporated that we used in section 10.6.1 to show how this works. Remember, Yukon common stock sells for $40 per share, is expected to pay a dividend of $3.64 at the end of the year, and is expected to grow at a 4 percent rate into the foreseeable future. The cost of *internal* equity as computed previously is

$$k_e = \frac{\$3.64}{\$40.00} + 4\%$$

$$= 9.10\% + 4\%$$

$$= 13.10\%$$

The cost of *external* equity for Yukon Dazzling Resorts requires an estimate of issuance costs. This estimate could be provided by Yukon's investment banker. Suppose in this case issuance costs are expected to be $6 per share. Then the cost of external equity using the dividend valuation model is

$$k_{ne} = \frac{\$3.64}{(\$40 - \$6)} + 4\%$$

$$= \frac{\$3.64}{\$34} + 4\%$$

$$= 10.71\% + 4\%$$

$$= 14.71\%$$

The dividend valuation model is the only model generally used to estimate the impact of issuance costs on the cost of *external* equity, but three different methods are generally used for estimating the cost of *internal* equity. A firm might use all three methods to generate a cost of internal equity estimate, or it might use just one of the three methods. What if a firm does not use the dividend valuation model to estimate the cost of *internal* equity? Does the firm have to use the dividend valuation model to estimate the cost of *external* equity? No, the dividend valuation model can be used to estimate the cost adjustment for external equity, and then this cost adjustment can be used in conjunction with any other method to derive a final cost estimate for external equity. Look back at our Yukon Dazzling Resorts example. Using the dividend valuation model, the cost of internal equity is 13.10 percent and the cost of external equity is 14.71 percent. The adjustment for issuance costs is 1.61 percent. In other words, issuance costs add 1.61 percent to the cost of Yukon's *internal* equity to arrive at Yukon's cost of *external* equity.

$$\text{adjustment for issuance costs} = 14.71\% - 13.10\% = 1.61\%$$

This adjustment can then be added to any cost of *internal* equity the firm decides to use. If the firm uses a 13.4 percent cost of *internal* equity from the CAPM method, then the cost of *external* equity is 15.01 percent.

$$k_{ne} = 13.40\% + 1.61\% = 15.01\%$$

If the firm uses a 13.5 percent cost of *internal* equity from the bond yield plus risk premium method, then the cost of *external* equity is 15.11 percent.

$$k_{ne} = 13.50\% + 1.61\% = 15.11\%$$

Suppose the firm uses a 13.33 percent cost of *internal* equity from averaging the three model estimates together as

$$k_e = \frac{(13.10\% + 13.40\% + 13.50\%)}{3} = 13.33\%$$

Adjusting this 13.33 percent cost of *internal* equity for issuance costs gives us a 14.94 percent cost of *external* equity.

$$k_{ne} = 13.33\% + 1.61\% = 14.94\%$$

10.8 Computation of the Weighted Average Cost of Capital

Now that we know how to compute the components' cost of capital, we are ready to complete the weighted average cost of capital estimation. In section 10.2, we presented the equation for weighted average cost of capital as

$$k_a = w_d \times k_d + w_p \times k_p + w_e \times k_e$$

In addition to the components' cost of capital, we need to know the target capital structure to calculate the weighted average cost of capital for a firm. We assume Yukon Dazzling Resorts Incorporated has a target capital structure of 40 percent long-term debt (w_d), 10 percent preferred stock (w_p), and 50 percent common equity (w_e). We also assume Yukon expects sufficient growth in retained earnings to meet the firm's needs for common equity funding.

Using the calculations for Yukon Dazzling Resorts from the previous sections, we have a 5.43 percent cost of long-term debt (k_d), a 10.31 percent cost of raising funds with preferred stock (k_p), and several estimates for the cost of internal equity (k_e). The cost of internal equity is estimated to be 13.10 percent using the dividend valuation model, 13.40 percent using the CAPM, and 13.50 percent using the bond yield plus risk premium method. We also computed a 13.33 percent cost of internal equity by averaging the three model estimates. Use 13.33 percent as Yukon's cost of internal equity. Now we have all the inputs we need to estimate the weighted average cost of capital.

$$k_a = w_d \times k_d + w_p \times k_p + w_e \times k_e$$
$$k_a = 0.40 \times 5.43\% + 0.10 \times 10.31\% + 0.50 \times 13.33\%$$
$$= 9.87\%$$

Therefore, Yukon Dazzling Resorts should use 9.87 percent as the minimum required rate of return when evaluating investments. An investment should be expected to return at least this amount before Yukon considers committing funds to an investment. An average return of 9.87 percent is required to pay off the firm's contractual obligations on bonds and preferred stock and still have enough left over to satisfy common shareholders with a sufficient return. Exhibit 10-1 summarizes this computation of the weighted average cost of capital, including the initial estimation of the component costs.

Exhibit 10-1
Computing the Weighted Average Cost of Capital

The weighted average cost of capital is computed using the following equation.

$$k_a = w_d \times k_d + w_p \times k_p + w_e \times k_e$$

Remember that the k_d, k_p, and k_e are the after-tax cost of funds raised from long-term debt, the cost of funds raised from preferred stock, and the cost of funds raised from common equity respectively. Also, w_d, w_p, and w_e represent a firm's target for the proportion of funds raised from long-term debt, preferred stock, and common equity respectively. These proportions represent a firm's target capital structure. Yukon Dazzling Resorts Incorporated has the following target capital structure.

$$w_d = 40\% \quad \text{(Long-term debt)}$$
$$w_p = 10\% \quad \text{(Preferred stock)}$$
$$w_e = 50\% \quad \text{(Common equity)}$$

Next, we estimate Yukon's after-tax cost of debt (k_d). Yukon believes one of its own 20-year bonds will sell at a market price of $1,000, with a 9 percent coupon rate and issuance costs of $5 for each $1,000 bond denomination. Also, Yukon's marginal tax rate is 40 percent. First, we need to compute the net proceeds from the bond issuance. It is just the $1,000 market price minus the $5 issuance cost per bond.

$$V_{net} = \$1,000 - 5 = \$995$$

Then we need to compute the before-tax interest rate on the bond to Yukon.

$$\$995 = \$90 \times \left[\frac{1 - \frac{1}{(1 + k_{dbt})^{20}}}{k_{dbt}} \right] + \frac{\$1,000}{(1 + k_{dbt})^{20}}$$

The easiest way to solve the preceding equation is with a business calculator, as illustrated in Appendix 4. Using this procedure, we obtain

$$PV = V_{net} = -\$995$$
$$PMT = C = \$90$$
$$N = n = 20$$
$$FV = M = \$1,000$$

(continued)

(continued)

And then compute I/Y or I/YR to obtain the before-tax interest cost.

$$I/Y = I/YR = k_{dbt} = 9.05\%$$

Then we can compute the after-tax cost of funds raised by the bond issuance.

$$k_d = 9.05\% \times (1 - 0.40) = 5.43\%$$

Next, we estimate Yukon's cost of raising funds with preferred stock. Yukon believes a perpetual preferred stock issue will sell at a market price of $100, the same as the par value. The company expects a 10 percent dividend rate and issuance costs of $3 per share. First, we need to compute the net proceeds from the preferred stock issuance. It is just the $100 market price minus the $3 issuance cost per share.

$$V_{net} = \$100 - 3 = \$97$$

The cost of funds raised by issuing preferred stock is

$$k_p = \frac{\$10}{\$97} = 10.31\%$$

The last component cost of capital we need to estimate is the cost of internal equity. Three different basic methods are used to estimate the cost of internal equity: the dividend valuation model, the CAPM, and the bond yield plus risk premium.

We first consider estimating Yukon's cost of internal equity using the dividend valuation model. Suppose Yukon's common stock is selling for $40 per share, pays a current dividend (d_0) of $3.50 per share, and is expected to grow at a 4 percent rate into the foreseeable future. The dividend one year from today (d_1) is expected to be $3.64.

$$d_1 = d_0 \times (1 + g) = \$3.50 \times (1.04) = \$3.64$$

The cost of internal equity estimate is

$$k_e = \frac{\$3.64}{\$40.00} + 4\%$$
$$= 9.10\% + 4\%$$
$$= 13.10\%$$

Now we estimate Yukon's cost of internal equity using the CAPM. Suppose Yukon Dazzling Resorts Incorporated has a beta (β_r) estimated at 1.20, the expected risk-free rate of return (k_r) is 5 percent, and the expected market return (k_m) is 12 percent. Use the security market line equation to compute the investor's required rate of return for Yukon Dazzling Resorts (k_r).

$$k_r = R_f + (R_m - R_f) \times \beta_r$$
$$= 5\% + (12\% - 5\%) \times 1.20$$
$$= 5\% + 7\% \times 1.20$$
$$= 5\% + 8.4\%$$
$$= 13.4\%$$

For a third estimate of Yukon's internal cost of equity, we use the bond yield plus risk premium method. Yukon Dazzling Resorts Incorporated has bonds trading at an

(continued)

(continued)

8.5 percent yield. Suppose the typical risk premium over bond yield for an average company ($\beta_j = 1.0$) is 4 percent. But remember from our previous example that Yukon Dazzling Resorts Incorporated has a beta of 1.20. As such, we use a higher risk premium of 5 percent. We have not used a precise method to raise the risk premium to 5 percent. We know Yukon has above-average systematic risk from its beta ($\beta_r > 1.0$). We have just used our judgment to estimate a higher-than-average risk premium of 5 percent versus a 4 percent average risk premium. So, Yukon Dazzling Resorts' cost of internal equity using the bond yield plus risk premium method is

$$k_e = 8.5\% + 5.0\% = 13.5\%$$

We could use any one of the three estimates for the cost of Yukon's internal cost of equity, or we could use an average of the three estimates as follows:

$$k_e = \frac{(13.10\% + 13.40\% + 13.50\%)}{3} = 13.33\%$$

We can now complete the weighted average cost of capital computation for Yukon Dazzling Resorts.

$$k_a = w_d \times k_d + w_p \times k_p + w_e \times k_e$$
$$k_a = 0.40 \times 5.43\% + 0.10 \times 10.31\% + 0.50 \times 13.33\%$$
$$= 9.87\%$$

Therefore, Yukon Dazzling Resorts' weighted average cost of capital is 9.87 percent, and Yukon should use 9.87 percent as the minimum required rate of return when evaluating investments.

In the preceding weighted average estimation, we assumed Yukon expects sufficient growth in retained earnings to meet the firm's needs for common equity funding. What if this is not the case? How does this change the estimation of Yukon's weighted average cost of capital? We assume Yukon is considering investing up to $100 million in new projects for the coming year and thus needs the following amounts of funding from debt, preferred stock, and common equity.

Long-term debt funding = 0.40 × $100 million = $40 million
Preferred stock funding = 0.10 × $100 million = $10 million
Common equity funding = 0.50 × $100 million = $50 million

What if Yukon expects to have only $20 million of new retained earnings to help finance this growth? This does not meet Yukon's needs for equity funding and leaves a shortfall of $30 million in common equity. What can be done? Of course, Yukon Dazzling Resorts Incorporated can raise the other $30 million by selling new shares of common stock. Remember, we call this external equity. In section 10.7 we computed a 14.94 percent cost of external equity for Yukon using the average estimate for internal equity and then adding an adjustment for issuance costs. To estimate Yukon's weighted average cost of capital, we must adapt our equation to this different situation. Remember, 50 percent, or $50 million, of common equity is expected to be needed. Yukon expects to have

$20 million of new retained earnings, and this provides 20 percent of the $100 million investment budget. The other $30 million of common equity is provided externally through the sale of new common stock. This provides 30 percent of the $100 million investment budget. The estimate of the new weighted average cost of capital is

$$k_a = w_d \times k_d + w_p \times k_p + w_e \times k_e + w_{ne} \times k_{ne}$$
$$k_a = 0.40 \times 5.43\% + 0.10 \times 10.31\% + 0.20 \times 13.33\% + 0.30 \times 14.94\%$$
$$= 10.35\%$$

We have broken up the 0.50 weight for common equity into two components. Internal equity is weighted at 0.20 ($20 million of the $100 million investment budget), and external equity is weighted at 0.30 ($30 million of the $100 million investment budget). Of course, the use of external equity raises the cost of capital because Yukon Dazzling Resorts is paying issuance costs for part of the common equity. Now Yukon Dazzling Resorts should use 10.35 percent as the minimum required rate of return when evaluating investments.

10.9 Using the Weighted Average Cost of Capital

A weighted average cost of capital is estimated for a period of time. Typically, a firm uses a time frame of six months or a year to estimate its marginal cost of capital. Suppose a year is used. A firm estimates its cost of new funds (cost of debt, preferred stock, and equity) over the coming year and uses the estimate to compute a weighted average cost of capital. This weighted average cost of capital is then used as a minimum required rate of return to evaluate possible investments over the next year. If capital costs change significantly during the year, then the weighted average cost of capital should be computed once again with the new estimates. This new weighted average cost of capital would then be used to evaluate any projects from this time forward.

It might be attractive to take a simpler approach to using the cost of capital. For example, suppose Yukon Dazzling Resorts plans to build a new hotel in the coming year at a cost of $40 million, entirely funded with proceeds from a bond sale. It is tempting to evaluate this project at the 5.43 percent after-tax cost of debt we estimated in section 10.4. It is much easier to compute just the after-tax cost of debt than the entire weighted average cost of capital. Also, all funding for this project comes from the bond sale, so would it be appropriate to use just the cost of debt to evaluate this project? No, it would not; below, we consider the possible consequences of making investment decisions in this fashion.

If the after-tax cost of debt is the minimum required rate of return for the new hotel, then any expected return above 5.43 percent makes the new hotel project an acceptable investment. If this hotel project is accepted and financed with a $40 million bond issue, then Yukon Dazzling Resorts will need to use preferred stock and common equity financing for later projects. Remember, only 40 percent of Yukon's capital is targeted to come from debt, whereas the other 60 percent should be raised from preferred stock issuance and common equity. Thus, later investment projects would need to be financed with preferred stock costing 10.31 percent, internal equity costing 13.33 percent, or external equity costing 14.94 percent. Using the same method of analysis, later investment projects will need to return a minimum of 10.31 percent, 13.33 percent, or 14.94 percent, depending on the source of funds used to finance the projects. If some projects are evaluated with a 5.43 percent minimum required rate of return, other projects at 10.31 percent, other projects at 13.33 percent, and still other projects at 14.94 percent, depending on the source of funds, the firm will be challenged and may experience dysfunction in its investment decision making. A project financed with debt would be acceptable with only a 6 percent expected rate of return, whereas another project financed with equity would be unacceptable with a 12 percent expected rate of return.

We advocate using a weighted average cost of capital, even if all components of capital are not used to finance an investment project. This notion is called *separating the financing decision from the investment decision*. In other words, as a firm evaluates investment projects, it should not consider the amount of funding from long-term debt, preferred stock, and equity. Instead, assume funds for the project are drawn from long-term debt, preferred stock, and equity in the same proportions as the firm's target capital structure. This means the firm can use its weighted average cost of capital to evaluate all projects, regardless of whether they are financed with long-term debt, preferred stock, common equity, or some combination of the three components.

10.10 SUMMARY

This chapter:

- Explained a firm's cost of capital
- Outlined the reasons why a firm's cost of capital should be measured on a marginal, after-tax basis and should measure only the cost of long-term sources of funds
- Discussed the relative risk of bonds, preferred stock, and common stock to an investor
- Explained how to estimate the cost of debt
- Explained how to estimate the cost of preferred stock
- Explained how to estimate the cost of common equity, both internal and external
- Discussed the reasons why internal equity (new retained earnings) has a cost
- Explained how to compute the weighted average cost of capital
- Explained how to use the weighted average cost of capital and introduced the concept of separating the financing decision from the investment decision

Key Terms

Cost of capital	Marginal measurement
External equity	Required rate of return
Flotation costs	Target capital structure
Issuance costs	Weighted average cost of capital

Discussion Questions

1. What is riskier from an investor's point of view: a firm's bonds, preferred stock, or common stock?

2. Why do a firm's retained earnings have a cost?

3. How are retained earnings different from funds raised by the issuance of bonds, preferred stock, or common stock?

4. Which is better for evaluating a firm's new investment proposals, the marginal cost of capital or the historical cost of capital?

5. There are two reasons why the cost of debt is less than the cost of funds raised from preferred stock or common stock. What are the two reasons?

6. Why is the cost of external equity greater than the cost of internal equity?

7. Why is computing a firm's cost of debt just like computing the investor's yield to maturity, as we learned in Chapter 8?

8. Is a firm's amount of retained earnings shown on its current balance sheet a good measure of the amount of internal equity available for new investments? Explain your answer.

9. What are the three alternative methods used to estimate the cost of internal equity?

10. Explain what is meant by the concept of separating the financing decision from the investment decision.

Problems

Problems designated with EXCEL can be solved using Excel spreadsheets accessible at www.pearsoned.ca/chatfield.

1. Stage West of Canada Casinos recently sold an issue of 15-year maturity bonds. The bonds were sold at $955 each. After issuance costs, Stage West received $948 each. The bonds have a $1,000 maturity value and a 7 percent coupon rate. The coupon is paid annually. What is the after-tax cost of debt for these bonds if Stage West's effective tax rate is 40 percent?

2. Niagara Restaurants expects to sell a new bond issue at its par value. The coupon rate is $8\frac{3}{8}$ percent, and the coupon is paid annually. Because issuance costs are so small, Niagara plans to ignore their impact on the after-tax cost. What is the after-tax cost of these $1,000 par value bonds if Niagara's effective tax rate is 40 percent?

3. Rocky Mountain Travel Incorporated plans to issue preferred stock at a price of $50 per share. The dividend will be $4.30 per share, and issuance costs are expected to be $3.00 per share. What is the cost to Rocky Mountain Travel of raising funds with preferred stock?

4. Canuck Tours Incorporated plans to issue a 20-year bond. Canuck Tours expects the $1,000 par value bonds to sell for $995 each. Issuance costs are expected to be $5 per $1,000 bond, and the coupon rate is $11\frac{7}{8}$ percent. If the effective tax rate is 40 percent, what is the after-tax cost of debt to Canuck Tours?

5. Norman Entertainment Corporation recently sold an issue of preferred stock at $45 per share. The dividend is $7.55, and the issuance costs are $4 per share. What is the cost to Norman Entertainment of raising funds with preferred stock?

6. Grace Fine Dining Trust is financed 100 percent with equity and intends to remain this way. Grace's common stock beta is 1.20, the expected market return (average market

return) is 12 percent, and the risk-free rate is 5 percent. What are the cost of equity and the weighted average cost of capital for Grace?

7. Sullivan & Associates expects to pay a common stock dividend of $2.00 per share next year (d_1). Dividends are expected to grow at a 5 percent rate for the foreseeable future. Sullivan's common stock is selling for $20 per share, and issuance costs are $3.00 per share.

   a. What is Sullivan's cost of internal equity?

   b. What is Sullivan's cost of external equity?

8. I Am Canadian Casinos' common stock beta is 0.85. The expected market return (average market return) is 14 percent, and the risk-free rate is 6 percent. What is I Am Canadian Casinos' cost of internal equity?

9. Hannibal's Restaurants expects to pay a common stock dividend of $4.35 per share next year (d_1). Dividends are expected to grow at a 3 percent rate for the foreseeable future. Hannibal's common stock is selling for $30 per share, and issuance costs are $4.25 per share.

   a. What is Hannibal's cost of internal equity?

   b. What is Hannibal's cost of external equity?

10. Cleopatra's Resorts Incorporated has a current capital structure that is 60 percent equity, 30 percent debt, and 10 percent preferred stock. This is considered optimal. Cleopatra's is considering a $100 million capital budgeting project. During the coming year Cleopatra's expects to have $20 million of retained earnings available to finance this capital budgeting project. The marginal tax rate is 40 percent.

    ■ Cleopatra's can sell $1,000 par value bonds with a 9 percent coupon rate to net $980 after issuance costs. The bonds mature in 15 years, and coupon payments are paid annually.

    ■ Preferred stock can be sold at a $50 price with a $5 annual dividend. Flotation or issuance costs will be $3 per preferred share.

    ■ Common stock can be sold at a $25 price. The common dividend is expected to be $3 next year. Dividends have been growing at an annual compound rate of 4 percent annually and are expected to continue growing at that rate into the foreseeable future. Flotation or issuance costs will be $4 per common share.

    Calculate Cleopatra's weighted average cost of capital that is appropriate to use in evaluating this capital budgeting project.

11. Poon Noodle House's current capital structure is 70 percent equity, 25 percent debt, and 5 percent preferred stock. This is considered optimal. Poon is considering a $50 million capital budgeting project. During the coming year Poon expects to have $15 million of retained earnings available to finance this capital budgeting project. The marginal tax rate is 40 percent.

    ■ Poon can raise long-term debt at a pretax interest rate of 7 percent.

    ■ Preferred stock can be sold at a $25 price with a $2 annual dividend. Flotation or issuance costs will be $3 per preferred share.

    ■ Common stock can be sold at a $20 price. The common dividend is expected to be $3 next year. Dividends have been growing at an annual compound rate of 4 percent annually and are expected to continue growing at that rate into the foreseeable future. Flotation or issuance costs will be $4 per common share.

    Calculate Poon's weighted average cost of capital that is appropriate to use in evaluating this capital budgeting project.

Chapter 11

Introduction to Capital Budgeting and Cash Flow Estimation

Chapter Objectives

This chapter covers the following topics:

1   Capital budgeting and why good capital budgeting decisions are crucial to the long-term success of a hospitality firm

2   The different types of capital budgeting decisions

3   The basic principles for estimating the cash flows associated with a capital budgeting project

4   How to estimate a capital budgeting project's net investment

5   How to estimate a capital budgeting project's net cash flows

6   How to compute the after-tax cash flow from the sale of a depreciable asset

7   Depreciation and its impact on a capital budgeting project's net cash flows

11.1 Introduction

Capital budgeting is generally viewed as the decision-making process used in the acquisition of long-term physical assets. Long-term assets are those with economic lives of more than one year or one operating cycle, whichever is the greater of the two. Capital budgeting decisions lead to capital investments in various capital projects. Cash expenditures to acquire a long-term asset or cash expenditures that are expected to generate a long-term positive cash flow represent capital investment. An example is a hotel's investment in a new fire alarm system—it might not generate a future cash flow, but it is a long-term asset satisfying legal requirements and ethical goals. An employee-training program is also a capital investment—it does not entail the acquisition of a physical asset, but is expected to generate a long-term positive cash flow through more-productive employees. Therefore, investments in capital budgeting projects are capital investments, but not all capital investments are investments in capital budgeting projects, such as the employee-training program in our example. Exhibit 11-1 provides a listing of capital budget projects.

Traditional capital budgeting projects include capital investments in a new hotel, a casino expansion, the addition of a new restaurant to a hotel, the addition of new laundry

> **Exhibit 11-1**
> **Classification of Capital Budgeting Projects**
>
> Classification by purpose:
>
> 1. Growth projects, such as expanding the hotel from 200 rooms to 300 rooms
> 2. Cost-reduction projects to increase efficiency, such as replacing old air conditioners with new air conditioners to save energy and maintenance costs
> 3. Projects required by government regulation or motivated by ethical considerations, such as adding a new fire alarm and fire suppression system to a hotel or restaurant
>
> Classification by type of decision:
>
> 1. Independent project decisions, such as whether or not Swiss Chalet should open a new business in downtown Edmonton
> 2. Mutually exclusive project decisions, such as whether or not Swiss Chalet should open a new business in downtown Edmonton or in Red Deer. If the decision is to do one or the other, but not both, then it is a mutually exclusive decision.

facilities to a hotel, the addition of a new bar to a restaurant, the replacement of a sprinkler system with a new updated fire suppression system—the list could go on and on. In this chapter, we introduce the concept of capital budgeting decisions and also discuss the information needed to proceed with a capital budgeting decision.

Capital budgeting decisions are crucial to most firms' long-term success because they require large investments of cash and the decisions have a long-lasting impact on a firm's cash flows. If a firm makes good capital budgeting decisions, then it will have good hotels, resorts, restaurants, or bars generating a positive cash flow for a long period of time. If a firm makes bad capital budgeting decisions, then it is shackled with bad projects and has invested cash that does not generate a sufficient return. Bad capital budgeting decisions are usually costly to reverse. What does one do with an unsuccessful hotel, restaurant, or bar? Continue to operate it with cash losses, or sell it at a significant loss.

A firm's capital budgeting decisions determine its future course by determining what services will be offered, how they will be offered, and where they will be offered. A firm's future long-term cash flow and health is dependent on good capital budgeting decisions, and so firms should have good, sound procedures in place to evaluate capital budgeting projects and all capital investments. Without prudent capital budgeting decisions a future for the hospitality operation may be in jeopardy.

According to Statistics Canada, there were more than 7,300 business failures—representing a rate of about 7 organizations for every 1,000—in 2005. In particular, there were 833 business failures from the accommodation and food services sectors, the vast majority occurring in Ontario and affecting 359 hospitality operations.

Good capital budgeting decisions create projects that return positive cash flows for a long period of time. Poor capital budgeting decisions create projects that lose money for a long period of time, or that incur a large one-time loss when the failed project is sold for a loss.

In December 2007 one of Canada's most respected microbreweries, Walkerville Brewing Company (WBC), declared bankruptcy. WCB was the winner of a gold medal at the Canadian Brewing Awards in 2007 for its Premium Blonde, and a bronze medal at the 2006 World Beer Cup for its Walkerville Lager. It was also named Canadian Brewery of the Year in 2004.

The company found it very difficult to compete against the bigger breweries in an intensified and somewhat saturated marketplace. As a result, an escalation of marketing, working capital, and capital improvement needs ensued that ultimately put Walkerville on the path to bankruptcy.

At the time of this writing, more than 30 microbreweries are operating in Ontario. All require sound financial planning practices, which includes practical capital budgeting.

Several financial suitors have expressed interest in acquiring the microbrewery. Whoever becomes the new owner will immediately need to craft a well-articulated, strategic-fit capital budget.

11.2 Classifying Capital Budgeting Projects

Capital budgeting projects can be classified according to their purpose. A firm might take on a project in order to grow, to reduce costs, to replace assets, or to meet legal requirements and ethical goals. Replacement capital budgeting decisions often come under the classification of cost reduction, and we treat it as one category.

Many capital budgeting projects are clearly for the purpose of growing the firm and increasing the firm's future cash flows. This would include expanding existing facilities or investing in new, additional facilities.

Capital budgeting projects may also be mainly motivated to decrease future operating costs. This could include new, more energy efficient air-conditioning units, new kitchen equipment requiring less maintenance, or new hotel laundry facilities to replace a more expensive outside vendor. These capital budgeting decisions are usually, but not always, a decision to replace inefficient or old assets. And sometimes a replacement decision is motivated not by cost considerations but simply because it is required if a firm wants to continue in a certain business.

Some capital budgeting projects may be motivated not by growth or cost-reduction considerations but rather by government regulation or ethical considerations. These would include the installation of fire alarm and fire suppression systems, equipment to minimize pollution, and other investments to promote the safety of employees, customers, and the community.

It is also useful to classify capital budgeting projects by the type of decision being made as well as by purpose. All capital budgeting decisions can be classified as independent decisions or mutually exclusive decisions. Classification of a project as independent or mutually exclusive impacts the method of capital budgeting analysis, as we will see later in the chapter.

Independent capital budgeting decisions are decisions that stand alone; the capital budgeting project is analyzed in isolation and is not compared to other projects. The decision whether to build a new hotel is independent. The decision whether to build a new hotel in either Toronto or Mississauga is not independent but mutually exclusive—you will build one or the other, but not both. If you decide to build one, then you exclude the other. The distinction between independent and mutually exclusive projects is important. An

independent project is analyzed to determine whether it will increase the value of the firm, whereas the analysis of **mutually exclusive projects** must go one step further. We must ask not only whether a new hotel in Toronto will increase the value of the firm, but also whether a new hotel in Mississauga will increase the value of the firm. If the answer is yes to both questions, then we must also decide which of the two projects increases the value of the firm the most—because the projects are mutually exclusive, and we can invest in only one or the other.

Many capital budgeting projects are naturally mutually exclusive. The decision to replace kitchen equipment may include a choice of new kitchen equipment from three different companies. Now, you must decide not only whether this investment will increase the value of your firm, but also which company's kitchen equipment will increase the value of your firm *the most*.

11.3 The Capital Budgeting Decision and Cash Flow Estimation

How a capital budgeting project impacts a firm's future cash flows should be estimated prior to making an investment decision. The information required to evaluate a large project of a major corporation comes from many sources. Information from marketing personnel about product demand, pricing, and competition is needed to estimate future revenues. Other examples include information from purchasing personnel about material costs, information from human resources personnel about employee expenses, and information from other sources about estimated future operating costs. If the evaluation is of a significant project for a small firm, then all this information may be provided by one person or a few personnel. And if a project is sufficiently small or obviously beneficial to a firm's health, it may not be worth performing a formal capital budgeting analysis. The proposal by a restaurant to add a new toaster for several hundred dollars or the proposal by a hotel to buy a new computer monitor for its front desk operations almost certainly does not require a formal capital budgeting process for a management decision.

Capital budgeting decision methods are based on cost–benefit analysis. The cost of starting a project is quantified and called the **net investment**. The benefit of a project is the increased future cash flow. This is quantified on an annual basis and called the **net cash flow**. Different capital budgeting methods then compare the net investment to the net cash flows to decide whether a project is a worthy investment.

Some basic principles should be followed when forecasting cash flows in the process of estimating a project's net investment and net cash flows. Cash flows should be estimated on an incremental basis, not on a total basis. *Incremental basis* means the change in cash flows caused by an investment in a project. If a hotel is considering an investment to expand one of its restaurants, then only the expected change in sales revenue caused by the expansion should be considered in the capital budgeting analysis. Incremental sales revenue means the change in sales revenue. The total sales revenue would not be the relevant number because a portion of total sales revenue will exist with or without the expansion. See Exhibit 11-2 for a visual perspective of estimating cash flows.

Always consider the impact of taxes on cash flow. Taxes are a real cost. But, of course, consider only incremental taxes caused by a capital budgeting investment.

Exhibit 11-2
Basic Principles for Estimating Cash Flows

1. Estimate cash flows on an incremental basis. Consider the change in cash flows brought about by a capital budgeting project, not the total cash flows.

2. Estimate cash flows on an after-tax basis. Taxes are a real cost and require a real commitment of cash. Be sure to always consider tax impacts.

3. Estimate the impact of indirect effects. If a project will bring in more customers to your other business lines or cannibalize your other business lines, this will change overall firm cash flow.

4. Understand that sunk costs are irrelevant cash flows; opportunity costs are relevant cash flows.

The indirect effects of a project on cash flows, in addition to the direct effects, should always be taken into account. Suppose a casino is considering an investment to add a new restaurant to the several restaurants already operating in the casino. One needs to consider not only the cash flow directly generated by the new restaurant, but also any reduction in cash flow at the casino's other restaurants resulting from competition with the new restaurant. Also relevant is any new cash flow at the casino generated from new customers attracted to the new restaurant. All cash flows resulting from a project, either negative or positive, are relevant.

Last but not least, costs need to be estimated on an **opportunity cost** basis (whereby the financial resources allocated and consumed on one particular project as opposed to another represent a potential opportunity lost), not on historical or sunk costs. **Sunk costs** are costs that have been paid in the past, and are thus irrelevant because the costs have been paid whether a project is accepted or rejected. Suppose Mayfield Hospitality is considering building a new restaurant on land purchased in Calgary years ago for $100,000, but the land is worth $500,000 today net of taxes and brokerage fees. The relevant cost to use in the capital budgeting analysis is the $500,000, not the $100,000. This is the opportunity Mayfield Hospitality is truly giving up if it invests in the new restaurant. The $100,000 was paid years ago, and this will not change whether the corporation builds the new restaurant or not. The $100,000 is a sunk cost and is no longer relevant.

11.3.1 NET INVESTMENT ESTIMATION

The *net investment* is the cash outflow at the beginning of a project's economic life. Sometimes it is called the *initial outlay* or the *initial investment*. It is just another project cash flow, but because it is a net outflow and occurs at the beginning it is usually differentiated from other project cash flows. Sometimes the net investment is defined as the cash outflow occurring at the single point in time that the project's life begins. Yet many projects require cash flows over several months or even years before the project is ready to start generating cash inflows. We define the net investment cash flows as the net cash outflows required to ready a project for its basic function or operation. For many projects, this takes place at virtually a single point in time, such as a new toaster for a restaurant or a new computer monitor for a hotel's front desk operations. But for many projects the net investment covers a period of time, such as the building of a new restaurant or hotel or the remodelling of an existing restaurant or hotel. In such a situation, capital expenditures take place over several months or years before the project is finished and ready for operation.

Any cash flow required to start a project or caused by a project is relevant to the project analysis. If the cash flow occurs before the project is ready for operation, we label it as part of the net investment. Most of these cash flows are obvious, including the cost of the asset and any installation cost, delivery cost, or tax effects. Possibly not so obvious is the investment required in net working capital and the after-tax salvage value from assets being replaced.

Some capital budgeting projects are expected to grow the firm through increased future sales and cash flows. These projects generally require an increase in current assets to support this growth. This might include more cash to handle a greater number of transactions, more accounts receivable as more credit is granted to customers to generate more sales, and more inventory to support the increased sales. Often, growth spontaneously generates greater current liabilities, including more accounts payable as increased inventory is purchased on credit, and more accruals as increased wages are generated and additional taxes are owed on greater income.

Net working capital is current assets minus current liabilities, and thus the expected increase in net working capital measures the dual impact of increased current assets and increased current liabilities. Growth-oriented capital budgeting projects generally increase net working capital because current assets are likely to increase more than current liabilities. If a project is expected to need increased net working capital prior to commencing operations, then this increased net working capital needs to be estimated and included as a cash outflow in the net investment estimation.

Some capital budgeting decisions are replacement decisions in which the firm is considering the replacement of old assets with new assets. In these cases, the old assets usually still have some value and can be salvaged for a positive cash flow. This cash flow needs to be estimated on an after-tax basis and included in the net investment as a cash inflow. Because net investment is defined as a cash outflow, the after-tax salvage value from replaced assets will decrease a project's net investment.

The tax impact on replaced assets depends on the market value of the assets relative to the book value. An asset's book value is the remaining asset acquisition cost that has not yet been depreciated. If an asset's market value is equal to its book value, there is no tax effect. If an asset's market value is greater than the book value but less than the acquisition cost, the excess of the market value over the book value is taxed as ordinary income. If an asset's market value is greater than the acquisition cost, the excess above the acquisition cost is taxed as a **capital gain**, and the amount of the market value equal to the difference between the acquisition cost and the book value is taxed as ordinary income. If the market value is less than the book value, the difference is treated as a tax-deductible expense that causes less taxes to be paid than otherwise. The effect for most firms is like a tax refund equal to the difference (book value minus market value) times the marginal tax rate.

A project's net investment estimation can be expressed as follows:

NINV = Asset cost + Delivery cost + Installation cost + Incremental net working
     capital − After-tax salvage value from replaced assets

Exhibit 11-3 illustrates the application of this equation in a net investment example.

Exhibit 11-3
A Net Investment Example

White Snow Restaurants is considering adding a new line of food to the menu. White Snow has already spent $1,000 to survey customers about their acceptance and interest in this new food choice. At this point the decision is whether to invest in the additional kitchen equipment and working capital required to proceed with the new venture. The new equipment will cost $30,000, freight for the equipment is $500, and installation cost is $1,500. The new equipment will replace the functions of some old kitchen equipment as well as allowing the preparation of new menu items. The old kitchen equipment can be salvaged for $4,000 after tax. Also, White Snow will need to carry an additional $2,000 in food inventory to offer the new menu items. What is the net investment for this project?

$$\text{NINV} = \$30,000 + \$500 + \$1,500 + \$2,000 - \$4,000 = \$30,000$$

Notice the $1,000 survey cost is not included in the net investment. The $1,000 has been paid, and it will stay paid, whether the project is accepted or not. Therefore, it is no longer relevant to the decision at this point. Notice the $2,000 for additional inventory is included. This $2,000 is not an expense because it has just been exchanged for another asset. Instead of $2,000 in cash, White Snow will have $2,000 in inventory. But it is an opportunity cost. The opportunity to use the $2,000 is lost as long as White Snow retains the extra $2,000 in inventory. Therefore, it is appropriate to show it as a cash outflow in the net investment.

11.3.2 NET CASH FLOW ESTIMATION

An estimate of project cash flows is needed for a capital budgeting analysis. The cash flows required at the beginning of a project's life to ready the project for basic operation are called the *net investment cash flows*. The cash flows after this point are called the *net cash flows*, or annual cash flows. The net investment cash flows are usually cash outflows, whereas the net cash flows are usually cash inflows. A project's net cash flows need to be estimated for each year of the project's expected economic life.

We begin a project's annual net cash flow estimation by projecting the expected change in a firm's net income. But we are interested in cash flow, not profit. We need to adjust net income to estimate cash flow. This is accomplished by adding depreciation to net income. Depreciation is properly considered in the net income calculation so as to estimate taxes correctly. But it needs to be added back in the net cash flow calculation to reflect that it is not an out-of-pocket expense.

If a project requires net working capital increases after the net investment period, then each year's net cash flow needs to be adjusted accordingly. Many times a project not only causes immediate growth in a firm's sales, but also continues to grow the firm's sales over the life of the project. In this case, net working capital likely continues to grow over the life of the project as well, to support the growth in sales. This needs to be reflected in the project's net cash flow calculations. In the following explanation of net cash flow calculations, we use the symbol Δ quite often. A Δ means the change in something. Thus, if a firm's net income increased from \$100,000 to \$115,000, then ΔNet income = \$115,000 − \$100,000 = \$15,000. Also, t stands for the marginal tax rate. If a firm's taxable income increases by \$100 and the firm's taxes increase by \$40, then the firm's marginal tax rate (t) is 40 percent. The following equation shows the calculations of net cash flow more explicitly.

$$NCF = \Delta\text{Net income} + \Delta\text{Depreciation} - \Delta\text{Net working capital}$$

The ΔNet income can be estimated by forecasting the ΔEarnings before taxes and multiplying by one minus the marginal tax rate.

$$NCF = \Delta\text{Earnings before taxes} \times (1 - t) + \Delta\text{Depreciation}$$
$$- \Delta \text{ Net working capital}$$

The ΔEarnings before taxes can be estimated by forecasting the ΔSales revenue, the ΔCash expenses, and the ΔDepreciation and combining them to calculate the ΔEarnings before taxes.

$$NCF = (\Delta\text{Sales revenue} - \Delta\text{Cash expenses} - \Delta\text{Depreciation}) \times (1 - t)$$
$$+ \Delta\text{Depreciation} - \Delta\text{Net working capital}$$

Exhibit 11-4 continues with the net investment example begun in Exhibit 11-3 to illustrate the calculation of a project's net cash flows.

Essentially, the change in earnings before tax is first calculated. If a variable has a positive impact on profit, it is added; if it has a negative impact on profit, it is subtracted. For instance, if a project is a growth project and leads to higher cash expenses, then the increased cash expenses have a negative impact on profits and are subtracted in the net cash flow calculation. Of course, hopefully the increased sales revenue more than offsets this. But if a project's motivation is reduced costs, then the resulting reduction in cash expenses has a positive impact on profits and is added (actually, the negative change in cash expenses is subtracted for a net positive impact) in the net cash flow calculation.

The net cash flow calculations should not include additional interest expense generated by the financing of the project. Certainly all costs are relevant, including financial costs. Financial costs are generally taken into account by the use of a required rate of return. Most capital budgeting decision methods used to recommend acceptance or rejection of a project take this required rate of return into account. **Required rates of return** are essentially a measure of the firm's cost of capital and therefore take into account the interest cost of debt and other financial costs as explained in the previous chapter. Thus there is no need to include financial costs at this stage of the analysis.

The end of a project's economic life often brings one-time cash flows in addition to the basic operating cash flow. We call these *terminal, nonoperating cash flows* because they come at a project's termination, and they are not regular, recurring, operating cash flows. One possible terminal, nonoperating cash flow is the salvage value of assets acquired as a

Exhibit 11-4
A Net Cash Flow Example

Continuing with the example in Exhibit 11-3, in which White Snow Restaurants is considering an investment to introduce a new menu line, the change in deprecia-tion will need to be calculated to estimate the net cash flows for the project. Suppose the economic life of the project is five years, but the new equipment is to be depreciated straight-line over eight years to a zero value. The old equipment being replaced has been fully depreciated to a zero value. Depreciable expense from the new equipment will include the cost of the asset, delivery cost, and installation cost.

$$\text{Depreciable expense} = \$30,000 + \$500 + \$1,500 = \$32,000$$

Annual depreciation on the new equipment will be $32,000 allocated evenly over the eight-year depreciable life.

$$\text{Annual depreciation} = \$32,000/8 = \$4,000 \text{ annually}$$

White Snow expects sales to gradually increase for the first three years from this new menu line. The following table reflects the expected sales increase expected each year as well as the associated increase in cash expenses and increased invest-ment in new working capital.

Year	ΔSales revenue	ΔCash expenses	ΔNet working capital
1	$ 20,000	$10,000	$ 500
2	$ 50,000	$25,000	$ 500
3	$100,000	$50,000	$1,000
4	$100,000	$50,000	
5	$100,000	$50,000	

White Snow expects sales to increase until the third year. Naturally, costs will increase along with sales, and additional working capital, especially inventory, will be needed to support the increased sales. The net cash flows can now be calcu-lated assuming a marginal tax rate of 40 percent and using the equation for net cash flow from earlier.

$NCF_1 = (\$20,000 - 10,000 - 4,000) \times (1-40\%) + 4,000 - 500 = \$7,100$

$NCF_2 = (\$50,000 - 25,000 - 4,000) \times (1-40\%) + 4,000 - 500 = \$16,100$

$NCF_3 = (\$100,000 - 50,000 - 4,000) \times (1-40\%) + 4,000 - 1,000 = \$30,600$

$NCF_4 = (\$100,000 - 50,000 - 4,000) \times (1-40\%) + 4,000 = \$31,600$

$NCF_5 = (\$100,000 - 50,000 - 4,000) \times (1-40\%) + 4,000 = \$31,600$

The cash flow for the fifth and last year will also include salvage value of the equipment plus the return of net working capital invested over the life of the project.

(*continued*)

(continued)

Remember, there was a $2,000 investment in net working capital (inventory) at the very beginning from the calculation of the net investment in Exhibit 11-3. This additional cash flow at the end of the project life is the terminal, nonoperating cash flow. Suppose the equipment can be salvaged for $12,000 after tax.

Terminal, nonoperating cash flow = $12,000 + 2,000 + 500 + 500 + 1,000 = $16,000

where the $12,000 is the salvage value, the $2,000 is the inventory investment in the beginning, and the $500, $500, and $1,000 are the investments in net working capital in years 1, 2, and 3 respectively. The total cash flow for the fifth and last year is the net cash flow for year 5 plus the terminal, nonoperating cash flow.

Total cash flow year 5 = $31,600 + 16,000 = $47,600

The cash flows for the five Years can also be summarized in table form.

	Year 1	Year 2	Year 3	Year 4	Year 5
ΔSales revenue	$ 20,000	$ 50,000	$100,000	$100,000	$100,000
ΔCash expenses	−10,000	−25,000	−50,000	−50,000	−50,000
ΔDepreciation	−4,000	−4,000	−4,000	−4,000	−4,000
ΔEarnings before taxes	$ 6,000	$ 21,000	$ 46,000	$ 46,000	$ 46,000
ΔTaxes	−2,400	−8,400	−18,400	−18,400	−18,400
ΔNet income	$ 3,600	$ 12,600	$ 27,600	$ 27,600	$ 27,600
ΔDepreciation	+4,000	+4,000	+4,000	+4,000	+4,000
ΔNet working capital	−500	−500	−1,000	0	0
Net cash flow	$ 7,100	$ 16,100	$ 30,600	$ 31,600	$ 31,600
After-tax salvage					+12,000
Net working capital return					+ 4,000
Total cash flow	$ 7,100	$ 16,100	$ 30,600	$ 31,600	$ 47,600

result of the project investment. If a project is truly finished, then we assume the firm will sell any remaining assets from the project. The after-tax salvage value of project assets should be added to the net cash flow for the last year. Also, all investments in net working capital (cash outflows) would generally be returned at the end of a project's life as cash inflows. An earlier investment to increase inventories and accounts receivable would probably be liquidated as the firm uses up the remaining inventory and collects its accounts receivable at the project's end. Often, though, the increased current assets would not be reduced because a successful project may be continued in the future by a replacement investment. But, even in this case, the cost of the increased net working capital should be assigned to the replacement project and the value of the increased net working capital still credited to the initial project's final-year net cash flow. If one does not assume the investments in net working capital are returned at the end of the project life, this implies the increased net working capital is lost, which is unlikely to be the case. A project's final-year cash flow will often be modified as follows.

$$\text{Final year } NCF = (\Delta\text{Sales revenue} - \Delta\text{Cash expenses} - \Delta\text{Depreciation})$$
$$\times (1 - t) + \Delta\text{Depreciation} + \Delta\text{Net working capital}$$
$$+ \text{After-tax salvage value}$$

where the ΔNet working capital is the sum of all the previous net working capital investments made including those in the net investment cash flows. Exhibit 11-5 provides an example to illustrate this calculation, along with a net cash flow calculation.

Exhibit 11-5
Capital Cost Allowance Rate Table

Class number	Description	CCA rate
1	Most buildings made of brick, stone, or cement acquired after 1987, including their component parts such as electric wiring, lighting fixtures, plumbing, heating and cooling equipment, elevators, and escalators	4%
3	Most buildings made of brick, stone, or cement acquired before 1988, including their component parts as listed in class 1 above	5%
6	Buildings made of frame, log, stucco on frame, galvanized iron, or corrugated metal that are used in the business of farming or fishing, or that have no footings below ground; fences and most greenhouses	10%
7	Canoes, boats, and most other vessels, including their furniture, fittings, or equipment	15%
8	Property that is not included in any other class such as furniture, calculators and cash registers (that do not record multiple sales taxes), photocopy and fax machines, printers, display fixtures, refrigeration equipment, machinery, tools costing $200 or more, and outdoor advertising billboards and greenhouses with rigid frames and plastic covers	20%
9	Aircraft, including furniture, fittings, or equipment attached, and their spare parts	25%
10	Automobiles (except taxis and others used for lease or rent), vans, wagons, trucks, buses, tractors, trailers, drive-in theatres, general-purpose electronic data processing equipment	30%
10.1	Passenger vehicles costing more than $30,000 if acquired after 2000	30%
12	Chinaware, cutlery, linen, uniforms, dies, jigs, moulds or lasts, computer software (except systems software), cutting or shaping parts of a machine, certain property used for earning rental income such as apparel or costumes, and videotape cassettes; certain property costing less than $200 such as kitchen utensils, tools, and medical or dental equipment	100%
13	Property that is leasehold interest (the maximum CCA rate depends on the type of leasehold and the terms of the lease)	N/A

(continued)

(continued)

14	Patents, franchises, concessions, and licences for a limited period—the CCA is limited to whichever is less: ■ the capital cost of the property spread out over the life of the property; or ■ the undepreciated capital cost of the property at the end of the taxation year	N/A
	Class 14 also includes patents, and licences to use patents for a limited period, that you elect not to include in class 44.	40%
16	Automobiles for lease or rent, taxicabs, and coin-operated video games or pinball machines; certain tractors and large trucks acquired after December 6, 1991, that are used to haul freight and that weigh more than 11,788 kilograms	
17	Roads, sidewalks, parking lot or storage areas, telephone, telegraph, or nonelectronic data communication switching equipment	8%
38	Most power-operated movable equipment acquired after 1987 used for moving, excavating, placing, or compacting earth, rock, concrete, or asphalt	30%
39	Machinery and equipment acquired after 1987 that is used in Canada primarily to manufacture and process goods for sale or lease	25%
43	Manufacturing and processing machinery and equipment acquired after February 25, 1992, described in class 39 above	30%
44	Patents and licences to use patents for a limited or unlimited period that the corporation acquired after April 26, 1993—however, you can elect not to include such property in class 44 by attaching a letter to the return for the year the corporation acquired the property. In the letter, indicate the property you do not want to include in class 44.	25%
45	Computer equipment that is "general purpose electronic data processing equipment and system software" included in paragraph I of class 10 acquired after March 22, 2004	45%
46	Data network infrastructure equipment that supports advanced telecommunication applications, acquired after March 22, 2004. It includes assets such as switches, multiplexers, routers, hubs, modems, and domain name servers that are used to control, transfer, modulate, and direct data, but does not include office equipment such as telephones, cell phones, or fax machines, or property such as wires, cables, or structures.	30%

Source: Reproduced with permission of the Canada Revenue Agency and the Minister of Public Works and Government Services Canada, 2008

11.3.3 ESTIMATION OF AFTER-TAX SALVAGE VALUES

Capital budgeting projects usually require large investments in depreciable assets. The salvage values of these depreciable assets often increase a project's cash flow at the end of the project's life. Also, replacement decision capital budgeting projects often can reduce the amount of the net investment at the beginning of the project's life by the salvage value of old assets being replaced. The tax effects from these salvage values are also an important input to the analysis, either reducing or increasing the salvage value on an after-tax basis. As an example, suppose the Rodd Hotels Corporation is salvaging or selling an old asset for its market value, and the asset's book value is $10,000. An asset's book value is equal to its acquisition cost minus accumulated depreciation. An asset's acquisition costs include costs for installation and delivery. Suppose Rodd's old asset was originally acquired for $100,000, and $90,000 has been depreciated. Then the book value is $10,000. Acquisition cost of $100,000 minus accumulated depreciation of $90,000 equals $10,000. Section 11.3.4 discusses depreciation, and Exhibit 11-6 provides more detail on computing after-tax salvage values with an example. But for now we continue with this example and consider the tax consequences to the Rodd Hotel Corporation from salvaging an old asset.

Exhibit 11-6
Estimating After-Tax Salvage Values

We will continue the example from Exhibits 11-3 and 11-4 to further illustrate the calculation of after-tax salvage values. White Snow's new kitchen equipment will generate $32,000 in depreciable expenses including asset cost, delivery cost, and installation cost. Depreciation will be straight-line to a zero value over eight years for depreciation of $4,000 per year. But the economic life of the project is only five years, meaning White Snow plans to finish with the new equipment in five years. At the end of five years, the book value of the new equipment will be $12,000. This is the amount of depreciation still remaining. It can be calculated as the depreciation still remaining after five years.

3 years $\times$ $4,000 depreciation per year = $12,000 book value

or it can be calculated as the acquisition cost minus accumulated depreciation.

$32,000 − 5 years $\times$ $4,000 depreciation per year = $12,000 book value

When White Snow disposes of the equipment in five years, the salvage price and the book value together determine the tax impact from the disposal as follows.

1. If the equipment is sold for its book value, there is no tax impact.

After-tax salvage value = $12,000

2. If the equipment is sold for more than its book value but less than its acquisition cost, the sale price over and above the book value is a recapture of depreciation and taxed as ordinary income. Suppose the equipment is sold for $20,000.

After-tax salvage value = $20,000 − ($8,000 $\times$ 40%)
= $20,000 − 3,200 = $16,800

where $8,000 is the recapture of depreciation.

3. If the equipment is sold for less than its book value, taxes on other firm income are reduced by an amount equal to this loss (the amount less than the book value) times the marginal tax rate. Suppose the equipment is sold for $7,000.

After-tax salvage value = $7,000 + (5,000 $\times$ 40%)
= $7,000 + 2,000 = $9,000

where $5,000 is the loss calculated as the book value minus the sale price.

(*continued*)

(*continued*)

4. If the equipment is sold for more than its book value and more than its acquisition, there are two different taxes to calculate. First is the recapture of depreciation calculated as the difference between the acquisition cost and the book value. This is taxed as ordinary income. Second is the capital gain calculated as the sale price minus the acquisition cost. This is taxed as a capital gain. Suppose the equipment is sold for $42,000, and the capital gains tax rate is 25 percent.

After-tax salvage value = $42,000 − (20,000 × 40%) − (10,000 × 25%)
After-tax salvage value = $42,000 − 8,000 − 2,500 = $31,500

Following is a summary of these calculations in one table. Keep in mind the original acquisition cost of the equipment is $32,000, and at the end of the five-year economic life accumulated depreciation is $20,000 and the book value is $12,000.

	Equal book value	More than book value	Less than book value	More than acquisition cost
Sale price	$12,000	$20,000	$7,000	$42,000
Book value	12,000	12,000	12,000	12,000
Depreciation recapture	0	8,000	−5,000	20,000
Capital gain	0	0	0	10,000
Ordinary income taxes				
40% × Depreciation recapture	0	3,200	−2,000	8,000
Capital gains taxes				
25% × Capital gain	0	0	0	2,500
After-tax salvage value				
Sale price − Taxes	**$12,000**	**$16,800**	**$9,000**	**$31,500**

If an asset is sold for its book value, there is no tax effect. If the Rodd Hotel Corporation sells the asset for exactly the book value of $10,000, there are no taxes owed and no reduced taxes. The after-tax salvage value is $10,000 because there is no tax impact.

If an asset is sold for more than its book value but less than its original acquisition cost, taxes are owed on the gain over and above the book value. If the Rodd Hotel Corporation sells the asset for $15,000, then taxes are owed on the $5,000 received above the book value of $10,000. This $5,000 is calculated by subtracting the $10,000 book value from the $15,000 sale price. If we assume a 40 percent marginal tax rate, 40% × $5,000 = $2,000 would be owed in taxes, and the Rodd Hotel Corporation would receive $13,000 after tax from the salvage value.

If an asset is sold for less than its book value, taxes are reduced on other corporate income by an amount equal to the loss times the marginal tax rate. If the Rodd Hotel Corporation sells the asset for $7,000, there is a $3,000 loss calculated by subtracting the $10,000 book value from the $7,000 sale price. This loss will lower taxes on other corporate income by $3,000 × 40% = $1,200. Because the Rodd Hotel Corporation will pay $1,200 less in taxes than otherwise, the net salvage value is actually $8,200. This is calculated by adding the $7,000 sale price to the $1,200 reduction in taxes.

If an asset is sold for more than its acquisition cost, ordinary income taxes are owed on the accumulated depreciation (acquisition cost minus book value), and capital gains taxes are owed on the gain over and above the original acquisition cost. If the Rodd Hotel

Corporation sells the asset for $130,000, then ordinary income taxes are owed on the $90,000 accumulated depreciation at 40 percent equal to $36,000, and additional capital gains taxes are owed on the gain over the $100,000 original cost. If the capital gains rate is 40 percent, this would be $30,000 × 40% = $12,000 for a total of $48,000 in taxes owed, leaving a net salvage value of $82,000 ($130,000 − $48,000). Depending on tax regulations, the capital gains tax rate sometimes has been the same as the ordinary income tax rate and sometimes has been below the ordinary income tax rate. This situation is rare. It is unusual for depreciable assets to appreciate in value, but it is possible.

11.3.4 DEPRECIATION

Long-term physical assets are depreciated over time rather than expensed immediately. **Depreciation** is the allocation of a capital expenditure over several years. The exact length of time depends on the type of asset. Depreciation has two basic functions. One is for financial reporting purposes, and the other is for calculating tax-deductible expenses and, subsequently, the income taxes owed by a firm. Depreciation is a legitimate tax-deductible expense. Different methods of calculating depreciation are used depending on the purpose. For financial reporting purposes, an asset is generally depreciated to an estimated salvage value using one of several methods. Canada Revenue Agency provides businesses with a table that identifies the rates of depreciation for certain asset classes.

As identified above, the cost of depreciable assets—such as buildings, furniture, and equipment—cannot be deducted as an upfront expense when calculating net income for tax purposes. In recognition of the reality that eventually these assets wear out, their utility is consumed, or they become obsolete over time and need to be replaced, Canada Revenue Agency promotes the use of the **capital cost allowance (CCA)**. The CCA is a non-refundable tax deduction that reduces taxes owed by permitting the cost of business-related assets to be deducted from income over a prescribed number of years.

For example, Graham Thompson's Hamburger Haven has computer equipment that was acquired in 2007. As indicated in the CCA table provided in Exhibit 11-5, Graham's computer equipment qualifies under asset class 45 and therefore is subject to a depreciation rate of 45 percent per annum. Accordingly, if the computer equipment cost a total of $4,000, the following depreciation charges would apply.

Year	1	2	3
Asset dollar value	$4,000	$4,000	$4,000
Depreciation amount	$1,800	$1,800	$ 400
Accumulated depreciation	$1,800	$3,600	$4,000
Book value	$2,200	$ 400	$ 0

Depreciation is a tax-deductible expense. But it is an expense allocation for a past cash outflow made in a previous period of time; it is not a cash outflow in the current period. Depreciation does reduce taxes in the current period. Because of the reduced taxes, depreciation causes current net cash flows to be higher than otherwise. For example, consider the net cash flow equation.

$$NCF = (\Delta\text{Sales revenue} - \Delta\text{Operating costs} - \Delta\text{Depreciation}) \times (1 - t)$$
$$+ \Delta\text{Depreciation} - \Delta\text{Net working capital}$$

Suppose a new project is expected to increase sales revenue by $100,000 a year, operating costs by $40,000 a year, and depreciation by $20,000 a year; the marginal tax rate is 40 percent; and there is no expected change in net working capital. The net cash flow is $44,000 per year. If depreciation increases by $30,000 instead of $20,000 per year, the net cash flow is $48,000 per year. The impact of depreciation on a project's cash flows is further illustrated in Exhibit 11-7.

Exhibit 11-7
The Impact of Depreciation on Net Cash Flow

If a capital budgeting project is expected to increase sales revenue by $100,000 a year and increase cash expenses by $40,000 a year and depreciation by $20,000 a year, the net cash flow is

$$NCF = (\$100,000 - 40,000 - 20,000) \times (1 - 40\%) + 20,000 = \$44,000$$

The change in earnings after tax is $24,000 (earnings after tax is from the preceding equation before adding back the $20,000 depreciation).

If depreciation is expected to be $30,000 higher each year instead of $20,000, the net cash flow is

$$NCF = (\$100,000 - 40,000 - 30,000) \times (1 - 40\%) + 30,000 = \$48,000$$

The change in earnings after tax is $18,000 (from the preceding equation before adding back the $30,000 depreciation). Following is a summary of these two calculations in one table.

	Depreciation = $20,000	Depreciation = $30,000
ΔSales revenue	$100,000	$100,000
ΔCash expenses	−40,000	−40,000
ΔDepreciation	−20,000	−30,000
ΔEarnings before taxes	$ 40,000	$ 30,000
ΔTaxes (40%)	−16,000	−12,000
ΔNet income	$ 24,000	$ 18,000
ΔDepreciation	+20,000	+30,000
Net cash flow	**$ 44,000**	**$ 48,000**

The impact of depreciation on firm profit and cash flow is summarized as follows.

	Profit	Cash flow
Depreciation increases	Decreases	Increases
Depreciation decreases	Increases	Decreases

11.4 SUMMARY

This chapter:

- Introduced capital budgeting and explained why good capital budgeting decisions are crucial to the long-term success of a hospitality firm
- Discussed the different types of capital budgeting decisions
- Introduced the basic principles for estimating the cash flows associated with a capital budgeting project
- Explained how to estimate a capital budgeting project's net investment
- Explained how to estimate a capital budgeting project's net cash flows
- Explained how to compute the after-tax cash flow from the sale of a depreciable asset
- Explained depreciation and its impact on a capital budgeting project's net cash flows

Key Terms

Capital budgeting

Capital cost allowance (CCA)

Capital gain

Depreciation

Independent project

Mutually exclusive project

Net cash flow

Net investment

Opportunity costs

Required rates of return

Sunk costs

Discussion Questions

1. Why are good capital budgeting decisions crucial to the long-term viability of a firm?
2. What is the difference between independent projects and mutually exclusive projects?
3. Explain why larger depreciation increases a capital budgeting project's net cash flow.
4. What is the difference between an opportunity cost and a sunk cost?
5. Define the net investment for a capital budgeting project. What is included in a capital budgeting project's net investment?
6. Define the net cash flows for a capital budgeting project. What is included in a capital budgeting project's net cash flows?
7. Capital budgeting projects can be classified according to the purpose of the project. List and explain the three categories for classifying projects according to their purpose.
8. The impact of indirect effects of a capital budgeting project should be included in cash flow estimation. Give some examples of indirect effects, and explain why they are important and should be considered in the capital budgeting decision process.
9. Explain how the net investment for a replacement capital budgeting project is likely to be different from the net investment for a pure growth-oriented capital budgeting project.
10. If a depreciable asset is sold for its book value, there are no tax consequences. But if a depreciable asset is sold for a value different from its book value, there are tax consequences. Explain the preceding statements.

Problems

1. Niagara Casino Corporation is considering an expansion of its busiest casino. Niagara Casino has already conducted and paid $50,000 for a marketing survey. The expansion will cost $2.5 million for the assets including delivery costs and all construction costs. In addition, $500,000 in net working capital will be needed immediately. Compute the net investment of this expansion project.

2. Vancouver Sushi Incorporated is considering the replacement of its sushi display cases. The current cases were purchased three years ago at a total cost of $40,000 and are being depreciated straight-line to a zero value over eight years. If Vancouver Sushi sells these sushi display cases at the following prices, what are the after-tax cash flows to Vancouver Sushi? Use 40 percent for the effective tax rate.

    a. $25,000

    b. $30,000

    c. $35,000

    d. $10,000

3. Graham Thompson is considering opening a new Hamburger Haven complete with a pub in the southwest part of town. The building will cost $1.5 million, and fixtures such as bars, kitchen equipment, and so on will cost another $200,000, including installation costs. Stocking the restaurant and pub with inventory before it opens will cost another $100,000. Land for the building site cost Thompson $300,000 several years ago, but now the land could be sold to net $1,000,000 after tax. Compute the net investment for the new Hamburger Haven restaurant and pub.

4. Montreal Casinos is considering replacing its craps tables. They were purchased four years ago for a total cost of $100,000 and are being depreciated straight-line to a zero value over ten years. If these craps tables are sold at the following prices, what are the after-tax cash flows to Montreal Casinos? Use 40 percent for the effective tax rate.

    a. $75,000

    b. $60,000

    c. $20,000

5. Bob's Outdoor Adventures is considering replacing its fleet of Hummers. A new fleet of specially configured Hummers will cost $800,000, including all shipping, dealer prep, documentation, and title costs. The old fleet can be sold for $200,000 and the remaining book value on the old fleet is $150,000. Compute the net investment for this replacement project. Use 40 percent for the effective tax rate.

6. A project is expected to increase a firm's sales revenues by $100,000 annually, increase its cash expenses by $45,000 annually, and increase its depreciation by $30,000 annually. The project has an expected economic life of seven years. What is the net cash flow each year? Use 40 percent for the effective tax rate. Assume there is no working capital to be liquidated at the end of seven years, and there is also no salvage value at the end of seven years.

7. A project is expected to increase a firm's sales revenues by $20,000 annually, decrease its cash expenses by $25,000 annually, and increase its depreciation by $15,000 annually. The project has an expected economic life of 10 years. What is the net cash flow each year? Use 40 percent for the effective tax rate. Assume there is no working capital to be liquidated at the end of 10 years, and there is also no salvage value at the end of 10 years.

8. A project is expected to decrease a firm's cash expenses by $150,000 annually and increase its depreciation by $80,000 annually. The project has an expected economic life

of eight years. What is the net cash flow each year? Use 40 percent for the effective tax rate. Assume there is no working capital to be liquidated at the end of eight years, and there is also no salvage value at the end of eight years.

9. Maxine's Fabulous Foods Incorporated is planning to add a new line of strawberry jam that will require the acquisition of new processing equipment. The equipment will cost $1,000,000, including installation and shipping. It will be depreciated straight-line to a zero value over the 10-year economic life of the project. Interest cost associated with financing the equipment purchase is estimated to be $40,000 annually. The expected salvage value of the machine at the end of 10 years is $200,000.

   One year ago a marketing survey was performed to gauge the likely success of this new project. The survey cost $25,000 and was paid last year.

   If this new equipment is acquired, it will also allow the replacement of old equipment used for other food lines. This old equipment can be salvaged for $150,000 and has a book value of $200,000. The remaining depreciation on the old equipment is $40,000 annually for five more years.

   Additional net working capital of $85,000 will be needed immediately. When the project is terminated in 10 years, there no longer will be a need for this incremental working capital.

   Maxine expects to sell $300,000 worth of this new jam annually. The cost of producing and selling the jam is estimated to be $50,000 annually (not including depreciation or interest expense). The marginal tax rate is 40 percent.

   a. Compute the net investment.

   b. Compute the net cash flow for the first year.

   c. Compute the net cash flow for the final year (year 10), including all terminal cash flows.

10. Rocky Mountain Resorts is planning to expand. This will require the acquisition of new equipment. The equipment will cost $200,000, including delivery and installation. It will be depreciated straight-line to a zero value over the five-year economic life of the project. Interest costs associated with financing the equipment purchase are estimated to be $15,000 annually. The expected salvage value of this new equipment at the end of five years is $25,000.

   Additional net working capital of $30,000 will be needed immediately. When the project is terminated in five years, there no longer will be a need for this incremental working capital. If new equipment is acquired, existing equipment can be salvaged for $10,000. The existing equipment has been completely depreciated.

   Rocky Mountain Resorts expects the expansion to increase sales by $100,000 annually. Cash operating costs are expected to increase by $40,000 annually (not including depreciation or interest expense). The marginal tax rate is 40 percent.

   a. Compute the net investment.

   b. Compute the net cash flow for the first year.

   c. Compute the net cash flow for the last year (year 5), including all terminal cash flows.

Chapter 12
Capital Budgeting Decision Methods

Chapter Objectives

This chapter covers the following topics:

1   How to compute a capital budgeting project's payback period, discounted payback period, net present value, profitability index, internal rate of return, and modified internal rate of return

2   How to use capital budgeting decision methods on independent capital budgeting projects

3   How to use capital budgeting decision methods on mutually exclusive capital budgeting projects

4   How to evaluate a capital budgeting project with cash flows that are considered to be not normal

5   The advantages and disadvantages of each of the capital budgeting decision methods

12.1 Introduction

In this chapter, we present the traditional methods used to evaluate capital budgeting projects. These methods can also be used to evaluate other capital investments besides traditional capital budgeting projects. Nontraditional capital projects might include investments in employee training, advertising campaigns, a permanent increase in inventory, repayment of a bond to be funded with a new, lower-interest-rate bond, or research and development expenditures.

The cost of acquiring a project is measured as the project's **net investment**, and the benefits from a project are measured as the project's **net cash flows**. Once a project's net investment and net cash flows have been estimated, a decision method is used to recommend either acceptance or rejection of the project. The decision methods are based on a comparison of the project costs with the project benefits. Some capital budgeting decision methods perform the cost–benefit analysis by determining how long it takes for the project benefits to recover the project cost (payback period and discounted payback period). The **discounted payback period** considers the time value of money (TVM) in determining this period of time, whereas the **payback period** does not take into account the time value of money. Other methods perform a straightforward comparison of the benefits and cost while taking into account the time value of money (net present value and profitability index). The **net present value** method is the difference between benefits and costs, and the **profitability index** is the ratio of benefits to costs. And, finally, some methods determine the annual percentage rate of return that a project's benefits provide to a project investment. These last methods are called the **internal rate of return** and the **modified internal rate of return.** This chapter presents these six different capital budgeting decision methods and explains the strengths and weaknesses of each. To simplify the comparison, the discussion will ignore the concepts of capital cost allowance and tax shields introduced in section 11.3.

12.2 Capital Budgeting Decision Methods

To assist in the presentation of the six capital budgeting methods, two capital budgeting examples will be used. The Maple Leaf restaurant is considering two possible projects. The first is an expansion of its very successful restaurant. The restaurant manager estimates the cash flows from the expansion will be as follows.

Maple Leaf Expansion Project	
Year	Cash flow
0	−$200,000
1	$ 70,000
2	$ 70,000
3	$ 70,000
4	$ 70,000
5	$ 70,000

The expansion project has a $200,000 net investment and positive net cash flows of $70,000 a year for five years, as estimated in the preceding table. The second project is to build a new restaurant on the other side of town. The manager estimates the cash flows from the new restaurant as follows.

Maple Leaf New-Restaurant Project	
Year	Cash flow
0	−$300,000
1	$ 50,000
2	$ 70,000
3	$100,000
4	$120,000
5	$150,000

The new-restaurant project has a $300,000 net investment and positive net cash flows of $50,000, $70,000, $100,000, $120,000, and $150,000 respectively for years 1 through 5, as estimated in the preceding table.

12.2.1 PAYBACK PERIOD

A project's payback period is the amount of time required for the net cash flows to recover the net investment. Generally, the more quickly a project pays back, the better the project. It is quite simple to calculate the payback period for a project with net cash flows that are the same each year, such as the Maple Leaf expansion project.

$$\text{Payback period} = \frac{\$200,000}{\$70,000} = 2.86 \text{ years}$$

But the calculation is a bit more difficult for a project with uneven net cash flows, such as the Maple Leaf new-restaurant project. It is best calculated by constructing a cash flow table and adding a cumulative cash flow column.

Maple Leaf New-Restaurant Project		
Year	Cash flow	Cumulative cash flow
0	–$300,000	–$300,000
1	$ 50,000	–$250,000
2	$ 70,000	–$180,000
3	$100,000	–$ 80,000
4	$120,000	
5	$150,000	

Keeping a running total of the cash flow column creates the new column, labelled "Cumulative cash flow." Year 0 is just the –$300,000 net investment, the initial capital outlay, the same as the "Cash flow" column. Year 1 is –$300,000 plus $50,000, which equals a cumulative cash flow of –$250,000 for year 1. Year 2 is –$250,000 plus $70,000, which equals a cumulative cash flow of –$180,000. Year 3 is –$180,000 plus $100,000, which equals a cumulative cash flow of –$80,000. It is obvious the year 4 cash flow of $120,000 is more than enough to pay back the remaining –$80,000 of the net investment, and therefore we know the payback period is more than three years but less than four years. Again, with –$80,000 of the net investment remaining after year 3, the payback period has to be more than three years. But with a cash flow of $120,000 in year 4, the payback period must be less than four years. Now it remains only to calculate what proportion of year 4 it will take to pay back the remaining –$80,000. This will be $\frac{\$80,000}{\$120,000} = 0.67$ of the fourth year, giving us a payback period of 3.67 years. Or, we could show the calculation for the new restaurant as

$$\text{Payback period} = 3 + \frac{\$80,000}{\$120,000} = 3 + 0.67 = 3.67 \text{ years}$$

According to the payback period calculations, the expansion project is better because it pays back more than three-fourths of a year faster (3.67 – 2.86 = 0.81 years) than the new-restaurant project. But does this mean the expansion project is a better investment for Maple Leaf? No, of course not. The payback period can be a useful measure of a project's liquidity risk. It is proper to say that Maple Leaf expects to recoup the net investment more quickly on the expansion than on the new restaurant, but it would be stretching logic to make much more out of the payback period calculation.

The payback period has several serious weaknesses. First, it does not take into account the time value of money. We learned in Chapter 7 that the time when money is received has a significant impact on the money's value. Thus, $100 received today is more valuable than $100 received in two years. In the payback calculation, this time value of money is not considered.

Second, there is no objective criterion for what is an acceptable payback period. Certainly a corporation can require that all projects pay back in less than three years or four years, or some other finite number of years. But this is subjective: there is nothing objective about a certain number of years' cutoff point that maximizes firm value. Two analysts considering the same project with the same data could make different accept/reject decisions using the payback period. For example, one analyst could use a two-year cutoff for payback and reject the expansion project, and the other analyst could use a three-year cutoff for payback and accept the expansion project.

Third, cash flows after the payback period have no impact on the payback period calculation. For example, suppose the expansion project had a $100,000 expected net cash flow in year 5 instead of $70,000. This would clearly make the project more attractive, but the project's payback period does not reflect this. Because cash flows after the payback period are ignored, the payback period would still be 2.86 years.

The payback period can be a useful measure of a project's liquidity risk, but this method has three serious drawbacks as indicated. A better measure of liquidity risk is the discounted payback period.

12.2.2 DISCOUNTED PAYBACK PERIOD

The discounted payback period improves on the payback period by considering the time value of money. A project's discounted payback period is the amount of time required for the net cash flow's present values to recover the net investment. The present values are typically calculated by discounting the net cash flows at the required rate of return. Generally, the shorter a project's discounted payback, the better the project. If the required rate of return is known and a project's cash flows have been estimated, the first step in the discounted payback's calculation is to discount the project's cash flows at the required rate of return (calculate the present values of the cash flows). Then the discounted payback period is calculated the same as the regular payback period, except the present values of the cash flows are used.

We illustrate the discounted payback with examples from the Maple Leaf restaurant. Let the required rate of return equal 10 percent.

Maple Leaf Restaurant Expansion Project			
Year	Cash flow	PV of cash flow	Cumulative
0	−$200,000	−$200,000	−$200,000
1	$ 70,000	$ 63,636	−$136,364
2	$ 70,000	$ 57,851	−$ 78,513
3	$ 70,000	$ 52,592	−$ 25,921
4	$ 70,000	$ 47,811	
5	$ 70,000	$ 43,464	

The "PV of cash flow" column is simply the cash flow discounted back at 10 percent rounded to the nearest dollar. For example, $70,000 discounted at 10 percent for one year equals $63,636 rounded to the nearest dollar. $70,000 discounted at 10 percent for two years equals $57,851, and so on for years 3, 4, and 5. The present value of the –$200,000 net investment is still –$200,000 because it is literally a present value at time zero (today). The "Cumulative" column is the accumulation of the "PV of cash flow" column. For example, the –$200,000 present value cash flow from year 0 plus the $63,636 present value cash flow from year 1 accumulate to –$136,364 (year 1 under "Cumulative"). The –$136,364 cumulative cash flow from year 1 plus the $57,851 present value cash flow from year 2 accumulate to –$78,513 (year 2 under "Cumulative"). The –$78,513 cumulative cash flow from year 2 plus the $52,592 present value cash flow from year 3 accumulate to –$25,921 (year 3 under "Cumulative"). After year 3 there still remains $25,921 of the net investment not recovered from the present value of the net cash flows. Therefore, the discounted payback period must be more than three years. Because the $47,811 present value cash flow from year 4 is more than enough to recover the remaining net investment of $25,921, the discounted payback period for the expansion project will be more than three years but less than four years as follows.

$$\text{Discounted payback period} = 3 \text{ years} + \frac{\$25,921 \text{ not yet recovered after 3 years}}{\$47,811 \text{ PV of cash flow from year 4}}$$

$$= 3 + 0.54 = 3.54 \text{ years}$$

The calculation for the Maple Leaf new-restaurant project is similar to the calculation for the expansion project.

Maple Leaf New-Restaurant Project

Year	Cash flow	PV of cash flow	Cumulative
0	−$300,000	−$300,000	−$300,000
1	$ 50,000	$ 45,455	−$254,545
2	$ 70,000	$ 57,851	−$196,694
3	$100,000	$ 75,131	−$121,563
4	$120,000	$ 81,962	−$ 39,601
5	$150,000	$ 93,138	

This table is constructed just like the table used to calculate the discounted payback period for the Maple Leaf expansion project. The third column, "PV of cash flow," is the present value of each cash flow discounted at the 10 percent required rate of return for the appropriate number of years. The "Cumulative" column accumulates the values from the "PV of cash flow" column. After four years, there is still $39,601 remaining from the net investment not yet recovered from the present value of the net cash flows. The present value of the cash flow from the fifth year is more than enough to pay back this remaining $39,601, and therefore the discounted payback period must be more than four years but less than five years. The discounted payback period for the new-restaurant project is

$$\text{Discounted payback period} = 4 + \frac{\$39,601}{\$93,138} = 4 + 0.43 = 4.43 \text{ years}$$

Again, the discounted payback period indicates the Maple Leaf expansion project pays back more quickly than the new-restaurant project, even when considering the time value of money. The expansion project expects to recover the net investment in 3.54 years and the new-restaurant project in 4.43 years. The shorter discounted payback still does not imply the expansion is a better project. It does imply the expansion recovers its net investment more quickly and has less liquidity risk than the new-restaurant project.

The discounted payback period is an improvement on the payback period. First, it does take into account the time value of money by discounting future cash flows back to the present. All cash flows are standardized by considering and accumulating only present values.

The discounted payback period improves on the second weakness of the payback period. This second weakness is the lack of an objective criterion for use with the payback period. The discounted payback period, however, has an objective criterion under certain circumstances. Consider the two projects just discussed. Both projects have only positive cash flows after the net investment. Projects with all-positive net cash flows after the net investment are considered normal projects. The expansion project has a discounted payback period of 3.54 years, indicating the net investment is recovered in 3.54 years with the required 10 percent rate of return. If all the cash flows occur as expected for 3.54 years, Maple Leaf has earned its 10 percent required rate of return. All cash flows after 3.54 years provide Maple Leaf with a return over and above 10 percent because the project is normal, and all remaining cash flows are positive. A similar analysis can be applied to the Maple Leaf new-restaurant project. Its discounted payback period is 4.43 years, and it is a normal project. If cash flows occur as expected, the new-restaurant project earns the 10 percent required rate of return in 4.43 years, and the positive cash flows continuing thereafter will provide additional returns over and above 10 percent.

A normal capital budgeting project with a discounted payback period less than its economic life is an acceptable project. It is expected to increase firm value. This is true for the two examples used previously. Both projects are expected to return more than the 10 percent required rate of return because their discounted payback periods are less than their five-year economic lives. If a project is not normal, we cannot use this decision rule to determine a project's acceptability. For example, suppose the Maple Leaf expansion project expected a negative cash flow in the fifth year instead of a positive $70,000. Without doing some additional calculations, we could not say the project returned more than 10 percent just because the net investment was recovered in 3.54 years. The negative cash flow in the fifth year could cause the accumulated present values of the net cash flows to be less than the net investment. This would in turn lead to a rate of return less than 10 percent.

The discounted payback period can be used to determine the acceptability of normal projects, but it cannot be used to determine which project is best for the firm. The Maple Leaf expansion project has a quicker discounted payback period than the new-restaurant project. This does indicate better liquidity risk for the expansion project and a quicker recovery of the project's net investment. It does not indicate that the expansion project is better, or that it will increase firm value more than the new-restaurant project.

The discounted payback period offers a partial solution to the lack of an objective criterion to use with the payback period. To decide the acceptability of a project, there is an objective criterion to use with the discounted payback period on normal projects. A discounted payback period that is less than the economic life indicates an acceptable normal project. However, when comparing mutually exclusive projects to one another, there is no objective criterion to use with the discounted payback period.

Finally, the discounted payback period does not improve on the third weakness of the payback period. Cash flows after the discounted payback period have no impact on the discounted payback period. Again, suppose the expansion project had a $100,000 expected net cash flow in year 5 instead of $70,000. This would clearly make the project more attractive, but the project's discounted payback period would still be 3.54 years.

The discounted payback period is an improved measure of liquidity risk relative to the payback period. It can also be used to decide the acceptability of normal projects. But it should be used only in conjunction with other capital budgeting decision methods.

12.2.3 NET PRESENT VALUE

A project's net present value (NPV) is the sum of the present values of the net cash flows discounted at the required rate of return minus the net investment. All capital budgeting decision methods are basically a form of cost–benefit analysis, but the net present value method is the most straightforward application of cost–benefit analysis. Net present value is simply the benefits, as measured by the sum of the present values of the net cash flows, minus the cost, as measured by the net investment. If a project's benefits exceed the cost, the net present value is positive, and the project is acceptable. If a project's benefits are less than the cost, the net present value is negative, and the project is unacceptable.

$$NPV = \text{Sum of present values of net cash flows} - \text{Net investment}$$

A more complete NPV equation is:

$$NPV = \text{Sum of present values of net cashflow} - \text{net investment} + \text{present value of tax shields} - \text{present value of lost tax shields due to salvage}$$

For the sake of simplicity, the tax shields are ignored in the discussion.

The net present value for the Maple Leaf expansion project using the 10 percent required rate of return is

$$NPV = \$70,000 \times \left[\frac{1 - \dfrac{1}{(1 + 10\%)^5}}{10\%} \right] - \$200,000$$

Finding the present value of the $70,000 net cash flows each year for five years discounted as an annuity payment at a 10 percent required rate of return,

$$NPV = \$265,355 - \$200,000 = \$65,355$$

The Maple Leaf expansion project has a positive net present value of $65,355, indicating the project is acceptable.

The net present value for the Maple Leaf new-restaurant project is

$$NPV = \frac{\$50,000}{(1 + 10\%)} + \frac{70,000}{(1 + 10\%)^2} + \frac{100,000}{(1 + 10\%)^3} + \frac{120,000}{(1 + 10\%)^4} + \frac{150,000}{(1 + 10\%)^5} - \$300,000$$

Finding the present value of the five uneven net cash flows at a 10 percent required rate of return,

$$NPV = \$353,537 - \$300,000 = \$53,537$$

Appendix 5 shows how to compute NPV with a business calculator.

The Maple Leaf new-restaurant project has a positive net present value of $53,537, indicating this project is also acceptable.

A positive net present value indicates a project is acceptable. A negative net present value indicates a project is unacceptable. Beyond a project's acceptability, a project's net present value imparts additional information. It is also an estimate of the change in firm value caused by investment in the project. In other words, the value of the Maple Leaf restaurant is expected to increase by $65,355 if an investment is made in the expansion project, and the firm value is expected to increase by $53,537 if an investment is made in the new-restaurant project.

Using net present value to make capital budgeting decisions is consistent with maximizing firm value because net present value is a measure of a project's contribution to firm value. The Maple Leaf expansion project is expected to add $65,355 to firm value over and above a 10 percent return on the $200,000 net investment. The new-restaurant project is expected to add $53,537 to firm value over and above a 10 percent return on the $300,000 net investment. Both projects are expected to provide more than the 10 percent required return to invested funds. The restaurant expansion project provides more value over and above the 10 percent required return ($63,355 expansion project *NPV* versus $53,537 new-restaurant project *NPV*). Therefore, if there are no other significant differences between the two projects, the restaurant expansion increases firm value the most and is the better project. Other possible significant differences that could nullify this conclusion include different project risk levels not taken into account, or that one project fits better into Maple Leaf's long-term strategic plan. If the projects are independent, then both projects are acceptable and could be funded. If the projects are mutually exclusive, then the available information indicates the expansion project will increase firm value the most and should be accepted.

12.2.4 PROFITABILITY INDEX

A capital budgeting project's profitability index (*PI*) is similar to a project's net present value because both methods compare a project's cost to its benefits. The net present value achieves this by subtracting the cost (net investment) from the benefits (sum of present values of net cash flows). The profitability index is constructed by taking the ratio of the benefits to the cost. In other words, the sum of the present values of net cash flows is divided by the net investment.

$$PI = \frac{\text{Sum of present values of net cash flows}}{\text{Net investment}}$$

The profitability index for the Maple Leaf restaurant expansion is

$$PI = \frac{\$70{,}000 \times \left[\dfrac{1 - \dfrac{1}{(1 + 10\%)^5}}{10\%} \right]}{\$200{,}000}$$

Find the present value of the $70,000 net cash flows each year for five years discounted as an annuity payment at a 10 percent required rate of return.

$$PI = \frac{\$265,355}{\$200,000} = 1.33$$

This can also be calculated by adding one to the ratio of the NPV and the net investment as follows.

$$PI = 1 + \frac{NPV}{\text{Net investment}} = 1 + \frac{\$65,355}{\$200,000}$$
$$PI = 1 + 0.33 = 1.33$$

The profitability index for the Maple Leaf new-restaurant project is

$$PI = 1 + \frac{\$53,537}{\$300,000} = 1 + 0.18 = 1.18$$

A profitability index greater than one provides an indicator that the project is acceptable and is consistent with a positive net present value. However, a profitability index that is less than one would indicate an unacceptable project and is consistent with a negative net present value. Further, a profitability index of exactly one indicates a project that is expected to earn exactly the required rate of return. The Maple Leaf expansion project's profitability index of 1.33 indicates it is expected to earn the 10 percent required rate of return, plus provide a net present value of $0.33 per $1.00 of net investment. The new-restaurant project's profitability index of 1.18 indicates it is expected to earn the 10 percent required rate of return, plus provide a net present value of $0.18 per $1.00 of net investment.

The profitability index method is most useful when a firm faces capital rationing, which exists when a firm can invest only a limited amount in capital budgeting projects regardless of the number, size, and expected returns of the capital budgeting projects available. When a firm faces capital rationing, it should choose the combination of capital budgeting projects to maximize the total net present value—or, in other words, to maximize firm value. The higher a project's profitability index, the more net present value it provides per dollar invested. Under capital rationing it may not be possible to invest in all projects with a positive net present value. Therefore, the firm needs to focus on projects providing the most net present value per dollar invested, and this is explicitly measured by a project's profitability index.

The profitability index is an appropriate indicator of a project's acceptability. In many circumstances, it can also be used to determine the preferred project in mutually exclusive comparisons. But this capital budgeting decision method is not used to a great extent, except in capital rationing situations.

12.2.5 INTERNAL RATE OF RETURN

A capital budgeting project's internal rate of return is the rate of return causing the project's net present value to equal zero. It is a project's true annual percentage rate of return based on the estimated cash flows. A project's internal rate of return is compared to the project's required rate of return. If the internal rate of return exceeds the required rate of return, the project is acceptable and is expected to increase firm value. If the internal rate of return is less than the required rate of return, the project is unacceptable and is expected to decrease firm value.

The equation used to compute internal rate of return (*IRR*) for the Maple Leaf expansion project can be adapted from the *NPV* equation. The equation previously used to compute *NPV* is

$$NPV = \$70{,}000 \times \left[\frac{1 - \dfrac{1}{(1 + 10\%)^5}}{10\%} \right] - \$200{,}000$$

The internal rate of return is the interest rate that makes the *NPV* equal zero. Therefore, *IRR* is substituted for the 10 percent interest rate in the *NPV* equation, and the *NPV* is set equal to zero.

$$\$70{,}000 \times \left[\frac{1 - \dfrac{1}{(1 + IRR)^5}}{IRR} \right] - \$200{,}000 = 0$$

If the *NPV* is zero then the sum of the present values of net cash flows exactly equals the net investment, and the equation for computing *IRR* can also be expressed as

$$\$70{,}000 \times \left[\frac{1 - \dfrac{1}{(1 + IRR)^5}}{IRR} \right] = \$200{,}000$$

Finding the internal rate of return for the expansion project is a matter of finding the interest rate that equates the present value of $70,000 a year for five years with $200,000. The expansion project's *IRR* is 22.11 percent. This is much higher than the 10 percent required rate of return, indicating the expansion project is acceptable.

The internal rate of return for the Maple Leaf new-restaurant project is

$$\frac{\$50{,}000}{(1 + IRR)} + \frac{70{,}000}{(1 + IRR)^2} + \frac{100{,}000}{(1 + IRR)^3} + \frac{120{,}000}{(1 + IRR)^4} + \frac{150{,}000}{(1 + IRR)^5}$$
$$-\$300{,}000 = 0$$

or

$$\frac{\$50{,}000}{(1 + IRR)} + \frac{70{,}000}{(1 + IRR)^2} + \frac{100{,}000}{(1 + IRR)^3} + \frac{120{,}000}{(1 + IRR)^4} + \frac{150{,}000}{(1 + IRR)^5} = \$300{,}000$$

If a project has uneven cash flows, as in this case, solving for the internal rate of return is tedious unless using a business calculator with a cash flow function or using a computer spreadsheet with an *IRR* function. The tedious method initially requires a guess at the *IRR*. Try 15 percent. Then, we need to calculate the preceding present values at a 15 percent interest rate, sum the present values, and compare to the $300,000 net investment. The sum of the present values equals $305,347, which is greater than the net investment. Next, choose a higher interest rate to lower the sum of the present values. Try 20 percent. At 20 percent, the sum of the present values equals $266,300. Now use these two guesses to close in on the answer. The difference between the two guesses is $39,047

($305,347 minus $266,300). The first guess is $5,347 above the $300,000 present value we are trying to achieve. This is 13.69 percent of the gap between the two guesses ($5,347 divided by $39,047), so to the 15 percent guess we should add 13.69 percent of 5 percent (20% minus 15%). *IRR* is approximately equal to 15% + 0.1369 × 5% = 15% + 0.68% = 15.68%.

Using the cash flow function on a calculator or a computer-based spreadsheet reveals a more accurate *IRR* of 15.63 percent. (Appendix 5 shows how to compute *IRR* with a business calculator.) This is higher than the 10 percent required rate of return, indicating the new-restaurant project is acceptable. If the two projects are independent, then both projects should be accepted based on the internal rate of return evidence. If the projects are mutually exclusive, then *IRR* indicates the expansion project is better. This ranking is consistent with the projects' *NPV* and therefore consistent with maximizing firm value. The internal rate of return usually ranks projects consistently with net present value, but not always. This is discussed later in this chapter.

12.2.6 MODIFIED INTERNAL RATE OF RETURN

The internal rate of return is a very popular capital budgeting decision method; however, the modified internal rate of return is a better measure of projects' relative profitability. The modified internal rate of return (*MIRR*) is the interest rate equating the present value of a project's investment costs with the present value of the terminal value of the project's net cash flows.

The present value of a project's investment costs is called a project's *beginning value*. The beginning value is the sum of the present values of all project investment outlays. If all investment outlays take place at the very beginning (time = 0), then the beginning value equals the net investment. If a project has investment outlays in the future, then the beginning value is the sum of the present values of the investment's outlays discounted at the project's required rate of return.

The terminal value of the project's net cash flows is the sum of the future values of the net cash flows at the end of the project's economic life. The terminal value assumes the net cash flows are invested at the project's required rate of return.

To calculate the modified internal rate of return for the Maple Leaf expansion project, we first calculate the project's beginning and terminal values.

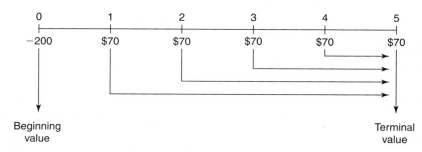

Beginning value = $200,000

$$\text{Terminal value} = \$70,000 \times \left[\frac{(1 + 10\%)^5 - 1}{10\%} \right] = \$427,357$$

The modified internal rate of return is the interest rate equating the present value of the terminal value with the beginning value. The modified internal rate of return for the Maple Leaf expansion project is

$$\$200{,}000 = \frac{\$427{,}357}{(1 + MIRR)^5} \qquad\qquad MIRR = 16.40\%$$

The modified internal rate of return of 16.40 percent is greater than the 10 percent required rate of return, indicating the expansion project is acceptable.

Next, we calculate the beginning value, the terminal value, and the modified internal rate of return for the Maple Leaf new-restaurant project.

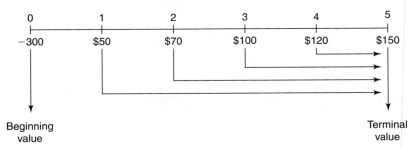

Beginning value = $200,000

Terminal value = $50,000 × (1 + 10%)^4 + 70,000 × (1 + 10%)^3
$\qquad\qquad$ + 100,000 × (1 + 10%)^2 + 120,000 × (1 + 10%) + 150,000

Terminal value = $569,375

The modified internal rate of return for the Maple Leaf new-restaurant project is

$$\$300{,}000 = \frac{\$569{,}375}{(1 + MIRR)^5} \qquad\qquad MIRR = 13.67\%$$

The modified internal rate of return of 13.67 percent is greater than the 10 percent required rate of return, indicating the expansion project is acceptable.

The six capital budgeting decision methods are summarized in Exhibit 12-1. To gain further understanding of how these methods are used in the hospitality industry, see Exhibit 12-2.

Exhibit 12-1
Capital Budgeting Decision Methods

Payback period is the number of years it takes for a project's net cash flows to recover the net investment. There is no objective criterion for deciding if a project is acceptable.

Discounted payback period is the number of years it takes for the present values of a project's net cash flows to recover the net investment. If the discounted payback

(continued)

(continued)

period is less than the project's economic life, an independent, normal project is acceptable and is expected to increase the value of the firm.

Net present value is the sum of the present values of the net cash flows minus the net investment. A net present value that is greater than zero indicates an acceptable independent project.

Profitability index is the sum of the present values of the net cash flows divided by the net investment. A profitability index that is greater than one indicates an acceptable independent project.

Internal rate of return is the interest rate at which a project's net present value equals zero. It is also the interest rate at which the sum of the present values of the net cash flows will equal the net investment. If an independent, normal project's internal rate of return is greater than the required rate of return, the project is acceptable.

Modified internal rate of return is the interest rate at which the project's present value of investment costs is equal to the present value of the project's terminal value of net cash flows. If the modified internal rate of return is greater than the required rate of return, the project is acceptable.

Exhibit 12-2
Capital Budgeting Decision Methods Used in the Hospitality Industry

Discounted cash flow techniques, such as internal rate of return and the net present value methods, are commonly used in the hospitality industry, as reported in two articles in *The Journal of Hospitality Financial Management.** One article surveyed firms in the hotel and gaming industry, and the other surveyed firms in the restaurant industry. Both articles show the primary methods used for capital budgeting decisions were first the internal rate of return method and second the net present value method. Also, the payback method was the most commonly used secondary method in both the hotel and gaming industry and the restaurant industry.

If you plan a career in the hospitality industry, certainly knowledge of capital budgeting techniques could be helpful, and it could be crucial, depending on positions held. Even if you do not plan to be in a finance-related position, knowledge of capital budgeting techniques can help you or your manager make better asset acquisition decisions. The top managers of large hospitality firms are knowledgeable of capital budgeting techniques and use these techniques to make asset acquisition decisions, as reported by these two studies.

*"A Survey of Capital-Budgeting Methods Used by the Hotel/Gaming Industry" by Stanley M. Atkinson and Stephen M. LeBruto, 5, no. 1 (1997), 23–31. Also "A Survey of Capital Budgeting Methods Used by the Restaurant Industry" by Robert A. Ashley, Stanley M. Atkinson, and Stephen M. LeBruto, 8, no. 1 (2000), 47–51.

12.3 Capital Budgeting Decision Methods and Independent Projects

Independent capital budgeting decisions are decisions that stand alone. An investment in an **independent project** is analyzed to determine whether it will increase the value of the firm. If a capital budgeting project is independent and normal, then any of the preceding capital budgeting decision methods besides the payback period can be used to determine the acceptability of the project. Following is a summary of the acceptability criteria for each of these five decision methods.

1. The discounted payback period is equal to or less than the economic life.
2. The net present value is equal to or greater than zero.
3. The profitability index is equal to or greater than one.
4. The internal rate of return is equal to or greater than the required rate of return.
5. The modified internal rate of return is equal to or greater than the required rate of return.

If a capital budgeting project is independent and normal, then the preceding five decision methods will provide consistent decisions regarding the project's acceptability. In other words, if one method indicates a project is acceptable, then all five methods will indicate the project is acceptable. If one method indicates a project is not acceptable, then all five methods will indicate the project is not acceptable.

12.4 Capital Budgeting Decision Methods and Mutually Exclusive Projects

Mutually exclusive capital budgeting projects require a different decision process from independent projects. One must decide not only whether a **mutually exclusive project** is acceptable and will increase the value of the firm, but also which one of the several acceptable mutually exclusive projects is expected to increase the value of the firm the most. In other words, when deciding among mutually exclusive projects, all acceptable projects need to be ranked, with only the best project accepted. The best project is expected to increase the value of the firm more than the other projects. The project with the highest net present value is, by definition, expected to increase the value of the firm the most. The mutually exclusive project with the highest profitability index, internal rate of return, and modified internal rate of return is usually the project expected to increase the value of the firm the most, but this is not always true. There is no reason to expect the mutually exclusive project with the shortest payback period or discounted payback period is the most valuable project. Short payback periods indicate lower liquidity risk, but not necessarily higher project value. So net present value, profitability index, internal rate of return, and modified internal rate of return generally rank mutually exclusive projects consistently, but there are several situations in which they may not be consistent. The first situation occurs when projects have different net investments (scale differences). The second occurs when projects' cash flows are timed differently. And the third occurs when projects have cash flows that are not normal.

12.4.1 SCALE DIFFERENCES

Scale differences among mutually exclusive projects create ranking problems when using the profitability index, the internal rate of return, and the modified internal rate of return. Differences in scale mean projects' net investments are different. For example, consider the following two mutually exclusive projects.

Year	Project A net cash flow	Project B net cash flow
0	−$1,000	−$1,500
1	700	1,000
2	700	1,000
3	700	1,000

Let the required rate of return equal 10 percent. The net present values for the two projects are as follows.

$$NPV_A = \$700 \times \left[\frac{1 - \frac{1}{(1 + 10\%)^3}}{10\%} \right] - \$1,000 = \$740.80$$

$$NPV_B = \$1,000 \times \left[\frac{1 - \frac{1}{(1 + 10\%)^3}}{10\%} \right] - \$1,500 = \$986.85$$

This indicates that project B is expected to increase the value of the firm the most and is the preferred project. The profitability index for each project is

$$\text{Profitability index}_A = 1 + \frac{\$740.80}{\$1,000} = 1.74$$

$$\text{Profitability index}_B = 1 + \frac{\$986.85}{\$1,500} = 1.66$$

Project A has a higher profitability index, even though project B is expected to increase the value of the firm the most. The internal rates of return are

$$\$700 \times \left[\frac{1 - \frac{1}{(1 + IRR_A)^3}}{IRR_A} \right] = \$1,000 \qquad IRR_A = 48.72\%$$

$$\$1,000 \times \left[\frac{1 - \frac{1}{(1 + IRR_B)^3}}{IRR_B} \right] = \$1,500 \qquad IRR_B = 44.63\%$$

Similar to the profitability index, the internal rate of return is higher for the inferior project (project A). The modified internal rates of return are

$$\text{Beginning value}_A = \$1{,}000$$

$$\text{Terminal value}_A = \$700 \times \left[\frac{(1 + 10\%)^3 - 1}{10\%} \right] = \$2{,}317$$

$$\$1{,}000 = \frac{\$2{,}317}{(1 + MIRR_A)^3} \qquad\qquad MIRR_A = 32.33\%$$

$$\text{Beginning value}_B = \$1{,}000$$

$$\text{Terminal value}_B = \$1{,}000 \times \left[\frac{(1 + 10\%)^3 - 1}{10\%} \right] = \$3{,}310$$

$$\$1{,}500 = \frac{\$3{,}310}{(1 + MIRR_B)^3} \qquad\qquad MIRR_B = 30.19\%$$

The modified internal rate of return ranks the two projects the same as the profitability index and internal rate of return. These rankings are inconsistent with the ranking of net present value. The net present value indicates project B will increase firm value by $246.05 more than project A. You might be tempted to choose project A as the best project because its net investment is $500 less than the net investment for project B, and you lose only $246.05 by choosing project A instead of project B. But keep the following in mind. Project B is expected to return 10 percent on the entire $1,500 net investment (including the extra $500 net investment relative to project A). Then, over and above this 10 percent return, project B provides increased firm value of $986.85. So after providing the 10 percent required rate of return on the extra $500 net investment, it still provides an additional $246.05 in value. When mutually exclusive projects are different in terms of scale, the net present value is the only method that always ranks the projects correctly.

12.4.2 CASH FLOW TIMING DIFFERENCES

The net cash flows in mutually exclusive projects may be timed quite differently. Some projects may have cash flows distributed evenly over their economic life, whereas other projects may have large cash flows early and small cash flows later, whereas still other projects may have small cash flows early and large cash flows later. Consider the following two mutually exclusive projects.

Year	Project A net cash flow	Project C net cash flow
0	−$1,000	−$1,000
1	700	0
2	700	0
3	700	2,500

Let the required rate of return equal 10 percent. The net present values for the two projects are as follows.

$$NPV_A = \$700 \times \left[\frac{1 - \dfrac{1}{(1 + 10\%)^3}}{10\%} \right] - \$1,000 = \$740.80$$

$$NPV_C = \frac{\$2,500}{(1 + 10\%)^3} - \$1,000 = \$878.29$$

This indicates that project C is expected to increase the value of the firm the most and is the preferred project. The profitability index for each project is

$$\text{Profitability index}_A = 1 + \frac{\$740.80}{\$1,000} = 1.74$$

$$\text{Profitability index}_C = 1 + \$878.29/\$1,000 \frac{\$878.29}{\$1,000} = 1.88$$

Project C has a higher profitability index and correctly ranks the two projects. The project internal rates of return are

$$\$700 \times \left[\frac{1 - \dfrac{1}{(1 + IRR_A)^3}}{IRR_A} \right] = \$1,000 \qquad IRR_A = 48.72\%$$

$$\frac{\$2,500}{(1 + IRR_C)^3} = \$1,000 \qquad IRR_C = 35.72\%$$

The internal rate of return is higher for the inferior project (project A) and therefore does not rank the projects correctly. The project modified internal rates of return are

$$\text{Beginning value}_A = \$1,000$$

$$\text{Terminal value}_A = \$700 \times \left[\frac{(1 + 10\%)^3 - 1}{10\%} \right] = \$2,317$$

$$\$1,000 = \frac{\$2,317}{(1 + MIRR_A)^3} \qquad MIRR_A = 32.33\%$$

$$\text{Beginning value}_C = \$1,000$$
$$\text{Terminal value}_C = \$2,500$$

$$\$1,000 = \frac{\$2,500}{(1 + MIRR_C)^3} \qquad MIRR_C = 35.72\%$$

Notice the modified internal rate of return is the same as the internal rate of return for project C. When a project has just two cash flows—a net investment and one cash flow at the end of the project's economic life—then modified internal rate of return equals the internal rate of return. The modified internal rate of return correctly ranks the two projects. When project cash flows are timed differently, the internal rate of return may not rank the projects correctly. But the net present value, the profitability index, and the modified internal rate of return do correctly select the best project under these circumstances.

12.5 Not-Normal Cash Flows

Capital budgeting projects with not-normal cash flows are possible but not very common in the hospitality industry. Normal project cash flows include a cash outflow (a negative cash flow) at the beginning of a project's life. We call this cash outflow the *net investment*. Normal projects then have positive cash flows (cash inflows) for the remainder of their life. We call these *net cash flows*. A project with not-normal cash flows will have at least one negative cash flow (outflow) following at least one positive cash flow (inflow). The following is an example of a project with not-normal cash flows.

Year	Project net cash flow
0	−$1,000
1	2,000
2	2,000
3	−3,200

The project starts out with a negative cash flow and is followed by two positive cash flows. This is normal so far. But the project has not-normal cash flows because the positive cash flow in year 2 is followed by a negative cash flow in year 3. This creates problems for using the payback period and discounted payback period methods. How can you calculate how long it takes to pay back the investment cash flows when you still have investment cash flows continuing at the end of the project's life? Therefore, both payback methods cannot be used in this scenario.

The net present value, profitability index, and modified internal rate of return handle this situation easily. Assuming a 10 percent required rate of return, the net present value for the above project is

$$NPV = \frac{\$2,000}{(1 + 10\%)} + \frac{2,000}{(1 + 10\%)^2} - \frac{3,200}{(1 + 10\%)^3} - 1,000$$

$$NPV = \$66.87$$

The profitability index is

$$\text{Profitability index} = 1 + \frac{\$66.87}{\$1,000} = 1.07$$

The modified internal rate of return begins with the calculation of the beginning value. This is the sum of the present value of the investment cash outflows.

$$\text{Beginning value} = \$1,000 + \frac{3,200}{(1 + 10\%)^3} = \$3,404.21$$

The terminal value is the sum of the future values of the net cash inflows.

$$\text{Terminal value} = \$2,000 \times (1 + 10\%)^2 + 2,000 \times (1 + 10\%) = \$4,620.00$$

$$\$3,404.21 = \frac{\$4,620}{(1 + MIRR)^3} \qquad MIRR = 10.72\%$$

All three methods indicate this project is acceptable. The problem is that the internal rate of return is not a viable decision method to use with not-normal cash flows because not-normal projects will have more than one internal rate of return. The internal rate of return calculation for this example is

$$\frac{\$2,000}{(1 + IRR)} + \frac{2,000}{(1 + IRR)^2} - \frac{3,200}{(1 + IRR)^3} = \$1,000$$

Both 6.83 percent and 125.81 percent work in the preceding equation, and they are both correct. (If you calculate the net present value at 6.83 percent and again at 125.81 percent, the net present value is zero in both cases. Remember, the *IRR* is the interest rate that causes *NPV* to equal zero.) There is no way to indicate which rate is more correct. Both 6.83 percent and 125.81 percent are the correct internal rate of return.

The internal rate of return is a very popular capital budgeting decision method. Unfortunately, it cannot be used for projects with not-normal cash flows (cash flows with more than one sign change). It doesn't matter if the projects being considered are independent or mutually exclusive. The internal rate of return method is not a viable decision method to use for projects with not-normal cash flows. Fortunately, most projects in the hospitality industry are normal projects, and thus the internal rate of return method usually works just fine. Exhibit 12-3 provides a summary of which capital budgeting decision methods properly rank mutually exclusive projects under various conditions.

Exhibit 12-3
Mutually Exclusive Projects and Capital Budgeting Decision Methods

Mutually exclusive projects present an additional challenge to capital budgeting decision making. In addition to deciding whether projects are acceptable, the manager must decide which project is best. A capital budgeting decision method should be able to rank projects with the number one–ranked project expected to increase firm value the most. The following table describes which capital budgeting decision methods perform correctly with mutually exclusive projects and under what conditions.

Properly Rank Mutually Exclusive Projects

Capital budgeting decision methods	Different size net investments (scale differences)	Cash flow timing differences	Not-normal cash flows
Payback period	No	No	No
Discounted payback period	No	No	No
Net present value	Yes	Yes	Yes
Profitability index	No	Yes	Yes
Internal rate of return	No	No	No
Modified internal rate of return	No	Yes	Yes

12.6 The Use of Capital Budgeting Decision Methods

We have indicated a possible problem with the use of the profitability index, the internal rate of return, and the modified internal rate of return when making mutually exclusive capital budgeting decisions. Scale differences between projects can cause all three of these methods to be inconsistent with value maximization. Additionally, projects with cash flows timed quite differently and projects with not-normal cash flows create problems with the use of the internal rate of return, as explained earlier. Fortunately, most mutually exclusive capital budgeting decisions in the hospitality industry do not have these conditions, and therefore all four methods (NPV, PI, IRR, and MIRR) usually render correct decisions in real life. But one needs to be aware of the possible problems and adapt appropriately where needed.

We have presented six capital budgeting decision methods in this chapter. Clearly, we favour net present value as the best single decision method, but all six methods have their advantages and disadvantages. The use of computer spreadsheets makes it quite easy to calculate all six methods, and we recommend consideration of all the methods in order to obtain as much information as possible about a project. Certainly the best single indicator of a project's profitability is the net present value. But the payback methods provide information about a project's risk and liquidity. A project with a payback period of two years is less risky and more liquid than a project with a payback period of five years. And the profitability index, internal rate of return, and modified internal rate of return provide information on risk not inherent in the net present value. For example, if two projects have the same net present value but vastly disparate net investments, the project with the smaller net investment has a greater margin for safety. The profitability index, internal rate of return, and modified internal rate of return will indicate this, but this information is not inherent in the net present value. The following example illustrates this concept.

Year	Project D net cash flow	Project E net cash flow
0	−$5,000	−$50,000
1	3,000	−1,096
2	3,000	−1,096
3	3,000	−1,096

Using a 10 percent required rate of return, we obtain the following calculations.

$NPV_D = \$2,460.56$ $NPV_E = \$2,462.63$

Profitability index$_D$ = 1.49   Profitability index$_E$ = 1.05

$IRR_D = 36.31\%$ $IRR_E = 12.78\%$

$MIRR_D = 25.70\%$ $MIRR_E = 11.78\%$

Both projects have a similar net present value, but project D has much more room for error. If project D's net cash flows decline by more than 32 percent, from $3,000 annually to $2,011 annually, the project still recovers its net investment and earns the 10 percent required rate of return (NPV > $0). But if project E's net cash flows decline by less than

5 percent, from $21,096 annually to $20,105 annually, the project will not earn its 10 percent required return on the $50,000 net investment ($NPV < \$0$). Additionally, project D places only $5,000 at risk, whereas project E places $50,000 at risk. Project D's higher profitability index, internal rate of return, and modified internal rate of return indicate project D's higher margin for safety.

The net present value is the best single indicator of a project's profitability, but it reveals nothing about the margin of safety. The profitability index, the internal rate of return, and the modified internal rate of return indicate not only that both projects are profitable, but also that their much higher levels for project D show a much higher margin for safety with project D versus project E. Exhibit 12-4 summarizes the advantages of the various capital budgeting decision methods. Appendix 6 works through a comprehensive "new hotel" capital budgeting example to arrive at the net present value for the project.

Exhibit 12-4
The Advantages of Capital Budgeting Decision Methods

Payback period provides a measure of liquidity and risk. The shorter the payback period, the quicker a project's net investment is expected to be recovered and the better the liquidity and the lower the risk. It provides no information on project profitability.

Discounted payback period is a better measure of risk and liquidity than payback period because it accounts for the time value of money. The shorter the discounted payback period, the quicker a project's net investment is expected to be recovered and the better the liquidity and lower the risk. If the discounted payback period is less than the economic life, it does indicate a normal, independent project is acceptable.

Net present value is the single best measure of project profitability. It does not provide much information about project risk unless it is evaluated in conjunction with other information. Net present value is consistent with value maximization.

Profitability index is a relative measure of profitability and provides some information about project risk. In general, the higher a project's profitability index, the lower the amount of risk, and therefore a greater margin of safety can be assumed. However, the profitability index may not rank mutually exclusive projects correctly when scale differences exist between projects.

Internal rate of return is a relative measure of profitability and also provides some information about project risk. The higher a project's internal rate of return, the lower the amount of risk, and therefore a greater margin of safety can be assumed. The internal rate of return may not rank mutually exclusive projects correctly.

Modified internal rate of return is a relative measure of profitability and provides some information about project risk. The higher a project's modified internal rate of return, the greater the margin of safety. The modified internal rate of return may not rank mutually exclusive projects correctly when scale differences exist between projects.

12.7 SUMMARY

This chapter:

- Explained how to compute a capital budgeting project's payback period, discounted payback period, net present value, profitability index, internal rate of return, and modified internal rate of return

- Explained how to use capital budgeting decision methods on independent capital budgeting projects

- Explained how to use capital budgeting decision methods on mutually exclusive capital budgeting projects

- Explained how to evaluate a capital budgeting project with cash flows that are considered to be not normal

- Discussed the advantages and disadvantages of each of the capital budgeting decision methods

Key Terms

Discounted payback period

Independent project

Internal rate of return

Modified internal rate of return

Mutually exclusive project

Net cash flows

Net investment

Net present value

Payback period

Profitability index

Discussion Questions

1. How can a capital budgeting decision be viewed in the context of cost–benefit analysis?

2. How is the discounted payback period an improvement on the payback period?

3. Explain how using the net present value method to make a capital budgeting decision is consistent with the objective of maximizing a firm's value.

4. How are the net present value method, the profitability index, and the internal rate of return similar to one another?

5. How is the modified internal rate of return different from the internal rate of return? How is the modified internal rate of return an improvement on the internal rate of return?

6. Each of the following capital budgeting decision methods provides a consistent decision on an independent capital budgeting project with normal cash flows. What should be the appropriate, suggested, or rule-based decision criteria for each of these methods?

   a. Discounted payback period

   b. Net present value

   c. Profitability index

   d. Internal rate of return

   e. Modified internal rate of return

7. Why is a capital budgeting decision involving independent projects different from a decision involving mutually exclusive projects?

8. What are the characteristics of mutually exclusive capital budgeting projects that may cause the net present value and internal rate of return methods to rank the projects differently?

9. What are the advantages of using the payback period or discounted payback period methods along with other methods when making a capital budgeting decision?

10. What is the advantage of using the internal rate of return method along with net present value when making a capital budgeting decision?

Problems

Problems designated with EXCEL can be solved using Excel spreadsheets accessible at www.pearsoned.ca/chatfield.

1. An independent capital budgeting project has a net investment of $100,000 and is expected to generate net cash flows of $40,000 annually for four years. The required rate of return is 12 percent.

   a. Compute the payback period.

   b. Compute the discounted payback period.

   c. Should the project be accepted? Explain your answer.

2. An independent capital budgeting project is expected to have the following cash flows.

Year	Cash flows
0	−$500,000
1	$100,000
2	$150,000
3	$250,000
4	$300,000

   a. Compute the payback period.

   b. Compute the discounted payback period using an 11 percent required rate of return.

   c. Should the project be accepted? Explain your answer.

3. An independent capital budgeting project has a net investment of $1 million and is expected to generate net cash flows of $300,000 annually for five years. The required rate of return is 18 percent.

   a. Compute the net present value.

   b. Compute the profitability index.

   c. Should the project be accepted? Explain your answer.

4. An independent capital budgeting project is expected to have the following cash flows.

Year	Cash flows
0	−$225,000
1	$ 75,000
2	$125,000
3	$200,000

a. Compute the net present value at a 17 percent required rate of return.

b. Compute the profitability index at a 17 percent required rate of return.

c. Should the project be accepted? Explain your answer.

5. An independent capital budgeting project has a net investment of $4.5 million and is expected to generate net cash flows of $1.5 million annually for five years. The required rate of return is 14 percent.

a. Compute the internal rate of return.

b. Compute the modified internal rate of return.

c. Should the project be accepted? Explain your answer.

6. An independent capital budgeting project is expected to have the following cash flows.

Year	Cash flows
0	−$875,000
1	$400,000
2	$500,000
3	$600,000

a. Compute the internal rate of return.

b. Compute the modified internal rate of return using a 13 percent required rate of return.

c. Should the project be accepted? Explain your answer, assuming 13 percent is the required rate of return.

7. The following table shows the cash flows for two mutually exclusive capital budgeting projects. The required rate of return for both projects is 10 percent.

Year	Project X cash flows	Project Y cash flows
0	−$120,000	−$120,000
1	$100,000	$ 20,000
2	$ 40,000	$ 50,000
3	$ 10,000	$100,000

a. Compute the net present value for both projects.

b. Compute the internal rate of return for both projects.

c. Compute the modified internal rate of return for both projects.

d. Which project should be accepted? What causes net present value and internal rate of return to rank the projects differently?

8. The following table shows the cash flows for two mutually exclusive capital budgeting projects. The required rate of return for both projects is 13 percent.

Year	Project P cash flows	Project Q cash flows
0	-$250,000	-$250,000
1	0	$120,000
2	0	$120,000
3	0	$120,000
4	0	$120,000
5	$900,000	$120,000

a. Compute the net present value for both projects.

b. Compute the internal rate of return for both projects.

c. Compute the modified internal rate of return for both projects.

d. Which project should be accepted? What causes net present value and internal rate of return to rank the projects differently?

9. The following table shows the cash flows for two mutually exclusive capital budgeting projects. The required rate of return for both projects is 15 percent.

Year	Project A cash flows	Project B cash flows
0	-$300,000	-$500,000
1	$100,000	$200,000
2	$175,000	$250,000
3	$200,000	$300,000

a. Compute the net present value for both projects.

b. Compute the internal rate of return for both projects.

c. Compute the modified internal rate of return for both projects.

d. Which project should be accepted? What causes net present value and the internal rate of return to rank the projects differently? Does the modified internal rate of return rank the projects consistently with the net present value? Explain your answer.

10. Graham's Fine Restaurants is considering two mutually exclusive projects with the following cash flow streams.

Year	Project A net cash flow	Project B net cash flow
0	-$90,000	-$100,000
1	$40,000	$ 30,000
2	$40,000	$ 50,000
3	$40,000	$ 25,000
4	$40,000	$ 55,000

a. Compute the net present value (NPV) for both projects using a 15 percent required rate of return.

b. Compute the internal rate of return (IRR) for both projects.

c. Which project should the firm accept and why?

11. Niagara Resorts is considering the acquisition of a new cruise boat for guests. It is estimated to cost $400,000, including delivery. It will require an immediate increase of $50,000 in net working capital. The salvage value of the new boat is expected to be $100,000 at the end of 10 years. The capital cost allowance rate pertaining to the new boat is 15%.

    Estimated annual additional revenues from the new boat are $150,000. Estimated annual additional costs are $80,000. The marginal tax rate is 40 percent.

    a. If Niagara Resorts requires a 16 percent rate of return on projects such as this, calculate the net present value (*NPV*) for the new cruise boat. Include in your calculation the net present value of the tax shields and the lost tax shields due to salvage.

    b. Should Niagara Resorts invest in the new cruise boat? Why or why not?

12. Mayfield Hotels is considering installing its own vending machines throughout one of its hotels. The vending machines will cost $100,000. An additional $7,000 will be needed for delivery and installation. Another $3,000 will be needed for initial net working capital. The vending machines are expected to have a salvage value of $5,000 at the end of 10 years. The capital cost allowance rate pertaining to the machines is 20%.

    The vending machines are expected to increase annual revenue by $20,000 and to increase annual cash operating costs by $7,000. Mayfield's effective tax rate is 40 percent, and the required rate of return is 14 percent.

    a. Compute the net present value (*NPV*). Include in your calculation the net present value of the tax shields and the lost tax shields due to salvage.

    b. Should the project be accepted?

EXCEL 13. A capital budgeting project has the following expected cash flows.

Year	Cash flows
0	−$ 400,000
1	$ 850,000
2	$ 150,000
3	$ 150,000
4	−$2800,000

    a. What is different about this capital budgeting project?

    b. Compute the net present value for this project at required rates of return of 0 percent, 3.55 percent, 15 percent, 20 percent, 25 percent, and 118.32 percent.

    c. What can you say about this project's internal rate of return?

    d. How would you make a decision to accept or reject this project?

Chapter 13
An Introduction to Hotel Valuation

Chapter Objectives

This chapter covers the following topics:

1   The reasons for performing hotel appraisals

2   The agency relationships inherent in the hotel appraisal process

3   The different types of users and preparers of market studies and appraisals

4   The process of hotel valuation

5   The different components of hotel market analysis

6   The cost approach

7   The sales comparison approach

8   The income capitalization approach

13.1 Introduction

An appraisal is an opinion of value at a certain point in time. Hotel valuation, or hotel appraisal, is an important aspect of hospitality financial management and is generally considered a specialization within the appraisal profession. Although hotel appraising follows all the standard appraisal procedures, hotels are operated differently from other types of commercial real estate endeavours such as shopping malls, apartment buildings, or office complexes. A hotel is both a business and a real estate asset.

This chapter is intended to be only an introduction to the topic of hotel valuation. We have included the section in this textbook because students may someday be asked to appraise a hotel. On the other hand, a hotel manager could also be expected to commission an appraisal and needs to understand how the value was determined. The overall objective of this chapter is to provide a general introduction to hotel appraising for the hospitality student.

13.2 Reasons for a Hotel Appraisal

Hotels are appraised for a variety of reasons. One general reason is because the owners of the hotel are interested in the current market value of an asset they own. The **market value** is considered the most likely price a buyer and seller would agree to under normal

HVS International Hotel Appraisal Specialists

HVS International (formerly known as Hospitality Valuation Services) is one of the largest hotel appraisal organizations in the world. Starting with one office in Mineola, New York, the company now has offices in Toronto and Vancouver, as well as Europe, Australia, Singapore, Hong Kong, Dubai, and South America. They specialize in hotel market studies, appraising, and general hotel consulting. Since 1980 they have conducted consulting engagements with more than 10,000 hotels worldwide.

In addition to consulting engagements, the company publishes a wide variety of surveys about the industry. Some of these include an overview of the lodging industry, hotel wage surveys, and franchise fee analyses. Additionally, they track hotel sales transactions with date, sales price, and capitalization rate information. Finally, they also produce software that can quantify rooms demand as well as forecast income and expenses. The company also sends via e-mail a daily lodging report that discusses important events affecting the hotel industry.

Of importance to students is the weekly lodging report for the Canadian hotel industry entitled "Canadian Weekly Lodging Outlook, 2008," which provides the reader with a detailed perspective on how Canada's largest hotel markets are performing with respect to occupancy, average daily rate, and RevPAR. This information is available on a weekly basis from the HVS Web site (www.hvs.com) at no cost to the user.

circumstances. It is also important to recognize that each appraisal has an effective date. After that date market conditions could change, altering the cash flows and thus the value of the property.

Lenders are also interested in the hotel's value to help assess the risk of their investment. Furthermore, because many loans to hotels are made by commercial banks, federal law requires most commercial loans to be backed by an appraisal. This is because the hotel property represents collateral for the loan from the lender. Lenders write a loan representing a certain proportion of the market value (say, 60 percent) of the hotel property. As long as the market value of the hotel remains above the amount of the loan, the lender's loan is not at risk. If the hotel is involved in a bankruptcy proceeding, the hotel can be sold and the loan will be repaid. However, if the market value is below the amount of the loan, the lender is "exposed" and is at much greater risk. This is one of the reasons why the market value of the property is important.

Other appraisals involve those completed for tax assessment purposes. An assessed value is often different from market value; assessments are made by government authorities in order to charge real estate taxes to pay for improvements to local communities such as roads and schools. Many hotels appeal their assessments to lower the amount of real estate taxes they are required to pay. Another type of value is liquidation value—the price the property would obtain in a very quick sale. This is not the same as market value because the seller is being forced to sell the property under duress. Although there are many different types of value, the focus of this chapter is on market value.

13.2.1 PARTIES INVOLVED IN THE PROCESS

As previously discussed, appraisals are usually completed so that lenders can have some level of confidence about the value of the property that is backing up the loan. Appraisals are now required for commercial properties such as hotels if the loan is being made by a bank whose deposits are federally insured. In earlier chapters, we discussed agency relationships between owners and managers and owners and lenders. In fact, the appraisal process also involves agency relationships.

In the 1980s, hotel developers (who were also borrowers) would commission appraisals directly from appraisal firms. As the principal in this agency relationship, the developer would want to secure the necessary loan for the hotel project. The appraiser, who was required to obtain a large amount of information about the project, could rely significantly on the information from the developer. This information could be incomplete or biased in a way that affected the appraised value. The failure of numerous banks and savings and loans companies in the 1980s exposed some of the problems in the appraisal process regarding agency problems and motivations. Some research indicates that hotel appraised values may be subject to the agency relationships and economic circumstances surrounding the appraisal.[1]

Founded in 1938, the Appraisal Institute of Canada is the national professional association representing individuals who are qualified to perform real estate appraisals and property valuations. The AIC is dedicated to serving the public interest through continually advancing high standards for the appraisal profession by granting use of the CRA (Canadian Residential Appraiser), AACI (Accredited Appraiser Canadian Institute), and P.App (Professional Appraiser) designations.

The AIC has more than 5,150 members across Canada. Designated members provide reasoned valuations that are widely respected by the courts, real estate corporations, chartered banks, trust companies, mortgage lending institutions, all levels of government, and private individuals. Many users of appraisal services accept only appraisal reports completed by individuals who have earned use of the CRA, AACI, or P.App designation. The AIC office is located in Ottawa, with association offices in each province. Additional information is available from its Web site (www.aicanada.ca).

In the United States in the mid-1980s, the U.S. Congress held hearings examining the appraisal process and concluded that the direct hiring of appraisers by developers helped cause inaccurate appraisals. In 1989 the U.S. Congress passed the Federal Institutions Reform Recovery and Enforcement Act of 1989. This law required appraisals to be commissioned by lenders directly and helped lead to state licensing and regulation of commercial real estate appraisers. Although it is still not clear whether this legislation has helped remove bias from appraised values, it recognized the importance of agency relationships in the process and had a major impact on how appraisals were to be completed. Although anyone can conduct an appraisal, those completed for loan underwriting purposes must be completed by real estate appraisers who are accredited and licensed.

Many accounting firms have appraisers with professional designations; a variety of other firms also conduct hotel appraisals, including HVS International and PKF Consulting (www.pkfcanada.com/hotel-consulting-canada.htm).

13.3 The Hotel Appraisal Process

Throughout this textbook we have shown that the value of an asset is the present value of its economic benefits. Accordingly, the hotel appraisal attempts to assess the future economic benefits of a hotel. Therefore, it is the job of the appraiser to attempt to

---

[1]For further reading, see. M. Dalbor and W. Andrew, "Agency Problems in the Hotel Appraisal Process: An Exploratory Study," *International Journal of Hospitality Management 19* (2000), 353–60.

quantify those future benefits. More specifically, an appraiser is expected to carefully examine any factors that affect the size, timing, and risk associated with those benefits. The process follows a specific order and is described in the following sections.

13.3.1 PURPOSE OF THE APPRAISAL

The first step in the appraisal process is determining the nature of the appraisal problem. A major concern is which type of value is being appraised and for whom. As previously discussed, most appraisals are completed to determine market value. Another important question to be answered is the specific property to be appraised. It is not uncommon for a hotel to be appraised along with a parcel of "excess" land next to it or a freestanding restaurant that is adjacent to the property. In terms of the hotel itself, both existing and proposed hotels can be appraised.

Because a hotel appraisal is an appraisal of real estate, it is important to understand the definition of real estate. **Real estate** represents the land and everything permanently attached to it. Land is considered to be not only the ground surface but also that which extends through the earth and also into the sky. This use is somewhat restricted by rights granted to utilities, called easements. On the other hand, the FF&E—fixtures, furniture, and equipment—is often included in the market value of the hotel (because you cannot operate the hotel without FF&E), but it is considered personal property and its value is segregated from the rest of the hotel.

Real property includes real estate along with the benefits of ownership. Different parties may have different ownership interests in real estate. The ownership interest with the most rights is a **fee simple interest**, implying all privileges available for use and enjoyment of the real estate. This is the interest most valued in a hotel appraisal assignment. On the other hand, a landlord in an apartment building has what is known as a *leased fee interest*. A landlord must allow a tenant to use a certain space in the building that is known as a *leasehold interest*. Examples of special interests, called *partial interests*, include the right to minerals under the ground (mineral rights) or the air space above the property (air rights). Each of these types of interest can be valued, and it is imperative that the appraiser understands the interest to be valued before beginning the assignment.

13.3.2 DATA COLLECTION

This portion of the appraisal process is one of the most critical and most difficult. However, in recent years the availability of secondary data on the Internet has made this task easier. Nevertheless, the appraiser must always carefully consider the accuracy of the data obtained and attempt to verify the information whenever possible. This is particularly true for information that is not publicly available (such as information about a hotel in the competitive market). Information that is later discovered to be inaccurate can have a serious impact on the valuation conclusion.

We have stated previously that the value of an asset is the present value of its current and future economic benefits. Accordingly, any and all information that can affect the size, timing, and risk of these benefits needs to be examined. In general, the process begins with very general information about the market area and becomes progressively more specific. For our purposes, we discuss the process for appraising an existing hotel.

13.3.2.1 Market Area Information

Location is a key success factor for all types of real estate, and hotels are no exception. Moreover, a hotel's location relative to its surrounding geographic area is also important. The first unit of analysis that is taken into consideration is usually a county, city, or both. The factors to be examined are those that will impact future hotel room night demand. Although a historical analysis is important and often presented in appraisal reports, the focus should remain on the future growth prospects for an area. We need to remember that the value of an asset is based on the present value of its *future* economic benefits. It is rarely the case that the future represents simple repetition of the past.

Some of the key information that helps to indicate future room night demand includes information about:

■ *Local employment.* This category includes labour force, unemployment rates, breakdown of employment by sector, names of major employers, and employers entering or leaving the area. Many municipalities will discuss new employment entering an area; however, are any employers leaving the market? In other words, is there a *net gain* in employment? The nature of employment in the area also has a significant impact on the market orientation of room night demand in the area.

■ *Office and industrial space.* Information about total square footage, vacancy rates, historical absorption patterns, and future construction/expansion projects should be gathered and considered carefully by the appraiser.

■ *Convention activity.* This information includes the terms of facilities available to attract groups, the number of room nights generated by previous convention groups, and a forecast of future group bookings.

■ *Demographics.* These statistics include population and household income information.

■ *Higher-education facilities.* Colleges and universities usually create demand through medical and research facilities as well as special events such as graduation, parents' weekends, and sporting events.

■ *Tourism.* Tourism plays a key role in hotel room night generation. Natural features such as beaches as well as festivals, concerts, and exhibits are all factors that can generate significant demand.

■ *Sports tourism.* Sports tourism also plays a significant role in hotel room night demand. Take into consideration professional and amateur sports teams that play within the area during a scheduled season or for tournaments.

The sources for the foregoing information vary from area to area, but the local office of economic development, provincial or regional tourism offices, and the local chamber of commerce are good places to start. The previously identified factors represent a partial list of those that are typically considered in the area analysis section of a report. However, the appraiser needs to have a solid understanding of the key elements in the specific market in which the hotel is located. For example, an appraiser in Toronto must understand the impact of events like Caribana and the WinterCity Festival on the local hotel market. A careful analysis of these factors enables the appraiser to understand the segmentation of existing market demand as well as make estimates of future growth.

13.3.2.2 Submarket Analysis

One of the most important features of a quality hotel appraisal is a thorough assessment of the competitive market in which the hotel operates. If an appraiser merely assumes the current occupancy of the hotel will continue indefinitely, the appraiser has ignored the highly competitive nature of the hotel business. A hotel is not merely an apartment building with short-term leases; it is a business within a property that competes for business largely based on its specific location and reputation.

Accordingly, the establishment of the competitive market, or the competitive supply in which the subject property operates, is of critical importance. The names of the hotels with which the subject hotel competes are generally obtained from interviews with the general manager and/or sales managers of the subject hotel. This information can be verified later when interviewing other properties.

Hotels are considered to compete with the subject property based on the following factors.

- Location or proximity to the subject
- Comparable price
- Comparable quality
- Comparable amenities and facilities
- Accommodation for same type of demand

After the hotels in the area are chosen, a significant amount of information needs to be gathered. Even though it is fairly common for appraisers to take photographs of competitive hotels, the goal of the appraiser should be to provide a verbal description that is adequate for an outside reviewer who is unfamiliar with the market to understand the property. The following is a suggested list of information to be obtained from competitive hotels.

- Name and address
- Location relative to subject hotel
- Number of available rooms
- Potential expansion/renovation plans
- Rack room rates
- Historical average occupancy and average rates
- Allocation of accommodated demand by market segment
- Description of food and beverage facilities
- Description of meeting and banquet space
- Seasonality, number of fill nights, and estimate of turnaway demand
- Age
- List of hotels considered competitive

Some of the information on this list is sensitive or proprietary. Many hotel managers are reluctant to provide sensitive information, particularly about average rates and occupancy. One source of this information may be the local tax assessor, who calculates occupancy taxes. Another potential source may be other hotels; many hotels share this information with each other on an informal basis. Sometimes the respondent will answer about occupancy if the question is expressed in terms of a five-point range. Nevertheless, the appraiser must be careful about using sensitive information obtained from personal interviews because it could be biased.

Of particular importance regarding the information gathered from competitive properties is an accurate breakdown of the segmentation of demand. It is also important to understand that although there are some "standard" segments of demand—such as commercial transient, convention group, and leisure—not all hotels in all markets categorize their demand in the same fashion. For example, where does the market include bus groups of tourists? In group business or leisure business? Additionally, segments of demand may be specific to a particular market, such as military, airline crews, and long-term-stay/relocation demand. The appraiser is expected to classify demand in a manner emulating the competitive market. Market segmentation also has a significant effect on analyzing the average rate of the market.

Eventually, the appraiser should compile a spreadsheet detailing the composition of the competitive market in terms of historical supply and demand. A historical range of three to five years is fairly common but is not always obtainable. An example of historical supply and demand is shown in Exhibit 13-1.

Exhibit 13-1 details the historical performance of our hypothetical hotel market for one year (as previously mentioned, it is advantageous to have three to five years of historical data). The historical data is important for a number of reasons. First, it gives the appraiser important information about the current condition of the competitive hotel market. Second, it quantifies the demand by segment, and a historical analysis shows which segments have been increasing or decreasing in the number of occupied rooms. Finally, it relates information about how the subject hotel is competing in the marketplace in overall terms and by segment.

Exhibit 13-1 Historical Supply and Demand Analysis Occupancy and Average Rate Performance for Calendar Year 2008

Hotel	Rooms	Available rooms	Average rate	Occupancy %	Occupied rooms	Rooms revenue
Holiday Inn	200	73,000	$62.00	70	51,100	$3,168,200
Ramada Inn	165	60,225	59.00	64	38,544	2,274,096
Subject Hotel	175	63,875	63.00	68	43,435	2,736,405
Overall Market	540	197,100	$61.45	67.52	133,079	$8,178,701

Segmentation of Market Demand for Calendar Year 2008

Hotel	Commercial %	Group %	Tourist %	Commercial demand	Group demand	Tourist demand
Holiday Inn	45	25	30	22,995	12,775	15,330
Ramada Inn	20	15	65	7,709	5,782	25,053
Subject Hotel	55	30	15	23,889	13,031	6,515
Overall Market	41.1	23.7	35.2	54,593	31,588	46,898

Exhibit 13-2 Historical Supply and Demand Growth

Year	Available rooms	Occupied rooms	Average rate	Occupancy %	Rev PAR
2006	197,100	126,538	$58.60	64.20	$37.62
2007	197,100	128,903	$60.75	65.40	$39.73
2008	197,100	133,079	$61.45	67.52	$41.49
Growth[a]	0.00%	2.55%	2.40%	2.55	5.02%

Year	Commercial %	Group %	Tourist %	Commercial demand	Group demand	Tourist demand
2006	39.5	25.2	35.3%	49,983	31,886	44,669
2007	38.7	26.2	35.1%	49,885	33,773	45,254
2008	41.1	23.7	35.2%	54,593	31,588	46,898
Growth[a]	—	—	—	4.51%	−0.47%	2.46%

[a]Growth is expressed in compound annual terms.

An examination of Exhibit 13-2 reveals the estimated change in accommodated demand for the three-year period. Our simulated market reveals strong historical growth in commercial demand, a decrease in group business, and a modest increase in tourist demand. The appraiser must then attempt to relate the performance of the competitive market to the information about patterns for the overall area. It is important to remember that what is happening in the overall metropolitan area may not be analogous to patterns at competitive hotels. For example, it may be such that the overall market area has accommodated an increasing number of groups in the metropolitan area. However, they may not be staying at hotels in the competitive market, or they may be staying for a shorter period of time. Other factors could come into play, such as a renovation or removal of meeting space at one of the competitive properties during the period of analysis. Overall, it is not enough for appraisers to report what has happened in the competitive market in recent years; they must know *why* the demand changed.

The most common way to evaluate the occupancy and average daily rate (ADR) performance of the subject hotel is by relative comparisons. Although this can also be done with ADR, it is most commonly done with average annual occupancy. The performance of the subject hotel is judged based on the amount of demand it actually captured versus what it "should" have captured. For example, our hypothetical competitive market contains 540 total daily hotel rooms (197,100 annual). The subject hotel contains 175 rooms and represents approximately 32.41 percent of the total market. Therefore, all else being equal, the subject hotel should accommodate 32.41 percent of the demand in the market. This is called its **fair share**. This is also true for each of the three market segments. This is called a *market penetration analysis* and is shown for 2008 in Exhibit 13-3.

A market penetration analysis by segment can be completed for each year when historical data are available. In our example, we can see that the subject hotel has received more than its fair share of demand in two segments—commercial and group demand.

Exhibit 13-3 Historical Market Penetration Analysis for the Subject Hotel, Calendar Year 2008

Subject hotel rooms (annual)	63,875
Total rooms in competitive market	197,100
Subject fair share percentage	32.41%
Commercial demand in market	54,593
Subject hotel fair share	17,694
Demand accommodated	23,889
Market penetration rate	135.01%
Group demand in market	31,588
Subject hotel fair share	10,237
Demand accommodated	13,031
Market penetration rate	127.29%
Tourist demand in market	46,898
Subject hotel fair share	15,200
Demand accommodated	6,515
Market penetration rate	42.86%

The appraiser also needs to consider why this is the case. It is usually a function of the marketing strategy of the property along with location, facilities, and rack rate positioning. On the other hand, we can see the subject hotel has received far less of its fair share in the tourist segment. It might be the case that the subject hotel is not located near tourist attractions or simply does not discount its rates enough to attract the very rate-sensitive tourist demand segment. This is a common situation for many commercially oriented hotels that accommodate a significant amount of demand during the weeknights but have much lower occupancies on weekends. This has important implications for future occupancy projections for the subject hotel.

In terms of ADR, the subject hotel is currently the rate leader in this market. This is probably because the hotel accommodates a significant amount of commercial demand, which is much less rate sensitive than the other segments. It may also reflect a lack of discounting practised by the subject hotel in all market segments, something the appraiser should consider when making future projections regarding ADR for the subject hotel. Projections for the overall competitive market as well as the subject hotel are usually included in the income capitalization approach to value section of the appraisal report.

13.3.2.3 Neighbourhood Analysis

As the appraiser moves from a general form of analysis to a specific one, the next step in the appraisal process is an examination of the neighbourhood in which the subject hotel is located. The major feature of a neighbourhood is complementary land uses. Most jurisdictions have similar land uses in an area because of zoning regulations. However, commercial properties can be considered to be part of a neighbourhood because they serve the residents. Neighbourhoods are often bounded by geographic features and/or roads, but this is not always the case. The neighbourhood ends where there are no direct factors influencing the subject hotel.

Neighbourhoods, much like products, have life cycles. Appraisals usually define the life cycle by four distinct periods: growth, stability, decline, and revitalization. This can generally be assessed by examination of the effective age of the real estate in the neighbourhood, although no number definitively indicates when a neighbourhood has moved into the next stage of the cycle. Decline is often caused by a change in an exterior factor such as the closing of a major employer or a change in the transportation network. The appraiser can obtain historical prices for both commercial and residential sales to assess the pattern of increasing, decreasing, or stable values.

Another important aspect of the neighbourhood is the development activity around the subject hotel. This reveals the interest in the neighbourhood by developers and can help determine its stage in the life cycle. This development could also help supply demand for local hotels. This is particularly true for new office and/or industrial development that could house employers needing hotel rooms. Moreover, the appraiser should consider the investment demand for similar hotels in the neighbourhood. If there are a number of closed hotels or hotels that have been converted to other uses, this is another indication of the desirability of the neighbourhood in terms of hotel investment.

The final consideration in regard to the neighbourhood is the availability of nearby amenities. The proximity of the subject hotel to demand generators is always critical to success, but many hotels offer only limited amenities. Accordingly, although many hotels do not supply these amenities themselves, they choose to be located near amenities valued by their guests. A classic example is a limited-service hotel that is located next to a restaurant. However, there are many other potential examples. A location near a health club may be important to hotel guests; additionally, the proximity of a grocery store and a dry cleaner could be very helpful to a hotel that accommodates long-term-stay demand.

13.3.2.4 Analysis of Site and Improvements

The desirability of the site is a critical element of the analysis. Because many hotels rely significantly on drive-by traffic, aspects that can affect a hotel's ability to attract this type of demand need to be carefully considered. The first step in site description is the identification of the appropriate property. A mailing address is not a legal address; a legal address is usually found in the original deed of the property in governmental records. Properties also are identified by the tax assessor of the region with a tax identification number. The zoning regulations regarding the site should be verified to ensure the subject hotel is a conforming use. Any prospective changes in the zoning laws affecting the subject hotel should also be noted.

An inspection of the property is made to examine the physical characteristics of the site, including size, shape, and topography. Information regarding the flood plain (available from federal, provincial, and/or municipal government environmental offices) and availability of the necessary utilities should be verified. Although appraisers are usually not experts about environmental hazards, an appraiser may become aware of this type of problem. If this is the case, the appraiser should notify the client and defer this analysis to an appropriate expert.

The rest of the site analysis relates primarily to a prospective guest's desire to stay at the property. Is the hotel accessible? From how far away is the property visible? Is the property visible but difficult to get to? How far away from a major highway is it? Is there enough parking on-site? Does the hotel have a corner location or exposure to a major thoroughfare? Even such small factors as the availability of a left-hand turn signal into the property can affect its desirability. Sometimes a relatively poor site can hamper the performance of a well-constructed hotel property.

The improvements description is often obtained from a combination of sources: the client or an engineer, a physical building inspection, or an examination of the building plans. The purpose of the improvements description is largely to help complete the cost approach to value, if one is conducted. Other reasons are to help assess the effective age of the property (as opposed to merely the chronological age) and to assess the need for any cash expenditures to be made for repairs and deferred maintenance.

The improvements description includes structural items and the nature of the systems (electrical, heating and cooling, plumbing, air-conditioning, and fire safety). Interior finishes of the public areas and guest rooms should also be described. Included in this section should be a description of any other areas affiliated with the hotel such as a health club, pro shop, retail space, banquet space, and the like. Any deferred maintenance items noted have to be estimated and subtracted from the various conclusions to value estimated by the appraiser. This amount must be considered to enable the hotel to function in a competitive market. This is just one example of one of the appraiser's major tasks: to consider the property from a market participant's perspective.

13.3.3 HIGHEST AND BEST USE ANALYSIS

Highest and best use is defined as "the reasonably probable and legal use of vacant land or an improved property, which is physically possible, appropriately supported, financially feasible, and that results in the highest value."[2] The market analysis that has been completed up to this point is instrumental in determining the highest and best use for the property, both as if vacant and as if improved.

The overall idea of the highest and best use analysis is to find the property use that produces the greatest return to the land. What does acquired knowledge about the market suggest should occupy this parcel of land if it were vacant? It is possible for hotel market conditions to deteriorate to the point where other types of commercial development may be more productive. This, however, is rarely the case. If it were, the client would be notified, and the appraiser would be expected to support his or her conclusions in this regard.

The criteria for highest and best use as vacant and as improved are the same. The highest and best use must be legally permissible (relative to zoning), physically possible (size limitations), financially feasible, and maximally productive. The first two tests are relatively easy to assess. Information from the area and market analysis should help assess the latter two tests. These involve projecting income and expenses from each potential use. The economic benefits are subsequently discounted to determine feasibility and maximum return.

---

[2]Appraisal Institute, *The Appraisal of Real Estate* (10th ed.), p. 275.

In nearly all cases, however, the existing use as a hotel is the highest and best use as both vacant and improved. This does not mean, however, that there are no deferred maintenance items that could be subtracted from the final conclusion of value. Nevertheless, all hotel appraisals must contain statements regarding highest and best use as vacant and as improved.

13.4 Approaches to Value

Appraisers have three major valuation methods at their disposal to value an existing hotel: the cost approach, the sales comparison approach, and the income capitalization approach. The reason for using three different approaches is to provide a check for reasonableness of one value conclusion as compared to the others. Although many appraisers use all three approaches to value, this is not required. The appraiser is expected to value the property in a manner similar to that used by active hotel buyers and sellers in the marketplace. We discuss each of the three approaches next.

13.4.1 THE COST APPROACH TO VALUE

The cost approach is based on the principle whereby no one would pay more for a hotel property than the cost of construction. The market value determined using the cost approach is based on replacement cost, not reproduction cost. Reproduction cost would be the cost to reproduce the existing property exactly as constructed. On the other hand, the more common type of cost in this approach is replacement cost: constructing another hotel property with similar utility for the buyer, not the construction of an exact replica.

The cost approach is completed in a series of steps.

- Land valuation
- Cost of improvements, as if newly constructed
- Estimated value of FF&E (furniture, fixtures, and equipment)
- Depreciation from three sources:
  1. Physical deterioration
  2. Functional obsolescence
  3. Economic obsolescence

Even if a hotel appraisal does not contain a complete cost approach to value, an estimate of the land value is often calculated. The most common way to value land is through the use of comparable sales. Appraisers obtain land sales with similar characteristics including size, zoning, and overall utility to the subject. Common sources for vacant land sales include brokers, tax assessors, and public records. Sales prices must subsequently be adjusted to make them more comparable to the subject. Sales with superior attributes to the subject are adjusted downward; sales with inferior attributes are adjusted upward. Land value is often reported on a price per square foot or price per acre basis.

Information regarding improvements and FF&E can be obtained from a variety of sources. Developers and construction companies are excellent sources for this information. Other companies offer subscription services detailing cost of construction on a per-square-foot basis or a per-item basis. If the subject hotel was recently constructed, the construction information should be available from management or the owner. The costs of FF&E are updated every year in surveys published by HVS International, which estimates the costs per room depending on the market orientation of the hotel. Obviously, luxury hotels have more expensive furnishings than budget properties.

The estimate of depreciation from three sources is one of the most difficult tasks for an appraiser. The physical deterioration is probably the easiest component to assess and understand. These items are noted in the on-site inspection of the hotel. Functional obsolescence is the loss in value extracted by the market because of outmoded design of the hotel. Examples may include a hotel with guest rooms that are much smaller than the rest of the market, or use of an old-fashioned "two-pipe" heating and cooling system. Economic obsolescence is the loss in value due to factors outside the structure. A classic example for hotels is an older property located on a highway that is bypassed by a new highway. The loss is calculated by capitalizing the estimated loss in income. All depreciation is subsequently subtracted from the land value and the cost of new improvements.

Overall, the cost approach is rarely used to appraise existing hotels. Although it is sometimes used for new hotels, it is really best for special-use properties such as public buildings (libraries, museums, etc). The cost approach is heavily dependent on reliable information from recent land sales, which may not always be available. Second, the difficulty in accurately assessing all three types of depreciation can be formidable. The task becomes increasingly difficult as a hotel ages over time.

Finally, and most importantly, the task of the appraiser is to value the property in a manner that emulates the market. Because a hotel is an income-producing property, it is rare for a hotel investor to be concerned with the cost to build it. Accordingly, the appraiser may not utilize the cost approach to value in an appraisal of an existing hotel. Nevertheless, the appraiser must state why the cost approach was not used in the appraisal report.

13.4.2 THE SALES COMPARISON APPROACH

The sales comparison approach to value is based on the idea that hotels offering the same amount of utility should sell for the same price. Hotel sales can be obtained in a variety of places. Sources such as hotel brokers and public information sources such as provincial or municipal records can be examined. Another good source of information about hotel sales is from interviews with competitive hotels. Generally, hotels that compete with the subject or are located in the neighbourhood should be analyzed if not at least mentioned in the appraisal report. As the use of the World Wide Web has increased significantly in recent years, a variety of online sources for hotel information can be found. These sources can save time but usually charge for each comparable sale requested.

The methodology employed in land valuation is similar to that used in this approach. Once comparable sales are obtained, adjustments must be made to these sales. Appraisers must be careful to consider all the specific circumstances surrounding the sale of other hotels. Interests conveyed, use of special financing, deferred maintenance items, and other considerations need to be verified before the sale can be used in an approach to value. Other important information to be gathered from each sale (if possible) includes rooms revenue and income information. Each sale should be verified with a knowledgeable party related to the transaction.

A major problem when using this approach is the availability of recent sales. As the student may be aware, the hotel business is subject to general business cycles. Accordingly, there may be times when certain hotels or even particular hotel markets are not generating interest for hotel buyers and sellers. This requires appraisers to use older sales or sales in other competitive markets. Another important consideration is to understand the unique nature of hotels. It is very difficult to find two hotels exactly alike, which makes the adjustment process much more difficult.

Accordingly, techniques have been developed to help deal with the adjustment process. One can argue that if one hotel is superior to another, the superior hotel should earn higher income. In order to standardize the comparison, the income per room is utilized. The amount of **net operating income (NOI)** is obtained from each comparable sale and compared to the subject property. We discuss NOI in greater detail later in this chapter, but it is similar to earnings before interest, taxes, depreciation, and amortization. An example follows.

As shown in Exhibit 13-4, the appraiser assumes the adjustments are built into the differences in the NOI per room achieved by the two hotels. Hopefully, a relatively small range is produced, and the appraiser merely multiplies the adjusted price per room by the number of hotel rooms in the subject to find the value via the sales comparison approach.

The drawbacks to this method include the availability of NOI information from each comparable sale. Moreover, a significant portion of the income capitalization approach must be completed before the sales comparison approach can be finished. Additionally, the appraiser assumes the important differences to active market participants are reflected in the NOI. By using this approach, the appraiser cannot really pass judgment on the key individual factors of each comparable sale that may be either superior or inferior to the subject property.

After completing the table shown in Exhibit 13-4, the appraiser must still examine the sales and decide on a price per room. The appraiser may give more weight to one sale or another in the final value conclusion with this approach. However, much like the cost approach, it is not always the case that hotel investors consider the prices of other hotels when setting prices. Nevertheless, the sales comparison approach can be used to check the validity of value via the other approaches, particularly the income capitalization approach.

13.4.3 THE INCOME CAPITALIZATION APPROACH

The income capitalization approach is generally the most heavily relied on when an appraiser considers a final opinion of value. This is in consideration of the fact that a hotel is an income-producing property and is valued by active market participants based on the

Exhibit 13-4 NOI per Room Grid

Sale #	Subject NOI/room	Comparable NOI/room	Factor	Comparable price/room	Adjusted price/room
1	$5,000	$5,500	1.10	$65,000	$59,091
2	$5,000	$4,700	.94	$61,000	$64,893
3	$5,000	$5,400	1.08	$62,000	$57,407

present value of its economic benefits. The purpose of this section is to provide further insight into the process of how those benefits are determined.

The first step is to utilize the historical market information gathered by the appraiser during the fieldwork portion of the appraisal assignment. Exhibit 13-1 indicates the market achieved an occupancy of 67.52 percent for calendar year 2008 with an ADR of $61.45. The total amount of accommodated demand was 133,079. An examination of Exhibit 13-2 indicates no new supply in the past three years with overall occupied rooms increasing at a compound annual rate of 2.55 percent. It is important to notice how each of the segments has increased (or decreased) at different rates. The next step in the process is to project demand growth by market segment using the information gathered from interviews in the market and trends in the secondary data.

The amount of demand for 2008 shown in Exhibits 13-1 and 13-2 represents the amount of demand *accommodated,* which is not necessarily all the demand that could be captured by the competitive hotels. There may be demand in the market that is currently being turned away during peak periods that could be captured by new hotels. This amount of demand is estimated based on turnaway information from the hotel interviews. This demand cannot be accommodated until new rooms are added to the market. Additionally, there is usually a positive correlation between market occupancy and turnaway demand. The lower the market occupancy, in general, the smaller the amount of unaccommodated demand in the market.

Another type of demand is known as latent demand. This demand usually represents customers who are particularly loyal to one hotel franchise or another and will not stay in the market until this type of property becomes available. Hotel loyalty varies by franchise, but it is not uncommon for hotels to receive at least 15 to 20 percent of their occupied room nights from their reservation system. An estimate is made for the total latent demand for the new property and then allocated among the appropriate demand segments.

The projection of new supply is relatively easy because information on building permits is publicly available. Additionally, a physical inspection of the proposed hotel site may indicate construction activity. It can be difficult with proposed projects in terms of their timing. Building plans for new hotels must be submitted and approved, and financing must be obtained before construction begins. The appraiser must carefully investigate information about new hotels to determine size, timing, and market orientation of the new property. For the purposes of our hypothetical hotel market, we assume a 146-room Courtyard by Marriott is going to open at the beginning of 2011.

The base level of demand must be projected by segment. This is one of the most important yet difficult tasks in the market study section of the appraisal. The appraiser must carefully consider what has happened in the past. For example, our market shows strong increases in commercial demand, a modest increase in tourist demand, and a decrease in group demand. The increase in the first two segments may be attributable to more businesses opening and new tourist attractions. The decline in group demand may be attributable to factors such as renovation of hotel convention space in 2008 or a conscious effort by one of the competitive hotels to block out lower-priced group rooms in favour of commercial transient customers. Other factors from the market such as new employers must also be considered. A five-year projection period is often used because of the increasing uncertainty as the projection period increases. Our projections of market demand by segment are shown in Exhibit 13-5, and the projections of total demand and supply are shown in Exhibit 13-6.

Exhibit 13-5 Market Demand Projection

Commercial Demand Segment

Year	Projected growth rate (%)	Commercial segment (accommodated)	Latent demand	Total demand
2008	—	54,593	0	54,593
2009	2.0	55,685	0	55,685
2010	2.0	56,799	0	56,799
2011	1.0	57,367	10,000	67,367
2012	1.0	68,041	0	68,041
2013	1.0	68,721	0	68,721

Group Demand Segment

Year	Projected growth rate (%)	Group segment (accommodated)	Latent demand	Total demand
2008	—	31,588	0	31,588
2009	3.0	32,536	0	32,536
2010	2.0	33,186	0	33,186
2011	1.0	33,518	0	33,518
2012	1.0	33,853	0	33,853
2013	1.0	34,192	0	34,192

Tourist Demand Segment

Year	Projected growth rate (%)	Tourist segment (accommodated)	Latent demand	Total demand
2008	—	46,898	0	46,898
2009	2.0	47,836	0	47,836
2010	3.0	49,271	0	49,271
2011	2.0	50,256	10,000	60,256
2012	1.0	60,859	0	60,859
2013	1.0	61,467	0	61,467

Exhibit 13-6 Market Supply and Demand Projection

Year	Total demand	Total supply	Market occupancy %
2008	133,079	197,100	67.5
2009	136,057	197,100	69.0
2010	139,256	197,100	70.7
2011	161,141	250,390	64.4
2012	162,753	250,390	65.0
2013	164,380	250,390	65.7

13.4.3.1 Occupancy Projection/Market Penetration Analysis

The appraiser begins this section of the analysis with an examination of the historical penetration performance of the subject hotel. Once again, the analysis is conducted for the overall property as well as within the specific market segments. A penetration rate of 100 percent indicates the hotel is receiving its fair share of demand; penetration rates exceeding this amount indicate a competitive advantage of the hotel. On the other hand, penetration rates below 100 percent represent a competitive disadvantage. For example, the subject hotel is at a competitive disadvantage within the tourist demand segment.

A number of considerations need to be made when projecting occupancies for the subject. It should be understood that market penetration analysis is an extremely subjective method of projecting occupancies. Nevertheless, important factors to consider can help improve the quality of the analysis. The first consideration is the balance of supply and demand within the market. The projected market occupancies indicate an impact on the overall market from the addition of new hotel rooms (the Courtyard by Marriott). The appraiser needs to consider the impact of the opening of this new supply on the occupancy of the subject.

Additionally, the market orientation of the property should be considered. Based on the fieldwork interviews, the mix of demand at the subject hotel is 55 percent commercial individual and 30 percent group. Although a portion of the accommodated group demand may indeed stay on weekends, it is likely that this demand segment is accommodated during the week along with the commercial transient demand. This means the subject hotel may be achieving very high occupancies during the period from Sunday to Thursday night. Therefore, any additional room nights accommodated by the subject hotel will have to occur on weekends. This simply may not be possible, and therefore the hotel may not be able to increase occupancy above its current level.

The appraiser must also carefully consider a win–lose scenario based on the market occupancies projected. It is sometimes the case that an appraiser can make overly aggressive projections for the hotel being appraised. However, the appraiser should remember that the accommodation of demand in the future is essentially a zero-sum game—any demand accommodated by the subject property is demand that cannot be accommodated by any other property. Therefore, a thoughtful exercise is for the appraiser to divide up the accommodated demand among all the hotels in the market—both existing and projected—in order to project occupancies for each of the properties. Which hotels are going to have a competitive advantage, and which will be at a disadvantage? This type of analysis helps keep the appraiser in perspective in terms of the overall market.

The objective of the market penetration analysis is to project occupancy for the subject hotel over the projection period. For new hotels, appraisers usually show an occupancy buildup of three or four years to a stabilized occupancy. Some appraisals assume this occupancy level will continue throughout the projection period. Although this may or may not occur, the appraiser must choose a stabilized year of operation to use a particular year for a value using a direct capitalization technique. In other cases, the stabilized occupancy represents an average, with actual occupancies potentially falling above or below the number. The projected occupancies are shown in Exhibit 13-7.

As shown in Exhibit 13-7, the hotel is projected to maintain approximately the same mix of accommodated demand over the projection period. The occupancy declines somewhat after the opening of the Courtyard by Marriott. Given the expected market orientation

Exhibit 13-7 Market Penetration Analysis

	2009	2010	2011	2012	2013
Commercial demand	55,685	56,799	67,367	68,041	68,721
Fair share %	32.41%	32.41%	25.51%	25.51%	25.51%
Fair share demand	18,048	18,409	17,185	17,357	17,531
Penetration rate	135%	135%	135%	135%	134%
Accommodated demand	24,364	24,852	23,200	23,432	23,492
% of total accommodated	55.7%	55.6%	53.9%	53.9%	53.8%
Group demand	32,536	33,186	33,518	33,853	34,192
Fair share %	32.41%	32.41%	25.51%	25.51%	25.51%
Fair share demand	10,545	10,756	8,550	8,631	8,722
Penetration rate	125%	125%	160%	160%	159%
Accommodated demand	13,181	13,445	13,680	13,810	13,868
% of total accommodated	30.1%	30.1%	31.8%	31.8%	31.8%
Tourist demand	47,836	49,271	60,256	60,859	61,467
Fair share %	32.41%	32.41%	25.51%	25.51%	25.51%
Fair share demand	15,504	15,969	15,371	15,525	15,680
Penetration rate	40%	40%	40%	40%	40%
Accommodated demand	6,202	6,386	6,149	6,210	6,272
% of total accommodated	14.2%	14.3%	14.3%	14.3%	14.4%
Total accommodated demand	43,747	44,683	43,029	43,452	43,632
Total available rooms	63,875	63,875	63,875	63,875	63,875
Subject hotel occupancy	68.5%	70.0%	67.4%	68.0%	68.3%

of the new hotel, the impact on the subject property is primarily in the commercial transient and group segments. By the fourth year of the projection period, the subject hotel is expected to achieve a stabilized occupancy level of approximately 68 percent. Many hotel appraisals round the occupancy to the nearest whole number. However, this rounding can have an increasing impact on the financial projections of the hotel, particularly for larger hotels. This effect is not necessarily intentional but reflects an estimated number consistent with the other estimates used in the market penetration analysis.

13.4.3.2 Average Daily Rate Projection

The projection of ADR for the subject hotel is almost as important as the occupancy projection. However, the forecast of ADR is generally less problematic. An existing hotel should have historical records available regarding the ADR ratio for the property. The historical growth in average rate is a consideration in future expected rate growth. Other important information to gather is rack rates from competitive hotels. By comparing the rack rates of competitive hotels with actual achieved rates for those hotels, the appraiser can gather information about discounting policies. Additionally, the appraiser can evaluate discounting policies within market segments.

The overall ADR is going to be affected by demand in each market segment, rack rates per segment, discounting within each segment, and the mix of single and double rooms. Most of this information should be available from the sales and marketing department of the subject hotel. Once each of these elements is known, then a relatively sophisticated ADR projection can be made.

On the other hand, there are other simple ways to project ADR for an existing hotel. If the projected mix of accommodated demand is not going to change, then the appraiser may estimate future ADR by simply using the existing ADR and compounding it into the future with a growth rate. Another method is a market positioning approach that compares the rack rates and achieved average rates of those properties with the subject. Given the location, facilities, and amenities of the subject hotel, this should affect how the subject hotel positions itself relative to the competition. This estimated rate is then projected into the future based on future growth rates.

The most sophisticated methodology makes use of the market penetration analysis previously conducted. The mix of demand from the stabilized year is utilized along with rack rates, discounted rates, and estimates of single versus double occupancy. An example of this is shown in Exhibit 13-8.

As shown in Exhibit 13-8, the weighted average rate equals $66.30, which rounds to approximately $66.50. (Average rates were once rounded to the nearest $1, but because of the potential impact on the financial results they are often rounded to the nearest $0.50 or $0.25.) The ADR is inflated based on expected rates of inflation, obtainable from a variety of econometric forecasting sources. Given the estimated occupancies and assuming an inflation rate of 3 percent for each year of the projection period, Exhibit 13-9 shows the projected rooms revenue for the years 2009–2013.

The importance of rooms revenue cannot be overemphasized as it is generally the largest revenue category for a hotel, even a casino property. Additionally, the rooms division is often the most or second most profitable division within the hotel. Finally, the occupied room nights are the impetus for revenue generation in other areas of the hotel.

Exhibit 13-8 Estimated Average Daily Rate in a Stabilized Year

Segment	% of demand	% of single occupancy	Single rate	% at rate	Contribution
Commercial					
Full rate	54	90	$70	25	$ 8.51
Corporate rate	54	90	$63	75	$22.96
Group					
Full rate	32	50	$70	10	$ 1.12
Group rate	32	50	$60	90	$ 8.64
Tourist					
Full rate	14	10	$70	10	$ 0.10
Discounted rate	14	10	$59	90	$ 0.74

Segment	% of demand	% of double occupancy	Double rate	% at rate	Contribution
Commercial					
Full rate	54	10	$80	25	$ 1.08
Corporate rate	54	10	$73	75	$ 2.96
Group					
Full rate	32	50	$80	10	$ 1.28
Group rate	32	50	$70	90	$10.08
Tourist					
Full rate	14	90	$80	10	$ 1.01
Discounted rate	14	90	$69	90	$ 7.82
Estimated average daily rate					$66.30
Rounded					$66.50

Exhibit 13-9 Projected Rooms Revenue for the Subject Hotel

Year	Occupied rooms (rounded)	ADR	Rooms revenue
Stabilized	43,500	$66.50	$2,892,750
2009	43,700	$68.50	$2,993,450
2010	44,700	$70.50	$3,151,350
2011	43,000	$72.50	$3,117,500
2012	43,500	$75.00	$3,262,500
2013	43,600	$77.00	$3,357,200

13.4.3.3 Preparation of Financial Estimates

As previously discussed, most hotel appraisals require an estimate of market value. This has important implications regarding how the appraisal is to be completed. For one, the appraiser is expected to emulate the marketplace in terms of the valuation methodology employed. Additionally, the revenue and expense projections are expected to be market oriented. This means that as of the date of appraisal, the hotel property is assumed to be under the guise of competent and efficient management. This has implications for all expense categories, including marketing and maintenance. Accordingly, this implicitly affects occupancy and average rate estimates as well.

A logical starting point for the compilation of financial estimates is an in-depth analysis of the historical financial statements of the subject property. In fact, appraisal practice currently requires presentation of three years of historical income statements in the final appraisal report (assuming the property is at least three years old). An appraiser may present more than three years of data if it is available. The appraiser can analyze the historical revenues and expenses in a number of ways, including

- Total dollars
- Percentage of total or departmental revenue
- Dollars per occupied room
- Dollars per available room

Most appraisers utilize the last three methods of comparison to analyze income statement line items. Additionally, most appraisers use more than one method of comparison to provide a check for the reasonableness of the estimates.

However, because the appraiser is projecting market-oriented revenues and expenses, one cannot merely rely on the historical income statements of the subject hotel. The appraiser must also analyze the income statements of comparable properties that are similar to the subject in size, facilities, and average rate. Many appraisal firms have a database of comparable hotel income statements to draw on for analysis. And accounting and consulting firms—such as PKF Consulting—annually survey hotels in Canada and the United States and publish these figures. PKF's "Trends in the Hotel Industry" is a commonly used publication, although it is not the only one available. Consulting firms charge fees for a subscription, but these publications may be available in your local or campus library.

The hotel data found in these publications should be analyzed in a fashion similar to the analysis of the subject hotel. Approximately three to five other hotels are used for comparison purposes, and a range is obtained for each income statement line item. The appraiser usually chooses an amount within the indicated range unless there is specific evidence regarding a certain item to justify a selection outside the range of the comparables.

An income statement is first produced for a representative year in current-value dollars. This statement should follow the Uniform System of Accounts format discussed earlier in the text. The format is slightly different from what may be produced for internal hotel use. The general format is shown in Exhibit 13-10.

This format is very similar to the one presented earlier in the text with a few important exceptions. First of all, fixed expenses such as interest, depreciation, amortization,

---

Exhibit 13-10
Income Statement—Appraisal Format

Departmental revenues

Less: Departmental expenses

Equals: Operated department income

Less: Undistributed operating expenses

Equals: Income before fixed charges

Less: Property taxes

Less: Building and contents insurance

Less: Management fees

Equals: Income before reserve for replacement

Less: Reserve for replacement

Income before other fixed charges (NOI)

---

and income taxes are ignored for the purposes of the income projection. Interest expense is ignored because most hotel appraisals are completed assuming all equity financing. Income taxes are excluded because of the uncertainty regarding the marginal tax rate of the owner(s). Accordingly, because income taxes are deleted from the analysis, the tax shield from depreciation and amortization cannot be calculated.

An important item often excluded from statements of operations is the reserve for replacement. This reserve is an allocation to the replacement of FF&E, which wears out over time. Although the expense of capital expenditures does not appear in the operating statements of a hotel, these items are important to the cash flows of the property and are represented by this expense, which is typically shown as a percentage of revenues. Historically, a range of 3 to 5 percent of gross revenues has been most often used by appraisers and consultants for this line item. However, studies of these expenditures reveal this range to be too low. A more appropriate allocation should be 5 to 7 percent of gross revenues.

Once an income statement for a typical year is compiled, the projected financial statements are completed using the previously determined ADR and occupancy. However, some important adjustments need to be made from the base-year estimate. First, inflation rates need to be considered to reflect dollar values in future years. Although it is common for all revenues and expenses to be inflated at the same rate, this is usually not appropriate. Wage rates most likely increase at a different rate from property insurance or utilities. Accordingly, the rate of future increases utilized in the report should be discussed.

Another important feature of the projection is the breakdown between fixed and variable components of revenue and expense items. In general, items before undistributed operating expenses tend to have a more significant variable component than fixed. On the other hand, expenses such as administrative and general, maintenance, and energy are primarily fixed. The appraiser must calculate the variable component (usually on a per-occupied-room basis) as well as the fixed component for each item on the income statement. Both elements are inflated and totalled to compile the NOI for the number of years in the future required by the appraisal assignment.

13.4.4 DIRECT CAPITALIZATION

The direct capitalization technique involves the use of a stabilized year's NOI in a present value of perpetuity formula. The formula to determine the value is as follows.

$$\text{Market value} = \frac{\text{Stabilized NOI}}{\text{Overall capitalization rate}}$$

Assuming we have compiled the financial statements in a manner consistent with the preceding text, we have derived the NOI stream for the subject hotel as shown in Exhibit 13-11.

Exhibit 13-11 indicates an NOI of $832,000 in a stabilized year in current-value dollars. The denominator of the formula can be obtained in two ways. The first is a derivation from comparable sales. If the appraiser uses rates obtained from comparable sales, the details of the transaction must be verified. Was the property stabilized at the time of sale? Were there any deferred maintenance items at the property? Did the NOI estimates of the comparable sales include a reserve for replacement? Overall, to be useful the income projection for the comparable sales must be completed in a manner similar to the projection for the subject property. If reliable income information has been obtained from the comparable sales, the overall capitalization rate is found as follows.

$$\text{Overall rate} = \frac{\text{Stabilized NOI}}{\text{Sales price}}$$

We then examine the range of overall capitalization rates for our sales. Hopefully, the sales help form a relatively small range for the appraiser to derive an overall capitalization rate from this method. If the appraiser has found five other sales with overall capitalization rates ranging from 11.5 percent to 14 percent, the appraiser may select a 13 percent rate to use for the direct capitalization method.

Another method of finding an overall capitalization rate is the band of investment method. It involves using a weighted average of a capitalization rate for debt and a required rate of return on equity. The overall capitalization rate is derived in the following manner.

Exhibit 13-11 NOI Stream for the Subject Hotel	
Year	**NOI**
Stabilized	$ 832,000
2006	$ 748,000
2007	$ 827,000
2008	$ 857,000
2009	$ 938,000
2010	$1,007,000

$$\text{Overall capitalization rate} = (\text{Loan to value \%} \times \text{Mortgage constant})$$
$$+ (\text{Equity \%} \times \text{Return on equity})$$

As previously mentioned, the mortgage constant is the rate of capitalization for debt. It is the ratio of annual debt service to the amount of the original loan. For example, assume a hotel is constructed with a $5,000,000 loan at an interest rate of 10 percent for 20 years. The mortgage constant is as follows.

$$\text{Annual payment} = \frac{\$5,000,000}{8.5136} = \$587,296$$

$$\text{Mortgage constant} = \frac{\$587,296}{\$5,000,000} = 0.1175$$

After consulting the market participants, the appraiser finds 70 percent loan-to-value ratios to be typical for hotels, and equity investors are requiring returns of 18 percent. The overall capitalization rate is as follows.

$$\text{Overall capitalization rate} = (0.70 \times 0.1175) + (0.30 \times 0.18) = 13.63 \text{ percent}$$

The two rates should be reasonably similar, although differences may occur because of changes in investment terms since the comparable hotels were sold. Assuming the appraiser uses a 13 percent overall capitalization rate, the value conclusion would be as follows.

$$\text{Value via direct capitalization} = \frac{\$832,000}{0.13} = \$6,400,000$$

Accordingly, the value using this approach is $6,400,000 (rounded). However, given the competitive nature of hotel markets and the changes in NOI from year to year, the use of an average NOI is usually not appropriate. Although this approach may be used by apartment building or office building investors from time to time, it is rarely used for hotel properties. Therefore, we attempt to value the property utilizing the projected NOI stream.

13.4.5 YIELD CAPITALIZATION

Generally, the discounting of the projected NOI stream is more widely used by active market participants because of the variability in the NOI stream for most hotel properties until the property becomes stabilized. Projection periods can vary from three to ten years or more, although a five- to ten-year projection period is fairly common.

The value of the subject hotel is arrived at in a manner similar to that for a share of stock—it is the present value of current and future economic benefits. The NOI is discounted using an equity yield rate. Equity yield rates are best obtained through surveys of hotel buyers in the marketplace. Appraisers may also subscribe to newsletters containing investor opinions about yield rates of return on different types of commercial real estate. The **equity yield rate** is the long-term holding period return for an equity investor.

Most appraisers also assume the hotel will be sold after a certain period of time. Accordingly, the sales price should be based on the present value of economic benefits.

Exhibit 13-12 Net Sales Price Calculation

NOI from Year 5 inflated by 3%	$1,037,000.00	
Terminal capitalization rate (TCR)	0.14	
Gross sales price (GSP)	$7,407,142.86	GSP = (NOI/TCR)
Less: Broker's fee (2%)	($ 148,142.86)	
Net sales price	$7,259,000.00	

In our case, year 5's NOI is inflated to represent an estimate of NOI for year 6. The present value of this NOI is based on a simple perpetuity formula. The NOI is divided by a **terminal capitalization rate**, or a "going-out" rate. This rate is similar to the overall capitalization rate discussed in the previous section except for the notion that the investor is bearing more risk at the time of sale because of general uncertainty farther into the future as well as the increasing age of the property. Finally, a broker's fee of 2 to 3 percent should be deducted from the gross sales price to obtain the net price. This net sales price is subsequently discounted at the equity yield rate with the rest of the NOI stream. The net sales price is also called the *reversion value*. The calculation for the net sales price for the subject hotel is shown in Exhibit 13-12.

With the NOI stream for the subject hotel from Exhibit 13-11 and the net sales price from the preceding text, we can find the market value of the property by finding the present value of these benefits. Assuming an equity yield of 14 percent, the present value calculation is shown in Exhibit 13-13.

There is a relatively small difference in the value conclusions between the direct and yield capitalization methods. It is not unusual for the two conclusions to differ slightly; the direct capitalization usually serves only as a check against the value conclusion via yield capitalization.

Exhibit 13-13 Estimate of Market Value for the Subject Hotel Utilizing Yield Capitalization

Year	NOI	PV factor at 14%	Present value
1	$ 748,000	0.8772	$ 656,146
2	$ 827,000	0.7695	$ 636,377
3	$ 857,000	0.6750	$ 578,475
4	$ 938,000	0.5921	$ 555,390
5	$1,007,000	0.5194	$ 523,036
Reversion[a]	$7,259,000	0.5194	$3,770,325
Total present value			$6,719,749
Rounded			$6,720,000

[a]The sale of the property is assumed to occur at the end of year 5.

13.5 A Rule of Thumb Approach and Revenue Multipliers

At least two other appraisal approaches that utilize income statement information can be considered rule-of-thumb techniques. The first is based on project cost. If the ADR is $63, then the value should be approximately $63,000 per room. In the case of the subject hotel, $63,000 multiplied by 175 equals $11,025,000. This number is not very close to the value conclusions from the income capitalization approach. Sometimes this approach is remarkably accurate, but at other times it does not seem very useful. And therein lies the problem with rule-of-thumb approaches—sometimes they work, and sometimes they do not. The problem is that we cannot be sure when they will work. Although some useful economic intuition underlies these approaches, they simply may not be applicable to all types of hotels in all hotel markets.

A much more commonly used technique is a gross revenue multiplier. However, because the majority of revenue generated by a hotel is in the rooms department, a gross rooms revenue multiplier is often used. The multipliers vary by hotel type and market, but the range of gross rooms revenue multipliers is between two and five times. For the subject hotel, the gross rooms revenue multiplier is calculated as follows.

Value conclusion via direct capitalization	$6,400,000
Divided by rooms revenue (stabilized year)	$2,892,750
Equals	2.2

This approach to value is really a combination of the income capitalization and sales comparison approaches because the sales prices and rooms revenue information are obtained from comparable sales. Once again, this method can be used but rarely stands alone in a formal written appraisal report. It also requires the sales used to be very comparable to the subject.

13.6 Final Reconciliation of Value

The final section of the appraisal report is a reconciliation of the different approaches to value used by the appraiser. It reports the values obtained through the approaches used (cost, sales comparison, and income capitalization). The final value is based on the previous value conclusions and the appraiser's judgment regarding the underlying reliability of each approach. If, for example, the appraiser could find only a few sales that were not very comparable, the appraiser may place very little reliance on this approach. The value conclusion should not merely be a simple average of the approaches used. It can be within the range of values indicated or it can be the actual value obtained from one of the approaches. The key is for the appraiser to justify the final value conclusion. In most hotel appraisals, the income capitalization approach usually receives the most significant consideration.

13.7 SUMMARY

This chapter:

- Explained the major reasons for performing hotel appraisals
- Explored the agency relationships inherent in the hotel appraisal process
- Introduced the different types of users and preparers of market studies and appraisals
- Explained the process of hotel valuation
- Introduced the different components of hotel market analysis
- Explained the cost approach
- Explained the sales comparison approach
- Explained the income capitalization approach

Key Terms

Equity yield rate

Fair share

Fee simple interest

Market value

Net operating income (NOI)

Real estate

Terminal capitalization rate

Discussion Questions

1. What are the reasons for appraising hotels?
2. What are the steps in the appraisal process?
3. Why is the submarket (competitive market) analysis so important for hotels?
4. What are the major features of the site analysis?
5. What are the three major approaches to value? Which one is most commonly used for hotel valuation?
6. What are some limitations associated with the cost approach to value?
7. How are occupancies for appraised hotels determined?
8. In terms of the income capitalization approach, how are most hotel properties valued? Why?
9. Where do hotel revenue and expense projections come from?
10. How does the appraiser reconcile the different approaches to value?

Problems

Problems designated with EXCEL can be solved using Excel spreadsheets accessible at www.pearsoned.ca/chatfield.

1. You are provided with the following information about a hotel and its competitive market.

	Number of rooms	Total demand	Commercial demand	Group demand	Tourist demand
Market	500	118,625	73,547	33,215	11,863
Subject	100	24,820	17,374	1,241	6,205

Calculate the subject hotel's total penetration rate and penetration rate by segment. Comment on these penetration rates for the subject.

2. You collect the following information from comparable sales.

	Hotel sale #1	Hotel sale #2	Hotel sale #3	Hotel sale #4
Sales price	$10,000,000	$7,500,000	$6,000,000	$9,500,000
Rooms revenue	$ 4,500,000	$3,000,000	$2,200,000	$5,000,000

If the hotel you are appraising is a 250-room property with a 65 percent occupancy and ADR of $80, what is a reasonable value for the hotel?

3. An appraiser has collected the following information about some recent sales in the competitive market area.

	Hotel sale #1	Hotel sale #2	Hotel sale #3	Hotel sale #4
Sales price	$12,000,000	$4,500,000	$5,000,000	$6,500,000
Number of rooms	250	130	140	155
NOI	$ 1,560,000	$ 520,000	$ 650,000	$ 900,000

The subject hotel has 175 rooms and a stabilized NOI of $1,250,000. Can you form an opinion of value?

4. A recent survey of hotel investors indicated expected equity yield rates of 16 percent. The hotel you are appraising could be financed today with a $7,000,000 loan at an interest rate of 9 percent for 15 years. The typical loan-to-value ratio is approximately 60 percent. Calculate the mortgage constant and the overall capitalization rate.

5. You have determined the NOI of the hotel you are appraising to be $1,350,000. The expected equity yield for hotel investments is currently 18 percent. The mortgage constant for typical hotel investments is 12 percent, and hotels are currently financed with 65 percent debt.

Determine an estimated value for your hotel using direct capitalization.

6. You collect the following information sales during your fieldwork.

	Hotel sale #1	Hotel sale #2	Hotel sale #3
NOI	$ 1,500,000	$ 800,000	$ 900,000
NOI as % of revenue	20%	18%	24%
Sales price	$12,500,000	$6,200,000	$6,500,000
Overall cap rate	12%	12.9%	13.85%

However, on further investigation, you discover that although all of the comparable hotel sales are stabilized, a reserve for replacement has not been deducted. Provide the revised range of overall capitalization rates after adjusting for a 5 percent reserve for replacement.

7. You have made the following five-year projection for a hotel you are appraising.

Year	NOI
1	$250,000
2	$306,000
3	$315,000
4	$328,000
5	$341,000

Cash flows are expected to increase by approximately 4 percent per year after the projection period. Overall capitalization rates are currently 12 percent; these can be expected to increase by 150 basis points at the termination of the investment. Furthermore, sales brokerage fees are 3 percent of the sales price.

Determine the terminal value of this property.

8. According to your interviews with hotel investors, equity yield rates are 14 percent. Year 6 NOI is expected to be 3 percent higher than year 5. Terminal capitalization rates are expected to be 13 percent at the time of sale. Brokers charge 3 percent of the gross sales price to market the property. You have also estimated the following NOI stream for the first five years of the property. **EXCEL**

Year	NOI
1	$875,000
2	$901,000
3	$928,000
4	$956,000
5	$985,000

Calculate the market value of the property using the income capitalization approach.

Chapter 14
Capital Structure

Chapter Objectives

This chapter covers the following topics:

1   The meaning of a firm's capital structure

2   The meaning of optimal capital structure

3   Financial risk, business risk, and the trade-off between these two risks

4   The trade-off between the benefits of debt financing and the costs of debt financing

5   The various factors affecting a firm's capital structure such as taxes, bond ratings, and industry standards

14.1 Introduction

Capital structure is a firm's mix of debt and equity financing. More precisely, it is a firm's proportion of long-term financing provided by debt, preferred stock, and common equity. A firm's capital structure is a relevant input into the weighted average cost of capital estimation. Recall from Chapter 10 the weighted average cost of capital equation:

$$k_a = w_d \times k_d + w_p \times k_p + w_e \times k_e$$

where w represents the firm's target capital structure and is measured as a proportion. All the w's must add up to 100 percent.

$$w_d + w_p + w_e = 100\%$$

The terms of the equation are defined as

w_d = the proportion of debt in the capital structure
w_p = the proportion of preferred stock in the capital structure
w_e = the proportion of equity in the capital structure
k_d = the after-tax cost of debt
k_p = the cost of funds raised from preferred stock
k_e = the cost of funds raised from common equity

The weighted average cost of capital is an average cost of a firm's various components of capital. The weights in the average cost of capital are a measurement of a firm's target capital structure. The focus of this chapter is how a firm's capital structure affects its cost of capital and its stock price. An **optimal capital structure** should minimize a firm's cost of capital and maximize its stock price. A firm's capital structure is affected by many different factors, including

- Financial risk and business risk
- Taxes
- Costs of financial distress
- Agency costs
- Creditor requirements and bond rating factors
- Industry standards
- Desire by owners to retain firm control
- Risk aversion by management
- Borrowing capacity
- Profitability

Even though it is not possible to precisely determine a firm's optimal capital structure, we cover the basic issues involved to assist managers in better understanding capital structure decisions they may face.

14.2 Financial Risk

Financial risk is the risk arising from a firm's use of fixed-cost sources of financing. Fixed-cost sources of financing include both debt and preferred stock. Debt and preferred stock create risk because they have fixed financial costs such as interest expense and preferred dividend payments. If the firm cannot afford to pay these fixed financial costs, financial distress occurs. Increasing use of debt and preferred stock increases the fixed costs a firm must pay regardless of its level of sales and profitability.

A firm's use of debt and preferred stock financing is called *financial leverage*. Thus, a firm using debt or preferred stock as part of its capital structure is said to be using financial leverage. Financial leverage increases the risk on the owners of a firm by increasing the volatility of a firm's return on equity or its earnings per share. When times are good, financial leverage causes owners' returns to increase more than otherwise. But when times are bad, financial leverage causes owners' returns to decrease more than otherwise. Consider the example in Exhibit 14-1, which illustrates this concept.

In Exhibit 14-1, Fried's Gourmet Catering Company has $400,000 in total assets. In the first column, Fried's is all equity financed with no debt. The next column shows 25 percent of assets financed with debt, and the last column has 50 percent of assets financed with debt. Starting with earnings before interest and taxes (EBIT) of $50,000, we subtract interest expense to obtain earnings before taxes (EBT) and then subtract taxes to obtain net income. Return on equity is then computed by dividing net income by the amount of equity. Notice that with more debt there is more interest expense to pay, and Fried's net income declines (as interest expense goes from 0 to $10,000 to $20,000 and net income goes from $30,000 to $24,000 to $18,000 respectively). Debt financing not only increases interest expense but also replaces equity financing. So, despite the lower net income, our example shows return on equity increasing with more financial

Exhibit 14-1 Fried's Gourmet Catering Company Financial Leverage and Return on Equity

EBIT = $50,000

Financial leverage	0%	25%	50%
Total assets	$400,000	$400,000	$400,000
Debt	0	100,000	200,000
Equity	400,000	300,000	200,000
EBIT	$ 50,000	$ 50,000	$ 50,000
−Interest (10%)	0	10,000	20,000
EBT	50,000	40,000	30,000
−Tax (40%)	20,000	16,000	12,000
Net income	30,000	24,000	18,000
ROE (Net income/equity)	7.5%	8%	9%
If EBIT increases to $100,000			
EBIT	$100,000	$100,000	$100,000
−Interest (10%)	0	10,000	20,000
EBT	100,000	90,000	80,000
−Tax (40%)	40,000	36,000	32,000
Net income	60,000	54,000	48,000
ROE (Net income/equity)	15%	18%	24%
If EBIT decreases to $15,000			
EBIT	$ 15,000	$ 15,000	$ 15,000
−Interest (10%)	0	10,000	20,000
EBT	15,000	5,000	−5,000
−Tax (40%)	6,000	2,000	−2,000
Net income	9,000	3,000	−3,000
ROE (Net income/equity)	2.25%	1%	−1.5%

leverage (return on equity increases from 7.5 percent to 8 percent to 9 percent). This is due to the smaller amounts of equity used with more debt financing.

The second part of Exhibit 14-1 shows the benefits of financial leverage when times are good. If EBIT is $100,000 instead of $50,000, of course return on equity will improve for Fried's. In the case of no financial leverage, return on equity doubles from 7.5 percent to 15 percent, whereas in the case of 50 percent debt financing return on equity more than doubles—from 9 percent to 24 percent.

The third and last part of Exhibit 14-1 shows the downside of financial leverage when times are bad. If EBIT is $15,000 instead of $50,000, of course return on equity will decline for Fried's. In the case of no financial leverage, return on equity drops significantly from 7.5 percent to 2.25 percent. In the case of 50 percent debt financing, return on equity drops drastically from 9 percent to −1.5 percent.

Exhibit 14-1 illustrates the positive impact of financial leverage on returns to owners. But it also shows the higher risk incurred by taking on financial leverage. Financial leverage increases the volatility of owners' returns. Exhibit 14-1 shows owners' returns varying from 2.25 percent to 15 percent with no financial leverage and from −1.5 percent to 24 percent with 50 percent financial leverage.

$$(\text{Debt/equity} = \frac{\$200,000}{\$400,000} = 50\%)$$

Keep in mind that Exhibit 14-1 shows only three possible scenarios for the EBIT level. Many other scenarios are possible. Essentially, the greater the financial leverage, the greater the possible variance in owners' returns. But as long as EBIT is greater than zero, Fried's return on equity will be positive if no financial leverage is used. Financial leverage can increase the return to owners, but it also increases the risk of those returns and increases the risk that those returns will be negative.

14.3 Business Risk

All firms have a risk involved with the basic operations of the business. Even in the absence of debt, there is a risk that sales may be low, cost of goods sold may be high, or operating expenses may be high. Any of these factors could cause a firm's EBIT to be low or even negative and in turn cause the firm's returns to owners to be low or negative. This basic risk inherent in the operations of a firm is called **business risk**. Business risk can be viewed as the volatility of a firm's EBIT.

Many factors influence business risk, and they can be categorized two ways. First are those factors affecting a firm's sales revenues, and second are those factors affecting costs. Many factors can affect a firm's sales, including

■ *Volatility of demand for a firm's product and services.* This includes sensitivity to the business cycle. Sales of hospitality firms tend to fluctuate a great deal along with the business cycle, so hospitality firms generally have a high degree of business risk.

■ *Volatility of price for a firm's product and services.* More stable selling prices lead to more stable sales revenue and lower business risk. Whether a firm has significant market power or operates in a very competitive market can play a large role. A firm with significant market power can control, to some extent, the selling price and generally has less business risk than firms operating in competitive markets.

■ *Diversification that reduces a firm's business risk.* It can take place in several different ways. A geographically diversified firm will not suffer the same decrease in sales from a regional recession as a firm operating only in that one particular region. A firm diversified across the low, middle, and high ends of a market will survive a decline in one segment of the market better than a firm operating in only one sector.

Because a firm's cost of goods sold and operating costs are deducted from sales revenue to arrive at EBIT, the volatility of a firm's costs is a determinant of business risk. Many factors can affect a firm's costs, including

■ *The inherent volatility of a firm's input costs.* For example, any company extensively using energy sources such as oil, gas, or electricity has more business risk than otherwise because the cost of energy is highly volatile.

■ *The degree to which a firm's operating costs are fixed rather than variable.* Fixed costs do not decline when a firm's sales decline. Fixed operating costs may include the wages and salaries of personnel that cannot be laid off, insurance premiums, and property taxes. As such, when a firm's sales decline, higher fixed costs cause a greater decline in EBIT than otherwise. Higher fixed costs are associated with higher business risk.

A firm's level of business risk is determined to some extent by the market it operates in as well as the management of the firm. For example, restaurants are generally hurt by recessions because people do not eat out as much during bad economic times. But management can minimize this to an extent by advertising or by other methods used to induce customers to patronize restaurants.

Generally, the higher a firm's business risk, the less the firm's use of financial leverage in its optimal capital structure. Remember, the use of financial leverage means a firm is using fixed-cost sources of financing to include debt or preferred stock financing. Increasing the use of financial leverage means increasing the level of EBIT a firm needs to generate in order to meet its obligations to pay for these fixed-cost sources of financing. If we look back at Exhibit 14-1, we see that the more financial leverage used by Fried's Gourmet Catering Company (debt ratio increasing from 0% to 25% to 50%), the more EBIT is needed to just cover the interest expense ($0, $10,000, and $20,000 respectively). In fact, if we look at the case of "If EBIT decreases to $15,000" in Exhibit 14-1, we see that owners' returns are negative when financial leverage is the highest (debt ratio = 50%), and owners' returns are the highest when there is no financial leverage (debt ratio = 0%).

More financial leverage means a firm requires a greater level of EBIT just to cover fixed financial expenses. More business risk means a firm's EBIT is more volatile. Of course, having a high level of financial leverage and a high level of business risk is a very risky combination. High financial leverage requires a high level of EBIT for firm survival, and a high level of business risk means the firm is not very certain of generating a high level of EBIT. Generally, firms with relatively more business risk should take on relatively less financial leverage to obtain the optimal capital structure.

14.4 Capital Structure Theory

There are many different theories of capital structure. Here we present a basic capital structure theory based on the trade-offs between the tax effects of using debt financing and the additional distress costs and agency costs arising from the use of debt financing. It is a basic theory that helps to illustrate the issues involved in the determination of a firm's optimal capital structure. In the following discussion, we assume a firm's capital structure consists of only long-term debt and common equity. By assuming a firm does not use other sources of capital (short-term debt and preferred stock), we make the discussion easier to understand but do not affect the relevance of our results.

A firm's weighted average cost of capital is estimated as follows.

$$k_a = w_d \times k_d + w_p \times k_p + w_e \times k_e$$

But if a firm has no preferred stock financing, then we eliminate the preferred stock component from the equation.

$$k_a = w_d \times k_d + w_e \times k_e$$

14.4.1 THE COST OF DEBT VERSUS THE COST OF EQUITY

A firm's cost of debt is always less than the cost of equity (k_e) because debt has less seniority risk and has a fixed return. In other words, in the case of financial difficulty, a firm will make payments to debt holders before making payments to owners (equity). The return on debt is also fixed and not dependent on the profitability of the firm, whereas the return on equity generally varies up and down with the profitability of the firm. Furthermore, the interest cost of debt (k_d) is a tax-deductible cost, and the cost of equity (k_e) is not tax deductible. Between the lower seniority risk, the more certain return, and the tax-deductibility of interest expense, the cost of a firm's debt is generally much lower than the cost of a firm's equity. It may appear a firm should use as much debt and as little equity as possible so as to minimize the weighted average cost of capital. But this logic ignores the higher risk and the resulting financial distress costs and higher agency costs brought on by more debt financing.

14.4.2 THE COST OF FINANCIAL DISTRESS

The costs of financial distress are brought on by the use of debt financing. The more debt financing used, the greater a firm's cost of financial distress. Bankruptcy costs represent one type of financial distress. In the case of bankruptcy, a firm's assets often decline in value as the various parties to the bankruptcy argue over the firm's reorganization or its liquidation. The bankruptcy proceedings often take years, and in the meantime assets are declining in value and investors' funds are tied up, receiving little or no return. There are also lawyers' fees, other legal fees, and accounting costs to be paid in a bankruptcy proceeding.

Even in the absence of bankruptcy, there may be significant financial distress costs. If a firm has a very high debt load and is viewed as risky and possibly near bankruptcy, it will usually change customer and supplier actions. Do you really want to stay at a hotel that might close down during the middle of your stay? Do you want to prepay for a cruise if there is a good chance the cruise ship company will stop operations and declare bankruptcy before you set foot on the boat? A company in financial distress may lose customers.

Financial distress may not just drive away customers—suppliers will also be reluctant to sell unless they receive cash on delivery. Do you really want to sell a shipment of steaks to a restaurant on credit if you know the restaurant is struggling to make enough income to pay the interest expense on its debt?

Financial distress also may cause management to take actions that are harmful to the value and long-term health of the company but that ensure the survival of the company in the short term. For example, valuable assets may be liquidated at bargain basement prices, key employees may be let go, and crucial maintenance may be delayed. While trying to preserve their jobs, management may actually reduce firm value.

We can see that financial distress includes not only bankruptcy costs but also costs arising from the impact of financial distress on customers, suppliers, and management. Financial distress is generally caused by the use of debt financing. The presence of fixed interest expense puts pressure on a firm to earn an EBIT level at least sufficient to pay the fixed interest expense. Thus, the more debt financing used the greater the possibility of financial distress.

14.4.3 THE AGENCY COST OF DEBT FINANCING

The concept of agency problems and agency costs was introduced in earlier chapters. One potential agency problem is the relationship between a firm's owners (shareholders) and creditors (bondholders). Remember, the owners of a firm receive both the upside benefits and the downside costs of risk. If the firm performs superbly and firm value increases (upside benefits), the owners receive the benefits because they hold the residual value of the firm. If the firm performs poorly, the owners lose out (downside costs). But creditors are very limited on receiving any benefits from risk. If the firm performs superbly, the creditors typically receive the fixed interest rate promised and no more. If the firm performs poorly, the creditors could lose everything. Therefore, the owners may have an incentive to increase risk and thus increase the possibility of upside benefits. Creditors do not have this same incentive because they will not gain anything more than the interest promised. Selling off low-risk assets and acquiring high-risk assets or issuing additional debt and investing in high-risk projects could accomplish this. The firm's expected profitability may be expected to increase, but since the creditors' return is fixed there is no benefit to the creditors, only a greater risk of not being paid.

Because managers may take actions to benefit owners (shareholders) to the detriment of creditors (bondholders), bonds are protected by restrictive contractual stipulations. These stipulations restrict actions a firm might take possibly to include management decisions that are quite reasonable. For example, a firm might be precluded from issuing additional debt or investing in particular segments of the economy. As a result, the restrictions can reduce the efficiency of a firm's operations.

In addition to the loss of efficiency caused by restrictive contractual stipulations, there will be monitoring costs to ensure the firm follows the restrictions. So agency problems increase the cost of debt beyond the interest expense and the financial distress costs. At low levels of debt financing, creditors are not likely to demand extensive contractual protection because the risk from possible agency problems is low. At higher levels of debt financing, owners have more to gain if management takes actions unfavourable to creditors. Thus, at higher debt levels creditors are likely to require more extensive contractual protection and require more monitoring of the firm's actions. As a result, these agency costs are expected to increase along with interest rates as a firm uses greater amounts of debt financing in its capital structure.

14.4.4 FINANCIAL LEVERAGE AND THE COST OF DEBT

In summary, as a firm uses more debt financing in its capital structure the interest costs of debt, the financial distress costs of debt, and the agency costs of debt will increase. Even though a firm's cost of debt is less than its cost of equity, there is a trade-off cost to using more debt. The higher risk in general, the greater financial distress costs, and the agency costs of using more debt typically restrict a firm to using much less than 100 percent debt in its capital structure.

Consider Exhibits 14-2, 14-3, and 14-4 to better understand the relationships among the costs of financial distress, agency costs, and optimal capital. In Exhibit 14-2 the horizontal axis measures a firm's debt ratio (debt/assets), and the vertical axis measures the

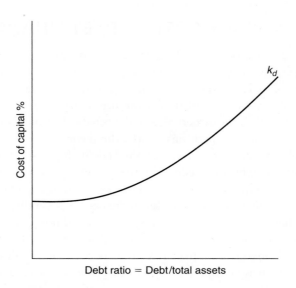

Exhibit 14-2 Financial Leverage and the Cost of Debt

cost of capital as a percentage. The line represents a firm moving from no-debt financing (at the origin, far left) to progressively more and more debt financing. We see the cost of debt financing growing at an increasing rate as the firm becomes increasingly risky, with greater proportions of debt in its capital structure. With more debt financing comes higher costs of financial distress and greater agency costs, as explained previously.

Exhibit 14-3 Financial Leverage and the Cost of Equity

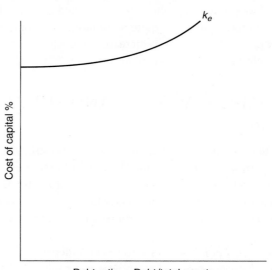

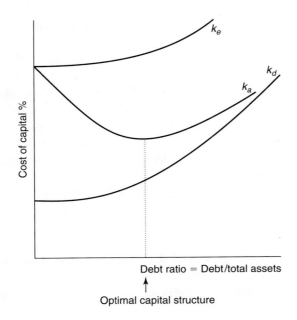

Exhibit 14-4 Financial Leverage and the Optimal Capital Structure

14.4.5 FINANCIAL LEVERAGE AND THE COST OF EQUITY

Exhibit 14-3 illustrates the relationship between the cost of equity and financial leverage. It is similar to Exhibit 14-2, except that we replace the cost of debt with the cost of equity. Remember, Exhibit 14-1 shows that financial leverage increases the risk of owners' return. More financial leverage causes greater risk. We cannot specify this relationship precisely, but more debt financing creates more risk to owners and thus increases the cost of equity. Also, the cost of equity will increase at an increasing rate with more debt financing. This is illustrated in Exhibit 14-3.

14.4.6 THE WEIGHTED AVERAGE COST OF CAPITAL AND OPTIMAL CAPITAL STRUCTURE

Now we again consider the weighted average cost of capital when a firm uses only debt and equity financing. In Exhibit 14-4 we show both the cost of debt and the cost of equity and the impact of financial leverage. Additionally, we show the resulting weighted average cost of capital. Remember, the weighted average cost of capital is computed with the following equation.

$$k_a = w_d \times k_d + w_e \times k_e$$

Therefore, if a firm is all equity financed ($w_e = 100\%$) with no debt ($w_d = 0\%$), the weighted average cost of capital is equal to the cost of equity. This can be seen in

Exhibit 14-4 along the vertical axis where the debt ratio is 0 and the k_e curve and the k_a curve intersect.

As a firm uses some debt financing ($w_d > 0\%$ and $w_e < 100\%$), the weighted average cost of capital (k_a) should initially decrease as it moves away from the cost of equity (k_e) and approaches the cost of debt (k_d). But as a firm's use of debt financing in the capital structure increases, the cost of equity and the cost of debt both increase at an increasing rate due to higher risk, greater financial distress costs, and greater agency costs. At some point, as more financial leverage is used and the weighted average cost of capital (k_a) approaches the cost of debt (k_d), the weighted average cost of capital will begin to increase with more financial leverage. This means the weighted average cost of capital (k_a) is at a minimum when debt is used in the capital structure, but debt is less than 100 percent of capital. The proportion of debt and equity financing at this minimum point (where cost of capital is minimized) is called the *optimal capital structure*.

It is extremely difficult to precisely calculate a firm's optimal capital structure. Even if we could precisely compute it, a firm's optimal capital structure changes over time. However, it is generally felt that a firm's weighted average cost of capital (k_a) curve is fairly flat over a large range of capital structures. This means that if a firm's actual capital structure is 30 percent debt financing and its optimal capital structure is 35 percent debt financing, its cost of capital will not be appreciably higher than its minimum possible cost of capital.

By combining the trade-off between the benefits of debt financing and the costs of debt financing, we can see why most firms use a significant amount of both debt and equity financing. The tax deductibility of interest provides an incentive to use debt in a firm's capital structure. But financial distress costs and agency costs become greater than the tax advantage if financial leverage is too high. The amount of financial leverage where this trade-off is optimized is called the optimal capital structure. It is at this point that the firm's weighted average cost of capital is minimized.

14.5 Other Significant Factors in the Determination of a Firm's Capital Structure

We have already discussed the relevance of financial risk, business risk, the tax-deductibility of the cost of debt, financial distress, and agency costs to a firm's capital structure decisions. Many other practical factors have a significant impact on a firm's capital structure decision. In this section, we discuss other factors likely to be relevant to a firm's capital structure.

14.5.1 INDUSTRY STANDARDS

Generally, when investors and other interested parties evaluate a firm's capital structure it is compared to what is typical for other firms in the same industry. So a large casino/hotel's capital structure will be compared to a typical large casino/hotel's capital structure. The capital structure of a chain of family restaurants will be compared to the capital structure of a typical chain of family restaurants. There will always be some variation in the capital structures of different firms in the same industry. But there is substantial evidence indicating that firms' capital structures tend toward an industry average with the averages varying from industry to industry. This is not surprising because, as we previously discussed, business risk is a significant factor impacting a firm's capital structure, and business risk is heavily influenced by industry. So if a firm's industry significantly influences business risk, and a firm's business risk significantly influences capital structure, then a firm's industry must significantly influence capital structure as well.

14.5.2 CREDITOR AND RATING AGENCY REQUIREMENTS

Firms need to follow previous debt agreements entered into. For example, a firm may have previously borrowed money and agreed to keep its debt ratio (total debt/total assets) to less than 50 percent. The firm's capital structure is restricted to debt-financing no more than 50 percent of assets until this loan is repaid. Firms must also be concerned with the ability to borrow in the future and also the cost of borrowing in the future. This is determined by investors' perceptions and also by ratings on a firm's debt provided by rating agencies such as Canadian Bond Rating Services, Moody's Investors Service, or Standard & Poor's Corporation. (We previously discussed bond ratings by these companies in Chapter 8.) A high bond rating, such as Aaa by Moody's or AAA by Standard & Poor's, lowers a firm's cost of debt, whereas a low bond rating, such as Ca by Moody's or Cc by Standard & Poor's, raises a firm's cost of debt. Strong financial leverage ratios—such as a low debt ratio and a high "times interest earned" ratio—help to convince creditors and rating agencies of a firm's financial strength. This in turn helps to maintain high bond ratings and the ability to more easily borrow funds when needed in the future, and also the ability to borrow at lower interest rates.

In summary, if a firm uses a small amount of debt in its capital structure, the firm is more likely to appear financially strong and less risky. This helps to maintain high bond ratings and build a strong reputation among potential creditors. This in turn helps the firm to more easily borrow in the future as needed as well as to keep interest rates lower than otherwise.

14.5.3 THE NEED FOR EXCESS BORROWING CAPACITY

Firms are said to have a certain borrowing capacity. A firm would not be able to borrow beyond its capacity without paying excessively high interest rates. Successful, ongoing firms not currently in financial distress generally maintain an excess borrowing capacity. This allows a firm the flexibility to handle future developments. For example, what if an excellent project is identified but a company's investors do not know about the project despite management's confidence? If management believes the stock price is currently undervalued because it does not reflect the future earnings from this project, management may be discouraged from issuing stock to raise investment funds. But if a firm has a sufficient reserve of borrowing capacity, the project can be funded with the proceeds of new debt. In summary, successful firms usually maintain excess borrowing capacity so they have the financing flexibility to properly react to investment opportunities as they become available. The desire to maintain excess borrowing capacity tends to reduce the use of debt in a firm's capital structure.

14.5.4 PROFITABILITY AND THE NEED FOR FUNDS

Highly profitable firms may have little need for debt because they generate much of the firm's funding internally. Remember, profits can be paid out as dividends to shareholders or reinvested in the firm. Reinvested profits are added to retained earnings on the balance sheet. If a firm generates high profits and reinvests much of the high profits in the firm, then the firm has a large continuous internal source of funds. This reduces the need to borrow and reduces the use of debt in a firm's capital structure.

14.5.5 MANAGERIAL RISK AVERSION

A firm's management may not desire a capital structure that is optimal for the shareholders. Management incentive is most likely to have less debt than is optimal for the owners. Management income and wealth are usually very dependent on the success of the one company they work for, and thus management may be unwilling to take on a lot of debt financing and the resultant financial risk. On the other hand, a firm's shareholders can easily diversify their investment portfolio through the purchase of common stock in several different firms. Thus a well-diversified shareholder is likely to be very tolerant to a firm's financial risk and willing to see a firm rely quite heavily on debt in the capital structure. For these reasons, management is likely to prefer the use of less debt in the capital structure than is optimal for well-diversified shareholders.

14.5.6 CORPORATE CONTROL

The impact of new securities on control of a firm may influence a firm's capital structure. Debt financing may be used to preserve control of a firm. If a few individuals currently control a firm, the controlling owners may not be willing to issue additional common stock unless they can afford to purchase the stock themselves. If the firm sells the new common stock to others, the control of the existing shareholders will be weakened or possibly eliminated through dilution. Debt could be used to raise new funds instead of a common stock issuance.

Avoiding a corporate takeover is another incentive for a firm to increase the use of debt in its capital structure. A firm with too little debt in its capital structure may be an excellent takeover target. Management generally desires to avoid a takeover because they run a significant risk of job loss in a takeover. The desire to avoid a takeover may motivate management to use more debt in its capital structure. Of course, takeovers are a control issue; a takeover is just a change in control of a firm.

On the other hand, another control issue could cause a firm to use more equity and less debt financing in its capital structure than otherwise. If a firm is facing financial distress, raising funds with more debt might seriously weaken the firm. This could force a turnover of control to creditors (based on previous credit agreements). Management facing such a situation may be motivated to issue common stock in place of additional debt in order to reduce the risk of losing control to creditors and possibly losing their jobs.

Corporate control can certainly be one of many variables significantly influencing a firm's capital structure. But whether corporate control concerns suggest the use of more debt or more equity depends on the specific situation.

14.6 SUMMARY

This chapter:

- Explained the meaning of a firm's capital structure
- Explained the meaning of optimal capital structure
- Discussed financial risk, business risk, and the trade-off between these two risks
- Examined the trade-off between the benefits of debt financing and the costs of debt financing
- Introduced the various factors affecting a firm's capital structure such as taxes, bond ratings, and industry standards

Key Terms

Business risk
Capital structure
Optimal capital structure

Discussion Questions

1. Under what circumstances can short-term debt be considered part of a firm's capital structure?
2. An optimal capital structure is optimal in what sense?
3. Explain the difference between financial risk and business risk.
4. What are the benefits of debt financing?
5. What are the costs of debt financing?
6. What factors affect a firm's level of business risk?
7. Why does a firm's financial leverage affect its cost of equity?
8. How can a firm's level of profitability affect its capital structure?
9. Explain how concerns by both owners and management about corporate control can affect a firm's capital structure.
10. Financial leverage is a double-edged sword in that it can either benefit or hurt the owners of a firm. Explain what this statement means.

Problems

1. An investment-banking firm has estimated the following after-tax cost of debt and cost of equity for Mann's Fine Dining Establishments Incorporated.

Proportion of debt	After-tax cost of debt	Cost of equity
0%		13.5%
10%	5.5%	13.6%
20%	5.6%	13.8%
30%	5.8%	14.1%
40%	6.2%	14.6%
50%	6.8%	15.4%
60%	7.7%	16.4%
70%	8.9%	17.7%

What is Mann's Fine Dining Establishments Incorporated's optimal capital structure?

2. Ramdeen's Restaurant has estimated the following cost of debt (before-tax) and cost of equity.

Proportion of debt	Before-tax cost of debt	Cost of equity
0%		11.2%
10%	7.0%	11.1%
20%	7.1%	11.3%
30%	7.3%	11.9%
40%	7.7%	12.7%
50%	8.4%	13.7%
60%	9.5%	14.9%
70%	10.9%	17.7%

What is Ramdeen's Restaurant's optimal capital structure assuming a 40 percent effective tax rate?

3. An investment-banking firm has estimated the following after-tax cost of debt and the cost of equity for Christianson's Extravagant Tours Incorporated.

Proportion of debt	After-tax cost of debt	Cost of equity
0%		10.4%
10%	3.5%	10.5%
20%	3.6%	10.8%
30%	3.8%	11.3%
40%	4.3%	12.0%
50%	5.0%	12.9%
60%	6.0%	14.1%
70%	7.2%	15.5%

What is Christianson's Extravagant Tours Incorporated's optimal capital structure?

4. Park Plaza Hotels has estimated the following cost of debt (before-tax) and cost of equity.

Proportion of debt	Before-tax cost of debt	Cost of equity
0%		14.3%
10%	9.5%	14.4%
20%	9.6%	14.7%
30%	9.7%	15.2%
40%	10.1%	16.0%
50%	10.8%	17.0%
60%	11.8%	18.5%
70%	13.0%	20.5%

What is Park Plaza Hotels' optimal capital structure assuming a 40 percent effective tax rate?

Chapter 15
Mergers and Acquisitions

Chapter Objectives

This chapter covers the following topics:

1   The reasons for a merger

2   The reasons for an acquisition

3   Possible motives for merger and acquisition strategy and action by a hospitality organization

4   Synergy and its relevance to a merged organization

15.1 Introduction

Mergers and acquisitions (M&A) represent a corporate strategy to buy, sell, unite, or execute some other form of business transaction involving two or more existing companies in a manner that is either friendly (in agreement with the acquired company's agenda) or hostile (against the acquired company's agenda).

A business **merger** is the product created when two or more companies agree to band together for strategic reasons. The merged companies believe mutual benefits are to be gained as a result of the merger and therefore work together toward a positive union. A merger usually occurs with two companies only, and this form of business combination is by mutual consent. Executives from the target company work cooperatively and collaboratively in providing assistance to the purchasing company in a due diligence process to help ensure the deal enjoys a smooth transition and becomes significantly beneficial to all parties.

A business **acquisition** is the product created when one company purchases another company. This transaction occurs in a number of different ways and can be either a friendly takeover or a hostile takeover. A **friendly takeover** usually represents consent and approval by the takeover target for the purchasing company to acquire the target company. A **hostile takeover** usually represents non-consent and disapproval by the takeover target. The target company expresses an opinion that in its best judgment the purchasing company is not perceived to be, or embraced as, a suitable buyer. The target company may believe that if the prospective purchaser acquires the target company the corporate culture or core products will change, and that these changes (real or perceived) would hurt the welfare of the company and its stakeholders.

Sometimes the only real threat to the target company is to self-preservation of its board of directors and senior executive team, and therefore they naturally oppose a takeover by the prospective purchaser.

However, regardless of whether the intention of the planned M&A transaction is altruistic, in most scenarios the main purpose of participating in an M&A is to achieve growth. The proposed M&A might involve carving up and selling off the assets of the target company—however, this type of action is more popular in Hollywood movies than within the corporate world. A key point is that the most common planned outcome of a hospitality company's participation in M&A activity is that the hospitality enterprise wants to successfully achieve growth.

Accordingly, most hospitality enterprises have ambitious expansion plans and therefore have an inherent major goal to grow that may be achieved vis-à-vis M&A activity. Specific growth objectives by the hospitality enterprise may include an increase in sales, dollar value of total assets, number of business units, number of business divisions, customer base, market share, profitability, geographical presence, product portfolio, or brand equity. These growth objectives can be accomplished by investing internally, sometimes referred to as **self-propelled expansion**, or by acquiring existing businesses, expanding externally, or some combination of both.

All internal and external expansion opportunities/possibilities should be subject to a rigorous evaluation process, regardless of what action the hospitality enterprise chooses to pursue for a growth strategy. Accordingly, any form of expansion being considered must demonstrate some degree of potential contribution to the overall value and welfare of the organization. Therefore, if the project under consideration does not show any evidence of adding shareholder value, or of improving the hospitality enterprise's financial position or performance, then it should be removed from the strategic planning realm.

It is also advocated that all internal expansion considerations be treated with the capital budgeting decision models presented in Chapters 11 and 12. For effective evaluation of external expansion opportunities/possibilities, the following discussion on mergers and acquisitions becomes important and relevant. It is also significant to note that M&A activity usually has more complex legal and tax implications than expansion activity that is undertaken internally.

M&A activity is alive and well in Canada. According to Crosbie & Company, a Toronto-based firm that specializes in providing expertise for M&A transactions, in 2007 a total of $370 billion in M&A transactions (1,941 deals) were made in Canada. These significant numbers represent new M&A records for the country.

In particular, such positive factors as globalization, a strong Canadian dollar, low interest rates, favourable demographic shifts, solvent corporate balance sheets, and a continued optimistic perspective on the Canadian economy as a whole helped drive the record M&A activity for Canada in 2007.

Two of the largest M&A transactions that occurred in the third quarter of 2007 were the $2.5-billion acquisition of Legacy Hotels REIT by InnVest REIT, Caisse de dépôt et placement du Québec, and Westmont Hospitality Group, and the $1.2-billion takeover of CHIP REIT by British Columbia Investment Management Corporation.

In 2006–2007, perhaps the most significant hotel company deals included the $4.2 billion acquisition of Four Seasons Hotel and Resorts by Kingdom Hotels International and Bill Gates's Cascade Investments, and the earlier $4.5-billion acquisition of Fairmont Hotels and Resorts by Kingdom Hotels International and Colony Capital. These two deals qualified as being in the "top ten" category for largest M&A transactions in 2006–2007.

An interesting and significant aspect to M&A activity is that once an organization becomes an acquisition target there is almost immediate upward pressure on the market value of the target company's share price. This outcome occurs because the purchasing company makes an offer to acquire the target company's outstanding shares at a premium price. This premium-price offering makes the proposed M&A transaction much more attractive for current shareholders, target-company board members, and senior company executives. In a friendly takeover situation the premium offered is usually at least 20 percent greater than the current market value. However, if the takeover attempt is hostile then the premium price offered can be as much as 35 percent more than the current market value of the target company's share price.

When Carl Icahn attempted to acquire Fairmont Hotels and Resorts in 2006 his actions resembled those of a hostile takeover. Accordingly, the market value of Fairmont stock went from $34.90 per share in November 2005 to a high of $45.00 per share on January 30, 2006, when the company was sold to its white knight, Saudi Prince Alwaleed bin Talal bin Abdulaziz Alsaud. (A **white knight** is a favourable and accepted suitor for the target company; in general, the white knight is perceived as being non-threatening.) This hostile takeover attempt turned into a friendly takeover in which the share price of Fairmont stock increased almost 30 percent in less than two months. The transaction turned out to be a very lucrative and rewarding financial gain for Fairmont shareholders.

15.2 Motives for M&A Activity

As previously identified, involvement by a hospitality enterprise in M&A activity should lead to a positive outcome. Within this notion, there are three main categorical types of M&A activity: horizontal, vertical, and conglomerate integration.

15.2.1 HORIZONTAL M&A

Horizontal integration occurs when the hospitality enterprise acquires a target company that is usually found within its own competitive set and is currently servicing the market with a similar product or service. The term "horizontal" makes sense because the target company can be found on a level playing field with the purchasing company. The typical benefits that can be achieved by the purchasing company from this type of M&A transaction would include achieving economies of scale, securing intellectual capital and human resources, increasing market share and/or entering new markets, and market penetration.

An example of horizontal M&A activity within the lodging industry is found with Kingdom Hotels International acquiring Fairmont Hotels and Resorts in 2006, and then once again with Kingdom's acquisition of Four Seasons Hotels and Resorts in 2007. As a result of these acquisitions Kingdom Hotels is now in a stronger position to enjoy greater economies of scale, new intellectual capital, enhanced and proven lodging systems technology, a more robust pool of human resources, improved brand equity, increased market share, and new geographical markets.

15.2.2 VERTICAL M&A

Vertical integration occurs when the hospitality enterprise purchases a complementary, supporting, or leading company that is currently integrated or will become integrated with the existing hospitality company. This can include forward integration or backward integration. **Forward integration** typically takes place when a manufacturer or supplier acquires a distributor or retail outlet—a forward market channel. **Backward integration** takes place when a distributor or retailer acquires a supplier—a backward product distribution channel. The principal motives for vertical M&A activity include improved economies of scale, greater control over the core product and thus less risk of vulnerability, and improved brand equity and synergy.

A hypothetical example of a backward vertical M&A transaction would be WestJet Airlines acquiring Imperial Esso for greater control over the availability and cost of jet fuel. A hypothetical example of a forward vertical M&A activity would be Niagara's Best Beer Company acquiring Canyon Creek Chophouse Restaurants so that Best Beer would be distributed and sold consistently throughout the Canyon Creek restaurant chain.

15.2.3 CONGLOMERATE M&A

Conglomerate integration occurs when the purchasing company acquires a target company that does not have a direct or indirect relationship to the purchasing company. The main goal of the purchasing company involved in a conglomerate M&A transaction is to spread risk by diversification. Through a diversified corporate portfolio the parent company generally has less exposure, reduced risk, and therefore a mitigated vulnerability to volatile swings in consumer and corporate preferences as well as the economic climate.

A hypothetical example of a conglomerate M&A transaction would be Niagara Casinos acquiring Poole Construction Limited (PCL) of Edmonton. PCL probably does not, and will not, have an impact on the gaming business today or in the future from a horizontal or vertical integration perspective. However, imagine Niagara Casinos decides to build a new physical structure; then, in all likelihood, PCL would provide the construction expertise. But that is an unlikely scenario! Therefore, unless that example were actually to take place, the successful target acquisition of PCL by Niagara Casinos would represent a conglomerate M&A transaction. We can assume there is no direct or indirect impact on Niagara Casinos as an entertainment and gaming company with the acquisition of PCL. But, it has now successfully diversified its company holdings and thus reduced its overall risk value as a result of acquiring a business found in a completely different industry, construction.

15.2.4 INTELLECTUAL CAPITAL

As identified in the introductory discussion in this chapter, from a theoretical perspective the company's board of directors and its senior executive team are supposed to act in the best interests of the company's shareholders in order to maximize shareholder wealth. However, the harsh reality is that often they do not. Instead, they may make decisions and take actions in the best interests of themselves—and not the shareholders, employees, and other stakeholders. This is where an agency issue arises.

In the Fairmont Hotels and Resorts case, Carl Icahn made it clear he was not happy with Fairmont's CEO, Bill Fatt, or the financial performance of the hotel company. Consequently, he sent aggressive and hostile messages that, should he gain control and ownership of Fairmont, Bill Fatt and his senior executive team would be gone.

Along this train of thought a potential motive for an M&A transaction could be to replace existing management with a new management team, or to provide additional fresh intellectual capital to assist and influence the existing management team. It is anticipated that with the introduction of a new management team, or at least a change in the complexion of the existing management team, the agency issue would become resolved.

Returning to the Fairmont example, it is easy to see why Bill Fatt and his senior executive team would be resistant to a possible hostile takeover attempt by Carl Icahn.

15.3 Synergy

A possible justification for an M&A transaction to occur is that there is a calculated expectation that the post–M&A transaction company, the product company of the M&A transaction, will be able to enjoy synergic related benefits. **Synergy** occurs when the total value of the new business combination is greater than the individual values of the M&A transaction companies added together. This positive effect of synergy is often referenced as the "one plus one now equals three" scenario.

For example, if pre-merger Niagara Hotels is believed to be worth $52 million and Halifax Hotels is believed to be worth $38 million, the new merged company (Niagara–Halifax Hotels) might now be valued at $95 million. As a result of synergy, there is now an additional $5 million in organizational value that did not exist prior to the merger.

Synergy can be created and occurs as a result of the merged company eliminating redundant costs, driving economies of scale, enjoying the benefits of greater purchasing power, having stronger influence or market power within the competitive set, promoting greater efficiencies, implementing easier and improved access to financing, and eliminating underperforming or idle human resources.

Synergy also occurs when there is a pooling of product research and development initiatives and programs, marketing strategies, human resource training and development, and organizational technology. Basically, the potential for synergic benefits arises whenever the strengths and competitive advantages of one company can be passed on to the other company.

15.4 SUMMARY

This chapter:

- Examined the reasons for a merger
- Examined the reasons for an acquisition
- Explored possible motives for merger and acquisition strategy and action by a hospitality organization
- Introduced the concept of synergy and its relevance to a merged organization

Key Terms

Acquisition

Backward integration

Conglomerate integration

Forward integration

Friendly takeover

Horizontal integration

Hostile takeover

Merger

Self-propelled expansion

Synergy

Vertical integration

White knight

Discussion Questions

1. What is an acquisition?

2. What is a merger?

3. When does an acquisition become hostile?

4. What is a white knight?

5. What is vertical integration and how is it different from horizontal integration?

6. What is a conglomerate?

7. Why would one company want to acquire another company?

8. What was the most significant M&A transaction for the Canadian lodging industry in 2006? Why did this event happen?

9. What was the most significant M&A transaction for the Canadian lodging industry in 2007? Why did this event happen?

10. What is synergy? Provide an example using companies from the Canadian food service industry.

APPENDIX 1 Using a Business Calculator Programmed for Financial Mathematics

Using a business calculator programmed to perform financial mathematics is a fast, efficient way to solve time value of money (TVM) problems, and most of you will probably depend on these calculators for this course. The Hewlett-Packard hp 10BII and the Texas Instruments BA II Plus are both excellent financial calculators. In this section we provide three rules to prepare your calculator for the computation of TVM problems. We also offer some tips for using, understanding, and getting the most out of your calculator. Understanding the information in this appendix will help you avoid making mistakes.

RULE #1: CLEAR THE FINANCIAL REGISTERS

The financial registers consist of five keys (keys are represented by [ ]): [N] for n number of periods or n number of annuity payments, [I/YR] or [I/Y] for the i interest rate per period, [PV] for the present value of a lump sum or the present value of an annuity, [PMT] for the annuity payment (this is not relevant for lump-sum calculations), and [FV] for the future value of a lump sum or the future value of an annuity. The basic clear key on your calculator clears only the display; it does not clear the financial registers. It is important to clear the financial registers because the last value entered into any financial register key (n, i, PV, PMT, or FV) is stored until cleared. You may not use all five financial register keys for every problem. Thus, mistakes are likely to happen as you move from one problem to the next unless you clear the financial registers as explained.

Hewlett-Packard hp 10BII

[orange], [C ALL]   [C ALL] is the secondary function for the [C] key

Texas Instruments BA II Plus

[2nd], [CLR TVM]   [CLR TVM] is the secondary function for the [FV] key

RULE #2: SET THE NUMBER OF PERIODS PER YEAR

Many business calculators allow the user to preset the number of compounding periods to something other than once per year. However, as a general rule, it is usually easiest to set compounding periods to once per year. This will help you to avoid mistakes and provide a uniform, consistent method of solving TVM problems. Many business calculators default to 12 compounding periods a year when a new battery powers up the calculator. We will show you how to set the calculators to one compounding period per year.

Hewlett-Packard hp 10BII

[1], [orange], [P/YR]   [P/YR] is the secondary function for the [PMT] key

Texas Instruments BA II Plus

[2nd], [P/Y], [1], [ENTER], [CE/C]   [P/Y] is the secondary function for the [I/Y] key

RULE #3: SET BEGIN OR END MODE

When computing problems that call for annuity payments, setting your calculator for ordinary annuity or annuity due is imperative. An ordinary annuity is one with payments at the end of each period. An annuity due is one with payments at the beginning of each period. This is explained more thoroughly later in this appendix. Setting the calculator for ordinary annuity or annuity due is necessary only when solving annuity problems. When solving lump-sum problems, it does not matter.

Hewlett-Packard hp 10BII

If BEGIN is displayed on the bottom of the calculator screen (slightly left of centre), then the calculator is in the *annuity due* mode and is set for an annuity due calculation. If BEGIN is not displayed on the calculator screen as noted, then the calculator is in the *ordinary annuity* mode and is set for an ordinary annuity. To change from one mode to the other, enter the following key strokes.

[orange], [BEG/END]   [BEG/END] is the secondary function for the [MAR] key

It does not matter if the calculator is in the BEGIN mode or the END mode; [orange], [BEG/END] will change it to the other mode.

Texas Instruments BA II Plus

If BGN is displayed on the top, right-hand side of the calculator screen, then the calculator is in the annuity due mode and is set for an annuity due calculation. If BGN is not displayed on the calculator screen as noted, then the calculator is in the ordinary annuity mode and is set for an ordinary annuity. To change from one mode to the other, enter the following key strokes.

[2nd], [BGN], [2nd], [SET], [CE/C]   [BGN] is the secondary function for the
[PMT] key and [SET] is the secondary function for the [ENTER] key

It does not matter if the calculator is in the BEGIN mode or the END mode, [2nd], [BGN], [2nd], [SET], [CE/C] will change it to the other mode.

ADDITIONAL TIPS ON CALCULATOR USE

Let us illustrate a basic calculation on each calculator. Consider an earlier example where $1,000 is invested for two years at 5 percent annually. Let us calculate the future value on each calculator. The last step for each calculator is **bold-faced** to indicate the step that computes the final answer.

Hewlett-Packard hp 10BII

[orange], [C ALL], [1,000], [PV], [2], [N], [5], [I/YR], **[FV]** and **−1,102.50** should appear on the screen.

Texas Instruments BA II Plus

[2nd], [CLR TVM], [1,000], [PV], [2], [N], [5], [I/Y], **[CPT], [FV]** and **FV = −1,102.50** should appear on the screen.

The order of entering the input information (present value, number of period, etc.) does not matter if the proper key ([PV], [N], etc.) is hit after the information is entered. Notice the future value actually comes out to a negative number (−1,102.50) on both calculators. Does this suggest you now owe the bank money? Of course you do not owe the bank money. This negative answer is simply an artifact of how the calculator was programmed. The logic is as follows. By placing a positive number in the [PV] register, you are receiving this money. When you solve for future value, the negative number computer for [FV] is saying this is the amount you need to pay back. Thus negative numbers indicate payments or cash outflows, and positive numbers indicate receipts or cash inflows. If the input dollar value is a payment (receipt), then the computed number must be a receipt (payment). Because the $1,000 is a payment by you to the bank, the intent of the calculator for this problem is that the $1,000 should be entered as a negative [PV]. The computed number will be a positive [FV] because it is a receipt to you from the bank. Negative numbers can be entered to the calculator by using the [+/−] key to change a number from positive to negative.

We suggest you generally ignore the sign in front of numbers when computing a dollar value. This will be the case when solving for [PV], [FV], or [PMT]. But when solving for the interest rate ([I/YR] or [I/Y]), or the [N], you will generally be entering two dollar values to the calculator as some combination of [PV], [FV], and [PMT]. In this case, you will need to enter one of the dollar values as a positive number and the other dollar value as a negative number. Let us illustrate this with an example. Suppose you plan to invest $1,000 today and leave it invested for eight years. What interest rate is required to end up with a future value of $2,000 in eight years?

Hewlett-Packard hp 10BII

[orange], [C ALL], [1,000], [PV], [2,000], [+/−], [FV] [8], [N], **[I/YR]** and **9.05** should appear on the screen, indicating a 9.05 percent return will grow $1,000 to $2,000 in eight years. But try the calculation again without converting the $2,000 future value to

a negative number (leave out the [+/−] after the [2,000]). **no Solution** will show on the screen. It does not matter if the [1,000] or the [2,000] is made negative. As long as the other is positive, the calculator will properly compute the answer.

Texas Instruments BA II Plus

[2nd], [CLR TVM],   [1,000], [PV],   [2,000], [+/−], [FV]   [8], [N],   **[CPT], [I/Y]** and **I/Y = 9.05** should appear on the screen. If both the [1,000] and [2,000] are entered as positive numbers or both are entered as negative numbers, then **Error 5** will show on the screen. Again, just be sure one of the two is positive and the other is negative, and the calculator will properly compute the answer.

APPENDIX 2 Using a Financial Calculator to Compute Effective Annual Rates

A financial calculator can be used very quickly and simply to compute annual interest rates. Compute the future value of a lump sum for one year at the interest rate that is not compounded annually. If you use an easy number to work with as the present value lump sum, then the effective annual rate will be obvious from your computed future value. For example, say we invested $100 for one year at a 10 percent annual rate, compounded semi-annually. Our future value is $110.25. Because we started out with $100, clearly the effective annual rate must be 10.25 percent because we earned $10.25 on a $100 investment ($10.25/$100.00 = 10.25%).

Let us try another example. Invest $100 for one year at a 6 percent annual rate, compounded monthly.

$$FV_1 = \$100 \times \left(1 + \frac{6\%}{12}\right)^{12 \times 1} = \$100 \times (1.005)^{12} = \$106.17$$

This can be obtained on your financial calculator with the following steps.

1. Be sure to properly clear out your calculator and prepare it for a new time value of money problem.
2. Enter PV = $100.
3. Enter i = 0.50% (the interest rate per monthly compounding period: $\frac{6\%}{12}$).
4. Enter n = 12 (12 monthly compounding periods in one year).
5. Compute FV = $106.17.

Because you have earned $6.17 on a $100 investment in one year, the effective annual rate is 6.17%.

When using a business calculator to solve time value of money problems in Chapter 7, we always were dealing with four variables. We entered the information for three variables into the calculator, and the calculator would compute the value of the fourth unknown variable. Using the business calculator to efficiently calculate bond value is quite similar, but different in one significant way. We are now dealing with five variables. The five variables are (1) the present value of the bond, (2) the coupon payment, (3) the maturity value, (4) the number of coupon payments to maturity, and (5) the investor's required rate of return. We will enter four known variables (2 through 5) and solve for the value of the bond (variable 1). It is important to enter the coupon payment and the maturity value with the same sign because they are both cash flows to be received by the investor. Let us compute the value for the Gretzky Resorts' corporate bond example used in Chapter 8. The annual coupon payment is $100, the maturity value is $1,000, the number of years to maturity is 15, and the investor's required rate of return is 10 percent.

Hewlett-Packard hp 10BII

[orange], [C ALL], [100], [PMT], [1,000], [FV], [15], [N], [10], [I/YR], **[PV]** and $-1,000.00$ should appear on the screen.

Texas Instruments BA II Plus

[2nd], [CLR TVM], [100], [PMT], [1,000], [FV], [15], [N], [10], [I/Y], **[CPT]**, **[PV]** and **PV** $= -1,000.00$ should appear on the screen.

Notice that the answer provided by the calculator has a negative sign in front of the 1,000.00. As we explained in Appendix 1, this negative sign can be ignored when simply computing the present value of a bond.

APPENDIX 4 Using a Business Calculator to Compute a Bond's Yield to Maturity

Using the business calculator to calculate the yield to maturity on a bond is quite similar to solving for the bond value. Once again, we are dealing with five variables: (1) the present value of the bond, (2) the coupon payment, (3) the maturity value, (4) the number of coupon payments to maturity, and (5) the investor's rate of return. We will enter four known variables (1 through 4) and solve for the investor's rate of return (variable 5). This investor's rate of return is actually the yield to maturity. One key difference here is that we are now entering into the calculator three known cash values. The three cash values are the bond value (*PV*), the bond's coupon payment (*PMT*), and the bond's maturity value (*FV*). It is crucial to use the proper signs on these three variables; otherwise, an incorrect yield to maturity will result. If you consider the logic of each of the cash values, it is not too difficult to understand the correct signs for each number. The bond value (*PV*) is what the investor pays to invest in the bond, and thus it should have a negative sign. The coupon payment (*PMT*) and maturity value (*FV*) are both cash flows the investor receives and should thus have positive signs. It is important to enter the coupon payment and the maturity value with the same sign because they are both cash flows to be received by the investor. We compute the yield to maturity for the Gretzky Resorts' corporate bond example used in Chapter 8. The bond can be purchased for $900, the annual coupon payment is $100, the maturity value is $1,000, and the number of years to maturity is 15.

Hewlett-Packard hp 10BII

[orange], [C ALL], [900], [+/−], [PV], [100], [PMT], [1,000], [FV], [15], [N], [I/YR] and **11.42** should appear on the screen, indicating the yield to maturity is 11.42 percent.

Texas Instruments BA II Plus

[2nd], [CLR TVM], [900], [+/−], [PV], [100], [PMT], [1,000], [FV], [15], [N], [CPT], [I/Y] and **I/Y = 11.42** should appear on the screen, indicating the yield to maturity is 11.42 percent.

APPENDIX 5 Using a Financial Calculator to Compute *NPV* and *IRR*

Several business calculators have a cash flow function for the computation of project net present values (*NPV*) and internal rates of return (*IRR*). We will show how to use the cash flow function on two business calculators to compute the *NPV* and *IRR* for both the Maple Leaf expansion project and the Maple Leaf new-restaurant project introduced in Chapter 12.

First, we calculate the Maple Leaf expansion project's *NPV* and *IRR*. The cash flows are as follows.

Year	Cash flow
0	−$200,000
1	$ 70,000
2	$ 70,000
3	$ 70,000
4	$ 70,000
5	$ 70,000

Using the Hewlett-Packard hp 10BII calculator step-by-step:

1. Clear the calculator: [orange], [C ALL].
   Notice [C ALL] is the secondary key for [C].

2. Enter the $200,000 net investment: [200,000], [+/−], [CFj].
   When you hold down [CFj], you will see a "0" on the left side of the screen. This indicates −$200,000 is the cash flow at time "0."

3. Enter the $70,000 annual net cash flow: [70,000], [CFj].
   When you hold down [CFj], you will see a "1" on the left side of the screen. This indicates $70,000 is the cash flow at time "1."

4. Let $70,000 be the annual cash flow for 5 years: [5], [orange], [Nj].

Notice [Nj] is the secondary key for [CFj]. When you hold down [Nj], you will see a "1" on the left side of the screen. This indicates the cash flow for year "0" ($70,000) will occur for "5" years.

5. Enter the 10% required rate of return: [10], [I/YR]. You will see "10.00."

6. Compute the *NPV*: [orange], [NPV]. Notice [NPV] is the secondary key to [PRC]. You will see "65,355.07." This means the *NPV* is $65,355.07.

7. Compute the *IRR*: [orange], [IRR/YR]. Notice [IRR/YR] is the secondary key to [CST]. You will see "22.11." This means the *IRR* is 22.11%.

Using the Texas Instruments BA II Plus calculator step-by-step:

1. Prepare the calculator to use the cash flow function: [CF]. You will see "$CF_0 = 0.00$" or there may be some other number there besides 0.00.

2. Clear the cash flow function: [2ND], [CLR Work]. Notice [CLR Work] is the secondary key to [CE/C]. You will see "$CF_0 = 0.00$."

3. Enter the $200,000 net investment: [200,000], [+/−], [ENTER]. You will see "$CF_0 = -200,000.00$." This indicates −$200,000 is the cash flow at time "0."

4. Prepare the calculator for the first net cash flow: [↓] key. You will see "C01" on the left and "0.00" on the right.

5. Enter the $70,000 annual net cash flow: [70,000], [ENTER]. You will see "C01 = 70,000.00." This indicates $70,000 is the cash flow at time "1."

6. Let the cash flow for time "1" be the annual cash flow for 5 years: [↓], [5], [ENTER]. You will see "F01 = 5.00."

7. Prepare to calculate NPV: [NPV]. You will see "I = 0.00."

8. Enter the 10% required rate of return: [10], [ENTER]. You will see "I = 10.00."

9. Compute the NPV: [↓], [CPT]. You will see "NPV = 65,355.07." This means the NPV is $65,355.07.

10. Compute the IRR: [IRR], [CPT]. You will see "IRR = 22.11." This means the IRR is 22.11%.

Next we will calculate the NPV and IRR for the Maple Leaf new-restaurant project. The cash flows are as follows.

Year	Cash flow
0	−$300,000
1	$ 50,000
2	$ 70,000
3	$100,000
4	$120,000
5	$150,000

Using the Hewlett-Packard hp 10BII calculator step-by-step:

1. Clear the calculator: [orange], [C ALL]. Notice [C ALL] is the secondary key to [C].

2. Enter the $300,000 net investment: [300,000], [+/−], [CFj]. When you hold down [CFj], you will see a "0" on the left side of the screen. This indicates −$300,000 is the cash flow at time "0."

3. Enter the $50,000 net cash flow for year 1: [50,000], [CFj]. When you hold down [CFj], you will see a "1" on the left side of the screen. This indicates $50,000 is the cash flow at time "1."

4. Enter the $70,000 net cash flow for year 2: [70,000], [CFj]. When you hold down [CFj], you will see a "2" on the left side of the screen. This indicates $70,000 is the cash flow at time "2."

5. Enter the $100,000 net cash flow for year 3: [100,000], [CFj]. When you hold down [CFj], you will see a "3" on the left side of the screen. This indicates $100,000 is the cash flow at time "3."

6. Enter the $120,000 net cash flow for year 4: [120,000], [CFj]. When you hold down [CFj], you will see a "4" on the left side of the screen. This indicates $120,000 is the cash flow at time "4."

7. Enter the $150,000 net cash flow for year 5: [150,000], [CFj]. When you hold down [CFj], you will see a "5" on the left side of the screen. This indicates $150,000 is the cash flow at time "5."

8. Enter the 10% required rate of return: [10], [I/YR]. You will see "10.00."

9. Compute the *NPV*: [orange], [NPV]. Notice [NPV] is the secondary key to [PRC]. You will see "53,537.08." This means the NPV is $53,537.08.

10. Compute the *IRR*: [orange], [IRR/YR]. Notice the [IRR/YR] is the secondary key to [CST]. You will see "15.63." This means the IRR is 15.63%.

Using the Texas Instruments BA II Plus calculator step-by-step:

1. Prepare the calculator to use the cash flow function: [CF]. You will see "$CF_0$50.00," or there may be some other number there besides 0.00.

2. Clear the cash flow function: [2ND], [CLR Work]. Notice [CLR Work] is the secondary key to [CE/C]. You will see "$CF_0$50.00."

3. Enter the $300,000 net investment: [300,000], [+/−], [ENTER]. You will see "CF_0 = −300,000.00." This indicates −$300,000 is the cash flow at time "0."

4. Prepare the calculator for the first net cash flow: [↓]. You will see "C01 = 0.00."

5. Enter the $50,000 net cash flow for year 1: [50,000], [ENTER]. You will see "C01 = 50,000.00." This indicates $50,000 is the cash flow at time "1."

6. Enter the $70,000 net cash flow for year 2: [↓], [↓], [70,000], [ENTER]. You will see "C02 = 70,000.00." This indicates $70,000 is the cash flow at time "2."

Notice we skipped by the "F01 = 0.00." This is the frequency for how many times the first cash flow will occur. If a cash flow occurs only once, you may skip "F01" because it will default to "1" automatically. Because all our cash flows occur once in this example, we will skip the cash flow frequency key for all cash flows.

7. Enter the $100,000 net cash flow for year 3: [↓], [↓], [100,000], [ENTER]. You will see "C03 = 100,000.00." This indicates $100,000 is the cash flow at time "3."

8. Enter the $120,000 net cash flow for year 4: [↓], [↓], [120,000], [ENTER]. You will see "C04 = 120,000.00." This indicates $120,000 is the cash flow at time "4."

9. Enter the $150,000 net cash flow for year 5: [↓], [↓], [150,000], [ENTER]. You will see "C05 = 150,000.00." This indicates $150,000 is the cash flow at time "5."

10. Prepare to calculate *NPV*: [NPV]. You will see "I = 0.00."

11. Enter the 10% required rate of return: [10], [ENTER]. You will see "I = 10.00."

12. Compute the *NPV*: [↓], [CPT]. You will see "NPV = 53,537.08." This means the NPV is $53,537.08.

13. Compute the *IRR*: [IRR], [CPT]. You will see "IRR = 15.63." This means the IRR is 15.63%.

APPENDIX 6 Hospitality Capital Budgeting Example

Assume you are working for Brennan Corporation and the company is trying to decide whether to build a new hotel. You are to consider the total net investment in the hotel and five years of cash flows. At the end of five years, you will sell the property.

Operating Information—Proposed Brennan Hotel	
Hotel size (rooms)	100
Occupancy/ADR year 1	68%/$80
Occupancy/ADR year 2	72%/$83
Occupancy/ADR year 3	74%/$86
Occupancy/ADR year 4	74%/$89
Occupancy/ADR year 5	74%/$92
Cash expenses year 1	$1,100,000
Cash expenses year 2	$1,300,000
Cash expenses year 3	$1,400,000
Cash expenses year 4	$1,500,000
Cash expenses year 5	$1,500,000

The following provides some additional information about the property's fixed assets.

Fixed Asset Information—Proposed Brennan Hotel	
Land cost	$1,000,000
Building cost	$5,000,000
Equipment cost	$2,000,000
Building life	39 years—no salvage
Equipment life	7 years—no salvage

The following provides information about the financing of the hotel.

Financing Information—Proposed Brennan Hotel	
Amount of loan	$4,800,000
Amount of equity	$3,200,000
Cost of debt (before tax)	9%
Cost of equity	14%
Average tax rate	30%
Working capital needed year 1	$ 200,000
Working capital needed year 2	$ 100,000

The hotel will be sold based on a projection of year 6 cash flow. This is estimated to be 4 percent higher than year 5's cash flow. Additionally, the purchaser will capitalize year 6 cash flow at the weighted average cost of capital.

Step 1. Calculate the revenue stream generated by the hotel using the number of rooms, occupancy, and average rate. The cash expenses are then subtracted from revenue. Note that although interest expense is a cash expense, it is excluded from our analysis because we are using the weighted average cost of capital that accounts for the interest expense as well as the tax benefits from the interest expense. The depreciation calculations should be based on the straight-line method described in the chapter and with the assumption that there is no salvage value.

Asset	Cost	Life	Salvage	Annual amount
Building	$5,000,000	39	$0	$128,205
Equipment	$2,000,000	7	$0	$285,714
Total	$7,000,000	—	—	$413,919

The total amount of depreciation, $413,919, is shown on the income statement to reduce our taxable income. After taxes are calculated, it is added back to net income because of its status as a noncash expense. This is shown in Exhibit A6-1.

Step 2. The next step is to calculate the net investment and the net incremental cash flows from the operation of the property. Exhibit A6-1 shows the operating cash inflows. We now must consider the cash outflows for the property. These would include the cost of the asset (including delivery and setup cost of equipment) as well as the working capital expenditures during the first two years of operation.

If the cash outflows and inflows occur during the same period, we can add them together to find the net cash flows. This is shown in Exhibit A6-2.

Step 3. The benefits of ownership of an asset can generally be categorized into two broad categories: dividends (operating cash flows) and capital gains (proceeds from sale). Because we already have calculated the net operating cash flows, we must determine the gross sales price of the property before taxes and commissions.

Exhibit A6-1 Operating Cash Flows

Year	Revenue	Less: Cash expenses	Less: Depreciation	Equals: Taxable income	Less: Income taxes	Equals: Net income	Plus: Depreciation Equals: Operating cash flow
1	$1,985,600	$1,100,000	$413,919	$471,681	$141,043	$330,638	$744,557
2	$2,181,240	$1,300,000	$413,919	$467,321	$140,196	$327,125	$741,044
3	$2,322,860	$1,400,000	$413,919	$508,941	$152,682	$356,259	$770,178
4	$2,403,890	$1,500,000	$413,919	$489,971	$146,991	$342,980	$756,899
5	$2,484,920	$1,500,000	$413,919	$571,001	$171,300	$399,701	$813,620

Exhibit A6-2 Calculation of Net Operating Cash Flows

Year	Initial investment	Working capital	Operating cash flow	Net cash flow
0	($8,000,000)	—	—	($8,000,000)
1	—	($200,000)	$744,557	$ 544,557
2	—	($100,000)	$741,044	$ 641,044
3	—	—	$770,178	$ 770,178
4	—	—	$756,899	$ 756,899
5	—	—	$813,620	$ 813,620

As discussed in the introduction of the example, the gross sales price is based on a projection of year 5's operating cash flow. This amount is expected to be 4 percent higher than that of year 5. Therefore, year 6's net operating cash flow must be

$$\$813,620 + 4\% = \$846,165$$

Investors often base sales prices on projected future benefits. Assuming this level of benefits will continue forever (like a perpetuity), the gross sales price is based on dividing the cash flow by a discount rate.

Step 4. Calculating the weighted average cost of capital is important because it is going to be used to determine the gross sales price as well as the net present value of the project overall. The calculation is as follows.

$$60\% \times [.09(1 - 30\%)] + [40\% \times .14] = 9.38$$

Therefore, the gross sales price is the year 6 operating cash flow divided by this discount rate.

$$\$846,165/.0938 = \$9,020,949$$

Step 5. We now have to calculate the net sales price, which is the gross sales price less any taxes and commissions. Assuming the property was appraised at the sale, let us assume the following values at the date of sale.

Asset	Acquisition cost	Book value	Value at sale
Land	$1,000,000	$ 1,000,000	$1,600,000
Building	$5,000,000	$4,358,975[a]	$5,700,000
Equipment	$2,000,000	$ 571,430[b]	$1,720,949

[a]$5,000,000 − (5 × $128,205) = $4,358,975
[b]$2,000,000 − (5 × $285,714) = $571,430

The following chart details the calculation of capital gains and recaptured depreciation taxes. We assume a flat income tax rate of 30 percent for both types of taxes.

Asset	Recaptured depreciation (cost less book value)	Recaptured depreciation tax	Capital gain (sales price less cost)	Capital gains tax
Land	N/A	N/A	$600,000	$180,000
Building	$ 641,025	$192,308	$700,000	$210,000
Equipment	$1,428,570	$428,571	($279,051)	($ 83,715)
Totals		$620,879		$306,285

Therefore, the total taxes at sale equal $620,879 + $306,285, or $927,164. Additionally, assume we used the services of a hotel broker who charges us a commission equal to 2 percent of the hotel sales price. Two percent of $9,020,949 equals $180,419. In summary, the net sales price is shown as follows.

Gross sales price	$9,020,949
Less: Recaptured depreciation tax	$ 620,879
Less: Capital gains tax	$ 306,285
Less: Sales commission	$ 180,419
Equals: Net sales price	$7,913,366

Therefore, the net cash flow from sale is $7,913,266.

Step 6. In addition to the sale of the property, we assume we will collect all of our receivables and sell our inventory. Thus, the working capital expenditures we made at the beginning of the project (a cash outflow) will become a cash inflow upon sale of the hotel. A total of $300,000 in working capital will become an inflow at the end of year 5 and be added to the positive net cash flow from the sale of the property.

Step 7. We can now organize the net cash flows on a timeline or in a table as follows.

Year	Initial investment	Working capital	Operating cash flow	Termination cash flow	Net cash flow
0	($8,000,000)	—	—	—	($8,000,000)
1	—	($200,000)	$744,557	—	$ 544,757
2	—	($100,000)	$741,044	—	$ 641,044
3	—	—	$770,178	—	$ 770,178
4	—	—	$756,899	—	$ 756,899
5	—	$300,000	$813,620	$7,913,366	$9,026,986

Step 8. We now have one net cash flow per year organized in such a fashion where we can calculate net present value, payback, or internal rate of return. As discussed in the chapter, net present value is the best criterion for a capital budgeting project. Therefore, we will calculate *NPV* using the weighted average cost of capital previously calculated (9.38 percent). This is shown in Exhibit A6-3.

Exhibit A6-3 Calculation of Net Present Value

Year	Net cash flow	PV Factor at 9.38%	PV of cash flow
0	($8,000,000)	1.00	($8,000,000)
1	$ 544,757	.9142	$ 498,017
2	$ 641,044	.8358	$ 535,785
3	$ 770,178	.7642	$ 588,570
4	$ 756,899	.6986	$ 528,770
5	$9,026,986	.6387	$5,765,536
Total			($ 83,322)

According to the net present value, the project should be rejected. The project costs $83,322 more than the benefits it generates (in present value terms).

Step 9. Now is a good time to re-examine our analysis. After going through this process, it may seem disappointing to arrive at a rejection decision. Some may argue that the project should go ahead because "we've already spent all this time and money on it." This is not the appropriate way to look at those costs. First, those costs are now sunk costs and are irrelevant in the analysis. Second, it is well worth the price (probably a few thousand dollars) to reject a project that could destroy $83,322 of shareholder wealth.

At this point, a tweaking process may begin in which analysts will change assumptions to increase cash flows. This may involve increasing occupancies, reducing expenses, or even altering discount rates, which is appropriate if there are serious errors in the preliminary analysis. However, a trained hotel analyst knows that reducing critical expenses such as training and advertising could have a serious negative impact on future cash flows, causing a drop in revenue that outweighs the expense savings.

In the fall of 2008, Canadians, like their global brethren, became a part of real-time history. Not since the world's great financial challenges—the market panic of 1907 and the stock market crash of 1929—have Canada and the rest of the world experienced a financial storm of this magnitude and severity. To date, several iconic financial institutions have been severely and in some cases mortally affected, including Lehman Brothers, Goldman Sachs, and AIG.

In the summer and fall of 2008, the TSX shed almost 6,400 points or approximately 42% of its market value. This represents a significant loss of wealth. In lay terms, for every dollar you invested during June, 2008, you would have lost about $0.42 on average. To this end, those who will be hardest hit by this quick negative change are existing pensioners and those on the cusp of retirement. Other potential victims of this financial disaster include small businesses, in particular mom-and-pop hospitality enterprises, as well as you and me, Canadian consumers.

At the time of this writing, October 24, 2008, we have an understanding of what went terribly wrong and a hope that the actions taken by the Canadian government and the Bank of Canada, as well as their political and central bank counterparts around the world, will help alleviate and eventually resolve the crisis. The big unknowns of today are first, how significant will the financial damage be to both the markets and society, and second, how much time, faith, and tolerance will be required by consumers and investors alike before the markets start to recover and ultimately prosper again?

WHAT WENT WRONG?

To fully understand what went wrong, you need a brief primer on recent American financial history. Since the late 1980s, American consumers and corporations enjoyed easy access to relatively cheap capital complemented by low barriers to a wide variety of credit instruments. This cash/credit-friendly environment was further augmented by clever retail promotional finance packages, which offered purchase schemes that simply became too attractive to the consumer. Sales promotions such as no down payment, 0% interest, low introductory credit card interest rates, and deferred payment plans became popular. The average American home-owner believed that property values would continue to increase over time and therefore was unconcerned when a second or third mortgage was secured. The operating philosophy of the day was to secure the additional cash, continue to spend, and not worry about servicing the debt given the expectation that the ability to refinance would always be present. However, during 2007–2008 housing prices stabilized and in most markets, started to decline. Thus the possibility of refinancing became much more difficult, if not impossible. As a result approximately 1.3 million property foreclosures took place in the United States during 2007 alone.

With so many homeowners suddenly unable to make their house payments and eventually defaulting on the mortgage(s), the banks and investment firms (BIFs) found themselves with severely reduced cash flows. Compounding this challenge was the shocking revelation that the BIFs were not sufficiently capitalized to operate, due in most part to the absence of government regulation.

With this huge increase in consumer-defaulted debt and this rapid erosion of BIF assets and weak capitalization/liquidity, the BIFs stopped lending, causing the financial system to become completely paralyzed. Recognizing that all was not well on Wall Street, Bay Street, and Main Street, investors around the world started to sell off their stocks and other financial instruments. This alarming development has become self-perpetuating, as this negative market momentum starts to breed fear which in turn drives panic. Hence what is taking place now is almost a repeat performance of 1929.

THE THREAT TO THE HOSPITALITY INDUSTRY

With such low consumer confidence, scarce liquidity, a deteriorating economy, and a decrease in jobs, consumers will have less money to spend on dining outside of the home, airline tickets, entertainment, and overnight stays at hotels. Business travel and related expenditures will also decline. Consequently, with less demand for hospitality products and services, less revenue will be generated. As cash becomes scarcer, it will become much more difficult for hospitality enterprises to pay their employees, suppliers, and taxes. Furthermore, with much tighter credit markets, it will be a challenge to those enterprises to secure an operating line of credit. Many hospitality enterprises will not be able to manage their short-term maturing financial obligations and therefore will not survive this financial storm.

HOW CAN THIS BE FIXED?

Many valuable lessons have been learned from the hardship of the Great Depression. As a result, governments and central banks are actively engaged with "hands-on" intervention almost on a daily basis. Today, four tools are being employed to help the financial system and the economy survive.

1. **Reduced interest rates.** Since December 2007, the Bank of Canada (BOC) cut the ONLR (Overnight Lending Rate) by 225 basis points.

2. **Increase the money supply.** The BOC has pumped about $10 billion into the Canadian financial system by parking cash in money markets. The BOC plans to inject another $20 billion to keep credit and cash flowing.

3. **Purchase of bank debt.** The Government of Canada purchased $25 billion of mortgage debt from Canadian banks, reducing the risk to the banks and providing them with improved capitalization, which would ultimately flow through to businesses and consumers.

4. **Nationalization of BIFs.** Canada enjoys stringent banking regulations and therefore the Canadian banking system is very safe and secure. To this end, nationalization has not occurred. However, the U.S., England, and Germany have partially nationalized some banks. Nationalization provides some degree of ownership to government and ultimately the taxpayer. It also reduces the likelihood of a BIF going bankrupt and provides a layer of insurance to the other stakeholders such as employees, investors, and consumers.

As this crisis continues other government initiatives such as deposit and loan guarantee programs will emerge.

Glossary

Acquisition The product created when one company purchases another company; can be either a friendly takeover or a hostile takeover.

Agency problems Problems caused by conflicting interests among a corporation's various stakeholders.

Agency relationship Established when a management company signs an agreement to work for the owners of a corporation.

Amortization A method of cost allocation whereby specific charges are consistently appropriated over a long period (more than one operating cycle or one fiscal year, whichever is greater).

Amortization table Shows the amount of each mortgage payment, how much of each payment is allocated to interest and how much is allocated to repayment of the principal balance, and the remaining principal balance owed at the end of each month assuming payments are made on time.

Angel investor Affluent, commerce-minded individual who sees potential and promise in a proposed hospitality enterprise and is willing to provide the required startup capital in exchange for shares in the company.

Annuity A series of payments of a fixed amount for a specified number of periods of equal length.

Annuity due Contracts calling for annuity payments that stipulate the payment is made at the beginning of each period.

Backward integration Takes place when a distributor or retailer acquires a supplier—a backward product distribution channel.

Balance sheet Represents the financial position of a firm for a specific point in time.

Bank of Canada Canada's central bank.

Beta Measures the risk of an investment relative to the market portfolio.

Bond Any type of long-term debt security.

Bond raters Companies that rate bonds for default risk.

Bridge financing A type of short-term financing used by hospitality organizations.

Business risk The basic risk inherent in the operations of a firm.

Call feature A feature that can cause a bond to be paid off before maturity; if a bond is callable, the corporation can repay the bond early if it so wishes.

Canada Savings Bonds (CSBs) Interest-paying bonds that are on sale from October to April each year and can be redeemed by the holder at any time.

Canadian Deposit Insurance Corporation (CDIC) A federal government agency that insures Schedule I banks for up to $100,000 per account.

Capital asset pricing model (CAPM) Predicts the expected rate of return on an equity investment.

Capital budgeting The decision-making process used in the acquisition of long-term physical assets.

Capital cost allowance (CCA) A non-refundable tax deduction that reduces taxes owed by permitting the cost of business-related assets to be deducted from income over a prescribed number of years.

Capital gain Occurs when an asset's market value is greater than the acquisition cost.

Capital market line The borrowing–lending line that connects the risk-free asset with the market portfolio.

Capital outlays Required assets and resources that a hospitality organization must acquire as needed.

Capital structure A firm's mix of debt and equity financing.

Capitalization A method of cost allocation whereby specific charges are consistently appropriated over a long period (more than one operating cycle or one fiscal year, whichever is greater).

Coefficient of variation The ratio of standard deviation to return.

Common stock A security that corporations may issue to raise funds; the upside and downside returns very much depend on the financial success of the corporation.

Compound interest The concept of earning interest on interest.

Compounding The process of a present value earning interest and growing to a future value.

Conglomerate integration Occurs when the purchasing company acquires a target company that does not have a direct or indirect relationship to the purchasing company.

Correlation coefficient A quantitative measure of how assets are related to one another; usually exhibited by the assets moving in a similiar pattern or direction over time.

Cost of capital The rate of return required to keep investors satisfied.

Coupon payment The interest payment on a bond.

Coupon rate The interest rate on a bond.

Cumulative dividends If a corporation misses a dividend on cumulative preferred stock, then the missed dividend accumulates; the corporation can never again pay a common stock dividend until all missed accumulated preferred dividends have been paid.

Debenture A bond that is not secured by collateral.

Default Occurs when companies do not make interest payments on their bond issues on time.

Deferred annuity An annuity in which the first payment is deferred more than one year into the future.

Depreciation A method of cost allocation whereby specific charges are consistently appropriated over a long period (more than one operating cycle or one fiscal year, whichever is greater).

Discounted payback period The number of years it takes for the present values of a project's net cash flows to recover the net investment. If the discounted payback period is less than the project's economic life, an independent, normal project is acceptable and is expected to increase the value of the firm.

Discounting The process of computing the present value of a future value.

Diversification The investing strategy of holding more than one asset.

Dividend A firm's financial reward to its shareholders.

Dividend decision The decision a firm makes regarding whether to pay out earnings as dividends or to retain earnings for future growth.

Effective annual rate The actual annual interest rate paid or received when compounding periods are not annual.

Equity financing Financial resources secured as a result of the business owner investing his or her own money, selling company stock, having other investors make a financial commitment to the firm, or some combination of the above.

Equity kicker An arrangement in which an individual agrees to provide services to a hospitality enterprise in exchange for little or no pay but a significant portion of the company's shares.

Equity yield rate The long-term holding period return for an equity investor.

Expected return The weighted average of potential outcomes. Also called mean value.

External equity Capital generated by the sale of new common stock.

Fair share The number of rooms available at a subject hotel divided by the total number of rooms in the competitive market.

Federal Reserve A federal government institution in the United States.

Fee simple interest In real estate, the ownership interest with the most rights, implying all privileges available for use and enjoyment of the real estate.

Fiduciary duties Administrative services for estates, asset management, pension funds, living trusts, charitable trusts, and so on.

Financing decision The decision regarding how a firm should pay for the assets it decides to acquire.

Floating currency exchange The Canadian system; the dollar is subject to change dependent largely upon supply and demand factors.

Forward contract An agreement about a sale of an asset that will be delivered in the future.

Forward integration Takes place when a manufacturer or supplier acquires a distributor or retail outlet—a forward market channel.

Friendly takeover Usually represents consent and approval by the takeover target for the purchasing company to acquire the target company.

Future value The value of a sum of money in the future at a given rate of interest.

Futures contract Similar to a forward contract in that the contract involves a future delivery of an asset at a set price (called the forward price).

Holding period of return Rate of return on an investment over a given period.

Horizontal integration Occurs when the hospitality enterprise acquires a target company found within its own competitive set and currently servicing the market with a similar product or service.

Hostile takeover Usually represents non-consent and disapproval by the takeover target.

Income statement Details on the revenues and expenses of a hospitality operation for a period of time.

Indenture A credit contract whereby an investor in a corporate bond is essentially acting as a lender to the corporate bond issuer.

Independent project An independent capital budgeting decision that stands alone.

Interest rates Reflect the change in the value of money from time period to time period.

Internal rate of return The interest rate at which a project's net present value equals zero. It is also the interest rate at which the sum of the present values of the net cash flows will equal the net investment. If an independent, normal project's internal rate of return is greater than the required rate of return, the project is acceptable.

Internally generated funds Funds created in a hospitality organization as a result of revenues exceeding expenses.

Investment decision The selection by the hospitality firm of which assets to hold.

Issuance (flotation) costs Costs paid to issue or "float" securities to investors.

Leaseback transaction A type of long-term arrangement (10 to 20 years) whereby a hotel company secures 100 percent financing from an insurance company and retains the use of the hotel property.

Liquidity ratios Ratios used by various parties to help measure a firm's ability to pay its short-term debts.

Marginal measurement A measurement concerned with the cost of new funds used to finance new investments.

Market maker Someone who helps stabilize prices by helping to guarantee trades between buyers and sellers.

Market portfolio A theoretical portfolio of all the assets of value in the world held in the appropriate proportions to yield the highest level of return for the least amount of risk; the most efficient portfolio to hold.

Market value In real estate, the most likely price a buyer and seller would agree to under normal circumstances.

Merger The product created when two or more companies agree to band together for strategic reasons.

Modified internal rate of return The interest rate at which the project's present value of investment costs is equal to the project's terminal value of net cash flows. If the modified internal rate of return is greater than the required rate of return, the project is acceptable.

Monetary policy Government policy primarily concerned with the health of the economy and what the Bank of Canada can do to improve the likelihood Canadians will enjoy a robust and productive economy.

Mortgage-backed securities The product created when U.S. government agencies purchase mortgages from lenders and resell them to investors in the form of securities; the investors receive income from those making the mortgage payments. Also called pass-through securities.

Mortgage bond A bond collateralized by specific physical assets, such as equipment or real estate.

Mutually exclusive project A capital budgeting project that is considered relative to other capital budgeting projects to determine which one is best and which one should be accepted, if any.

Net cash flows The benefits returned from a project.

Net investment The costs of acquiring a project.

Net operating income (NOI) The income available to owners after fixed charges and a reserve for replacement, but before interest, taxes, depreciation, and amortization.

Net present value The sum of the present values of the net cash flows minus the net investment. A net present value that is greater than zero indicates an acceptable independent project.

Nominal annual interest rate An interest rate that does not factor in inflationary pressure, or make any adjustments for the actual purchasing power of the dollar.

Office of the Superintendent of Financial Institutions (OSFI) A federal government agency that monitors, evaluates, and polices all banks conducting business in Canada.

Opportunity costs The financial resources allocated and consumed on one particular project as opposed to another represent a potential opportunity lost.

Optimal capital structure Achieved when a business has access to required funds when they are needed and at the lowest possible cost.

Ordinary annuity Contracts calling for annuity payments that stipulate the payment is made at the end of each period.

Par value (face value) The principal of a bond.

Pass-through securities See Mortgage-backed securities.

Payback period The number of years it takes for a project's net cash flows to recover the net investment. There is no objective criterion for deciding if a project is acceptable.

Payments system The interexchange financial network that connects Canadian banks for the clearing and settlement of accounts.

Perpetuity An infinite annuity.

Preferred stock Stock that has seniority relative to common stock.

Present value The value today of a future value by factoring in the variables of time and interest (rate).

Primary market The initial sale of a stock.

Principal The original amount of money invested or borrowed; the face value of a bond.

Probability distribution A series of outcomes and the probabilities associated with each one.

Profitability index The sum of the present values of the net cash flows divided by the net investment. A profitability index that is greater than one indicates an acceptable independent project.

Prospectus Promotional written literature that presents the prospect of being financially rewarded for participating in certain investments.

Put feature A feature somewhat opposite to the call feature on a bond; allows an investor to demand the corporation repay the bond prior to maturity.

Real estate The land and everything permanently attached to it.

Restrictive covenants A number of restrictions on the corporation making a bond issue.

Risk The potential for outcomes to be different from our expectations.

Risk aversion How financial managers, consumers, and investors alike behave when presented with an investment decision that has a high degree of uncertainty.

Risk-free rate of return An essentially guaranteed return that is backed by the credit of the government.

Schedule I banks Banks that are authorized under the Bank Act to accept deposits.

Schedule II banks Foreign bank subsidiaries that are controlled and owned by foreign banks.

Schedule III banks Foreign bank lending branches that operate under precise restrictions and that do not have legal authority to accept deposits.

Secondary market Represents investors trading among themselves through brokers.

Seed money See Startup capital.

Self-propelled expansion Accomplishing growth objectives by investing internally.

Seniority The order in which a corporation would pay off its obligations in case of financial difficulty.

Sinking fund feature A feature that may cause early repayment of a bond; without a sinking fund, a corporation would pay only bond interest each year and no principal. At maturity, the entire principal then is due.

Solvency ratios Ratios that indicate the degree of financial leverage used by the company.

Spread The difference between the actual purchase price for a T-bill and the redemption value (that is, the face value) of the T-bill on the maturity date.

Standard deviation The square root of the variance.

Startup capital Identified aggregate financial requirement; often referred to as *venture capital* (private equity), or *seed money*.

Statement of cash flows Statement showing the sources and uses of cash over a period of time.

Statement of retained earnings Statement showing changes in the retained earnings portion of the balance sheet over a period of time.

Sunk costs Costs that have been paid in the past, and are thus irrelevant because the costs have been paid whether a project is accepted or rejected.

Synergy Occurs when the total value of the new business combination is greater than the individual values of the M&A transaction companies added together.

Systematic risk The type of risk involved in all assets that do not have a guaranteed return.

Target capital structure The proportion of various capital components a firm plans to use to fund investments.

Tax carryback An asset the federal government allows firms with an operating loss to use against previous taxation years.

Tax carryforward An asset the federal government allows firms with an operating loss to use against future taxation years.

Tax shield Occurs when depreciation, amortization, and/or capitalization charges are incurred.

Terminal capitalization rate Similar to the overall capitalization rate except for the notion that the investor is bearing more risk at the time of sale because of general uncertainty farther into the future as well as the increasing age of the property. Also called a "going-out" rate.

Time value of money The concept that a set amount of money has different values at different points in time.

Uniform System of Accounts A standardized income statement for hotels that provides numerous advantages to the hospitality industry: it allows new properties to understand immediately the proper format of their income statements, allows easier comparison between properties, and can be used for properties of all different sizes.

Unsystematic risk The component of total risk related to a specific business or industry.

Value creation The outcome of an asset's prospective benefits exceeding its costs.

Variance A quantifiable measure of the uncertainty of investing; the sum of the squared, weighted differences between each outcome and the expected value.

Venture capital *See* Startup capital.

Vertical integration Occurs when a hospitality enterprise purchases a complementary, supporting, or leading company that is currently integrated or will become integrated with the existing hospitality company. Can include forward integration or backward integration.

Weighted average cost of capital The firm's minimum required rate of return on investments.

White knight A favourable and accepted suitor for a company targeted for a takeover.

Working capital Current assets minus current liabilities; resources required as the hospitality business conducts operations on a day-to-day basis.

Yield to maturity An investor's rate of return if he or she buys a bond and holds it to maturity.

Zero-coupon securities Bonds that investors buy at a discount and that gain value as they near maturity; no interest payments are made.

Index